Internetworking With TCP/IP

Internetworking With TCP/IP

Vol I:

Principles, Protocols, and Architecture

Second Edition

DOUGLAS E. COMER

Department of Computer Sciences
Purdue University
West Lafayette, IN 47907

PRENTICE HALL
Englewood Cliffs, New Jersey 07632

Library of Congress Cataloging-in-Publication Data

Comer, Douglas E.
    Internetworking with TCP/IP / Douglas E. Comer. -- 2nd ed.
       p.   cm.
    Includes bibliographical references (v. 1, p.   ) and index.
    Contents: vol. 1. Principles, protocols, and architecture.
    ISBN 0-13-468505-9 (v. 1)
    1. Computer networks. 2. Computer network protocols. 3. Data
transmission systems.   I. Title.
    TK5105.5.C59 1991
    004.6--dc20   90-7829
                                                        CIP

Editorial/production supervision: Joe Scordato
Cover design: Karen Stephens
Cover illustration: Jim Kinstrey
Manufacturing buyers: Linda Behrens and Patrice Fraccio

The author and publisher of this book have used their best efforts in preparing this book. These efforts include the development, research, and testing of the theories and programs to determine their effectiveness. The author and publisher make no warranty of any kind, expressed or implied, with regard to these programs or the documentation contained in this book. The author and publisher shall not be liable in any event for incidental or consequential damages in connection with, or arising out of, the furnishing, performance, or use of these programs.

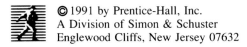 © 1991 by Prentice-Hall, Inc.
A Division of Simon & Schuster
Englewood Cliffs, New Jersey 07632

All rights reserved. No part of this book may be reproduced, in any form or by any means without permission in writing from the publisher.

Printed in the United States of America

10 9 8 7 6 5

UNIX is a registered trademark of AT&T Bell Laboratories. proNET-10 is a trademark of Proteon Corporation. VAX, Microvax, and LSI 11 are trademarks of Digital Equipment Corporation. Network Systems and HYPER-channels are registered trademarks of Network Systems Corporation.

ISBN 0-13-468505-9

Prentice-Hall International (UK) Limited, *London*
Prentice-Hall of Australia Pty. Limited, *Sidney*
Prentice-Hall Canada Inc., *Toronto*
Prentice-Hall Hispanoamericana, S. A., *Mexico*
Prentice-Hall of India Private Limited, *New Delhi*
Prentice-Hall of Japan, Inc., *Tokyo*
Simon & Schuster Asia Pte. Ltd., *Singapore*
Editora Prentice-Hall do Brasil, Ltda., *Rio de Janeiro*

To Chris

Contents

Chapter 9   Internet Protocol: Error and Control Messages (ICMP)   123

Chapter 10   Protocol Layering   139

Chapter 11   User Datagram Protocol   159

Chapter 12   Reliable Stream Transport Service (TCP)   171

Chapter 13   Routing: Cores, Peers, and Algorithms (GGP)   205

Chapter 14   Routing: Autonomous Systems (EGP)   223

Chapter 15   Routing: Interior Gateway Protocols (RIP, OSPF, HELLO)   243

Chapter 18   Client-Server Model Of Interaction   293

Chapter 19   Bootstrap Protocol (BOOTP)   303

Chapter 20   The Domain Name System   311

Chapter 21   The Socket Interface   335

Chapter 22   Applications: Remote Login (TELNET, Rlogin)   365

Chapter 23   Applications: File Transfer And Access (FTP, TFTP, NFS)   377

Chapter 24   Applications: Electronic Mail (822, SMTP)   391

Foreword

This second edition of Professor Douglas Comer's book provides an up-to-date overview and introduction to TCP/IP. There have been many requests for *the* article, report, or book to read to get started on understanding the TCP/IP protocols. This book satisfies those requests. Writing an introduction to TCP/IP for the uninitiated is a very difficult task. While combining the explanation of the general principles of computer communication with the specific examples from the TCP/IP protocol suite, Doug Comer has provided a very readable book.

While this book is specifically about the TCP/IP protocol suite, it is a good book for learning about computer communications protocols in general. The principles of architecture, layering, multiplexing, encapsulation, addressing and address mapping, routing, and naming are quite similar in any protocol suite, though, of course, different in detail (See Chapters 3, 10, 18, 20, and 26).

Computer communication protocols do not do anything themselves. Like operating systems, they are in the service of application processes. Processes are the active elements that request communication and are the ultimate senders and receivers of the data transmitted. The various layers of protocols are like the various layers in a computer operating system, especially the file system. Understanding protocol architecture is like understanding operating system architecture. In this book Doug Comer has taken the "bottom up" approach – starting with the physical networks and moving up in levels of abstraction to the applications.

Since application processes are the active elements using the communication supported by the protocols, TCP/IP is an "interprocess communication" (IPC) mechanism. While there are several experiments in progress with operating system style message passing and procedure call types of IPC based on IP, the focus in this book is on more traditional applications that use the UDP datagram or TCP logical connection forms of IPC (See Chapters 11, 12, 18, 20, and 22-25). Typically in operating systems there is a set of functions provided by the operating system to the application processes. This system call interface usually includes calls for opening, reading, writing, and closing files, among other things. In many systems there are similar system calls for IPC functions including network communication. As an example of such an interface Doug Comer presents an overview of the socket interface (See Chapter 21).

One of the key ideas inherent in TCP/IP and in the title of this book is "internetworking." The power of a communication system is directly related to the number of entities in that system. The telephone network is very useful because (nearly) all the telephones are in one network (as it appears to the users). Computer communication systems and networks are currently separated and fragmented. The goal of interconnection and internetworking, to have a single powerful computer communication network, is fundamental to the design of TCP/IP. Essential to internetworking is addressing (See Chapters 4, 5, 6, and 17), and a universal protocol – the Internet Protocol (See Chapters 7, 8, and 9). Of course, the individual networks have their own protocols which are used to carry the IP datagrams (See Chapter 2), and there must be a mapping between the individual network address and the IP address (See Chapters 5, 6, and 19).

To have an internetwork the individual networks must be connected. The connecting devices are called gateways. Further, these gateways must have some procedures for forwarding data from one network to the next. The data is in the form of IP datagrams and the destination is specified by an IP address, but the gateway must make a routing decision based on the IP address and what it knows about the connectivity of the networks making up the Internet. The procedures for distributing the current connectivity information to the gateways are called routing algorithms, and these are currently the subject of much study and development (See Chapters 13, 14, 15, 16, and 17).

Like all communication systems, the TCP/IP protocol suite is an unfinished system. It is evolving to meet changing requirements and new opportunities. Thus, this book is, in a sense, a snapshot of TCP/IP circa 1990. And, as Doug Comer points out, there are many loose ends (See Chapter 27). One area that has changed significantly since the first edition of this book is network management (See Chapter 25).

Most chapters end with a few pointers to material "for further study." Many of these refer to memos of the RFC series of notes. This series of notes is the result of a policy of making the working ideas and the protocol specifications developed by the TCP/IP research and development community widely available. This availability of the basic and detailed information about these protocols, and the availability of the early implementations of them, has had much to do with their current widespread use. This commitment to public documentation at this level of detail is unusual for a research effort, and has had significant benefits for the development of computer communication (See Appendices 1, 3, and 4).

This book brings together information about the various parts of the TCP/IP architecture and protocols and makes it accessible. Its publication is a very significant milestone in the evolution of computer communications.

Jon Postel,
Director, Communications Division
Information Sciences Institute
University of Southern California

June, 1990

Preface

In the last century, railroads revolutionized the world by providing a transportation network that moved raw materials and manufactured products. They made an industrialized society possible. Digital communication networks have started a new revolution by providing the technology that transports the data needed by a society in which information plays a key role. Networking already permeates industry, education, and government. It has already begun to change the way we view the world by shrinking geographic distances and forming new communities of people who interact frequently. More important, network growth is explosive. The revolution is well underway.

To understand networking and the selection of topics discussed in this book, it is important to realize that network research and development occurred in three stages. Before the 1960s, the main question was, "How can we transmit bits across a communication medium efficiently and reliably?" The results include the development of information theory, the sampling theorem, and other ideas commonly referred to as signal processing. Beginning around the mid 1960s, emphasis shifted to packet switching and the question became, "How can we transmit packets across a communication medium efficiently and reliably?" The results include the development of packet switching technologies, local area networks, and statistical analysis of network response to load. From approximately the mid 1970s to the present, emphasis has centered on network architecture and the question, "How can we provide communication services across a series of interconnected networks?" The results include the development of internetwork technologies, protocol layering models, datagram and stream transport services, and the client-server interaction paradigm.

Most textbooks and network courses concentrate on the first two stages of network research, presenting the well-known theories of data communications and queueing analysis. Although such information is important to engineers who design network technologies and hardware products, most network architects purchase commercially available network hardware. Instead of detailed knowledge about how bits or packets flow across communication media, they need to know how to interconnect such hardware and how to use the resulting system.

This text concentrates on the third stage of networking. It examines the architecture of interconnected networks and explains the principles and protocols that make such interconnected architectures function as a single unified communication system. More important, it shows how an interconnected architecture can be used for distributed computation.

The entire text focuses on the concept of internetworking in general and the TCP/IP internet technology in particular. Internetworking is a powerful abstraction that allows us to deal with the complexity of multiple underlying communication technologies. It hides the details of network hardware and provides a high level communication environment. As the book shows, the ultimate goal of internetworking is maximal interoperability, that is, maximizing the ability of programs on diverse computer and network systems to communicate reliably and efficiently.

The text reviews both the architecture of network interconnections as well as internet communication services and the protocols needed to provide those services. By the end of the book, the reader will understand how it is possible to interconnect multiple physical networks into a coordinated system, how internet protocols operate in that environment, and how application programs use the resulting system. As a specific example, the reader learns the details of the Connected (TCP/IP) Internet, including the architecture of the gateway system and the application protocols it supports. In addition, the book discusses some of the limitations of the internet approach.

Writing about internetworking is both exciting and challenging. It is challenging because, as in any rapidly changing research area, nothing is stable. It is exciting because the TCP/IP Internet is an active, rapidly expanding entity. Researchers working on it generate new ideas constantly and the possibilities seem endless. Looking back over TCP/IP and the evolution of the Internet makes it clear that much has been accomplished. Knowing that the research has taken a little over a decade makes one realize how intense the effort has been.

Designed as both a college text and as a professional reference, the book is written at an advanced undergraduate or graduate level. For professionals, the book provides a comprehensive introduction to the TCP/IP technology and the architecture of the Internet. Although it is not intended to replace protocol standards, the book is a good starting point for learning about internetworking because it provides a uniform overview that emphasizes principles. Moreover, it gives the reader perspective that can be extremely difficult to obtain from individual protocol documents.

When used in the classroom, the text provides more than sufficient material for a single semester network course at either the undergraduate or graduate level. Such a course can be extended to a 2-semester sequence if accompanied by programming projects and readings from the literature. For undergraduate courses, it can be taken at face value. Students should be expected to grasp the basic concepts described in the text, and they should be able to describe or use them. At the graduate level, students should be expected to use the material here as a basis for further exploration of current research. They should understand it well enough to answer exercises or solve problems that require them to explore subtleties and consequences. Many of the exercises suggest such subtleties; solving them often requires students to read protocol standards and apply creative energy to comprehend consequences.

At all levels, hands-on experience sharpens the concepts and helps students gain intuition. Thus, I encourage instructors to invent projects that force students to use internetwork services and protocols. Although such experimentation is safest when the instructional laboratory network is isolated from production computing facilities, we have found that students exhibit the most enthusiasm, and benefit the most, when they have access to the "real" TCP/IP Internet.

The book is organized into four main parts. Chapters 1 and 2 form an introduction that provides an overview and discusses existing technologies. In particular, Chapter 2 reviews physical network hardware. The intention is to provide basic intuition about what is possible, not to spend inordinate time on hardware details. Chapters 3-12 describe the TCP/IP Internet from the viewpoint of a single host, showing the basic services available and the protocols a host uses to access them. They cover the basics of Internet addressing and routing as well as the notion of protocol layering. Chapters 13-17 describe the architecture of an internet when viewed globally. They explore the core gateway system and the protocols gateways use to exchange routing information. Finally, Chapters 18-26 discuss application level services available in the Internet. They present the client-server model of interaction and give several examples of how one can organize client and server software. The last section discusses electronic mail and the domain name system, two topics that are extremely popular.

The chapters have been organized "bottom up." They begin with an overview of hardware and continue to build new functionality on top of it. This view will appeal to anyone who has developed Internet software because it follows the same pattern one uses in implementation. The concept of layering does not appear until Chapter 10. The discussion of layering emphasizes the distinction between conceptual layers of functionality and the reality of layered protocol software in which multiple objects appear at each layer.

Although it is difficult to omit any chapter completely, the instructor will find that students are often satisfied to know that something is possible without knowing the details. For example, one can skim through Chapters 5, 6, and 9 by covering only the functionality and not the details of the protocols. In addition, several chapters (especially 16) contain engineering techniques. While such techniques are crucial to efficient implementations, they can be skipped to save time.

A modest background is required to understand the material. The reader is expected to have programmed in a high level language and to be familiar with basic data structures like stacks, queues, and trees. Readers need basic intuition about the organization of computer software into an operating system that supports concurrent programming and application programs that users invoke to perform computation. Readers do not need sophisticated mathematics, nor do they need to know information theory or theorems from data communications; the book describes the physical network as a black box around which an internetwork can be built. It states design principles in English and discusses motivations and consequences.

Many people have contributed to this book. I thank Scott Ballew, Steve Chapin, Jim Griffioen, Chris Kent, Tim Korb, Dan Lynch, Thomas Narten, Vic Norman, Shawn Ostermann, John Steele, Mike StJohns, Dan Tormey, Raj Yavatkar, and Preston Wilson who all read drafts and made valuable comments. Craig Partridge supplied numerous suggestions, including a few exercises, and corrected several technical errors. He and Van Jacobson supplied the graph of Internet round trip delays in Chapter 12. Dave Stevens suggested both technical and grammatical improvements for the second edition. Barry Shein graciously allowed me to use his example UNIX client and server code in Appendix 1. Charlotte Tubis provided valuable editing. Special thanks go to my wife, Chris, who has read the text more times than I can count and made extensive suggestions.

Internetworking With TCP/IP

1

Introduction and Overview

1.1 The Need For An Internet

Data communication has become a fundamental part of computing. World-wide networks gather data about such diverse subjects as atmospheric conditions, crop production, and airline traffic. Groups establish electronic mailing lists so they can share information of common interest. Hobbyists exchange programs for their home computers. In the scientific world, data networks are essential because they allow scientists to send programs and data to remote supercomputers for processing, to retrieve the results, and to exchange scientific information with colleagues.

Unfortunately, most networks are independent entities, established to serve the needs of a single group. The users choose a hardware technology appropriate to their communication problems. More important, it is impossible to build a universal network from a single hardware technology because no single network suffices for all uses. Some users need a high-speed network to connect machines, but such networks cannot be expanded to span large distances. Others settle for a slower speed network that connects machines thousands of miles apart.

Recently, however, a new technology has emerged that makes it possible to interconnect many disparate physical networks and make them function as a coordinated unit. The new technology, called *internetworking*, or *internetting*, accommodates multiple, diverse underlying hardware technologies by adding both physical connections and a new set of conventions. The internet technology hides the details of network hardware and permits computers to communicate independent of their physical network connections.

The internet technology described in this book is an example of *open system interconnection*. It is called an *open system* because, unlike proprietary communication systems available from one specific vendor, the specifications are publicly available. Thus,

1

anyone can build the software needed to communicate across an internet. More important, the entire technology has been designed to foster communication between
machines with diverse hardware architectures, to use almost any packet switched network hardware, and to accommodate multiple computer operating systems.

To appreciate internet technology, think of how it affects research. Imagine for a
minute the effects of interconnecting all the computers used by scientists. Any scientist
would be able to exchange data resulting from an experiment with any other scientist.
It would be possible to establish national data centers to collect data from natural
phenomena and make the data available to all scientists. Computer services and programs available at one location could be used by scientists at other locations. As a
result, the speed with which scientific investigations proceed would increase. In short,
the changes would be dramatic.

1.2 The TCP/IP Internet

Government agencies have realized the importance and potential of internet technology for many years and have been funding research that will make possible a national internet. This book discusses principles and ideas underlying the leading internet
technology, one that has resulted from research funded by the *Defense Advanced
Research Projects Agency* (*DARPA*). The DARPA technology includes a set of network
standards that specify the details of how computers communicate, as well as a set of
conventions for interconnecting networks and routing traffic. Officially named the
TCP/IP Internet Protocol Suite and commonly referred to as *TCP/IP* (after the names of
its two main standards), it can be used to communicate across any set of interconnected
networks. For example, some corporations use TCP/IP to interconnect all networks
within their corporation, even though the corporation has no connection to outside networks. Other groups use TCP/IP for long haul communication among geographically
distant sites.

Although the TCP/IP technology is noteworthy by itself, it is especially interesting
because its viability has been demonstrated on a large scale. It forms the base technology for a large internet that connects most major research institutions, including university, corporate, and government labs. The *National Science Foundation* (*NSF*), the
Department of Energy (*DOE*), the *Department of Defense* (*DOD*), the *Health and Human Services Agency*, (*HHS*) and the *National Aeronautics and Space Administration*
(*NASA*) all participate, using TCP/IP to connect many of their research sites with those
of DARPA. The resulting entity, known as the *connected Internet*, the *DARPA/NSF Internet*, the *TCP/IP Internet*, or just the *Internet†*, allows researchers at connected institutions to share information with colleagues across the country as easily as they share it
with researchers in the next room. An outstanding success, the Internet demonstrates
the viability of the TCP/IP technology and shows how it can accommodate a wide
variety of underlying network technologies.

---

†We will follow the usual convention of capitalizing *Internet* when referring specifically to the connected
internet, and use lower case otherwise; we will also assume the term ''internet'' used without further qualifica-
tion refers to TCP/IP internets.

Most of the material in this book applies to any internet that uses TCP/IP, but some chapters refer specifically to the connected Internet. Readers interested only in the technology should be careful to watch for the distinction between the Internet architecture as it exists and general TCP/IP internets as they might exist. It would be a mistake, however, to ignore sections of the text that describe the connected Internet completely – many corporate networks are already more complex than the connected Internet of ten years ago, and many of the problems they face have already been solved in the connected Internet.

1.3 Internet Services

One cannot appreciate the technical details underlying TCP/IP without understanding the services it provides. This chapter reviews internet services briefly, highlighting the services most users access, and leaving to later chapters the discussion of how computers connect to a TCP/IP internet and how the functionality is implemented.

Much of our discussion of services will focus on standards called *protocols*. Protocols, like TCP and IP, give the formulas for passing messages, specify the details of message formats, and describe how to handle error conditions. Most important, they allow us to discuss communication standards independent of any particular vendor's network hardware. In a sense, protocols are to communication what programming languages are to computation. A programming language allows one to specify or understand a computation without knowing the details of any particular CPU instruction set. Similarly, a communication protocol allows one to specify or understand data communication without depending on detailed knowledge of a particular vendor's network hardware.

Hiding the low-level details of communication helps improve productivity in several ways. First, because programmers deal with higher-level protocol abstractions, they do not need to learn or remember as many details about a given hardware configuration. They can create new programs quickly. Second, because programs built using higher-level abstractions are not restricted to a particular machine architecture or particular network hardware, they do not need to be changed when machines or networks are reconfigured. Third, because application programs built using higher-level protocols are independent of the underlying hardware, they can provide direct communication for an arbitrary pair of machines. Programmers do not need to build special versions of application software to move and translate data between each possible pair of machine types.

We will see that all network services are described by protocols. The next sections refer to protocols used to specify application-level services as well as those used to define network-level services. Later chapters explain each of these protocols in more detail.

1.3.1 Application Level Internet Services

From the user's point of view, a TCP/IP internet appears to be a set of application programs that use the network to carry out useful communication tasks. We use the term *interoperability* to refer to the ability of diverse computing systems to cooperate in solving computational problems. We say that internet application programs exhibit a high degree of interoperability. Most users that access the Internet do so merely by running application programs without understanding the TCP/IP technology, the structure of the underlying internet, or even the path their data travels to its destination; they rely on the application programs to handle such details. Only programmers who write such application programs view the internet as a network and need to understand the details of the technology.

The most popular and widespread Internet application services include:

- *Electronic mail.* Electronic mail allows a user to compose memos and send them to individuals or groups. Another part of the mail application allows users to read memos that they have received. Electronic mail has been so successful that many Internet users depend on it for normal business correspondence. Although many electronic mail systems exist, it is important to understand that using TCP/IP makes mail delivery more reliable. Instead of relying on intermediate machines to relay mail messages, the TCP/IP mail delivery system operates by having the sender's machine contact the receiver's machine directly. Thus, the sender knows that once the message leaves the local machine, it has been successfully received at the destination site.

- *File transfer.* Although users sometimes transfer files using electronic mail, mail is designed primarily for short, text files. The TCP/IP protocols include a file transfer application program that allows users to send or receive arbitrarily large files of programs or data. For example, using the file transfer program, one can copy from one machine to another large data banks containing satellite images, programs written in FORTRAN or Pascal, or an English dictionary. The system provides a way to check for authorized users, or even to prevent all access. Like mail, file transfer across a TCP/IP internet is reliable because the two machines involved communicate directly, without relying on intermediate machines to make copies of the file along the way.

- *Remote login.* Perhaps the most interesting Internet application, remote login allows a user sitting at one computer to connect to a remote machine and establish an interactive login session. The remote login makes it appear that the user's terminal or workstation connects directly to the remote machine by sending every keystroke from the user's keyboard to the remote machine and displaying every character the remote computer prints on the user's terminal screen. When the remote login session terminates, the application returns the user to the local system.

We will return to each of these applications in later chapters to examine them in more detail. We will see exactly how they use the underlying TCP/IP protocols, and why having standards for application protocols has helped ensure that they are widespread.

1.3.2 Network-Level Internet Services

A programmer who writes application programs that use TCP/IP protocols has an entirely different view of an internet than a user who merely executes applications like electronic mail. At the network level, an internet provides two broad types of service that all application programs use. While it is unimportant at this time to understand the details of these services, they cannot be omitted from any overview of TCP/IP:

- *Connectionless Packet Delivery Service.* This service, explained in detail throughout the text, forms the basis for all other internet services. Connectionless delivery is an abstraction of the service that most packet-switching networks offer. It means simply that a TCP/IP internet routes small messages from one machine to another based on address information carried in the message. Because the connectionless service routes each packet separately, it does not guarantee reliable, in-order delivery. Because it usually maps directly onto the underlying hardware, the connectionless service is extremely efficient. More important, having connectionless packet delivery as the basis for all internet services makes the TCP/IP protocols adaptable to a wide range of network hardware.

- *Reliable Stream Transport Service.* Most applications need much more than packet delivery because they require the communication software to recover automatically from transmission errors, lost packets, or failures of intermediate switches along the path between sender and receiver. The reliable transport service handles such problems. It allows an application on one computer to establish a ''connection'' with an application on another computer, and then to send a large volume of data across the connection as if it were a permanent, direct hardware connection. Underneath, of course, the communication protocols divide the stream of data into small messages and send them, one at a time, waiting for the receiver to acknowledge reception.

Many networks provide basic services similar to those outlined above, so one might wonder what distinguishes TCP/IP services from others. The primary distinguishing features are:

- *Network Technology Independence.* While TCP/IP is based on conventional packet switching technology, it is independent of any particular vendor's hardware. The connected Internet includes a variety of network technologies ranging from networks designed to operate within a single building to those designed to span large distances. TCP/IP protocols define the unit of data transmission, called a *datagram*, and specify how to transmit datagrams on a particular network.

- *Universal Interconnection.* A TCP/IP internet allows any pair of computers to which it attaches to communicate. Each computer is assigned an *address* that is universally recognized throughout the internet. Every datagram carries the addresses of its source and destination. Intermediate switching computers use the destination address to make routing decisions.
- *End-to-End Acknowledgements.* The TCP/IP internet protocols provide acknowledgements between the source and ultimate destination instead of between successive machines along the path, even when the two machines do not connect to a common physical network.
- *Application Protocol Standards.* In addition to the basic transport-level services (like reliable stream connections), the TCP/IP protocols include standards for many common applications including electronic mail, file transfer, and remote login. Thus, when designing application programs that use TCP/IP, programmers often find that existing software provides the communication services they need.

Later chapters will discuss the details of the services provided to the programmer as well as many of the application protocol standards.

1.4 History And Scope Of The Internet

Part of what makes the TCP/IP technology so exciting is its almost universal adoption as well as the size and growth rate of the connected Internet. DARPA began working toward an internet technology in the mid 1970s, with the architecture and protocols taking their current form around 1977-79. At that time, DARPA was known as the primary funding agency for packet-switched network research and had pioneered many ideas in packet-switching with its well-known *ARPANET*. The ARPANET used conventional point-to-point leased line interconnection, but DARPA had also funded exploration of packet-switching over radio networks and satellite communication channels. Indeed, the growing diversity of network hardware technologies helped force DARPA to study network interconnection, and pushed internetworking forward.

The availability of research funding from DARPA caught the attention and imagination of several research groups, especially those researchers who had previous experience using packet switching on the ARPANET. DARPA scheduled informal meetings of researchers to share ideas and discuss results of experiments. By 1979, so many researchers were involved in the TCP/IP effort that DARPA formed an informal committee to coordinate and guide the design of the protocols and architecture of the evolving connected Internet. Called the Internet Control and Configuration Board (ICCB), the group met regularly until 1983, when it was reorganized.

The connected Internet began around 1980 when DARPA started converting machines attached to its research networks to the new TCP/IP protocols. The ARPANET, already in place, quickly became the backbone of the new Internet and was used for many of the early experiments with TCP/IP. The transition to Internet technology became complete in January 1983 when the Office of the Secretary of Defense mandated that all computers connected to long-haul networks use TCP/IP. At the same time, the *Defense Communication Agency* (DCA) split the ARPANET into two separate networks, one for further research and one for military communication. The research part retained the name ARPANET; the military part, which was somewhat larger, became known as the *MILNET*.

To encourage university researchers to adopt and use the new protocols, DARPA made an implementation available at low cost. At that time, most university computer science departments were running a version of the UNIX operating system available in the University of California's *Berkeley Software Distribution*, commonly called *Berkeley UNIX* or *BSD UNIX*. By funding Bolt Beranek and Newman, Inc. (BBN) to implement its TCP/IP protocols for use with UNIX, and funding Berkeley to integrate the protocols with its software distribution, DARPA was able to reach over 90% of the university computer science departments. The new protocol software came at a particularly significant time because many departments were just acquiring second or third computers and connecting them together with local area networks. The departments needed communication protocols and no others were generally available.

The Berkeley software distribution became popular because it offered more than basic TCP/IP protocols. In addition to standard TCP/IP application programs, Berkeley offered a set of utilities for network services that resembled the UNIX services used on a single machine. The chief advantage of the Berkeley utilities lay in their similarity to standard UNIX. For example, an experienced UNIX user can quickly learn how to use Berkeley's remote file copy utility (*rcp*) because it behaves exactly like the UNIX file copy utility except that it allows users to copy files to or from remote machines.

Besides a set of utility programs, Berkeley UNIX provides a new operating system abstraction known as a *socket* that allows application programs to access communication protocols. A generalization of the UNIX mechanism for I/O, the socket has options for several types of network protocols in addition to TCP/IP. Its design has been debated since its introduction, and many operating systems researchers have proposed alternatives. Independent of its overall merits, however, the introduction of the socket abstraction was important because it allowed programmers to use TCP/IP protocols with little effort. Thus, it encouraged researchers to experiment with TCP/IP.

The success of the TCP/IP technology and the Internet among computer science researchers led other groups to adopt it. Realizing that network communication would soon be a crucial part of scientific research, the National Science Foundation took an active role in expanding the TCP/IP Internet to reach as many scientists as possible. Starting in 1985, it began a program to establish access networks centered around its six supercomputer centers. In 1986 it expanded networking efforts by funding a new long haul backbone network, called the *NSFNET†*, that eventually reached all its supercomputer centers and tied them to the ARPANET. Finally, in 1986 NSF provided seed money for many regional networks, each of which now connects major scientific research institutions in a given area. All the NSF-funded networks use TCP/IP protocols, and all are part of the connected Internet.

---

†The term *NSFNET* is sometimes used loosely to mean all the NSF-funded networking activities, but we will use it to refer to the backbone. The next chapter gives more details about the technology.

Within seven years of its inception, the Internet had grown to span hundreds of individual networks located throughout the United States and Europe. It connected nearly 20,000 computers at universities, government, and corporate research laboratories. Both the size and the use of the Internet continued to grow much faster than anticipated. By late 1987 it was estimated that the growth had reached 15% per month and remained high for the following two years. By 1990, the connected Internet included over 3,000 active networks and over 200,000 computers.

Adoption of TCP/IP protocols and growth of the Internet has not been limited to government-funded projects. Major computer corporations are all connected to the Internet as well as many other large corporations including: oil companies, the auto industry, electronics firms, and telephone companies. In addition, many companies use the TCP/IP protocols on their internal corporate internets even though they choose not to be part of the connected Internet.

Rapid expansion introduced problems of scale unanticipated in the original design and motivated researchers to find techniques for managing large, distributed resources. In the original design, for example, the names and addresses of all computers attached to the Internet were kept in a single file that was edited by hand and then distributed to every site on the Internet. By the mid 1980s, it became apparent that a central database would not suffice. First, requests to update the file would soon exceed the capacity of people to process them. Second, even if a correct central file existed, network capacity was insufficient to allow either frequent distribution to every site or on-line access by every site.

New protocols were developed and a naming system was put in place across the connected Internet that allows any user to resolve the name of a remote machine automatically. Known as the *Domain Name System*, the mechanism relies on machines called *name servers* to answer queries about names. No single machine contains the entire domain name database. Instead, data is distributed among a set of machines that use TCP/IP protocols to communicate among themselves when answering a query.

1.5 The Original Internet Activities Board

Because the TCP/IP internet protocol suite did not arise from a specific vendor or from a recognized professional society, it is natural to ask, "who sets the technical direction and decides when protocols become standard?" The answer is a group known as the *Internet Activities Board* (*IAB*). The IAB provides the focus and coordination for much of the research and development underlying the TCP/IP protocols and guides the evolution of the connected Internet. It decides which protocols are a required part of the TCP/IP suite and sets official policies.

Formed in 1983 when DARPA reorganized the Internet Control and Configuration Board, the IAB inherited much of its charter from the earlier group. Its initial goals were to encourage exchange among the principals involved in research related to TCP/IP and the Internet and to keep researchers focused on common objectives. Through the first six years, the IAB evolved from a DARPA-specific research group into an autonomous organization. During these years, each member of the IAB chaired an *Internet Task Force* charged with investigating a problem or set of issues deemed to be important. The IAB consisted of approximately ten task forces, with charters ranging from one that investigated how the traffic load from various applications affects the Internet to one that handled short term Internet engineering problems. The IAB met several times each year to hear status reports from each task force, review and revise technical directions, discuss policies, and exchange information with representatives from agencies like DARPA and NSF who funded Internet operations and research.

The chairman of the IAB had the title *Internet Architect* and was responsible for suggesting technical directions and coordinating the activities of the various task forces. The IAB chairman established new task forces on the advice of the IAB and also represented the IAB to others.

Newcomers to TCP/IP are sometimes surprised to learn that the IAB did not manage a large budget; although it set direction, it did not fund most of the research and engineering it envisioned. Instead, volunteers performed much of the work. Members of the IAB were each responsible for recruiting volunteers to serve on their task forces, for calling and running task force meetings, and for reporting progress to the IAB. Usually, volunteers came from the research community or from commercial organizations that produced or used TCP/IP. Active researchers participated in Internet task force activities for two reasons. On one hand, serving on a task force provided opportunities to learn about new research problems. On the other hand, because new ideas and problem solutions designed and tested by task forces often became part of the TCP/IP Internet technology, members realized that their work had a direct, positive influence on the field.

1.6 The New IAB Organization

By the summer of 1989, both the TCP/IP technology and the connected Internet had grown beyond the initial research project into production facilities on which thousands of people depended for daily business. It was no longer possible to introduce new ideas by changing a few installations overnight. To a large extent, the literally hundreds of commercial companies that offer TCP/IP products determined whether products would interoperate by deciding when to incorporate changes in their software. Researchers who drafted specifications and tested new ideas in laboratories could no longer expect instant acceptance and use of their ideas. It was ironic that the researchers who designed and watched TCP/IP develop found themselves overcome by the commercial success of their brainchild. In short, TCP/IP became a successful, production technology and the market place began to dominate its evolution.

To reflect the political and commercial realities of both TCP/IP and the connected Internet, the IAB was reorganized in the summer of 1989. The chairmanship changed. Researchers were moved from the IAB itself to a subsidiary group and a new IAB board was constituted to include representatives from the wider community.

The new IAB organization and names for subparts can best be explained by the diagram in Figure 1.1.

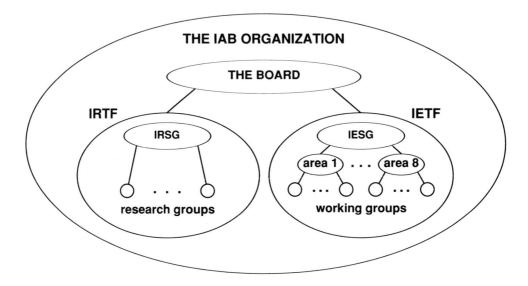

Figure 1.1 The structure of the IAB after the 1989 reorganization.

As Figure 1.1 shows, in addition to the Board itself, the IAB organization contains two major groups: the *Internet Research Task Force (IRTF)* and the *Internet Engineering Task Force (IETF)*.

As its name implies, the IETF concentrates on short-term or medium-term engineering problems. The IETF existed in the old IAB structure, and its success provided part of the motivation for reorganization. Unlike most IAB task forces, which were limited to a few individuals who focused on one specific issue, the IETF had grown to include dozens of active members who worked on many problems concurrently. Before the reorganization, the IETF had been divided into over 20 *working groups*, each working on a specific problem. Working groups held individual meetings to formulate problem solutions. In addition, the entire IETF met regularly to hear reports from working groups and discuss proposed changes or additions to the TCP/IP technology. Usually held three times annually, full IETF meetings attracted hundreds of participants and spectators. The IETF had become too large for the chairman to manage.

The reorganized IAB structure retained the IETF, but split it into eight areas, each with its own manager. The IETF chairman and the eight IETF area managers comprise the *Internet Engineering Steering Group (IESG)*, the individuals responsible for coordinating all efforts of IETF working groups.

Because the IETF was widely known throughout the Internet, and because its meetings were widely recognized and attended, the name "IETF" was preserved in the reorganization and still refers to the entire body, including the chairman, area managers, and all members of working groups. Similarly, the name "IETF working group" was retained.

Created during the reorganization, the Internet Research Task Force was given a name that denotes it as the research counterpart to the IETF. The IRTF coordinates research activities related to TCP/IP protocols or internet architecture in general. Like the IETF, the IRTF has a small group called the *Internet Research Steering Group* or *IRSG*, that sets priorities and coordinates research activities. Unlike the IETF, however, the IRTF is currently a much smaller organization. Each member of the IRSG chairs a volunteer *Internet Research Group* analogous to the IETF working groups; the IRTF is not divided into areas.

1.7 Internet Request For Comments

We have said that no vendor owns the TCP/IP technology nor does any professional society or standards body. Thus, the documentation of protocols, standards, and policies cannot be obtained from a vendor. Instead, DCA funds a group at *SRI International* to maintain and distribute information about TCP/IP and the connected Internet. Known as the *Network Information Center* or simply *The NIC*†, the group handles many administrative details for the Internet in addition to distributing documentation.

Documentation of work on the Internet, proposals for new or revised protocols, and TCP/IP protocol standards all appear in a series of technical reports called Internet *Requests For Comments*, or *RFCs*. (Preliminary versions of RFCs are known as *Internet drafts*.) RFCs can be short or long, can cover broad concepts or details, and can be standards or merely proposals for new protocols. The RFC editor is called the *Deputy Internet Architect*, and is a member of the IAB. While RFCs are edited, they are not refereed in the same way as academic research papers. Also, some reports pertinent to the Internet were published in an earlier, parallel series of reports called *Internet Engineering Notes*, or *IENs*. Although the IEN series is no longer active, not all IENs appear in the RFC series. There are references to RFCs and IENs throughout the text.

Both the RFC and IEN note series are numbered sequentially in the chronological order they are written. Each new or revised RFC is assigned a new number, so readers must be careful to obtain the highest numbered version of a document; an index is available to help identify the correct version.

The NIC distributes RFCs and IENs to the community. You can obtain RFCs from the NIC by postal mail, by electronic mail, or directly across the Internet using a file transfer program. Ask a local network expert how to obtain RFCs at your site, or refer to Appendix *1* for further instructions on how to retrieve them.

---

†Pronounced "The Nick" after its acronym.

1.8 Internet Protocols and Standardization

Readers familiar with data communication networks realize that many communication protocol standards exist. Many of them precede the Internet, so the question arises, "Why did the Internet designers invent new protocols when so many international standards already existed?" The answer is complex, but follows a simple maxim:

> *Use existing protocol standards whenever such standards apply; invent new protocols only when existing standards are insufficient, but be prepared to migrate to international standards when they become available and provide equivalent functionality.*

So, despite appearances to the contrary, the TCP/IP Internet Protocol Suite was not intended to ignore or avoid international standards. It came about merely because none of the existing protocols satisfied the need. The philosophy of adopting standards when they become available also means that when international standards arise and provide the same interoperability as TCP/IP, the Internet will migrate from TCP/IP to those new standards. These ideas agree with the federal government, which has adopted an Opens Systems Profile that specifies the adoption and use of the International Standards Organization's internet technology whenever the technology offers the equivalent functionality of TCP/IP.

1.9 Future Growth and Technology

Both the TCP/IP technology and the Internet continue to evolve. New protocols are being proposed; old ones are being revised. NSF has added considerable complexity to the system by introducing its backbone network, several regional networks, and hundreds of campus networks. Other groups continue to connect to the Internet as well. The most significant change comes not from added network connections, however, but from additional traffic. Physicists, chemists, and space scientists manipulate and exchange much larger volumes of data than computer science researchers who accounted for much of the early Internet traffic. These other scientists introduced substantial load when they began using the Internet, and the load has increased steadily as they continue to find new uses.

To accommodate growth in traffic, the capacity of the NSFNET backbone has already been increased twice, making the current capacity approximately 28 times larger than the original; an additional increase by another factor of 30 is scheduled for late 1990. At the current time, it is difficult to foresee an end to the need for more capacity.

Growth in demands for networking should not be unexpected. The computer industry has enjoyed a continual demand for increased processing power and larger data storage for many years. Users have only begun to understand how to use networks. In the future we can expect continual increases in the demand for communications. Thus, higher-capacity communication technologies will be needed to accommodate the growth.

Figure 1.2 summarizes expansion of the Internet and illustrates an important component of growth: the change in complexity arising because multiple autonomous groups manage parts of the connected Internet. The initial designs for many subsystems depended on centralized management. Much effort is needed to extend those designs to accommodate decentralized management.

	number of networks	number of computers	number of managers
1980	10	10^2	10^0
1990	10^3	10^5	10^1
1995	10^5	10^{10}	10^2

Figure 1.2 Growth of the connected Internet. In addition to traffic increases that result from increased size, the Internet faces complexity that results from decentralized management of both development and operations.

1.10 The FNC And The NREN

The *Federal Networking Council (FNC)*† serves to coordinate activities of federal agencies that fund research or development of TCP/IP and the Internet. The FNC currently consists of representatives from DARPA, NSF, NASA, DOE, DOD, and HHS. FNC members participate in IAB meetings and help suggest priorities for Internet research and engineering projects.

Aware of increasing needs of their agencies and national priorities for high-speed computing and communication, the FNC has worked with leaders in the technical community to produce a plan to evolve the current Internet into a *National Research and Education Network (NREN)*. According to the plan, the NREN will expand to eventually connect all educational institutions and research labs. Doing so will require higher speed communication technologies as well as a shift from federally funded backbone networks to commercially operated services. The FNC will use federal research funds to stimulate research and development of the needed technologies.

---

†The FNC was originally called the *Federal Research Internet Coordination Committee (FRICC)*.

1.11 Organization Of This Text

This text is organized into two volumes. Volume I presents the TCP/IP technology, applications that use it, and the architecture of the connected Internet in more detail. It discusses the fundamentals of protocols like TCP and IP, and shows how they fit together in an internet. In addition to giving details, it highlights the general principles underlying network protocols and explains why the TCP/IP protocols adapt easily to so many underlying physical network technologies. Volume II discusses in depth the internal details of the TCP/IP protocols and shows how programmers use them. It discusses the interface between programs and the protocols and shows how to create and manage corporate internets.

So far we have talked about the TCP/IP technology and the Internet in general terms, summarizing the services provided and the history of their development. The next chapter provides a brief summary of the type of network hardware used throughout the Internet. Its purpose is not to illuminate nuances of a particular vendor's hardware, but to focus on the features of each technology that are of primary importance to an internet architect. Later chapters delve into the protocols and the Internet, fulfilling three purposes: they explore general concepts and review the Internet architectural model, they examine the details of TCP/IP protocols, and they look at standards for high-level services like electronic mail and electronic file transfer. Chapters *3* through *12* review fundamental principles and describe the network protocols software found in any machine that uses TCP/IP. Later chapters describe services that span multiple machines, including the propagation of routing information, name resolution, and applications like electronic mail.

Several appendices follow the main text. The first appendix contains a guide to RFCs. It expands on the description of RFCs found in this chapter and gives examples of what can be found in RFCs. It describes in detail how to obtain RFCs from the NIC by electronic mail, postal mail, and file transfer. Finally, because the standard RFC index comes in chronological order, it presents a list of RFCs organized by topic to make it easier for beginners to find RFCs pertinent to a given subject.

The second appendix contains an alphabetical list of terms and abbreviations used throughout the literature and the text. Because beginners often find the new terminology overwhelming and difficult to remember, they are encouraged to use the alphabetical list instead of scanning back through the text.

Finally, the third appendix, intended as a reference, contains a list of the official Internet protocols. It includes a description of the IAB terminology for distinguishing between protocols that are ''recommended'' and those that are ''required,'' as well as listing the protocols themselves.

1.12 Summary

An internet consists of a set of connected networks that act as a coordinated whole. The chief advantage of an internet is that it provides universal interconnection while allowing individual groups to use whatever network hardware is best suited to their needs. We will examine principles underlying internet communication in general and the details of one internet protocol suite in particular. We will also discuss how internet protocols are used in an internet. Our example technology, called TCP/IP after its two main protocols, was developed by the Defense Advanced Research Projects Agency. It provides the basis for the connected Internet, a large, operational internet that connects most major scientific research institutions including many universities, corporations, and government laboratories. The connected Internet is expanding rapidly and has continuing support from the Defense Research Projects Agency, the National Science Foundation, the Department of Energy, the National Aeronautics and Space Administration, and other government agencies.

FOR FURTHER STUDY

Cerf's *The History Of The ARPANET* [1989] and *History of the Internet Activities Board* [RFC 1120] provide fascinating reading and point the reader to many early research papers on TCP/IP and internetworking. Denning [Nov-Dec 1989] provides a different perspective on the history of the ARPANET. Jennings et. al. [1986] discusses the importance of computer networking for scientists. Denning [Sept-Oct 1989] also points out the importance of internetworking and gives one possible scenario for a world-wide internet.

In [FCCSET], the Federal Coordinating Committee for Science, Engineering and Technology suggests networking should be a national priority. The FRICC presents their vision for a national internet capable of interconnecting all educational and research groups in the country and their plan for evolving the connected Internet toward that vision over the next few years [1989]. The Government Open System Profile report, GOSIP [1989], outlines government procurement procedures for OSI products.

The IETF publishes minutes from its regular meetings; these are available from the Corporation for National Research Initiatives in Reston, VA. The *Journal of Internetworking: Research and Experience* reports on internetworking research, with emphasis on experimental validation of ideas. The periodical *Connexions* [Lynch and Jacobsen 1987] contains articles about TCP/IP and the Internet as well as official statements of policy from the IAB. Finally, the reader is encouraged to remember that the TCP/IP protocol suite and the Internet continue to change; new information can be found in in RFCs and at conferences like the annual Interop conference [Lynch 1987].

EXERCISES

1.1 Explore application programs at your site that use TCP/IP.

1.2 Find out whether your site connects to the Internet.

1.3 TCP/IP products account for over a billion dollars per year in gross revenue. Read trade publications to find a list of vendors offering such products.

2

Review of Underlying Network Technologies

2.1 Introduction

It is important to understand that the Internet is not a new kind of physical network. It is, instead, a method of interconnecting physical networks and a set of conventions for using networks that allow the computers they reach to interact. While hardware technology plays only a minor role in the overall design, it is important to be able to distinguish between the low-level mechanisms provided by the hardware itself and the higher-level facilities that the Internet protocol software provides. It is also important to understand how the facilities supplied by packet-switched technology affect our choice of high-level abstractions.

This chapter introduces basic packet-switching concepts and terminology and then reviews some of the underlying network hardware technologies that have been used in TCP/IP internets. Later chapters describe how these networks are interconnected and how the TCP/IP protocols accommodate vast differences in the hardware. While the list presented here is certainly not comprehensive, it clearly demonstrates the variety among physical networks over which TCP/IP operates. The reader can safely skip many of the technical details, but should try to grasp the idea of packet switching and try to imagine building a homogeneous communication system using such heterogeneous hardware. Most important, the reader should look closely at the details of the physical address schemes the various technologies use; later chapters will discuss in detail how high-level protocols use these physical addresses.

2.2 Two Approaches To Network Communication

Whether they provide connections between one computer and another or between terminals and computers, communication networks can be divided into two basic types: *circuit-switched* and *packet-switched*†. Circuit-switched networks operate by forming a dedicated connection (circuit) between two points. The U.S. telephone system uses circuit switching technology – a telephone call establishes a circuit from the originating phone through the local switching office, across trunk lines, to a remote switching office, and finally to the destination telephone. While a circuit is in place, the phone equipment samples the microphone repeatedly, encodes the samples digitally, and transmits them across the circuit to the receiver. The sender is guaranteed that the samples can be delivered and reproduced because the circuit provides a guaranteed data path of 64 Kbps (thousand bits per second), the rate needed to send digitized voice. The advantage of circuit switching lies in its guaranteed capacity: once a circuit is established, no other network activity will decrease the capacity of the circuit. One disadvantage of circuit switching is cost: circuit costs are fixed, independent of traffic. For example, one pays a fixed rate when making a phone call, even when the two parties do not talk.

Packet-switched networks, the type usually used to connect computers, take an entirely different approach. In a packet-switched network, traffic on the network is divided into small pieces called *packets* that are multiplexed onto high capacity intermachine connections. A packet, which usually contains only a few hundred bytes of data, carries identification that enables computers on the network to know whether it is destined for them or how to send it on to its correct destination. For example, a file to be transmitted between two machines may be broken into many packets that are sent across the network one at a time. The network hardware delivers the packets to the specified destination, where network software reassembles them into a single file again. The chief advantage of packet-switching is that multiple communications among computers can proceed concurrently, with intermachine connections shared by all pairs of machines that are communicating. The disadvantage, of course, is that as activity increases, a given pair of communicating computers receives less of the network capacity. That is, whenever a packet switched network becomes overloaded, computers using the network must wait before they can send additional packets.

Despite the potential drawback of not being able to guarantee network capacity, packet-switched networks have become extremely popular. The motivations for adopting packet switching are cost and performance. Because multiple machines can share a network, fewer interconnections are required and cost is kept low. Because engineers have been able to build high speed network hardware, capacity is not usually a problem. So many computer interconnections use packet-switching that, throughout the remainder of this text, the term *network* will refer only to packet-switched networks.

---

†In fact, it is possible to build hybrid hardware technologies; for our purposes, only the difference in functionality is important.

2.3 Wide Area, Metropolitan Area, and Local Area Networks

Packet-switched networks that span large geographical distances (e.g., the continental U.S.) are fundamentally different from those that span short distances (e.g., a single room). To help characterize the differences in capacity and intended use, packet switched technologies are often divided into three broad categories: *wide area networks (WANs)*, *Metropolitan Area Networks (MANs)*, and *Local Area Networks (LANs)*.

WAN technologies, sometimes called *long haul networks*, allow endpoints to be arbitrarily far apart and are intended for use over large distances. Usually, WANs operate at slower speeds than other technologies and have much greater delay between connections. Typical speeds for a WAN range from 9.6 Kbps to 45 Mbps (million bits per second).

The newest type of network hardware, MAN technologies span intermediate geographic areas and operate at medium-to-high speeds. The name is derived from the ability of a single MAN to span a large metropolitan area. MANs introduce less delay than WANs, but cannot span as large a distance. Typical MANs operate at 56 Kbps to 100 Mbps.

LAN technologies provide the highest speed connections among computers, but sacrifice the ability to span large distances. For example, a typical LAN spans a small area like a single building or a small campus and operates between 4 Mbps and 2 Gbps (billion bits per second).

We have already mentioned the general tradeoff between speed and distance: technologies that provide higher speed communication operate over shorter distances. There are other differences among technologies in the three categories as well. In LAN technologies, each computer usually contains a network interface device that connects the machine directly to the network medium (e.g., a passive copper wire or coaxial cable). Often, the network itself is passive, depending on electronic devices in the attached computers to generate and receive the necessary electrical signals. In MAN technologies, a network contains active switching elements that introduce short delays as they route data to its destination. In WAN technologies, a network usually consists of a series of complex packet switches interconnected by communication lines. The size of the network can be extended by adding a new switch and another communication line. Attaching a computer to a WAN means connecting it to one of the packet switches. The switches introduce significant delays when routing traffic. Thus, the larger the WAN becomes the longer it takes to route traffic across it.

The goal of network protocol design is to hide the technological differences between networks, making interconnection independent of the underlying hardware. The next sections present six examples of network technologies used throughout the Internet, showing some of the differences among them. Later chapters show how the TCP/IP software isolates such differences and makes the communication system independent of the underlying hardware technology.

2.4 Ethernet Technology

Ethernet is the name given to a popular local area packet-switched network technology invented at Xerox PARC in the early 1970s. The version described here was standardized by Xerox Corporation, Intel Corporation, and Digital Equipment Corporation in 1978. As Figure 2.1 shows, an Ethernet consists of a coaxial cable about 1/2 inch in diameter and up to 500 meters long. A resistor is added between the center wire and shield at each end to prevent reflection of electrical signals. Called the *ether*, the cable itself is completely passive; all the active electronic components that make the network function are associated with computers that are attached to the network.

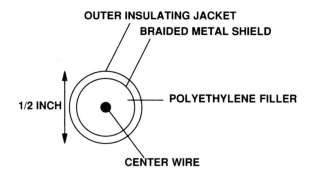

Figure 2.1 Coaxial cable used in an Ethernet

Ethernets may be extended with hardware devices called *repeaters* that relay electrical signals from one cable to another. Figure 2.2 shows a typical use of repeaters in an office building. A single backbone cable runs vertically up the building, and a repeater attaches the backbone to an additional cable on each floor. Computers attach to the cables on each floor. Only two repeaters can be placed between any two machines, so the total length of a single Ethernet is still rather short (1500 meters).

Extending an Ethernet by using repeaters has advantages and disadvantages. Repeaters are less expensive than other types of interconnection hardware, making them the least costly way to extend an Ethernet. However, repeaters have two disadvantages. First, because repeaters repeat and amplify all electrical signals, they also copy electrical disturbance or errors that occur on one wire to the other. Second, because they contain active electronic components and require power, they can fail. In an office environment, the failure may occur in an inconvenient location (e.g., above the ceiling or in a wiring closet), making it difficult to find and repair.

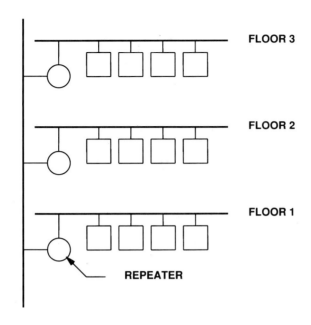

Figure 2.2 Repeaters used to join Ethernet cables in a building. At most two repeaters can be placed between a pair of communicating machines.

Connections to the ether are made by *taps* as Figure 2.3 shows. At each tap, a small hole in the outer layers of cable allows small pins to touch the center wire and the braided shield (some manufacturers' connectors require that the cable be cut and a ''T'' inserted). Each connection to an Ethernet has two major electronic components. A *transceiver* connects to the center wire and braided shield on the ether, sensing and sending signals on the ether. A *host interface* connects to the transceiver and communicates with the computer (usually through the computer's bus).

The transceiver is a small piece of hardware usually found physically adjacent to the ether. In addition to the analog hardware that senses and controls the ether, a transceiver contains digital circuitry that allows it to communicate with a digital computer. The transceiver can sense when the ether is in use and can translate analog electrical signals on the ether to (and from) digital form. The transceiver cable that runs between the transceiver and host interface carries power to operate the transceiver as well as signals to control its operation.

Figure 2.4 shows the interconnection between a host and a transceiver. Each host interface controls the operation of one transceiver according to instructions it receives from the computer software. To the operating system software, the interface appears to be an input/output device that accepts basic data transfer instructions from the computer, controls the transceiver to carry them out, interrupts when the task has been completed, and reports status information. While the transceiver is a simple hardware device, the host interface can be complex (e.g., it may contain a microprocessor used to control transfers between the computer memory and the ether).

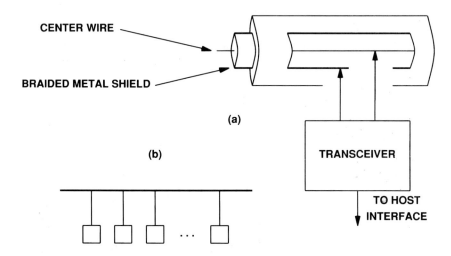

Figure 2.3 (a) A cutaway view of the cable showing the details of 2 electrical
connections between a transceiver and the cable at a tap, and (b)
the schematic diagram of an Ethernet with many taps.

2.4.1 Properties of an Ethernet

The Ethernet is a 10 Mbps broadcast bus technology with best-effort delivery semantics and distributed access control. It is a *bus* because all stations share a single communication channel; it is *broadcast* because all transceivers receive every transmission. The method used to direct packets from one station to just one other station or a subset of all stations will be discussed later. For now, it is enough to understand that transceivers do not filter transmissions – they pass all packets onto the host interface, which chooses packets the host should receive and filters out all others. Ethernet is called a *best-effort delivery* mechanism because it provides no information to the sender about whether the packet was delivered. For example, if the destination machine happens to be powered down, the packet will be lost but the sender will not be notified. We will see later how the TCP/IP protocols accommodate best-effort delivery hardware.

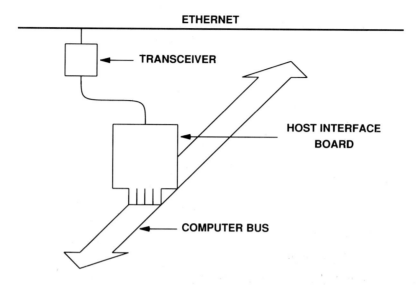

Figure 2.4 The connection between an Ethernet cable and a computer.

Ethernet access control is distributed because, unlike some network hardware, there is no central authority granting access. The Ethernet access scheme is called *Carrier Sense Multiple Access* with *Collision Detect* (*CSMA/CD*). It is *CSMA* because multiple machines can access the Ethernet simultaneously and each machine determines whether the ether is idle by sensing whether a carrier wave is present. When a host interface has a packet to transmit, it listens to the ether to see if a message is being transmitted (i.e., performs carrier sensing). When no transmission is sensed, the host interface starts transmitting. Each transmission is limited in duration (because there is a maximum packet size). Furthermore, the hardware must observe a minimum idle time between transmissions, which means that no single pair of communicating machines can use the network without giving other machines an opportunity for access.

2.4.2 Collision Detection and Recovery

When a transceiver begins transmission, the signal does not reach all parts of the network simultaneously. Instead it travels along the cable at approximately 80% of the speed of light. Thus, it is possible for two transceivers to both sense that the network is idle and begin transmission simultaneously. When the two electrical signals cross they become scrambled, such that neither is meaningful. Such incidents are called *collisions*.

The Ethernet handles collisions in an ingenious fashion. Each transceiver monitors the cable while it is transmitting to see if a foreign signal interferes with its transmission. Technically, the monitoring is called *collision detect* (*CD*), making the Ethernet a

CSMA/CD network. When a collision is detected, the host interface aborts transmission, waits for activity to subside, and tries again. Care must be taken or the network could wind up with all transceivers busily attempting to transmit and every transmission producing a collision. To help avoid such situations, Ethernet uses a binary exponential backoff policy where a sender delays a random time after the first collision, twice as long if a second attempt to transmit also produces a collision, four times as long if a third attempt results in a collision, and so on. The idea behind exponential backoff is that in the unlikely event many stations attempt to transmit simultaneously, a severe traffic jam could occur. In such a jam, there is high probability two stations will choose random backoffs that are close together. Thus, the probability of another collision is high. By doubling the random delay, the exponential backoff strategy quickly spreads the stations' attempts to retransmit over a reasonably long period of time, making the probability of further collisions extremely small.

2.4.3 Ethernet Capacity

The standard Ethernet is rated at 10 Mbps, which means that data can be transmitted onto the cable at 10 million bits per second. Although many recent computers can generate data at Ethernet speed, raw network speed should not be thought of as the rate at which two computers can exchange data. Instead, network speed should be thought of as a measure of network total traffic capacity. Think of a network as a highway connecting multiple cities. High speeds make it possible to carry high traffic loads, while low speed means the highway cannot carry as much traffic. A 10 Mbps Ethernet, for example, can handle a few computers that generate heavy loads, or many computers that generate light loads.

2.4.4 Ethernet Variations

Recent advances in technology have made it possible to build Ethernets that do not need the electrical isolation of coaxial cable. Called *twisted pair Ethernet*, the technology allows a conventional 10 Mbps Ethernet to pass across a pair of copper wires much like the ones used to interconnect telephones. The advantage of using twisted pair is that it reduces cost and makes it possible for many groups to use existing wiring instead of adding new cable.

When high capacity is not needed, the network can still use Ethernet-like technology, but operate at slightly lower speed. The advantages are primarily economic. Lower speed means less complicated hardware and lower cost. One reason lower speed networks cost less is that the interfaces require less buffer memory and can be built from inexpensive integrated circuits.

Costs can also be reduced if high-speed digital circuits can connect directly to the cable without using a transceiver. In such cases, an Ethernet can be implemented with standard coaxial cable like that used for cable television. Called *thin-wire Ethernet*, the thin cable is inexpensive, but supports somewhat fewer connections and covers slightly shorter distances than standard Ethernet cable. Workstation manufacturers find thin wire Ethernet an especially attractive system because they can integrate Ethernet hardware into single board computers and mount BNC-style connectors directly on the back of the machine.

Because they require no special tools, BNC connectors make it possible for users to connect workstations to Ethernets. Of course, allowing users to add their own machines to networks has disadvantages. It means that the network is susceptible to disconnection, incorrect wiring, or intentional abuse. In most situations, however, the advantages outweigh the disadvantages.

Another method of reducing costs uses a single physical cable to carry multiple, independent Ethernets. Known as *broadband*, the technology works much like broadcast radio. The transmitter multiplexes multiple Ethernets onto a single cable by assigning each Ethernet a unique frequency. Receivers must be "tuned" to the correct frequency so they receive only the desired signal and ignore others. Although the equipment needed to connect to a broadband cable is somewhat more expensive than equipment needed to connect to a conventional *baseband* cable, broadband eliminates the cost of laying multiple cables.

2.4.5 Ethernet Addressing

An Ethernet host interface provides an *addressing mechanism* that keeps unwanted packets from being passed to the host computer. Recall that each interface receives a copy of every packet – even those addressed to other machines. The hardware filters packets, ignoring those that are addressed to other machines and passing to the host only those packets addressed to it. The addressing mechanism and filter are needed to prevent a computer from being overwhelmed with incoming data.

To allow a computer to determine which packets are meant for it, each computer attached to an Ethernet is assigned a 48-bit integer known as its *Ethernet address*. Ethernet hardware manufacturers purchase blocks of Ethernet addresses† and assign them in sequence as they manufacture Ethernet interface hardware. Thus, no two hardware interfaces have the same Ethernet address.

Usually, the Ethernet address is fixed in machine readable form on the host interface hardware. Because Ethernet addresses belong to hardware devices, they are sometimes called *hardware addresses* or *physical addresses*. Note the following important property of Ethernet physical addresses:

> *Physical addresses are associated with the Ethernet interface hardware; moving the hardware interface to a new machine or replacing a hardware interface that has failed changes the physical address.*

Knowing that Ethernet physical addresses can change will make it clear why higher levels of the network software are designed to accommodate such changes.

---

†The Institute for Electrical and Electronic Engineers (IEEE) manages the Ethernet address space and assigns addresses as needed.

The 48-bit Ethernet address does more than specify a single hardware interface. It can be one of three types:

- The physical address of one network interface,
- The network *broadcast* address, or
- A *multicast* address.

By convention, the broadcast address (all 1s) is reserved for sending to all stations simultaneously. Multicast addresses provide a limited form of broadcast in which a subset of the computers on a network agree to respond to a multicast address. Every computer in a multicast group can be reached simultaneously without affecting computers outside the multicast group.

To accommodate broadcast and multicast addressing, Ethernet interface hardware must recognize more than its physical address. A host interface usually accepts at least two kinds of transmissions: those addressed to the interface physical address and those addressed to the broadcast address. Some interfaces can be programmed to recognize multicast addresses or even alternate physical addresses. When the operating system starts, it initializes the Ethernet interface, giving it a set of addresses to recognize. The interface then scans each transmission, passing on to the host only those transmissions designated for one of the specified addresses.

2.4.6 Ethernet Frame Format

The Ethernet should be thought of as a link-level connection among machines. Thus, it makes sense to view the data transmitted as a *frame*†. Ethernet frames are of variable length, with no frame smaller than 64 octets‡ or larger than 1518 octets (header, data, and CRC). As in all packet-switched networks, a frame must identify its destination. Figure 2.5 shows the Ethernet frame format that contains the physical source address as well as the physical destination address.

In addition to identifying the source and destination, each frame transmitted across the Ethernet contains a *preamble, type field, data field*, and *Cyclic Redundancy Check (CRC)*. The preamble consists of 64 bits of alternating *0*s and *1*s to help receiving nodes synchronize. The 32-bit CRC helps the interface detect transmission errors: the sender computes the CRC as a function of the data in the frame, and the receiver recomputes the CRC to verify that the packet has been received intact.

The frame type field contains a 16-bit integer that identifies the type of the data being carried in the frame. From the Internet point of view, the frame type field is essential because it means Ethernet frames are *self-identifying*. When a frame arrives at a given machine, the operating system uses the frame type to determine which protocol software module should process the frame. The chief advantages of self-identifying frames are that they allow multiple protocols to be used together on a single machine and they allow multiple protocols to be intermixed on the same physical network without interference. For example, one could have an application program using Internet protocols while another used a local experimental protocol. The operating system

---

†The term *frame* derives from communication over serial lines in which the sender "frames" the data by adding special characters before and after the transmitted data.
‡The term *octet* refers to an 8-bit quantity, often called a *byte*.

would decide where to send incoming packets based on their frame type. We will see that the TCP/IP protocols use self-identifying Ethernet frames to distinguish among several protocols.

Preamble	Destination Address	Source Address	Frame Type	Frame Data	CRC
64 bits	48 bits	48 bits	16 bits	368-12000 bits	32 bits

Figure 2.5 The format of a frame (packet) as it travels across an Ethernet. Fields are not drawn to scale.

2.4.7 Bridges and Their Importance

We already discussed the use of Ethernet repeaters as one technique for extending a physical Ethernet to multiple physical wire segments. Although repeaters were a popular extension many years ago, most sites now use *bridges* to interconnect segments. Unlike a repeater, which replicates electrical signals, a bridge replicates packets. In fact, a bridge is a fast computer with two Ethernet interfaces and a fixed program. The bridge operates both Ethernet interfaces in *promiscuous mode*, meaning that they capture all valid packets that appear on their respective Ethernets and deliver them to the processor in the bridge. If the bridge connects two Ethernets, E_1 and E_2, the software takes each packet arriving on E_1 and transmits it on E_2, and vice versa.

Bridges are superior to repeaters because they do not replicate noise, errors, or malformed frames; a completely valid frame must be received before it will be reproduced. Furthermore, bridge interfaces follow the Ethernet CSMA/CD rules, so collisions and propagation delays on one wire remain isolated from those on the other. As a result, an (almost) arbitrary number of Ethernets can be connected together with bridges. Note that bridges hide the details of interconnection: a set of bridged segments acts like a single Ethernet. A computer can communicate across a bridge using exactly the same hardware signals it uses to communicate on its own segment.

Most bridges do much more than replicate frames from one wire to another: they make intelligent decisions about which frames to forward. Such bridges are called *adaptive*, or *learning* bridges. An adaptive bridge consists of a computer with two Ethernet interfaces. The software in an adaptive bridge keeps two address lists, one for each interface. When a frame arrives from Ethernet E_1, the adaptive bridge adds the 48-bit Ethernet *source* address to the list associated with E_1. Similarly, when a frame arrives from Ethernet E_2, the bridge adds the source address to the list associated with E_2. Thus, over time the adaptive bridge will learn which machines lie on E_1 and which lie on E_2.

After recording the source address of a frame, the adaptive bridge uses the destination address to determine whether to forward the frame. If the address lists show that the destination lies on the Ethernet from which the frame arrived, the bridge does not forward the frame. If the destination is not in the address list (i.e., the destination is a broadcast or multicast address or the bridge has not yet learned the location of the destination), the bridge forwards the frame to the other Ethernet.

The advantages of adaptive bridges should be obvious. Because the bridge uses addresses found in normal traffic, it is completely automatic – humans are not required to program the bridge with specific addresses. Because a bridge isolates traffic when forwarding is unnecessary, it can be used to improve the performance of an overloaded network (note that bridges work exceptionally well to partition load in a workstation environment where sets of workstations direct most of their traffic to a file server). To summarize:

> *An adaptive Ethernet bridge connects two Ethernet segments, forwarding frames from one to the other. It uses source addresses to learn which machines lie on which Ethernet segment and it combines information learned with destination addresses to eliminate forwarding when unnecessary.*

From the TCP/IP point of view, bridged Ethernets are merely another form of physical network connection. The important point is:

> *Because the connection among physical cables provided by bridges and repeaters is transparent to machines using the Ethernet, we think of bridged Ethernets as a single physical network system.*

Most commercial bridges are much more sophisticated and robust than our description indicates. When first powered up, they check for other bridges and learn the topology of the network. They use a distributed spanning-tree algorithm to decide how to forward frames. In particular, the bridges decide how to propagate broadcast packets so only one copy of a broadcast frame is delivered to each wire. Without such an algorithm, Ethernets and bridges connected into a cycle would produce catastrophic results because they would forward broadcast packets in both directions simultaneously.

2.5 ProNET Token Ring Technology

ProNET-10 is the name of a commercial local area network product that offers an interesting alternative to the Ethernet. Based on networking research at universities, and manufactured by Proteon Incorporated, a proNET-10 consists of a passive wiring system that interconnects computers. Like the Ethernet, the low-speed version operates at 10 Mbps†, is limited to short geographic distances, and requires attached computers to have an active host interface.

Unlike the Ethernet or related bus technologies, proNET-10 requires hosts to be wired in a one-way ring and uses an access technology known as *token passing*. The primary distinguishing feature of token-passing systems is that they achieve fair access by having all machines take turns using the network. At any time, exactly one machine

---

†A related Proteon product operates at 80 Mbps.

holds a *token* which grants that machine the right to send a packet. After sending its packet, the machine passes the token to the next machine in sequence, and so on. Thus, when none of the machines has anything to send, they continually pass the token around; when they all have packets to send, they take turns sending them.

Although token passing can be used with Ethernet-like bus topologies, ring topologies like those used by proNET-10 make token passing especially simple because the physical connections determine the sequence through which the token passes. The key is that a given machine does not know the identity of the machine to which it passes the token. We will soon see why token circulation based on physical order is important, and how it can be used to make the ring more reliable.

To understand how a ring operates, we need to look at the hardware. Physically, the ring network is not a continuous wire – it consists of point-to-point connections among the host interfaces of computers on the net. At each host, one wire carries incoming signals, and another carries outgoing signals.

Conceptually, each host interface operates in one of three modes: *copy mode, transmit mode,* or *recovery mode.* As Figure 2.6 shows, the first two modes represent normal operation, with the choice depending on whether the machine currently holds the token.

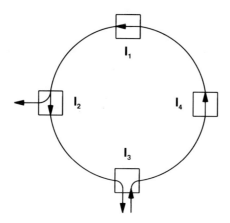

Figure 2.6 A token ring network with interface I_3 in transmit mode, holding the token and sending a packet to interface I_2. Other interfaces are in copy mode. The sender always receives back the bits being sent; other interfaces extract a copy of the packet for their host only if the address matches.

When not holding the token, an interface runs in copy mode, reading bits from the incoming wire and copying them to the outgoing wire. In copy mode, the interface also watches the data stream to find packets addressed to the local machine, placing a copy of such packets in the machine's memory. When holding the token, the interface operates in transmit mode, sending a packet on the outgoing wire and verifying correctness by reading it back from the incoming wire.

It is important to understand that ProNET-10 is a LAN technology that only has small propagation delays. When constructed from shielded copper cable, the ring can span at most a few adjacent buildings. When fiber optic cable is used, the ring can span longer distances (e.g., an entire campus). In any case, propagation delays are short. As a consequence, signals can propagate through the entire ring and return to the sender so quickly that the beginning of a packet completes its trip around the ring while the sender continues to transmit. The advantage of short propagation delay is that a station can determine quickly whether the ring is broken. It can also determine whether electrical interference or broken hardware along the path introduces any errors into the packet. We will discuss both of these features below.

2.5.1 ProNET-10 Addressing

Quite unlike the Ethernet, proNET-10 interface hardware does not have fixed addresses assigned by the manufacturer. Instead, each interface comes with a set of 8 switches that allows a system administrator to choose any of 255 possible addresses (thus, a given proNET-10 network is limited to 255 machines). The address must be selected and configured using physical switches on the board. It cannot be changed quickly or easily once the interface is installed, nor can it be changed by software. However, making an address configurable has two important advantages. First, it means that proNET-10 addresses can be much smaller than Ethernet addresses (8 bits instead of 48 bits). Second, it means:

> *Because customers can change proNET-10 addresses when installing boards, the network hardware address of a machine need not change when the host interface hardware is replaced.*

Of course, making hardware addresses configurable does have a disadvantage. Unlike Ethernet addresses, the configurable address scheme used by proNET-10 allows address conflicts. An installer is required to ensure that each interface on a given ring is assigned a unique address between 0 and 254. An address of all *1*s (255) is reserved for broadcast traffic. As we will see later, when using proNET-10 with TCP/IP, installers should avoid assigning any host address zero.

2.5.2 ProNET-10 Frame Format

Figure 2.7 shows the proNET-10 frame format. Fields are specified in bits because the network is bit-oriented and does not always align data on octet boundaries. The network hardware requires the data field to be an exact multiple of octets, making it easy to transfer data to the host computer's memory. Like the Ethernet, the hardware only understands some parts of the frame format; software supplies and uses other parts. From the internet designer's point of view, the distinction is unimportant.

Start of Msg.	Dest. Addr.	Src. Addr.	Frame Type	Frame Data	End of Msg.	Parity	Refuse
10 bits	8 bits	8 bits	24 bits	0-16352 bits	9 bits	1 bit	1 bit

Figure 2.7 The proNET-10 frame format. Fields are not shown to scale.

Each frame begins with a *start of message* field, followed by two octets of *destination* and *source* address. The *frame type* field consists of three octets, but only the first is currently used; the last two must contain 0. Following the *data* portion of the frame comes an *End of Message* field, a single *parity* bit, and a *refused* bit. Either another frame or the token follows immediately after the end of a frame. Note that, like the Ethernet, proNET-10 frames are self-identifying.

In contrast to Ethernet, which uses a complex 32-bit CRC to check for transmission errors, proNET-10 uses only a single parity. To understand why only one bit is needed, recall that proNET is a LAN technology with low propagation delay. Thus, the sending site receives a copy of the frame during transmission, and can easily compare bits in the copy to see if they have been changed. In fact, the parity bit is unnecessary except as a check on the *refused* bit.

The hardware uses a *flag* consisting of 7 contiguous 1 bits to distinguish fields like end-of-message from user data. The token and beginning of a frame also start with a flag. Whenever 7 contiguous 1 bits occur in the user's data, the hardware modifies the sequence to ensure that the receiver can distinguish it from a flag. The receiver reverses the modification to deliver exactly the same data that was sent.

2.5.3 proNET-10 Token Recovery

Because a token passing ring relies on all hosts to forward the token when they finish transmitting, failures at one node can stop the ring. Suppose, for example, that a malfunction or electrical interference damaged the token. Unless the ring included a mechanism to recover, all transmission would cease. To recover from token loss, the proNET-10 has each station run two timers. One timer, called a *flag timer*, is reset whenever the station detects an activity (e.g., a frame or a token) and the other, called a *token timer*, is reset when a token arrives. If either timer has expired when the station has a packet to send, the station changes to recovery mode and eventually generates a new token for the ring. On an otherwise idle ring, the token circulates continually. Thus, the flag timer expires quickly (after 3 ms) if the ring is completely idle. The token timer must allow for large packet transmissions by up to 255 other stations, so it has a much longer expiration time (400 ms). Ring technologies that allow more stations or larger packets use longer expiration times (e.g., proNET-80 uses 700ms).

Usually, the first station to enter recovery mode assumes it holds the token and transmits its packet. Following the packet, it transmits the token as if nothing had gone wrong. As it transmits, the station monitors the ring to check that the packet circulates

completely. If so, the ring has recovered and everything proceeds as usual. In the im-
probable case that two stations simultaneously attempt to transmit after a token loss,
they detect the problem because they do not receive back their own transmission. The
two stations back off, wait a random time, and try again. To guarantee that they do not
both wait exactly the same amount of time, each station computes a delay proportional
to its hardware address. Thus, if two boards begin circulating packets simultaneously,
only one survives. The recovery algorithm is both efficient and reliable. It guarantees
that in only a few trips around the ring, one station will decide it holds the token and all
other stations will agree.

2.5.4 proNET-10 Star-Shaped Ring

In practice, most installations configure proNET-10 networks into star-shaped rings
to improve reliability. The idea is to use a passive wire center as the hub of a physical
star topology even though the network operates logically as a ring. Figure 2.8 illustrates such a connection.

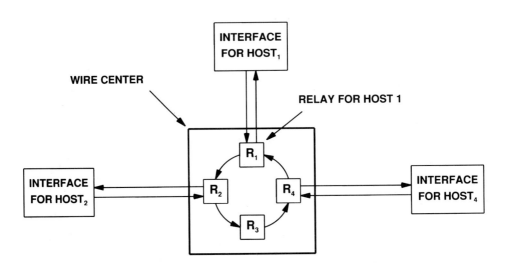

Figure 2.8 The connection of three hosts through a passive wire center. Because it receives no power, relay R_3 passes signals through directly. Logically, the network is a ring; physically, it is a star.

In the Figure, Relay R_3 does not receive power because there is no host connection. R_3
closes the ring and connects R_2 to R_4. Because other relays receive power, they connect
their respective hosts into the ring. Thus, an electrical signal sent from Host 4 passes
through relay R_4, to relay R_1, up to the interface on Host 1, back to relay R_1, over to relay R_2, and so on.

The wire center has no active components, but uses sensitive relays powered by current flowing over host connections. A host supplies low voltage direct current to power the relay as well as the signal that encodes data over a single set of wires. Electronics in the wire center separate the DC power from the AC signal. As long as a machine has power, its relay at the wire center keeps it connected into the ring. When the machine is powered down, however, current stops flowing to the wire center, and the corresponding relay changes state, disconnecting the host and connecting other machines into the ring. Thus, the network continues to operate even if some of the attached machines lose power (of course, a machine failure may stop the network for a few milliseconds while the remaining nodes recover the token). Adding to the reliability, the vendor has designed the proNET-10 interface on two boards, a controller that can participate in copy mode and token recovery without any help from the CPU, and a computer interface that depends on the CPU to read or write packets. Using two boards isolates the rest of the network from operating system failures on a given host.

2.6 ARPANET Technology

One of the oldest wide area packet-switched networks, the ARPANET, was built by the Defense Advanced Research Projects Agency (DARPA), at a time when the agency was still called ARPA. DARPA awarded a contract for the development of ARPANET software to Bolt, Beranek and Newman of Cambridge, MA in the fall of 1968. By September of 1969, the first pieces of the ARPANET were in place.

The ARPANET served as a testbed for much of the research in packet-switching. In addition to its use for network research, researchers in several universities, military bases, and government labs regularly used the ARPANET to exchange files and electronic mail and to provide remote login among their sites. In 1975, control of the network was transferred from DARPA to the U.S. Defense Communications Agency (DCA). The DCA made the ARPANET part of the Defense Data Network (DDN), a program that provides multiple networks as part of a world-wide communication system for the Department of Defense.

In 1983 the Department of Defense partitioned the ARPANET into two connected networks, leaving the ARPANET for experimental research and forming the *MILNET* for military use. MILNET is restricted to unclassified data. Although under normal circumstances, both ARPANET and MILNET agreed to pass traffic to each other, controls were established that allowed them to be disconnected†. Because the ARPANET and MILNET used the same hardware technology, our description of the technical details apply to both even though we refer mainly to the ARPANET. In fact, the technology is available commercially and has been used by several corporations to establish private packet switching networks.

Because the ARPANET was already in place and used daily by many of the researchers who developed the Internet architecture, it had a profound effect on their work. They came to think of the ARPANET as a dependable wide area backbone around which the Internet could be built. The influence of a single, central wide area

---

†Perhaps the best known example of disconnection occurred in November, 1988 when a *worm* program attacked the Internet and replicated itself as quickly as possible.

backbone is still painfully obvious in some of the Internet protocols that we will discuss later, and has prevented the Internet from accommodating additional backbone networks gracefully.

Physically, the ARPANET consisted of approximately 50 BBN Corporation C30 and C300 minicomputers, called *Packet Switching Nodes* or *PSNs*‡, scattered across the continental U.S. and western Europe (the MILNET has approximately 160 PSNs, including 34 in Europe and 18 in the Pacific and Far East). One PSN resided at each site participating in the network and was dedicated to the task of switching packets; it could not be used for general-purpose computation. Indeed, the PSN was considered to be part of the ARPANET and was owned and controlled by the *Network Operations Center (NOC§)* located at BBN in Cambridge, Massachusetts.

Point-to-point data circuits leased from long haul carriers connected the PSNs together to form a network. For example, leased data circuits connected the ARPANET PSN at Purdue University to the ARPANET PSNs at Carnegie Mellon and at the University of Wisconsin. Initially, most of the leased data circuits in the ARPANET operated at 56 Kbps, speeds considered extremely fast in 1968 but slow by current standards. Remember to think of the speed as a measure of capacity rather than a measure of the time it takes to deliver packets. As more computers used the ARPANET, capacity was increased to accommodate the load. For example, during the final year the ARPANET existed, many of the cross-country links operated over megabit-speed channels.

The idea of having no single point of failure in a system is common in military applications because reliability is important. When building the ARPANET, DARPA decided to follow the military requirements for reliability, so they mandated that each PSN had to have at least two leased line connections to other PSNs, and the software had to automatically adapt to failures and choose alternate routes. As a result, the ARPANET continued to operate even if one of its data circuits failed.

In addition to connections for leased data circuits, each ARPANET PSN had up to 22 *ports* that connected it to user computers, called *hosts*. Originally, all computers that needed to access the ARPANET connected directly to one of the ports on a PSN. Normally, direct connections were formed with a special-purpose interface board that plugged into the computer's I/O bus and attached to a PSN host port. When programmed properly, the interface allowed the computer to contact the PSN to send and receive packets.

The original PSN port hardware used a complex protocol for transferring data across the ARPANET. Fondly known as 1822, after the number of a technical report that described it, this bizarre protocol survives and is still used on PSN ports in the MILNET. In general, 1822 permits a host to send a packet across the ARPANET to a specified destination PSN and a specified port on that PSN. Performing the transfer is complicated, however, because 1822 offers reliable, flow-controlled delivery. To prevent a given host from saturating the net, 1822 limits the number of packets that can be in transit. To guarantee that each packet arrives at its destination, 1822 forces the sender to await a *Ready For Next Message (RFNM)* signal from the PSN before transmitting each packet. The RFNM acts as an acknowledgement. It includes a buffer

---

‡PSNs were initially called *Interface Message Processor*s or *IMP*s, and the terminology persists.
§called "the knock" after its acronym.

reservation scheme that requires the sender to reserve a buffer at the destination PSN before sending a packet.

Although there are many parts of 1822 not discussed here, the key idea to under-stand is that underneath all the detail, the ARPANET is merely a transfer mechanism. When a computer connected to one port sends a packet to another port, the data delivered is exactly the data sent. Because the ARPANET does not deliver a network-specific header, packets sent across it do not have a fixed field to specify packet type. Thus, unlike other network technologies, the ARPANET does not deliver self-identifying packets. In summary:

> *The ARPANET does not understand contents of packets that travel across it; it is only by convention that machines attached to the AR-PANET agree on the format and contents of packets sent or received at a specific PSN port.*

Unfortunately, 1822 was never an industry standard. Because few vendors manufacture 1822 interface boards it became difficult to connect new machines to the ARPANET. To solve the problem, DARPA developed a new PSN interface that uses an international data communications standard known as *CCITT X.25* (the designator was assigned by the standards committee that developed it). The first version of an X.25 PSN implementation used only the data transfer part of the X.25 standard (known as HDLC/LAPB), but later versions made it possible to use all of X.25 when connecting to a PSN (i.e., ARPANET appears to be an X.25 network). Many MILNET ports now use X.25.

Internally, of course, the ARPANET used its own set of protocols that are invisible to users. For example, there was a special protocol that allows one PSN to request status from another, another protocol that PSNs used to send packets among themselves, and still another that allowed PSNs to exchange information about link status and op-timal routes.

Because the ARPANET was originally built as a single, independent network to be used for research, its protocols and addressing structure were designed without much thought given to expansion. By the mid 1970's, it became apparent no single network would solve all communication problems, and DARPA began to investigate satellite and packet radio network technologies. This experience with a variety of network technolo-gies led to the concept of an internetwork.

Today, the ARPANET has quietly disappeared and been replaced by new technolo-gies. MILNET continues to form the backbone of the military side of the connected In-ternet. The MILNET Monitoring Center, located near Washington DC, monitors traffic 24 hours a day, detects malfunctions in the hardware and communications lines, and coordinates the installation of new software in the PSNs. DARPA is participating with the FNC to fund research and experimentation that will provide the basis for the Nation-al Research and Education Network. The NREN plan includes a DARPA-sponsored *Defense Research Internet (DRI)* and a provision to make some of the new backbone capacity available to researchers in a *National Network Testbed (NNT)*.

2.6.1 ARPANET Addressing

While the details of ARPANET addressing are unimportant, they illustrate how most wide area networks form physical addresses. Unlike local area networks like Ethernet or proNET-10, wide area networks usually imbed information in the address that helps the network route packets to their destination efficiently. In the ARPANET, each packet switch is assigned a unique integer, P, and each host port on the switch is numbered from 0 to $N-1$. Conceptually, a destination address consists of a pair of small integers, (P,N). In practice, the hardware uses a larger integer address, with some bits of the address used to represent N and others used to represent P.

2.7 National Science Foundation Networking

Realizing that data communication would soon be crucial to scientific research, in 1987 the National Science Foundation established a *Division of Network and Communications Research and Infrastructure* to help ensure that requisite network communications will be available for U.S. scientists and engineers. Although the division funds basic research in networking, its emphasis so far has been concentrated on providing seed funds to build extensions to the Internet.

NSF's Internet extensions form a three-level hierarchy consisting of a new cross-country backbone, a set of "mid-level" or "regional" networks that each span a small geographic area, and a set of "campus" or "access" networks. In the NSF model, mid-level networks attach to the backbone and campus networks attach to the mid-level nets. Researchers have a connection from their computer to the local campus network. They can use that connection to communicate with local researchers' computers across the local campus net, and they can communicate with researchers further away because their machine will route traffic across the local net and across the mid-level and backbone nets as needed.

2.7.1 The Original NSFNET Backbone

Of all the NSF-funded networks, the NSFNET backbone has the most interesting history and uses the most interesting technology. To date, the backbone has evolved in three major steps; it increased in size and capacity at the time the ARPANET declined until it became the dominant backbone in the Internet. The first version was built quickly, as a temporary measure. One early justification for the backbone was to provide scientists with access to NSF supercomputers. As a result, the first backbone consisted of six Digital Equipment Corporation LSI-11 microcomputers located at the existing NSF supercomputer centers. Geographically, the backbone spanned the continental United States from Princeton, NJ to San Diego, CA, using 56 Kbps leased lines as Figure 2.9 shows.

At each site, the LSI-11 microcomputer ran software affectionately known as *fuzz-ball*† code. Developed by Dave Mills, each fuzzball accessed computers at the local supercomputer center using a conventional Ethernet interface. It accessed leased lines leading to fuzzballs at other supercomputer centers using serial line controllers employing vendor link-level protocols. Fuzzballs contained tables with addresses of possible destinations and used those tables to direct each incoming packet toward its destination.

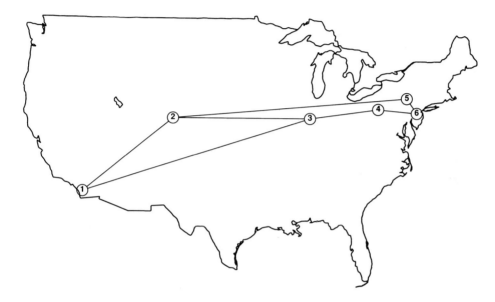

Figure 2.9 Circuits in the original NSFNET backbone with sites in (1) San Diego CA, (2) Boulder CO, (3) Champaign IL, (4) Pittsburgh PA, (5) Ithaca NY, and (6) Princeton NJ.

The primary connection between the original NSFNET backbone and the rest of the Internet was located at Carnegie Mellon, which had both an NSFNET backbone node and an ARPANET PSN. When a user, connected to NSFNET, sent traffic to a site on the ARPANET, the packets would travel across the NSFNET to CMU where the fuzzball would route them onto the ARPANET via a local Ethernet. Similarly, the fuzzball understood that packets destined for NSFNET sites should be accepted from the Ethernet and sent across the NSF backbone to the appropriate site.

---

†The exact origin of the term "fuzzball" is unclear.

2.7.2 The Second NSFNET Backbone 1988-1989

Although users were excited about the possibilities of computer communication, the transmission and switching capacities of the original backbone were too small to provide adequate service. Within months after its inception, the backbone became overloaded and its inventor worked to engineer quick solutions for the most pressing problems while NSF began the arduous process of planning for a second backbone.

In 1987, NSF issued a request for proposals from groups that wanted to establish and operate a new, higher-speed backbone. Proposals were submitted in August of 1987 and evaluated that fall. On November 24, 1987 NSF announced it had selected a proposal submitted by a partnership of: MERIT Inc., the statewide computer network run out of the University of Michigan in Ann Arbor, IBM Corporation, and MCI Incorporated. The partners proposed to build a second backbone network, establish a network operation and control center in Ann Arbor, and have the system operational by the following summer. Because NSF had funded the creation of several new mid-level networks, the proposed backbone was planned to serve more sites than the original. Each additional site would provide a connection between the backbone and one of the NSF mid-level networks.

The easiest way to envision the division of labor among the three groups is to assume that MERIT was in charge of planning, establishing, and operating the network center. IBM contributed machines and manpower from its research labs to help MERIT develop, configure, and test needed hardware and software. MCI, a long-distance carrier, provided the communication bandwidth using the optical fiber already in place for its voice network. Of course, in practice there was close cooperation between all groups, including joint study projects and representatives from IBM and MCI in the project management.

By the middle of the summer of 1988, the hardware was in place and NSFNET began to use the second backbone. Shortly thereafter, the original backbone was shut down and disconnected. Figure 2.10 shows the logical topology of the second backbone after it was installed in 1988.

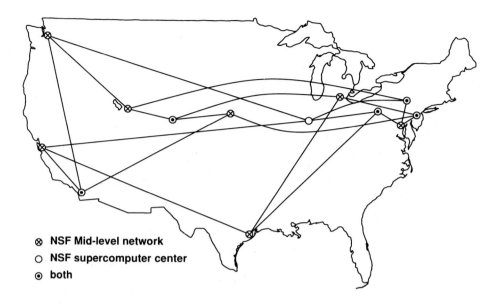

Figure 2.10 Logical circuits in the second NSFNET backbone from summer
1988 to summer 1989.

The technology chosen for the second NSFNET backbone was interesting. In essence, the backbone was a wide area network composed of packet switches interconnected by communication lines. As with the original backbone, the packet switch at each site connected to the site's local Ethernet as well as to communication lines leading to other sites.

Instead of using either fuzzballs or commercially available packet switches, the second backbone used custom made packet switches, created by placing several conventional computers in a large cabinet and interconnecting them as Figure 2.11 shows. The result is called a *nodal switching system (NSS)*. An NSS functions like a single packet switch.

Nodal Switching System

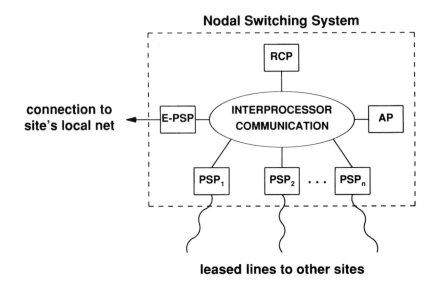

Figure 2.11 A Nodal Switching System (NSS) composed of multiple processors connected by an interprocessor communication mechanism.

As Figure 2.11 shows, an NSS contained a central interprocessor communication mechanism and three types of processors: Packet Switching Processors (PSPs), a Routing and Control Processor (RCP), and an Application Processor (AP). In the first implementation, the central interprocess communication mechanism was a conventional local area network† (an IBM Token Ring Network), and the processors were IBM RT-PCs.

Conceptually, each Packet Switching Processor in an NSS controls one of the leased lines leading to an NSS at another site. Physically, a leased line connects to an I/O interface in the PSP bus. A PSP performs two tasks: it accepts packets that arrive over the interprocessor communication net and transmits them across its leased line, and it accepts packets that arrive over its leased line and routes them across the interprocessor communication net to an outgoing line (i.e., to the processor controlling the line over which they must be sent). Because all Packet Switching Processors operate simultaneously, the NSS can switch packets in parallel. The whole NSS can be thought of as a multiprocessor that uses its interprocessor communication channel as a bus.

Even though an NSS had parallel capability, efficiency was important. Initial leased circuits operated at 448 Kbps, but the goal was to allow Packet Switching Processors to handle leased lines running at speeds of DS-1 (1.544 Mbps) through DS-3 (45 Mbps). At such speeds a processor has little time to perform computations for each packet. Thus, to make routing decisions efficient, PSPs use a table lookup similar to the one described in later chapters of this text. To further offload computational tasks, each NSS contains additional Routing and Control Processors that are used to compute

---

†The interprocessor communication LAN is entirely local to the NSS.

new routing tables or otherwise control the NSS. Application processors perform other tasks like network monitoring.

2.7.3 NSFNET Backbone 1989-1990

After measuring traffic on the second NSFNET backbone for a year, the operations center reconfigured the network by adding some circuits and deleting others. In addition, they increased the speed of circuits to DS-1 (1.544 Mbps). Figure 2.12 shows the revised connection topology, which provided redundant connections to all sites.

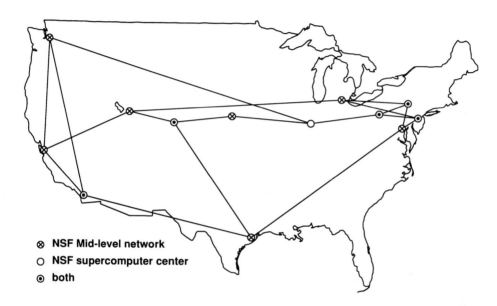

⊗ **NSF Mid-level network**

○ **NSF supercomputer center**

◉ **both**

Figure 2.12 Circuits in the second NSFNET backbone from summer 1989 to 1990.

2.7.4 Multiplexing and Programmable Connections

While the exact topology of NSFNET is unimportant, the technology used to reconfigure it is. As part of their proposal, MERIT, IBM, and MCI promised to explore new ways to make the network reconfigurable. What makes their proposed plan more interesting than most network plans is that it involves MCI, the vendor supplying the long-lines connection service.

To understand the possibilities for reconfiguration, consider what usually happens when a customer contacts a long-distance vendor to lease a digital data circuit. Although the customer may imagine wires hung in a direct line between the two sites, the vendor chooses a path for the circuit that takes advantage of existing cable. For example, the vendor may connect the customer through a local office, from there to a nearby large city where the vendor has trunk capacity, across the trunk to another large city near the destination, and finally down through a local office to the specified termination point. More important, with modern technology, the vendor does not supply a separate physical circuit. Instead, electronic equipment at one end of a trunk fiber *multiplexes* (combines) multiple circuits over the fiber and equipment at the other end *demultiplexes* (separates) them, making it possible for the vendor to add or reconfigure circuits electronically. For example, Figure 2.13 shows the location of optical fiber owned by MCI. Circuits in the NSFNET backbone are multiplexed onto this fiber.

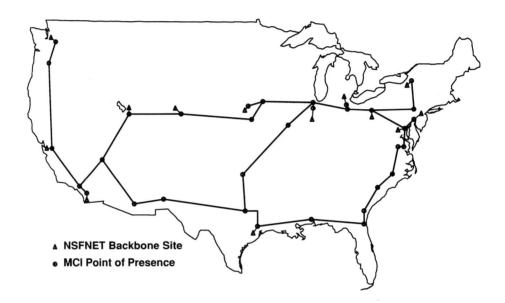

▲ **NSFNET Backbone Site**

● **MCI Point of Presence**

Figure 2.13 The MCI physical fiber installation over which NSFNET backbone circuits are allocated.

The MERIT/IBM/MCI proposal poses an interesting question: "If users had the ability to reconfigure circuits electronically, how could they improve networking?" The reconfiguration shown between Figures 2.11 and 2.12 illustrates one possibility. The owner of a network could watch network traffic over a long period of time and then reconfigure the circuits to provide a direct path between pairs of sites with the most traffic. In addition to adding circuits where needed, dynamic reconfiguration can allow the user to save money by eliminating costly direct paths between pairs of sites that have little or no traffic. Comparing Figures 2.11 and 2.12, we see that a direct path has been added between the sites in Seattle and the San Francisco Bay area, while the direct path between the site at Ann Arbor, Michigan and Houston, Texas has been eliminated. Of course, one cannot reconfigure underlying circuits without recomputing routes in packet switches.

If users had access to the same reconfiguration facilities as vendors, they could do much more than merely create or delete circuits. They could adjust circuit capacities on demand. Such adjustments could be important because it could mean saving enough money on unused circuit capacity to pay for more capacity when needed. Consider NSFNET, for example. At 8 AM on the east coast, users arrive at work and begin generating traffic, so higher capacity is needed for circuits connecting to machines in the east. Meanwhile, on the west coast, most users are still asleep, so little capacity is needed for circuits that connect to west coast machines. As the day proceeds capacity should gradually shift to the west coast circuits. By late afternoon, when users are leaving their offices in the east, west coast circuits need the greatest capacity.

From the suppliers point of view, giving customers reconfigurable circuit capacity means that customers still pay for a fixed capacity in the underlying physical network, but they are free to allocate their bandwidth however they choose. Figure 2.14 illustrates the idea.

As Figure 2.14 shows, a customer who pays for capacity T in the underlying physical network can choose to divide that capacity among multiple circuits. Of course, when configuring the capacity of individual circuits, a customer must make sure that not more than capacity T is allocated at any point along the physical cable. The chief drawback of this scheme is that to make valid capacity assignments, customers must know both the topology of the physical net and the paths in that net to which their circuits have been assigned.

Capacity T allocated from physical net

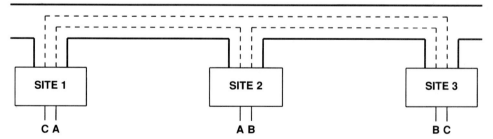

Figure 2.14 Three circuits (A, B, and C) that can be reconfigured as long as they use less than capacity T at any point in the backbone. For example, each can have capacity T/2 or, if A and B have capacity T/3, C can have capacity 2T/3.

2.7.5 NSFNET Mid-level Networks

NSF has funded many mid-level networks that span almost every state. A typical mid-level network includes 10 to 30 universities and corporations clustered in a geographic area. The original NSF goal was to cover initial costs and then encourage self-sufficiency by allowing each mid-level network to operate in fiscal and administrative autonomy. While some mid-level nets have achieved the goal of fiscal independence, others have found it difficult. Managers of mid-level networks have formed the *Federation of Academic Research Networks* (*FARNET*) to help coordinate technical work and lobby for additional government support.

Each mid-level network is free to choose whatever technology will serve it best; NSF will provide access from a mid-level net to the rest of the Internet via the NSFNET backbone. Most mid-level nets use point-to-point leased line interconnections similar to that of the NSFNET backbone; almost all plan to upgrade to higher speed lines over time.

2.7.6 NSFNET Access Networks

The family of NSF mid-level networks includes a motley collection of access networks. Some were funded as experiments using new technology (e.g., a satellite bridge), while others were funded to provide supercomputer access for a specific research individual or group. In the latter category, each supercomputer center includes a consortium of research groups that connect to it over leased lines. A consortium sometimes includes geographically distant sites, making these so-called *consortium networks* quite extensive.

2.7.7 NSFNET Campus Networks

The third tier in the NSF network family consists of campus networks that attach to mid-level nets. NSF decided to concentrate its funding on the backbone and mid-level nets, leaving universities and corporations free to choose their own local networking strategy. Most major research institutions already have a network in place at each campus; smaller corporations and schools are just beginning to consider the possibilities. The technologies used range in complexity and speed from single local area networks to complex network interconnections with backbones operating at gigabit speeds.

2.8 Other Technologies over which TCP/IP has been used

One of the major strengths of TCP/IP lies in the variety of physical networking technologies over which it can be used. We have already discussed several widely used technologies, including local area and wide area networks. This section briefly reviews others that help illustrate an important principle:

Much of the success of the TCP/IP protocols lies in their ability to ac-
commodate almost any underlying communication technology.

2.8.1 X25NET

CSNET†, an organization formed in 1980 to help provide Internet services to industry and small schools, used X25NET technology to connect some of its subscribers
to the Internet. Originally developed at Purdue University, X25NET runs Internet protocols over *Public Data Networks* (*PDN*s). The motivation is to allow organizations
that cannot afford direct ARPANET connections to lease a network connection from a
common carrier (e.g., AT&T) and use it to send Internet traffic.

Readers who know about public packet-switched networks may find X25NET
strange because such networks use the CCITT X.25 protocols exclusively while the Internet uses TCP/IP protocols. When used to transport TCP/IP traffic, however, the
underlying X.25 network merely provides a path over which Internet traffic can be
transferred. We have already stated that many underlying technologies can be used to
carry Internet traffic. The technique, sometimes called *tunneling*, simply means that a
complex network with its own protocols is treated like any other hardware delivery system. To send TCP/IP traffic through an X.25 ''tunnel,'' one makes an X.25 connection
and then sends TCP/IP packets as if they were data. The X.25 system carries packets
along its connection and delivers them to another X.25 endpoint, where they must be
picked up and forwarded on to their ultimate destination. Because tunneling treats
packets like data, it does not provide for self-identifying frames. Thus, it only works
when both ends of the X.25 connection agree *a priori* that they will exchange TCP/IP
packets.

What makes the use of X.25 peculiar is its interface. Unlike most network
hardware, X.25 protocols provide a reliable transmission stream, sometimes called a *virtual circuit*, between the sender and the receiver, while the Internet protocols have been
designed for a packet delivery system, making the two (apparently) incompatible.

Viewing X.25 connections merely as delivery paths produces a strange twist. It
turns out that X.25 networks exhibit substantially better throughput with multiple simultaneous connections. Thus, instead of opening a single connection to a given destination, an X25NET sender often opens multiple connections and distributes packets
among them to improve performance. The receiver accepts packets from all the X.25
connections and combines them together again.

The addressing scheme used by X.25 networks is given in a related standard
known as X.121. X.121 physical addresses each consist of a 14-digit number, with 10
digits assigned by the vendor that supplies the X.25 network service. Resembling telephone numbers, one popular vendor's assignment includes an area code based on geographic location. The addressing scheme is not surprising because it comes from an organization that determines international telephone standards. It is unfortunate, however,
because it makes assignment of Internet addresses difficult. Subscribers using X25NET
must each maintain a table of mappings between Internet addresses and X.25 addresses.

---

†CSNET and BITNET have merged; the new organization is CREN.

Chapter 6 discusses the address mapping problem in detail and gives an alternative to using fixed tables.

Because public X.25 networks operate independently of the Internet, a point of contact must be provided between the two. Both DARPA and CSNET operate dedicated machines that provide the interconnection between X.25 and the ARPANET. The primary interconnection is known as the *VAN gateway*. The VAN agrees to accept X.25 connections and route incoming Internet traffic to its destination.

X25NET is significant because it illustrates the flexibility and adaptability of the TCP/IP protocols. In particular, it shows how tunneling makes it possible to use an extremely wide range of complex network technologies in an internet.

2.8.2 Cypress

Most of the network technologies we have discussed so far are expensive. But Internet access need not be limited to large institutions that connect directly to major backbones like the NSFNET; many small schools and individuals need access as well. Small institutions cannot afford high speed leased lines, or the equipment that connects to it. Cypress is designed to fill that need by providing a low cost, low volume TCP/IP technology.

Cypress consists of minicomputers interconnected by low or medium speed (9.6 Kbps to 56 Kbps) leased lines. As Figure 2.15 shows, each minicomputer resides at a subscriber's site where it connects to the local computing environment over an Ethernet local area network. It connects to the rest of Cypress over leased serial lines. At least one site on a Cypress network connects to the Internet and passes traffic between the Cypress net and the rest of the Internet.

Originally, Cypress was designed to have a "growing vine" topology in which each new site leased a serial line to the closest existing site. The advantage of using a vine topology is low cost; the disadvantage is delay, which becomes noticeable for traffic that passes through several intermediate machines. The Cypress topology has changed for two reasons: first, NSFNET has increased the number of potential Internet connection points dramatically, and second, most subscribers seem to be willing to pay more to avoid delays. Thus, the Cypress network evolved to a single hub located at Purdue University, where it connects to NSFNET.

Cypress is based on a few key ideas. First, to achieve low cost, Cypress consolidates functionality by using a single computer to serve several purposes. Second, like Ethernet, the Cypress protocols use best-effort delivery, with no attempt made to correct errors or recover lost packets at the link level. Later chapters will explain why best-effort delivery works well in the TCP/IP environment. Third, Cypress operates as a network, not merely as a set of point-to-point links. Fourth, Cypress connects to a network at subscriber sites, not just to a single machine. Thus, many hosts at the subscriber's site can use the Cypress connection by treating it as their path to the rest of the Internet. Fifth, Cypress allows its packet switches to be monitored from any site in the Internet because it uses IP to transport monitoring information.

The minicomputers that comprise a Cypress network are called *implets*, and each implet provides three conceptual functions in a single machine. At the lowest level, an implet operates like a packet switch, accepting packets over serial lines and routing them on to their destination using the hardware address in a frame when selecting a route. At the next level, an implet connects two networks, the local Ethernet at the subscriber's site and the Cypress network. At the highest level, an implet is a general purpose computer that executes network control and monitoring programs as user processes.

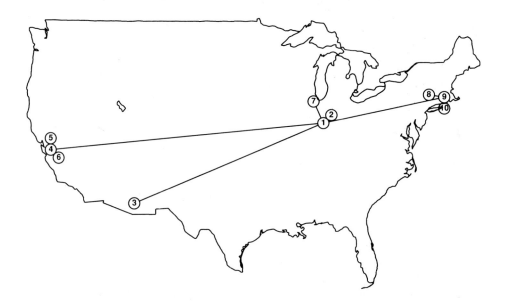

Figure 2.15 The Cypress network at its peak with sites at (1,2) Purdue, (3) Tucson AZ, (4,5,6) Palo Alto CA, (7) Chicago IL, (8) Williamstown MA, (9) Cambridge MA, and (10) Boston MA. At each site an implet connects to an Ethernet.

In addition to its technical contributions Cypress demonstrates three important ideas. First, it illustrates why network speed should be thought of as a measure of capacity. Sites with low traffic volumes perceive Cypress as an adequate, viable interconnection technology. Low speed does not mean limited functionality. Second, Cypress shows that the Internet protocols work well over a best-effort delivery system with minimum link level protocols. Third, Cypress shows that designing control and monitoring software to use the Internet protocols makes monitoring flexible and debugging easier.

2.8.3 Dial-up IP

Another interesting use of TCP/IP pioneered by CSNET involves running TCP/IP protocols over the dial-up voice network (i.e., the telephone system). CSNET member sites that use the Internet infrequently may not be able to justify leased line connections. For those sites, CSNET developed a dial-up IP system that works as expected: whenever a connection is needed, software at the member's site uses a modem to form a connection to the CSNET hub over the voice telephone network. A computer at the hub answers the phone call and, after obtaining valid authorization, forwards traffic between the site and other computers on the Internet.

2.8.4 Packet Radio

One of the most interesting DARPA experiments in packet switching resulted in a technology that used broadcast radio waves to carry packets. Designed for a military environment in which stations might be mobile, packet radio includes hardware and software that allow sites to find other sites, establish point-to-point communication, and then use the point-to-point communication to carry packets. Because sites change geographic location and may move out of communication range, the system must constantly monitor connectivity and recompute routes to reflect changes in topology. An operational packet radio system was built and used to demonstrate TCP/IP communication between a remote packet radio site and other sites on the Internet.

2.9 Summary And Conclusion

We have reviewed several network hardware technologies used by the TCP/IP protocols, ranging from high-speed, local area networks like Ethernet and proNET-10 to slower-speed, long haul networks like the ARPANET and Cypress. We have also seen that it is possible to run the TCP/IP protocols over other general-purpose network protocols using a technique called tunneling. While the details of specific network technologies are not important, a general idea has emerged:

> *The TCP/IP protocols are extremely flexible in that almost any underlying technology can be used to transfer TCP/IP traffic.*

FOR FURTHER STUDY

Early computer communication systems employed point-to-point interconnection, often using general-purpose serial line hardware that McNamara [1982] describes. Metcalf and Boggs [1976] introduced the Ethernet with a 3 Mbps prototype version. Digital [1980] specifies the 10 Mbps standard adopted by most vendors, with IEEE standard 802.3 reported in Nelson [1983]. Shoch, Dalal, and Redell [1982] provides an historical perspective of the Ethernet evolution. Related work on the ALOHA network is reported in Abramson [1970], with a survey of technologies given by Cotton [1979].

Token passing ring technology was proposed in Farmer and Newhall [1969]. Miller and Thompson [1982], as well as Andrews and Shultz [1982], give recent summaries. Another alternative, the slotted ring network, was proposed by Pierce [1972]. For a comparison of technologies, see Rosenthal [1982].

Details of the proposal for the second NSFNET backbone can be found in MERIT [November 1987]. Comer, Narten and Yavatkar [1987] first suggests using the technique of building a multiprocessor packet switch around a local area network bus; apparently it was discovered independently for the second NSFNET backbone proposal.

For more information on the ARPANET see Cerf [1989] and BBN [1981]. The ideas behind X25NET are summarized in Comer and Korb [1983], while Cypress is described in Comer, Narten, and Yavatkar [April 1987]. Lanzillo and Partridge [January 1989] describes dial-up IP.

Quarterman and Hoskins [1986] provides a summary of major wide area computer networks; Quarterman [1990] contains an updated list and offers more detail. LaQuey [1990] contains a directory of computer networks.

EXERCISES

2.1   Find out which network technologies your site uses.

2.2   What is the maximum size packet that can be sent on a high-speed network like NSC's Hyperchannel or Ultra Network Technologies' UltraNet?

2.3   What are the advantages and disadvantages of tunneling?

2.4   Read the Ethernet standard to find exact details of the inter-packet gap and preamble size. What is the maximum data rate Ethernet can deliver?

2.5   What characteristic of a satellite communication channel is most desirable? Least desirable?

2.6   Find a lower bound on the time it takes to transfer a 5 megabyte file across a network that operates at: 9600 bps, 56 Kbps, 10 Mbps, 100 Mbps, and 2 Gbps.

3

Internetworking Concept and Architectural Model

3.1 Introduction

So far we have looked at the low-level details of transmission across individual networks, the foundation on which all computer communication is built. This chapter makes a giant conceptual leap by describing a scheme that allows us to collect the diverse network technologies into a coordinated whole. The primary goal is a scheme that hides the details of underlying network hardware while providing universal communication services. The primary result is a high-level abstraction that provides the framework for all design decisions. Succeeding chapters show how we use this abstraction to build the necessary layers of internet communication software and how the software hides the underlying physical transport mechanisms. Later chapters also show how applications use the resulting communication system.

3.2 Application-Level Interconnection

Designers have taken two different approaches to hiding network details, using application programs to handle heterogeneity or hiding details in the operating system. Early heterogeneous network interconnections provided uniformity through application-level programs. In such systems, an application-level program, executing on each machine in the network, understands the details of the network connections for that machine and interoperates with the application programs across those connections. For example, some electronic mail systems consist of mailer programs that forward a memo one machine at a time. The path from source to destination may involve many different networks, but that does not matter as long as the mail systems on all the machines cooperate by forwarding each message.

Using application programs to hide network details may seem natural at first, but such an approach results in limited, cumbersome communication. Adding new functionality to the system means building a new application program for each machine. Adding new network hardware means modifying or creating new programs for each possible application. On a given machine each application program understands the network connections for that machine, resulting in duplication of code.

Users who are experienced with networking understand that once the interconnections grow to hundreds or thousands of networks; no one can possibly build all the necessary application programs. Furthermore, success of the step-at-a-time communication scheme requires correctness of all application programs executing along the way. When an intermediate program fails, the source and destination remain unable to detect or control the problem. Thus, systems that use intermediate programs cannot guarantee reliable communication.

3.3 Network-Level Interconnection

The alternative to providing interconnection with application-level programs is a system based on network-level interconnection. A network-level interconnection provides a mechanism that delivers packets from their original source to their ultimate destination in real time. Switching small units of data instead of files or large messages has several advantages. First, it maps directly onto the underlying network hardware, making it extremely efficient. Second, it separates data communication activities from application programs, permitting machines to handle network traffic without understanding the applications that use it. Third, it keeps the system flexible, making it possible to build general purpose network protocols. Fourth, it allows network managers to add new network technologies by modifying or adding a single piece of new network level software, while application programs remain unchanged.

The key to designing universal network-level interconnection can be found in an abstract communication system concept known as *internetworking*. The internetwork, or *internet*, concept is an extremely powerful one. It detaches the notions of communication from the details of network technologies and hides low-level details from the user. More important, it drives all software design decisions and explains how to handle physical addresses and routes. After reviewing basic motivations for internetworking, we will consider the properties of an internet in more detail.

Recall that we began with two fundamental observations about the design of communication systems:

- No single network can serve all users.
- Users desire universal interconnection.

The first observation is a technical one. Local area networks that provide the highest speed communication are limited in geographic span; wide area networks span large distances but cannot supply high speed connections. No single network technology satisfies all needs, so we are forced to consider multiple underlying hardware technologies.

The second observation is self-evident. Ultimately, we would like to be able to communicate between any two points. In particular, we desire a communication system that is not constrained by the boundaries of physical networks.

The goal is to build a unified, cooperative interconnection of networks that supports a universal communication service. Within each network, computers will use underlying technology-dependent communication primitives like the ones described in Chapter 2. New software, inserted between the technology-dependent communication mechanisms and application programs, will hide the low-level details and make the collection of networks appear to be a single large network. Such an interconnection scheme is called an *internetwork* or *internet*.

The idea of building an internet follows a standard pattern of system design: researchers imagine a high level computing facility and work from available computing technology, adding layers of software until they have a system that efficiently implements the imagined high-level facility. The next section shows the first step of the design process by defining the goal more precisely.

3.4 Properties Of The Internet

The notion of universal service is important, but it alone does not capture all the ideas we have in mind for a unified internet because there can be many implementations of universal services. In our design, we want to hide the underlying internet architecture from the user. That is, we do not want to require users or application programs to understand the details of hardware interconnections to use the internet. We also do not want to mandate a network interconnection topology. In particular, adding a new network to the internet should not mean connecting to a centralized switching point, nor should it mean adding direct physical connections between the new network and all existing networks. We want to be able to send data across intermediate networks even though they are not directly connected to the source or destination machines. We want all machines in the internet to share a universal set of machine identifiers (which can be thought of as *names* or *addresses*).

Our notion of a unified internet also includes the idea of network independence in the user interface. That is, we want the set of operations used to establish communication or to transfer data to remain independent of the underlying network technologies and the destination machine. Certainly, a user should not have to understand the network interconnection topology when writing application programs that communicate.

3.5 Internet Architecture

We have seen how machines connect to individual networks. The question arises, "How are networks interconnected to form an internetwork?" The answer has two parts. Physically, two networks can only be connected by a computer that attaches to both of them. A physical attachment does not provide the interconnection we have in mind, however, because such a connection does not guarantee that the computer will cooperate with other machines that wish to communicate. To have a viable internet, we need computers that are willing to shuffle packets from one network to another. Computers that interconnect two networks and pass packets from one to the other are called *internet gateways*† or *internet routers*.

Consider an example consisting of two physical networks shown in Figure 3.1. In the figure, machine *G* connects to both network *1* and network *2*. For *G* to act as a gateway, it must capture packets on network *1* that are bound for machines on network *2* and transfer them. Similarly, *G* must capture packets on network *2* that are destined for machines on network *1* and transfer them.

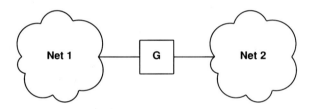

Figure 3.1 Two networks interconnected by *G*, a gateway (router).

3.6 Interconnection Through IP Gateways or Routers

When internet connections become more complex, gateways need to know about the topology of the internet beyond the networks to which they connect. For example, Figure 3.2 shows three networks interconnected by two gateways.

---

†The original literature used the term *gateway* but recently, vendors seem to prefer the term *IP router* – they are used interchangeably throughout this text.

Figure 3.2 Three networks interconnected by two gateways.

In this example, gateway G_1 must move from network *1* to network *2* all packets destined for machines on either network *2* or network *3*. As the size of the internet expands, the gateway's task of making decisions about where to send packets becomes more complex.

The idea of a gateway seems simple, but it is important because it provides a way to interconnect networks, not just machines. In fact, we have already discovered the principle of interconnection used throughout an internet:

> *In a TCP/IP internet, computers called gateways provide all interconnections among physical networks.*

You might suspect that gateways, which must know how to route packets to their destination, are large machines with enough primary or secondary memory to hold information about every machine in the internet to which they attach. However, gateways used with TCP/IP internets are usually minicomputers; they often have little or no disk storage and limited main memories. The trick to building a small internet gateway lies in the following concept:

> *Gateways route packets based on destination network, not on destination host.*

If routing is based on networks, the amount of information that a gateway needs to keep is proportional to the number of networks in the internet, not the number of machines.

Because gateways play a key role in internet communication, we will return to them in later chapters and discuss the details of how they operate and how they learn about routes. For now, we will assume that it is possible and practical to have correct routes for all networks in each gateway in the internet. We will also assume that only gateways provide connections between physical networks in an internet.

3.7 The User's View

Remember that TCP/IP is designed to provide a universal interconnection among machines independent of the particular networks to which they attach. Thus, we want the user to view an internet as a single, virtual network to which all machines connect despite their physical connections. Figure 3.3a shows how thinking of an internet instead of constituent networks simplifies the details and makes it easy for the user to conceptualize communication. In addition to gateways that interconnect physical networks, internet access software is needed on each host to allow application programs to use the internet as if it were a single, real physical network.

The advantage of providing interconnection at the network level now becomes clear. Because application programs that communicate over the internet do not know the details of underlying connections, they can be run without change on any machine. Because the details of each machine's physical network connections are hidden in the internet software, only that software needs to change when new physical connections appear or old ones disappear. In fact, it is possible to optimize routing by altering physical connections without even recompiling application programs.

A second advantage of having communication at the network level is more subtle: users do not have to understand or remember how networks connect or what traffic they carry. Application programs can be written that operate independent of underlying physical connectivity. In fact, network managers are free to change interior parts of the underlying internet architecture without changing application software in most of the computers attached to the internet (of course, network software must be reconfigured when a computer moves to a new network).

As Figure 3.3b shows, gateways do not provide direct connections among all pairs of networks. It may be necessary for traffic traveling from one machine to another to pass across several intermediate networks. Thus, networks participating in the internet are analogous to highways in the U.S. interstate system: each net agrees to handle transit traffic in exchange for the right to send traffic throughout the internet. Typical users are unaffected and unaware of extra traffic on their local network.

3.8 All Networks Are Equal

Chapter 2 reviewed example network hardware used to build TCP/IP internets and illustrated the great diversity of technologies. We have described an internet as a collection of cooperative, interconnected networks. It is now important to understand a fundamental concept: from the internet point of view, any communication system capable of transferring packets counts as a single network, independent of its delay and throughput characteristics, maximum packet size, or geographic scale. In particular, Figure 3.3b uses the same small cloud to depict all physical networks because TCP/IP treats them equally despite their differences. The point is:

The TCP/IP internet protocols treat all networks equally. A local area network like an Ethernet, a wide area network like the NSFNET backbone, or a point-to-point link between two machines each count as one network.

Readers unaccustomed to internet architecture may find it difficult to accept such a simplistic view of networks. In essence, TCP/IP defines an abstraction of "network" that hides the details of physical networks; we will learn that such abstractions help make TCP/IP extremely powerful.

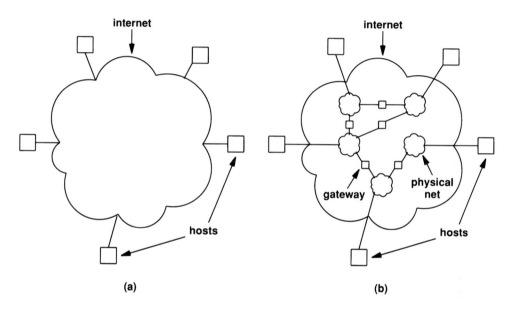

Figure 3.3 (a) The user's view of a TCP/IP internet in which each computer appears to attach to a single large network, and (b) the structure of physical networks and gateways that provide interconnection.

3.9 The Unanswered Questions

Our sketch of internets leaves many unanswered questions. For example, you might wonder about the exact form of internet machine addresses or how such addresses relate to the Ethernet, proNET-10, or ARPANET physical hardware addresses described in Chapter 2. The next three chapters confront these questions. They describe the format of IP addresses and illustrate how hosts map between internet addresses and physical addresses. You might also want to know exactly what a packet looks like when it travels through an internet, or what happens when packets arrive too fast for some host or gateway to handle. Chapter 7 answers these questions. Finally, you might wonder how multiple application programs executing concurrently on a single machine can send and receive packets to multiple destinations without becoming entangled in each other's transmissions or how internet gateways learn about routes. All of these questions will be answered as well.

Although it may seem vague now, the direction we are following will let us learn about both the structure and use of internet protocol software. We will examine each part, looking at the concepts and principles as well as technical details. We began by establishing a physical communication layer on which an internet is built. Each of the following chapters will explore one part of the internet software, until we understand how all the pieces fit together.

3.10 Summary

An internet is more than a collection of networks interconnected by computers. Internetworking implies that the interconnected systems agree to conventions that allow each computer to communicate with every other computer. In particular, an internet will allow two machines to communicate even if the communication path between them passes across a network to which neither connects directly. Such cooperation is only possible when computers agree on a set of universal identifiers and a set of procedures for moving data to its final destination.

In an internet, interconnections among networks are formed by computers called IP gateways, or routers, that attach to two or more networks. Gateways route packets between networks by receiving them from one network and sending them to another.

FOR FURTHER STUDY

Our model of an internetwork comes from Cerf and Cain [1983] and Cerf and Kahn [1974], which describe an internet as a set of networks interconnected by gateways and sketch an internet protocol similar to that eventually developed for the TCP/IP protocol suite. More information on the connected Internet architecture can be found in Postel [1980]; Postel, Sunshine, and Chen [1981]; and in Hinden, Haverty, and Sheltzer [1983]. Shoch [1978] presents issues in internetwork naming and addressing. Boggs *et. al.* [1980] describes the internet developed at Xerox PARC, an alternative to the TCP/IP internet we will examine. Cheriton [1983] describes internetworking as it relates to the V-system.

EXERCISES

3.1 Changing a gateway routing table can be tricky because it is impossible to change all gateways simultaneously. Investigate algorithms that guarantee to either install a change on all machines or install it on none.

3.2 In an internet, gateways periodically exchange information from their routing tables, making it possible for a new gateway to appear and begin routing packets. Investigate the algorithms used to exchange routing information.

3.3 Compare the organization of a TCP/IP internet to the style of internet designed by Xerox Corporation.

3.4 What processors have been used as gateways in the connected Internet? Does the size and speed of the gateways surprise you? Why?

4

Internet Addresses

4.1 Introduction

The previous chapter defined a TCP/IP internet as a virtual network built by interconnecting physical networks with gateways. This chapter discusses addressing, an essential ingredient that helps TCP/IP software hide physical network details and makes the internet appear to be a single, uniform entity.

4.2 Universal Identifiers

A communication system is said to supply *universal communication service* if it allows any host to communicate with any other host. To make our communication system universal, we need to establish a globally accepted method of identifying computers that attach to it.

Often, host identifiers are classified as *names*, *addresses*, or *routes*. Shoch [1978] suggests that a name identifies *what* an object is, an address identifies *where* it is, and a route tells *how* to get there. Although these definitions are intuitive, they can be misleading. Names, addresses, and routes really refer to successively lower level representations of host identifiers. In general, people usually prefer pronounceable names to identify machines, while software works better with more compact representations of identifiers that we think of as addresses. Either could have been chosen as the TCP/IP universal host identifiers. The decision was made to standardize on compact, binary addresses that make computations like routing decisions efficient. For now, we will discuss only binary addresses, postponing until later the questions of how to map between binary addresses and pronounceable names, and how to use addresses for routing.

4.3 Three Primary Classes Of IP Addresses

Think of an internet as a large network like any other physical network. The difference, of course, is that the internet is a virtual structure, imagined by its designers, and implemented entirely in software. Thus, the designers are free to choose packet formats and sizes, addresses, delivery techniques, and so on; nothing is dictated by hardware. For addresses, the designers of TCP/IP chose a scheme analogous to physical network addressing in which each host on the internet is assigned an integer address called its *internet address* or *IP address*. The clever part of internet addressing is that the integers are carefully chosen to make routing efficient. Specifically, an IP address encodes the identification of the network to which a host attaches as well as the identification of a unique host on that network. We can summarize:

> *Each host on a TCP/IP internet is assigned a unique 32-bit internet address that is used in all communication with that host.*

The details of IP addresses help clarify the abstract ideas. For now, we give a simplified view and expand it later. In the simplest case, each host attached to an internet is assigned a 32-bit universal identifier as its internet address. The bits of IP addresses for all hosts on a given network share a common prefix.

Conceptually, each address is a pair (*netid*, *hostid*), where *netid* identifies a network, and *hostid* identifies a host on that network. In practice, each IP address must have one of the first three forms shown in Figure 4.1†.

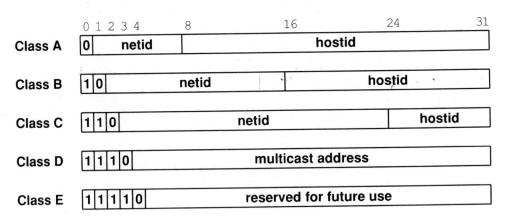

Figure 4.1 The five forms of Internet (IP) addresses. The three primary forms, Classes *A*, *B* and *C*, can be distinguished by the first two bits.

---

†The fourth form, reserved for internet multicasting, will be described in a later chapter; for now, we will restrict our comments to the forms that specify addresses of individual objects.

Given an IP address, its class can be determined from the three high-order bits, with two bits being sufficient to distinguish among the three primary classes. Class *A* addresses, which are used for the handful of networks that have more than 2^{16} (i.e., 65,536) hosts, devote 7 bits to netid and 24 bits to hostid. Class *B* addresses, which are used for intermediate size networks that have between 2^8 (i.e., 256) and 2^{16} hosts, allocate 14 bits to the netid and 16 bits to the hostid. Finally, class *C* networks, which have less than 2^8 hosts, allocate 21 bits to the netid and only 8 bits to the hostid. Note that the IP address has been defined in such a way that it is possible to extract the hostid or netid portions quickly. Gateways base routing on the netid and depend on such efficient extraction.

4.4 Addresses Specify Network Connections

To simplify the discussion, we said that an internet address identifies a host, but that is not strictly accurate. Consider a gateway that attaches to two physical networks. How can we assign a single IP address if the address encodes a network identifier as well as a host identifier? In fact, we cannot. When conventional computers have two or more physical connections they are called *multi-homed hosts*. Multi-homed hosts and gateways require multiple IP addresses. Each address corresponds to one of the machine's network connections. Looking at multi-homed hosts leads to the following important idea:

> *Because IP addresses encode both a network and a host on that network, they do not specify an individual machine, but a connection to a network.*

Thus, a gateway connecting *n* networks has *n* distinct IP addresses, one for each network connection.

4.5 Network And Broadcast Addresses

We have already cited the major advantage of encoding network information in internet addresses: it makes efficient routing possible. Another advantage is that internet addresses can refer to networks as well as hosts. By convention, hostid *0* is never assigned to an individual host. Instead, an IP address with hostid zero is used to refer to the network itself. In summary:

> *Internet addresses can be used to refer to networks as well as individual hosts. By convention, the network address has hostid with all bits 0.*

Another significant advantage of the internet addressing scheme is that it includes a *broadcast address* that refers to all hosts on the network. According to the standard, any hostid consisting of all *1s* is reserved for broadcast†. On many network technologies (e.g., Ethernet) broadcasting can be as efficient as normal transmission; on others (e.g., Cypress) broadcasting is supported by the network software, but requires substantially more delay than single transmission. Some networks do not support broadcast at all. Thus, having an IP broadcast address does not guarantee the availability or efficiency of broadcast delivery. In summary,

> *IP addresses can be used to specify a broadcast and map to hardware broadcast if available. By convention, a broadcast address has hostid with all bits 1.*

4.6 Limited Broadcast

Technically, the broadcast address we just described is called a *directed broadcast address* because it contains both a valid network id and the broadcast hostid. A directed broadcast address can be interpreted unambiguously at any point in an internet because it uniquely identifies the target network in addition to specifying broadcast on that network. Directed broadcast addresses provide a powerful (and somewhat dangerous) mechanism that allows a remote system to send a single packet that will be broadcast on the specified network.

From an addressing point of view, the chief disadvantage of directed broadcast is that it requires knowledge of the network address. Another form of broadcast address, called a *limited broadcast address* or *local network broadcast address*, provides a broadcast address for the local network independent of the assigned IP address. The local broadcast address consists of thirty-two *1s* (hence, it is sometimes called the ''all *1s*'' broadcast address). A host may use the limited broadcast address as part of a start-up procedure before it learns its IP address or the IP address for the local network. Once the host learns the correct IP address for the local network, however, it should use directed broadcast.

As a general rule, TCP/IP protocols restrict broadcasting to the smallest possible set of machines. We will see how this rule affects multiple networks that share addresses in Chapter 16 when we discuss subnet addressing.

4.7 Interpreting Zero To Mean ''This''

We have seen that a field consisting of *1s* can be interpreted to mean ''all,'' as in ''all hosts'' on a network. In general, internet software interprets fields consisting of *0s* to mean ''this.'' The interpretation appears throughout the literature. Thus, an IP address with hostid *0* refers to ''this'' host, and an internet address with network id *0* refers to ''this'' network. Of course, it is only meaningful to use such an address in a

---

†Unfortunately, an early release of TCP/IP code that accompanied Berkeley UNIX incorrectly used all zeroes for broadcast, and even though the Berkeley code has been repaired, the mistake still survives in some commercial systems derived from that code.

context where it can be interpreted unambiguously. For example, if a machine receives a packet in which the source address has netid set to *0* and the hostid matching its own, the receiver interprets the netid field to mean "this" network (i.e., the network over which the packet arrived).

Using netid *0* is especially important in those cases where a host wants to communicate over a network but does not yet know the network IP address. The host uses network id *0* temporarily, and other hosts on the network interpret the address as meaning "this" network. In most cases, replies will have the network address fully specified, allowing the original sender to record it for future use. Chapters 9 and 20 will discuss in detail how a host determines its network address and how it uses network id *0*.

4.7.1 Multicast Addressing

In addition to broadcasting, the IP address scheme supports a special form of multipoint delivery known as *multicasting*. Multicasting is especially useful for networks where the hardware technology supports multicast delivery. Chapter 17 discusses multicast addressing and delivery in detail.

4.8 Weaknesses In Internet Addressing

Encoding network information in an internet address does have some disadvantages. The most obvious disadvantage is that addresses refer to connections, not to hosts:

> *If a host moves from one network to another, its IP address must change.*

To understand the consequences, consider travelers who wish to disconnect their personal computers, carry them along on a trip, and reconnect them to the internet after reaching their destination. The personal computer cannot be assigned a permanent IP address because an IP address identifies the network to which the machine attaches.

Another weakness of the internet addressing scheme is that when any class *C* network grows to more than 255 hosts, it must have its address changed to a class *B* address. While this may seem like a minor problem, changing network addresses can be incredibly time-consuming and difficult to debug. Because most software is not designed to handle multiple addresses for the same physical network, administrators cannot plan a smooth transition in which they introduce new addresses slowly. Instead, they must abruptly stop using one network address, change the addresses of all machines, and then resume communication using the new network address.

The most important flaw in the internet addressing scheme will not become fully apparent until we examine routing. However, its importance warrants a brief introduction here. We have suggested that routing will be based on internet addresses, with the network id used to make routing decisions. Consider a host with two connections to the

internet. We know that such a host must have more than one IP address. The following is true:

> *Because routing uses the network portion of the IP address, the path
> taken by packets traveling to a host with multiple IP addresses
> depends on the address used.*

The implications are surprising. Humans think of each host as a single entity and want
to use a single name. They are often surprised to find that they must learn more than
one name and even more surprised to find that multiple names behave differently.

Another surprising consequence of the internet addressing scheme is that merely
knowing one IP address for a destination may not be sufficient; it may be impossible to
reach the destination using that address. Consider the example network shown in Figure 4.2. In the figure, two hosts, A and B, both attach to network *1*, and usually communicate directly using that network. Thus, users on host A should normally refer to
host B using IP address I_4. An alternate path from A to B exists through gateway G and
is used whenever A sends packets to IP address I_5. Now suppose B's connection to network *1* fails, but the machine itself remains running (e.g., a wire breaks between B and
network *1*). Users on A who specify IP address I_4 cannot reach B, although users who
specify address I_5 can. These problems with naming and addressing will arise again in
later chapters when we consider routing and name binding.

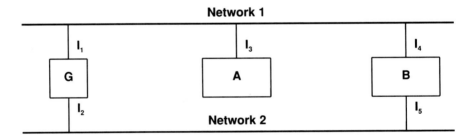

Figure 4.2 An example internet with a multi-homed host, B, that demonstrates a problem with the IP addressing scheme. If interface I_4
becomes disconnected, A must use address I_5 to reach B, routing
packets through gateway G.

4.9 Dotted Decimal Notation

When communicated to humans, either in technical documents or through application programs, IP addresses are written as four decimal integers separated by decimal
points, where each integer gives the value of one octet of the IP address†. Thus, the
32-bit internet address

---

†Dotted decimal notation is sometimes called *dotted quad notation.*

10000000   00001010   00000010   00011110

is written

128.10.2.30

We will use dotted decimal notation when expressing IP addresses throughout the remainder of this text.

4.10 Loopback Address

The class A network address 127.0.0.0 is reserved for *loopback* and is designed for testing and inter-process communication on the local machine. When any program uses the loopback address to send data, the protocol software in the computer returns the data without sending traffic across any network. The literature explicitly states that a packet sent to a network 127 address should never appear on any network. Furthermore, a host or gateway should never propagate routing or reachability information for network number *127*; it is not a network address.

4.11 Summary Of Special Address Conventions

In practice, IP uses only a few combinations of *0*s ("this") or *1*s ("all"). Figure 4.3 lists the possibilities.

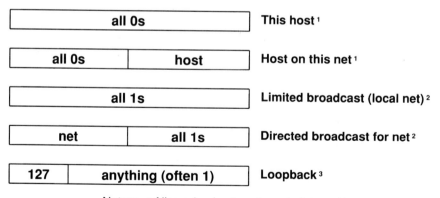

all 0s	This host [1]
all 0s | host	Host on this net [1]
all 1s	Limited broadcast (local net) [2]
net | all 1s	Directed broadcast for net [2]
127 | anything (often 1)	Loopback [3]

Notes: [1] Allowed only at system startup and is never a valid destination address.
[2] Never a valid source address.
[3] Should never appear on a network.

Figure 4.3 Special forms of IP addresses, including valid combinations of *0*s ("this"), *1*s ("all"). The length of the net portion of a directed broadcast depends on the network address class.

As the notes in the figure mention, using all *0*s for the network is only allowed during the bootstrap procedure. It allows a machine to communicate temporarily. Once the machine learns its correct network and IP address, it must not use network *0*.

4.12 Internet Addressing Authority

To insure that the network portion of an Internet addresses is unique, all Internet addresses are assigned by a central authority, the *Network Information Center (NIC)*. The central authority only assigns the network portion of the address and delegates responsibility for assigning host addresses to the requesting organization. Local area networks with a small number of attached machines (less than 255) are usually assigned Class C numbers because many local area networks are expected. Large networks, like the ARPANET, are assigned class A numbers because only a few large networks are expected.

It is only essential for the NIC to assign IP addresses for networks that are (or will be) attached to the connected Internet. An individual corporation could take responsibility for assigning unique network addresses within its TCP/IP internet as long as it never connects that internet to the outside world. Indeed, many corporate groups that use TCP/IP protocols do assign internet addresses on their own. For example, the NIC assigned address 10.0.0.0 to the ARPANET. If a college campus decides to use TCP/IP protocols on one Ethernet with only three hosts (and no other gateway connections), that college could choose to use address 10.0.0.0 for its local network. However, experience has shown that it is unwise to create a private internet using the same network addresses as the connected Internet because it prevents future interoperability and may cause problems when trying to exchange software with other sites. Thus, everyone using TCP/IP is strongly encouraged to take the time to obtain official Internet addresses from the NIC.

4.13 An Example

To clarify the IP addressing scheme, consider the example in Figure 4.4 that shows just a few of the connections and hosts on the Internet at the Purdue University Department of Computer Science in the mid-1980s. The example shows three networks: the ARPANET (10.0.0.0), an Ethernet (128.10.0.0), and a proNET-10 token ring network (192.5.48.0). Writing out the addresses in binary shows them to be class *A*, *B*, and *C*, respectively.

In the figure, four hosts attach to these networks, labeled *Arthur*, *Merlin*, *Guenevere*, and *Lancelot*. Machine *Taliesyn* serves as a gateway between the ARPANET and the proNET-10, and machine *Glatisant* serves as a gateway between the proNET-10 and the Ethernet. Host *Merlin* has connections to both the Ethernet and the proNET-10, so it can reach hosts on either network directly. Although a multi-homed host like *Merlin* can also operate as a gateway, *Merlin* is primarily a timesharing system and the additional work of routing packets would reduce the amount of processing available to users. Thus, a dedicated gateway, *Glatisant*, was installed to keep the gateway traffic load off the timesharing system. Traffic between these two networks was much higher than this configuration suggests because only a handful of the existing hosts are shown.

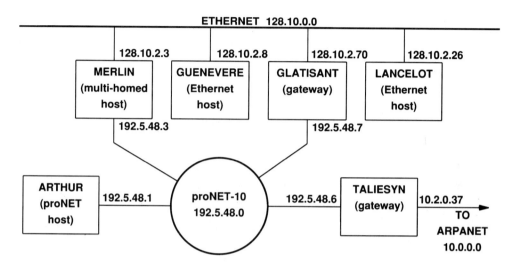

Figure 4.4 Example IP address assignments for hosts and gateways on an Ethernet, token ring network, and ARPANET.

Figure 4.4 shows the IP addresses for each network connection. *Lancelot*, which connects only to the Ethernet, has been assigned 128.10.2.26 as its only IP address. *Merlin* has address 128.10.2.3 for its connection to the Ethernet and 192.5.48.3 for its connection to the proNET-10. Choosing the same value for the low-order byte of its two addresses makes it easier for systems programmers to remember all of *Merlin's* Internet addresses.

4.14 Network Byte Order

To create an internet that is independent of any particular vendor's machine architecture or network hardware, we must define a standard representation for data. Consider what happens, for example, when one machine sends a 32-bit binary integer to another. The physical transport hardware moves the sequence of bits from the first machine to the second without changing the order. However, not all machines store 32-bit integers in the same way. On some (called *Little Endian*), the lowest memory address contains the low-order byte of the integer. On others (called *Big Endian*), the lowest memory address holds the high-order byte of the integer. Still others store integers in groups of 16-bit words, with the lowest addresses holding the low-order word, but with bytes swapped. Thus, direct copying of bytes from one machine to another may change the value of the number.

Standardizing byte-order for integers is especially important in an internet because internet packets carry binary numbers that specify information like destination addresses and packet lengths. Such quantities must be understood by both the senders and receivers. The TCP/IP protocols solve the byte-order problem by defining a *network standard byte order* that all machines must use for binary fields in internet packets. Each host converts binary items from the local representation to network standard byte order before sending a packet; it converts from network byte order to the host-specific order when a packet is received. Naturally, the user data field in a packet is exempt from this standard – users are free to format their own data however they choose. Of course, most users rely on standard application programs and do not have to deal with the byte order problem directly.

The internet standard for byte order specifies that integers are sent most significant byte first (i.e., *Big Endian* style). If one considers the successive bytes in a packet as it travels from one machine to another, a binary integer in that packet has its most significant byte nearest the beginning of the packet and its least significant byte nearest the end of the packet. Many arguments have been offered about which data representation should be used, and the internet standard still comes under attack from time to time. However, everyone agrees that having a standard is crucial, and the exact form of the standard is far less important.

4.15 Summary

TCP/IP uses 32-bit binary addresses as universal machine identifiers. Called internet or IP addresses, the identifiers are divided into three primary classes, allowing a few hundred networks with over a million hosts each, thousands of networks with thousands of hosts each, and over a million networks with up to 254 hosts each. To make such addresses easier for humans to understand, they are written in dotted decimal notation, with the values of the four octets written in decimal, separated by decimal points.

Because the IP address encodes network identification as well as the identification of a specific host on that network, routing is efficient. An important property of IP addresses is that they refer to network connections. Hosts with multiple connections have multiple addresses. One advantage of the internet addressing scheme is that the same form of address can be used to refer to hosts, networks, and all hosts on a network (broadcast). The biggest disadvantage of the IP addressing scheme is that if a machine has multiple addresses, knowing one address may not be sufficient to reach it when some network(s) are unavailable.

To permit the exchange of binary data among machines, TCP/IP protocols enforce a standard byte ordering for integers within protocol fields. In general, a host must convert all binary data from its internal form to network standard byte order before sending a packet, and it must convert from network byte order to internal order upon receipt.

FOR FURTHER STUDY

The internet addressing scheme presented here can be found in Reynolds and Postel [RFCs 990 and 997]. Official Internet addresses are assigned by the NIC (see Appendix 1 for an address and telephone number). Chapter 16 covers an important part of the Internet address standard called *subnet addressing*. Subnet addressing allows a single network address to be used with multiple physical networks. Chapter 17 shows how Class D addresses are assigned for internet *multicast*. Cohen [1981] explains bit and byte ordering, and introduces the terms ''Big Endian'' and ''Little Endian.''

EXERCISES

4.1   Exactly how many class *A*, *B*, and *C* networks can exist? Exactly how many hosts can a network in each class have? Be careful to allow for class *D* and *E* addresses.

4.2   A machine readable list of assigned addresses is sometimes called an internet *host table*. If your site has a host table, find out how many class *A*, *B*, and *C* network numbers have been assigned.

4.3   How many hosts are attached to each of the local area networks at your site? Does your site have any local area networks for which a Class *C* address is insufficient?

4.4   What is the chief difference between the IP addressing scheme and the U.S. telephone numbering scheme?

4.5   A single central authority cannot manage to assign Internet addresses fast enough to accommodate the demand. Can you invent a scheme that allows the central authority to divide its task among several groups but still ensure that each assigned address is unique?

4.6   Does network standard byte order differ from your local machine's byte order?

5

Mapping Internet Addresses to Physical Addresses (ARP)

5.1 Introduction

We have described the TCP/IP address scheme in which each host is assigned a 32-bit address and have said that an internet behaves like a virtual network, using only these assigned addresses when sending and receiving packets. We also reviewed several physical network technologies and noted that two machines on a given physical network can communicate *only if they know each other's physical network address*. What we have not mentioned is how a host or a gateway maps an IP address to the correct physical address when it needs to send a packet across a physical net. This chapter considers that mapping, showing how it is implemented for the two most common physical network address schemes.

5.2 The Address Resolution Problem

Consider two machines A and B that share a physical network. Each has an assigned IP address I_A and I_B and a physical address P_A and P_B. The goal is to devise low-level software that hides physical addresses and allows higher-level programs to work only with internet addresses. Ultimately, however, communication must be carried out by physical networks using whatever physical address scheme the hardware supplies. Suppose machine A wants to send a packet to machine B across a physical network to which they both attach, but *A* has only *B*'s internet address I_B. The question arises: how does *A* map that address to *B's* physical address, P_B?

The problem of mapping high-level addresses to physical addresses is known as the *address resolution problem* and has been solved in several ways. Some protocol suites keep tables in each machine that contain pairs of high-level and physical addresses. Others solve the problem by encoding hardware addresses in high-level addresses. Using either approach exclusively makes high-level addressing awkward at best. This chapter discusses two techniques for address resolution used by TCP/IP protocols.

5.3 Two Types Of Physical Addresses

There are two basic types of physical addresses, exemplified by the Ethernet, which has large, fixed physical addresses, and proNET-10, which has small, easily configured physical addresses. Address resolution is difficult for Ethernet-like networks, but easy for networks like proNET-10. We will consider the easy case first.

5.4 Resolution Through Direct Mapping

Consider a proNET-10 token ring network. Recall from Chapter 2 that it uses small integers for physical addresses and allows the user to choose a hardware address when installing an interface board in a computer. The key to making address resolution easy for a proNET-10 network lies in observing that as long as one has the freedom to choose both IP and physical addresses, they can be selected such that parts of them are the same. Typically, one assigns IP addresses with the host id portion equal to 1, 2, 3, and so on, and then, when installing network interface hardware, selects a physical address that corresponds to the IP address. For example, one would select physical address 3 for a machine with the IP address 192.5.48.3 because 192.5.48.3 is a class *C* address with the host portion equal to 3.

For networks like proNET-10, computing a physical address from an IP address is trivial. The computation consists of extracting the host id portion of the IP address. It is computationally efficient because it requires only a few machine instructions. It is easy to maintain because the mapping can be performed without reference to external data. Finally, new machines can be added to the network without changing data or recompiling code.

Conceptually, choosing a numbering scheme that makes address resolution efficient means selecting a function *f* that maps IP addresses to physical addresses. The designer may be able to select a physical address numbering scheme as well, depending on the hardware. Resolving IP address I_A means computing

$$P_A = f(I_A)$$

We want the computation of f to be efficient. If the set of physical addresses is constrained, it may be possible to arrange efficient mappings other than the one given in the example above. For instance, when using X.25, one cannot choose physical addresses. Usually, gateways on X.25 networks store pairs of IP and X.25 physical addresses in a table and search the table when resolving an IP address. To make address resolution efficient in such cases, software can use a hash function to search the table. Exercise 5.1 suggests another alternative.

5.5 Resolution Through Dynamic Binding

To understand why address resolution is difficult for some networks, consider Ethernet technology. Recall from Chapter 2 that an Ethernet has 48-bit physical addresses assigned by vendors when they manufacture interface boards. As a consequence, when hardware fails and requires that an interface board be replaced, the machine's physical address changes. Furthermore, because the Ethernet address is 48 bits long, there is no hope it can be encoded in a 32-bit IP address.

Designers of TCP/IP protocols found a creative solution to the address resolution problem for networks like the Chaosnet or Ethernet that have broadcast capability. The solution allows new machines to be added to the network without recompiling code, and does not require maintenance of a centralized database. To avoid maintaining a table of mappings, the designers chose to use a low-level protocol to bind addresses dynamically. Termed the *Address Resolution Protocol* (*ARP*), it provides a mechanism that is both efficient and easy to maintain.

As Figure 5.1 shows, the idea behind dynamic resolution with ARP is simple: when host A wants to resolve IP address I_B, it broadcasts a special packet that asks the host with IP address I_B to respond with its physical address, P_B. All hosts, including B, receive the request, but only host B recognizes its IP address and sends a reply that contains its physical address. When A receives the reply, it uses the physical address to send the internet packet directly to B. We can summarize:

> *The Address Resolution Protocol, ARP, allows a host to find the physical address of a target host on the same physical network, given only the target's IP address.*

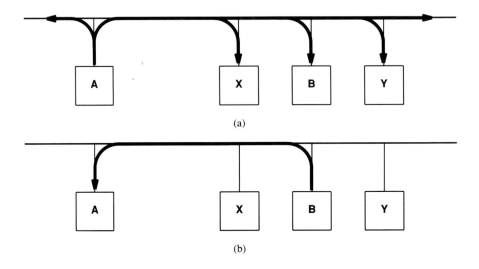

(a)

(b)

Figure 5.1 The ARP protocol. To determine P_B, B's physical address, from I_B, its IP address, (a) host A broadcasts an ARP request containing I_B to all machines, and (b) host B responds with an ARP reply that contains the pair (I_B, P_B).

5.6 The Address Resolution Cache

It may seem silly that for A to send a packet to B it first sends a broadcast that reaches B. Or it may seem even sillier that A broadcasts the question, "how can I reach you?" instead of just broadcasting the packet it wants to deliver. But there is an important reason for the exchange. Broadcasting is far too expensive to be used every time one machine needs to transmit a packet to another because it requires every machine on the network to process the broadcast packet. To reduce communication costs, hosts that use ARP maintain a cache of recently acquired IP-to-physical address bindings so they do not have to use ARP repeatedly. Whenever a host receives an ARP reply, it saves the machine's IP address and corresponding hardware address in its cache for successive lookups. When transmitting a packet, the host always looks in its cache for a binding before sending an ARP request. If the host finds the desired binding in its cache, it need not broadcast on the network. Experience shows that because most network communication involves more than one packet transfer, even a small cache is worthwhile.

5.7 ARP Refinements

Several refinements of ARP are possible. First, observe that if host *A* is about to use ARP because it needs to send to *B*, there is a high probability that host *B* will need to send to *A* in the near future. If we anticipate *B*'s need, we can avoid extra network traffic by arranging for *A* to include its IP-to-physical address binding when sending a request to *B*. Second, notice that because *A* broadcasts its initial request, all machines on the network receive it and can extract and store in their cache *A*'s IP-to-physical address binding. Third, when a new machine appears on the net (e.g., when an operating system reboots), we can avoid having every other machine run ARP by broadcasting the new machine's IP address and physical address pair.

The following rule summarizes refinements:

> *The sender's IP-to-physical address binding is included in every ARP broadcast; receivers update the IP-to-physical address binding information in their cache before processing an ARP packet.*

5.8 Relationship Of ARP To Other Protocols

ARP provides one possible mechanism to map from IP addresses to physical addresses; we have already seen that some network technologies do not need it. The point is that ARP would be completely unnecessary if we could make all network interfaces understand their IP address. Thus, ARP merely imposes a new address scheme on top of whatever low-level address mechanism the hardware uses. The idea can be summarized:

> *ARP is a low-level protocol that hides the underlying network physical addressing, permitting us to assign IP addresses of our choosing to every machine. We think of it as part of the physical network system, and not as part of the internet protocols.*

5.9 ARP Implementation

Functionally, ARP is divided into two parts. One part determines physical addresses when sending a packet, and the other part answers requests from other machines. Address resolution for outgoing packets seems straightforward, but small details complicate an implementation. Given a destination IP address the host consults its ARP cache to see if it knows the mapping from IP address to physical address. If it does, it extracts the physical address, places the data in a frame using that address, and sends the frame. If it does not know the mapping, it must broadcast an ARP request and wait for a reply.

Broadcasting an ARP request to find an address mapping can become complex. The target machine could be down or just too busy to accept the request. If so, the sender may not receive a reply or the reply may be delayed. Because the Ethernet is a best-effort delivery system, the initial ARP broadcast request can also be lost (in which case the sender should retransmit, at least once). Meanwhile, the host must store the original outgoing packet so it can be sent once the address has been resolved†. In fact, the host must decide whether to allow other application programs to proceed while it processes an ARP request (most do). If so, it must handle the case where an application generates additional ARP requests for the same address without broadcasting multiple requests for a given target.

Finally, consider the case where machine *A* has obtained a binding for machine *B*, but then *B*'s hardware fails and is replaced. Although *B*'s address has changed, *A*'s cached binding has not, so *A* uses a nonexistent hardware address, making successful reception impossible. This case shows why it is important to have ARP software treat its table of bindings as a cache and remove entries after a fixed period. Of course, the timer for an entry in the cache must be reset whenever an ARP broadcast arrives containing the binding (but it is not reset when the entry is used to send a packet).

The second part of the ARP code handles ARP packets that arrive from the network. When an ARP packet arrives, the software first extracts the sender's IP address and hardware address pair, and examines the local cache to see if it already has an entry for the sender. If a cache entry exists for the given IP address, the handler updates that entry by overwriting the physical address with the physical address obtained from the packet. The receiver then processes the rest of the ARP packet.

The receiver must handle two types of incoming ARP packets. If the incoming ARP packet is a request, the receiving machine must see if it is the target of the request (i.e., some other machine has broadcast a request for the receiver's physical address). If so, the ARP software forms a reply by supplying its physical hardware address, and sends the reply directly back to the requestor. The receiver also adds the sender's address pair to its cache if the pair is not already present. If the IP address mentioned in the ARP request does not match the local IP address, the packet is requesting a mapping for some other machine on the network and can be ignored.

The other interesting case occurs when an ARP reply arrives. Depending on the implementation, the handler may need to create a cache entry or the entry may already be present. In any case, once the cache has been updated, the receiver tries to match the reply with a previously issued request. Usually, replies arrive in response to a request, which was generated because the machine has a packet to deliver. Between the time the machine broadcasts its ARP request and receives the reply, application programs or higher-level protocols may generate additional requests for the same address; the software must remember that it has already sent a request and not send more. Usually, it places the additional requests on a queue. Once the reply arrives and the address binding is known, the ARP software removes items from the queue and supplies the address binding to each. If the machine did not previously issue a request for the IP address in the reply, it simply stops processing the packet.

---

†If the delay is significant, the host may choose to discard the outgoing packet(s).

5.10 ARP Encapsulation And Identification

When ARP messages travel from one machine to another, they must be carried in physical frames. Figure 5.2 shows that the ARP message is carried in the data portion of a frame.

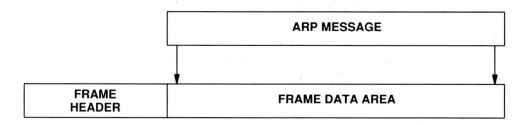

Figure 5.2 An ARP message encapsulated in a physical network frame.

To identify the frame as carrying an ARP request or ARP reply, the sender assigns a special value to the type field in the frame header and places the ARP message in the frame's data field. When a frame arrives at a host, the system examines the frame type to determine its contents. For example, on an Ethernet, frames carrying ARP messages have a type field of 0806_{16}. This is a standard value assigned by the authority that sets Ethernet standards.

5.11 ARP Protocol Format

Unlike most protocols, the data in ARP packets does not have a fixed-format header. Instead, the message is designed to be useful with a variety of network technologies. Thus, the first fields in the header contain counts that specify the lengths of succeeding fields. In fact, ARP can be used with arbitrary physical addresses and arbitrary protocol addresses. The example in Figure 5.3 shows the 28-octet ARP message format used on Ethernet hardware (where physical addresses are 48-bits or 6 octets long), when resolving IP protocol addresses (which are 4 octets long).

Figure 5.3 shows an ARP message with 4 octets per line, a format that is standard throughout this text. Unfortunately, unlike most of the remaining protocols, the variable-length fields in ARP packets do not align neatly on 32-bit boundaries, making the diagram difficult to read. For example, the sender's hardware address, labeled *SENDER HA*, occupies 6 contiguous octets, so it spans two lines in the diagram.

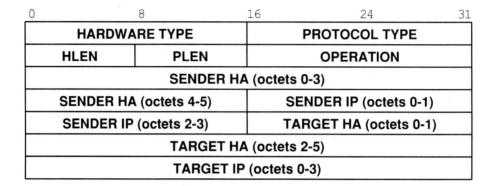

Figure 5.3 An example of ARP/RARP message format when used for IP-to-Ethernet address resolution. The length of fields depends on the hardware and protocol address lengths, which are 6 octets for an Ethernet address and 4 octets for an IP address.

Field *HARDWARE TYPE* specifies a hardware interface type for which the sender seeks an answer; it contains the value *1* for Ethernet. Similarly, field *PROTOCOL TYPE* specifies the type of high-level protocol address the sender has supplied; it contains 0800_{16} for IP addresses. Field *OPERATION* specifies an ARP request (*1*), ARP response (*2*), RARP† request (*3*), or RARP response (*4*). Fields *HLEN* and *PLEN* allow ARP to be used with arbitrary networks because they specify the length of the hardware address and the length of the high-level protocol address. The sender supplies its hardware address and IP address, if known, in fields *SENDER HA* and *SENDER IP*.

When making a request, the sender also supplies the target IP address (ARP), or target hardware address (RARP), using fields *TARGET HA* and *TARGET IP*. Before the target machine responds, it fills in the missing addresses, swaps the target and sender pairs, and changes the operation to a reply. Thus, a reply carries the IP and hardware addresses of the original requestor, as well as the IP and hardware addresses of the machine for which a binding was sought.

5.12 Summary

IP addresses are assigned independent of a machine's physical hardware address. To deliver an internet packet, the network software must ultimately map the IP address into a physical hardware address and use the hardware address to transmit the frame. If hardware addresses consist of small integers that can be changed easily, a direct mapping can be established by having the machine's physical address encoded in its IP address. Otherwise, the mapping must be performed dynamically. The Address Resolution Protocol (ARP) performs dynamic address resolution, using only the low-level net-

---

†RARP, another protocol that uses the same message format, will be described in the next chapter.

work communication system. ARP permits machines to resolve addresses without keeping a permanent record of bindings.

A machine uses ARP to find the hardware address of another machine by broadcasting an ARP request. The request contains the IP address of the machine for which a hardware address is needed. Each machine responds to requests that match its IP address by sending replies that contain the needed hardware address.

To make ARP efficient, each machine caches IP-to-physical address bindings. Because internet traffic tends to consist of a sequence of interactions between pairs of machines, the cache eliminates most ARP broadcast requests.

FOR FURTHER STUDY

The address resolution protocol used here is given by Plummer [RFC 826] and has become a TCP/IP internet protocol standard. Dalal and Printis [1981] describe the relationship between Ethernet and IP addresses, and Clark [RFC 814] discusses addresses and bindings in general. Parr [RFC 1029] discusses fault tolerant address resolution. The Internet Numbers document [RFC 1010] specifies values used to identify network frames. Comer [1987] presents an example ARP implementation for the Xinu operating system.

EXERCISES

5.1   Given a small set of physical addresses (positive integers), can you find a function f and an assignment of IP addresses such that f maps the IP addresses 1-to-1 onto the physical addresses and computing f is efficient?

5.2   In what special case does a host connected to an Ethernet not need to use ARP or an ARP cache before transmitting an IP datagram?

5.3   One common algorithm for managing the ARP cache replaces the least recently used entry when adding a new one. Under what circumstances can this algorithm produce unnecessary network traffic?

5.4   Should ARP update the cache if an old entry already exists for a given IP address? Why or why not?

5.5   Should ARP modify the cache even when it receives information without specifically requesting it? Why or why not?

5.6   Any implementation of ARP that uses a fixed-size cache can fail when used on a network that has many hosts and much ARP traffic. Explain how.

5.7   ARP is often cited as a security weakness. Explain why.

5.8   Explain what can happen if the hardware address field in an ARP response becomes corrupted during transmission. Hint: ARP implementations do not usually remove cache entries if they are frequently used.

5.9 Suppose machine C receives an ARP request sent from A looking for target B, and suppose C has the binding from I_B to P_B in its cache. Should C answer the request? Explain.

5.10 How can a workstation use ARP when it boots to find out if any other machine on the network is impersonating it? What are the disadvantages of the scheme?

6

Determining an Internet Address at Startup (RARP)

6.1 Introduction

We now know that physical network addresses are both low-level and hardware dependent, and we understand that each machine using TCP/IP is assigned one or more 32-bit IP addresses that are independent of the machine's hardware addresses. Application programs always use the IP address when specifying a destination. Hosts and gateways must use physical addresses to transmit datagrams across underlying networks; they rely on address resolution schemes like ARP to perform the binding.

Usually, a machine's IP address is kept on its secondary storage, where the operating system finds it at startup. The question arises, "How does a diskless machine, one without access to secondary storage, determine its IP address?" The problem is critical for diskless workstations that use IP addresses to communicate with a file server. Furthermore, because many diskless machines use standard TCP/IP file transfer protocols to obtain their initial boot image, they must obtain and use an IP address before the operating system runs. This chapter explores the question of how to obtain an IP address and describes a protocol that diskless machines use.

To allow a single software image to be used on a set of machines, it must be built without having the machine's IP address bound into the image. In particular, designers try to keep both bootstrap code and initial operating system images free from specific IP addresses, so the same image can be run on many machines. When such code starts execution on a diskless machine, it must use the network to contact a server to obtain the machine's IP address. The procedure sounds paradoxical: a machine communicates with a remote server to obtain an address needed for communication.

The paradox is only imagined because the machine *does* know how to communicate. It can use its physical address to communicate over a single network. Thus, the machine must resort to physical network addressing temporarily in the same way that operating systems use physical memory addressing to set up page tables for virtual addressing. Once a machine knows its internet address, it can communicate across an internet.

The idea behind finding an IP address is simple: the diskless machine sends a request to another machine, called a *server*†, and waits until the server sends a response. We assume the server has a disk where it keeps a database of internet addresses. In the request, the machine needing to know its internet address must uniquely identify itself, so the server can look up the correct internet address and send a reply. Both the machine that issues the request and the server that responds use physical network addresses during their brief communication. How does the diskless machine know the physical address of a server? Usually, it does not – it simply broadcasts the request to all machines on the local network. One or more servers respond.

When a diskless machine broadcasts a request, it must uniquely identify itself. What information can be included in its request that will uniquely identify the machine? Any unique hardware identification suffices (e.g., the CPU serial number). However, we want to choose an identification that can be obtained by an executing program. The objective is to create a single software image that can execute on an arbitrary processor. Furthermore, the length or format of CPU-specific information may vary among processor models, and we would like to devise a server that accepts requests from all machines on the physical network using a single format.

6.2 Reverse Address Resolution Protocol (RARP)

The designers of TCP/IP protocols realized that there is another piece of uniquely identifying information readily available, namely, the machine's physical network address. Using the physical address as a unique identification has two advantages. Because a host obtains its physical addresses from the network interface hardware, such addresses are always available and do not have to be bound into the operating system image. Because the identifying information depends on the network and not on the CPU vendor or model, all machines on a given network will supply uniform, unique identifiers. Thus, the problem becomes the reverse of address resolution: given a physical network address, devise a scheme that will allow a server to map it into an internet address.

A diskless machine uses a TCP/IP internet protocol called *RARP* (*Reverse Address Resolution Protocol*) to obtain its IP address from a server. RARP is adapted from the ARP protocol of the previous chapter and uses the same message format shown in Figure 5.3. In practice, the RARP message sent to request an internet address is a little more general than what we have outlined above: it allows a machine to request the IP address of a third party as easily as its own. It also allows for multiple physical network types.

---

†Chapter 18 discusses servers in detail.

Like an ARP message, a RARP message is sent from one machine to another encapsulated in the data portion of an Ethernet frame. An Ethernet frame carrying a RARP request has the usual preamble, Ethernet source and destination addresses, and packet type fields in front of the frame. The frame type contains the value 8035_{16} to identify the contents of the frame as a RARP message. The data portion of the frame contains the 28-octet RARP message.

Figure 6.1 illustrates how a host uses RARP. The sender broadcasts a RARP request that specifies itself as both the sender and target machine, and supplies its physical network address in the target hardware address field. All machines on the network receive the request, but only those authorized to supply the RARP service process the request and send a reply; such machines are known as *RARP servers*. For RARP to succeed, the network must contain at least one RARP server.

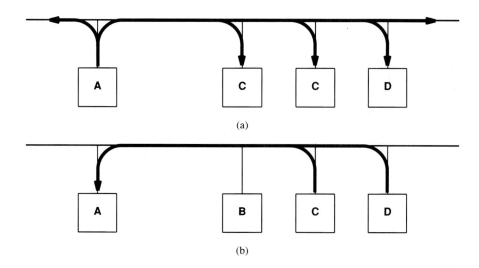

Figure 6.1 Example exchange using the RARP protocol. (a) machine *A* broadcasts a RARP request specifying itself as a target, and (b) those machines authorized to supply the RARP service (*C* and *D*) reply directly to *A*.

Servers answer requests by filling in the target protocol address field, changing the message type from *request* to *reply*, and sending the reply back directly to the machine making the request. The original machine receives replies from all RARP servers, even though only the first is needed.

Keep in mind that all communication between the machine seeking its IP address and the server supplying it must be carried out using only the physical network. Furthermore, the protocol allows a host to ask about an arbitrary target. Thus, the sender supplies its hardware address separate from the target hardware address, and the server is careful to send the reply to the sender's hardware address. On an Ethernet, having a field for the sender's hardware address may seem redundant because the information is also contained in the Ethernet frame header. However, not all Ethernet hardware provides the operating system with access to the physical frame header.

6.3 Timing RARP Transactions

Like any communication on a best-effort delivery network, RARP requests are susceptible to loss or corruption. Because RARP uses the physical network directly, no other protocol software will time the response or retransmit the request; RARP software must handle these tasks. In general, RARP is used only on local area networks like the Ethernet, where the probability of failure is low. If a network has only one RARP server, however, that machine may not be able to handle the load, so packets may be dropped.

Many diskless machines rely on RARP to boot and may choose to retry indefinitely until they receive a response. Other implementations announce failure after only a few tries to avoid flooding the network with unnecessary broadcast traffic (e.g., in case the server is unavailable). On an Ethernet, network failure is less likely than server overload. Making RARP software retransmit quickly may have the unwanted effect of flooding a congested server with more traffic. Using a large delay ensures that servers have ample time to satisfy the request and return an answer.

6.4 Primary And Backup RARP Servers

The chief advantage of having several machines function as RARP servers is that it makes the system more reliable. If one server is down, or too heavily loaded to respond, another answers the request. Thus, it is highly likely that the service will be available. The chief disadvantage of using many servers is that when a machine broadcasts a RARP request, the network becomes overloaded when all servers attempt to respond. On an Ethernet, for example, using multiple RARP servers makes the probability of collision high.

How can the RARP service be arranged to keep it available and reliable without incurring the cost of multiple, simultaneous replies? There are at least two possibilities, and they both involve delaying responses. In the first solution, each machine that makes RARP requests is assigned a *primary server*. Under normal circumstances, only the machine's primary server responds to its RARP request. All nonprimary servers receive the request but merely record its arrival time. If the primary server is unavailable, the original machine will timeout waiting for a response and then rebroadcast the request. Whenever a nonprimary server receives a second copy of a RARP request within a short time of the first, it responds.

The second solution uses a similar scheme but attempts to avoid having all nonprimary servers transmit responses simultaneously. Each nonprimary machine that receives a request computes a random delay and then sends a response. Under normal circumstances, the primary server responds immediately and successive responses are delayed, so there is low probability that they arrive at the same time. When the primary server is unavailable, the requesting machine experiences a small delay before receiving a reply. By choosing delays carefully, the designer can insure that requesting machines do not rebroadcast before they receive an answer.

6.5 Summary

At system startup, a diskless machine must contact a server to find its IP address before it can communicate using TCP/IP. We examined the RARP protocol that uses physical network addressing to obtain the machine's internet address. The RARP mechanism supplies the target machine's physical hardware address to uniquely identify the processor and broadcasts the RARP request. Servers on the network receive the message, look up the mapping in a table (presumably from secondary storage), and reply to the sender. Once a machine obtains its IP address, it stores the address in memory and does not use RARP again until it reboots.

FOR FURTHER STUDY

The details of RARP are given in Finlayson, *et. al.* [RFC 903]. Finlayson [RFC 906] describes workstation bootstrapping using the TFTP protocol. Comer [1987] describes an example implementation of RARP for the Xinu operating system.

Chapter 19 considers an alternative to RARP known as BOOTP. Unlike the low-level address determination scheme RARP supplies, BOOTP builds on higher level protocols like IP and UDP. Chapter 19 compares the two approaches, discussing the strengths and weaknesses of each.

EXERCISES

6.1   A RARP server can broadcast RARP replies to all machines or transmit each reply directly to the machine that makes the request. Can you characterize a system in which broadcasting replies to all machines is beneficial?

6.2   RARP is a narrowly focused protocol in the sense that replies only contain one piece of information (i.e., the requested IP address). When diskless machines boot, they usually want to know at least the time and their machine name in addition to their internet address. Extend RARP to supply the additional information.

6.3 How much larger will Ethernet frames become when information is added to RARP as described in the previous exercise?

6.4 Adding a second RARP server to a network increases reliability. Does it ever make sense to add a third? How about a fourth? Why or Why not?

6.5 The diskless workstations from one vendor use RARP to obtain their IP addresses, but always assume the response comes from the workstation's file server. The diskless machine then tries to obtain a boot image from that server. If it does not receive a response, the workstation enters an infinite loop broadcasting boot requests. Explain how adding a backup RARP server to such a configuration can cause the network to become congested with broadcasts. Hint: think of power failures.

7

Internet Protocol: Connectionless Datagram Delivery

7.1 Introduction

We have been reviewing pieces of network hardware and software that make internet communication possible, explaining the underlying network technologies and address resolution. This chapter considers the fundamental principle of connectionless delivery and discusses how it is provided by the *Internet Protocol* (*IP*), one of the two major protocols used in internetworking. We will study the format of IP datagrams and see how they form the basis for all internet communication. The next two chapters continue our examination of the Internet Protocol by discussing datagram routing and error handling.

7.2 A Virtual Network

Chapter 3 discussed an internet architecture in which gateway machines connect multiple physical networks. Looking at the architecture may be misleading, because the focus should be on the interface that an internet provides users, not on the interconnection technology.

A user thinks of an internet as a single virtual network that intercon-
nects all hosts, and through which communication is possible; its
underlying architecture is both hidden and irrelevant.

In a sense, an internet is an abstraction of physical networks because, at the lowest level, it provides the same functionality: accepting packets and delivering them. Higher
levels of internet software add most of the rich functionality users perceive.

7.3 Internet Architecture And Philosophy

Conceptually, a TCP/IP internet provides three sets of services as shown in Figure
7.1; their arrangement in the figure suggests dependencies among them. At the lowest
level, a connectionless delivery service provides a foundation on which everything rests.
At the next level, a reliable transport service provides a higher level platform on which
applications depend. We will soon explore each of these services, understand what they
provide, and see the protocols associated with them.

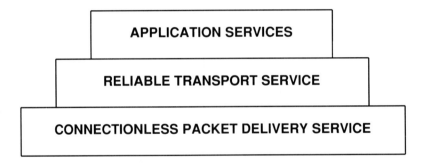

Figure 7.1 The three conceptual layers of internet services.

7.4 The Concept Of Unreliable Delivery

Although we can associate protocol software with each of the services in Figure
7.1, the reason for identifying them as conceptual parts of the internet is that they clearly point out the philosophical underpinnings of the design. The point is:

Internet software is designed around three conceptual networking ser-
vices arranged in a hierarchy; much of its success has resulted be-
cause this architecture is surprisingly robust and adaptable.

One of the most significant advantages of this conceptual separation is that it becomes possible to replace one service without disturbing others. Thus, research and development can proceed concurrently on all three.

7.5 Connectionless Delivery System

The most fundamental internet service consists of a packet delivery system. Technically, the service is defined as an unreliable, best-effort, connectionless packet delivery system, analogous to the service provided by network hardware that operates on a best-effort delivery paradigm. The service is called *unreliable* because delivery is not guaranteed. The packet may be lost, duplicated, delayed, or delivered out of order, but the service will not detect such conditions, nor will it inform the sender or receiver. The service is called *connectionless* because each packet is treated independently from all others. A sequence of packets sent from one machine to another may travel over different paths, or some may be lost while others are delivered. Finally, the service is said to use *best-effort delivery* because the internet software makes an earnest attempt to deliver packets. That is, the internet does not discard packets capriciously; unreliability arises only when resources are exhausted or underlying networks fail.

7.6 Purpose Of The Internet Protocol

The protocol that defines the unreliable, connectionless delivery mechanism is called the *Internet Protocol* and is usually referred to by its initials, *IP*†. IP provides three important definitions. First, the IP protocol defines the basic unit of data transfer used throughout a TCP/IP internet. Thus, it specifies the exact format of all data as it passes across a TCP/IP internet. Second, IP software performs the *routing* function, choosing a path over which data will be sent. Third, in addition to the precise, formal specification of data formats and routing, IP includes a set of rules that embody the idea of unreliable packet delivery. The rules characterize how hosts and gateways should process packets, how and when error messages should be generated, and the conditions under which packets can be discarded. IP is such a fundamental part of the design that a TCP/IP internet is sometimes called an *IP-based technology*.

We begin our consideration of IP in this chapter by looking at the packet format it specifies. We leave until later chapters the topics of routing and error handling.

7.7 The Internet Datagram

The analogy between a physical network and a TCP/IP internet is strong. On a physical network, the unit of transfer is a frame that contains a header and data, where the header gives information like the (physical) source and destination addresses. The internet calls its basic transfer unit an *Internet datagram*, sometimes referred to as an *IP*

---

†The abbreviation IP gives rise to the term "IP address."

datagram or merely a *datagram*. Like a typical physical network frame, a datagram is divided into header and data areas. Also like a frame, the datagram header contains the source and destination addresses and a type field that identifies the contents of the datagram. The difference, of course, is that the datagram header contains IP addresses whereas the frame header contains physical addresses. Figure 7.2 shows the general form of a datagram:

DATAGRAM HEADER	DATAGRAM DATA AREA

Figure 7.2 General form of an IP datagram, the TCP/IP analogy to a network frame. IP specifies the header format including the source and destination IP addresses. IP does not specify the format of the data area; it can be used to transport arbitrary data.

7.7.1 Datagram Format

Now that we have described the general layout of an IP datagram we can look at the contents in more detail. Figure 7.3 shows the arrangement of fields in a datagram:

0 4 8 16 19 24 31
VERS	HLEN	SERVICE TYPE	TOTAL LENGTH
IDENTIFICATION	FLAGS	FRAGMENT OFFSET
TIME TO LIVE	PROTOCOL	HEADER CHECKSUM
SOURCE IP ADDRESS
DESTINATION IP ADDRESS
IP OPTIONS (IF ANY)	PADDING
DATA
. . .

Figure 7.3 Format of an Internet datagram, the basic unit of transfer in a TCP/IP internet.

Because datagram processing occurs in software, the contents and format are not constrained by any hardware. For example, the first 4-bit field in a datagram (*VERS*) contains the version of the IP protocol that was used to create the datagram. It is used to verify that the sender, receiver, and any gateways in between them agree on the format of the datagram. All IP software is required to check the version field before processing a datagram to insure it matches the format the software expects. If standards change, machines will reject datagrams with protocol versions that differ from theirs, preventing them from misinterpreting datagram contents according to an outdated format. The current IP protocol version is *4*.

The header length field (*HLEN*), also 4 bits, gives the datagram header length measured in 32-bit words. As we will see, all fields in the header have fixed length except for the *IP OPTIONS* and corresponding *PADDING* fields. The most common header, which contains no options and no padding, measures 20 octets and has a header length field equal to *5*.

The *TOTAL LENGTH* field gives the length of the IP datagram measured in octets, including octets in the header and data. The size of the data area can be computed by subtracting the length of the header (*HLEN*) from the *TOTAL LENGTH*. Because the *TOTAL LENGTH* field is 16 bits long, the maximum possible size of an IP datagram is 2^{16} or 65,535 octets. In most applications this is not a severe limitation. It may become more important in the future when higher speed networks can carry data packets larger than 65,535 octets.

7.7.2 Datagram Type of Service and Precedence

The 8-bit *SERVICE TYPE* field specifies how the datagram should be handled and is broken down into five subfields as shown in Figure 7.4:

0	1	2	3	4	5	6	7
PRECEDENCE			D	T	R	UNUSED	

Figure 7.4 The five subfields that comprise the 8-bit type-of-service field.

Three *PRECEDENCE* bits specify datagram precedence, with values ranging from 0 (normal precedence) through 7 (network control), allowing senders to indicate the importance of each datagram. Although most host and gateway software ignores type of service, it is an important concept because it provides a mechanism that will eventually allow control information to have precedence over data. For example, if all hosts and gateways honor precedence, it is possible to implement congestion control algorithms that are not affected by the congestion they are trying to control.

Bits *D*, *T*, and *R* specify the type of transport the datagram desires. When set, the *D* bit requests low delay, the *T* bit requests high throughput, and the *R* bit requests high reliability. Of course, it may not be possible for an internet to guarantee the type of transport requested (i.e., it could be that no path to the destination has the requested property). Thus, we think of the transport request as a hint to the routing algorithms, not as a demand. If a gateway does know more than one possible route to a given destination, it can use the type of transport field to select one with characteristics closest to those desired. For example, suppose the gateway can select between a low capacity leased line or a high bandwidth (but high delay) satellite connection. Datagrams carrying keystrokes from a user to a remote computer could have the *D* bit set requesting that they be delivered as quickly as possible, while datagrams carrying a bulk file transfer could have the *T* bit set requesting that they travel across the high capacity satellite path.

It is also important to realize that routing algorithms must choose from among underlying physical network technologies that each have characteristics of delay, throughput, and reliability. Often, a given technology trades off one characteristic for another (e.g., higher throughput rates at the expense of longer delay). Thus, the idea is to give the algorithm a hint about what is most important; it seldom makes sense to specify all three types of service. To summarize:

> *We regard the type of transport specification as a hint to the routing algorithm that helps it choose among various paths to a destination based on its knowledge of the hardware technologies available on those paths. An internet does not guarantee the type of transport requested.*

7.7.3 Datagram Encapsulation

Before we can understand the next fields in a datagram, we need to consider how datagrams relate to physical network frames. We start with a question: "How large can a datagram be?" Unlike physical network frames that must be recognized by hardware, datagrams are handled by software. They can be of any length the protocol designers choose. We have seen that the current datagram format allots only 16 bits to the total length field, limiting the datagram to at most 65,535 octets. However, that limit could be changed in later versions of the protocol.

More fundamental limits on datagram size arise in practice. We know that as datagrams move from one machine to another, they must always be transported by the underlying physical network. To make internet transportation efficient, we would like to guarantee that each datagram travels in a distinct physical frame. That is, we want our abstraction of a physical network packet to map directly onto a real packet if possible.

The idea of carrying one datagram in one network frame is called *encapsulation*. To the underlying network, a datagram is like any other message sent from one machine to another. The hardware does not recognize the datagram format, nor does it understand the IP destination address. Thus, as Figure 7.5 shows, when one machine sends an IP datagram to another, the entire datagram travels in the data portion of the network frame.

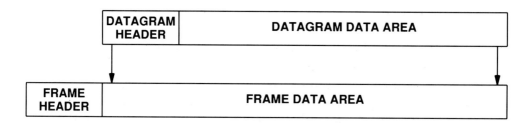

Figure 7.5 The encapsulation of an IP datagram in a frame. The physical network treats the entire datagram, including the header, as data.

7.7.4 Datagram Size, Network MTU, and Fragmentation

In the ideal case, the entire IP datagram fits into one physical frame, making
transmission across the physical net efficient.† To achieve such efficiency, the
designers of IP might have selected a maximum datagram size such that a datagram
would always fit into one frame. But which frame size should be chosen? After all, a
datagram may travel across many types of physical networks as it moves across an internet to its final destination.

To understand the problem, we need a fact about network hardware: each packet-
switching technology places a fixed upper bound on the amount of data that can be
transferred in one physical frame. For example, the Ethernet limits transfers to 1500‡
octets of data, while the proNET-10 allows 2044 octets per frame. We refer to these
limits as the network's *maximum transfer unit* or *MTU*. MTU sizes can be quite small:
some hardware technologies limit transfers to 128 octets or less. Limiting datagrams to
fit the smallest possible MTU in the internet makes transfers inefficient when those datagrams pass across a network that can carry larger size frames. However, allowing datagrams to be larger than the minimum network MTU in an internet means that a datagram may not always fit into a single network frame.

The choice should be obvious: the point of the internet design is to hide underlying
network technologies and make communication convenient for the user. Thus, instead
of designing datagrams that adhere to the constraints of physical networks, TCP/IP
software chooses a convenient initial datagram size and arranges a way to divide large
datagrams into smaller pieces when the datagram needs to traverse a network that has a
small MTU. The small pieces into which a datagram is divided are called *fragments*,
and the process of dividing a datagram is known as *fragmentation*.

As Figure 7.6 illustrates, fragmentation usually occurs at a gateway somewhere
along the path between the datagram source and its ultimate destination. The gateway
receives a datagram from a network with a large MTU and must route it over a network
for which the MTU is smaller than the datagram size.

---

†A field in the frame header identifies the data being carried. Ethernet uses the type value 0800₁₆ to
specify that the data area contains an encapsulated IP datagram.

‡The limit of 1500 comes from the Ethernet specification; when used with a SNAP header the IEEE
802.3 standard limits data to 1492 octets. Some hardware allows slightly larger transfers.

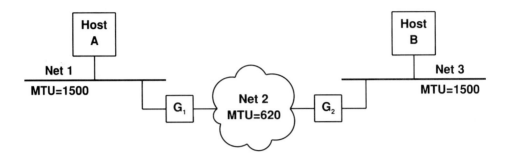

Figure 7.6 An illustration of where fragmentation occurs. Gateway G_1 fragments large datagrams sent from A to B; G_2 fragments large datagrams sent from B to A.

In the figure, both hosts attach directly to Ethernets which have an MTU of 1500 octets. Thus, both hosts can generate and send datagrams up to 1500 octets long. The path between them, however, includes a network with an MTU of 620. If host A sends host B a datagram larger than 620 octets, gateway G_1 will fragment the datagram. Similarly, if B sends a large datagram to A, gateway G_2 will fragment the the datagram.

Fragment size is chosen so each fragment can be shipped across the underlying network in a single frame. In addition, because IP represents the offset of the data in multiples of eight octets, the fragment size must be chosen to be a multiple of eight. Of course, choosing the multiple of eight octets nearest to the network MTU does not usually divide the datagram into equal size pieces; the last piece is often shorter than the others. Fragments must be *reassembled* to produce a complete copy of the original datagram before it can be processed at the destination.

The IP protocol does not limit datagrams to a small size, nor does it guarantee that large datagrams will be delivered without fragmentation. The source can choose any datagram size it thinks appropriate; fragmentation and reassembly occur automatically, without the source taking special action. The IP specification states that gateways must accept datagrams up to the maximum of the MTUs of networks to which they attach. In addition, gateways must always handle datagrams of up to 576 octets. (Hosts are also required to accept, and reassemble if necessary, datagrams of at least 576 octets.)

Fragmenting a datagram means dividing it into several pieces. It may surprise you to learn that each piece has the same format as the original datagram. Figure 7.7 illustrates the result of fragmentation.

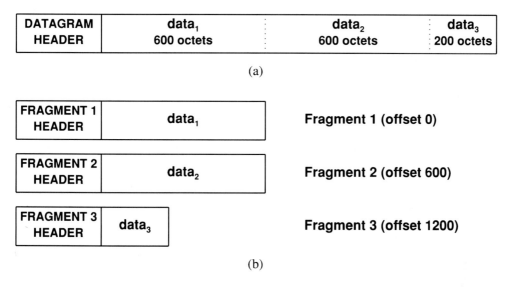

Figure 7.7 (a) An original datagram carrying 1400 octets of data and (b) the three fragments for network MTU of 620. Headers 1 and 2 have the *more fragments* bit set. Offsets shown are decimal octets; they must be divided by 8 to get the value stored in the fragment headers.

Each fragment contains a datagram header that duplicates most of the original datagram header (except for a bit in the *FLAGS* field that shows it is a fragment), followed by as much data as can be carried in the fragment while keeping the total length smaller than the MTU of the network over which it must travel.

7.7.5 Reassembly Of Fragments

Should a datagram be reassembled after passing across one network, or should the fragments be carried to the final host before reassembly? In a TCP/IP internet, once a datagram has been fragmented, the fragments travel as separate datagrams all the way to the ultimate destination where they must be reassembled. Preserving fragments all the way to the ultimate destination has two disadvantages. First, because datagrams are not reassembled immediately after passing across a network with small MTU, the small fragments must be carried from the point of fragmentation to the ultimate destination. Reassembling datagrams at the ultimate destination can lead to inefficiency: even if some of the physical networks encountered after the point of fragmentation have large MTU capability, only small fragments traverse them. Second, if any fragments are lost, the datagram cannot be reassembled. The receiving machine starts a *reassembly timer* when it receives an initial fragment. If the timer expires before all fragments arrive, the receiving machine discards the surviving pieces without processing the datagram. Thus, the probability of datagram loss increases when fragmentation occurs because the loss of a single fragment results in loss of the entire datagram.

Despite the minor disadvantages, performing reassembly at the ultimate destination works well. It allows fragments to be routed independently and does not require intermediate gateways to store or reassemble fragments.

7.7.6 Fragmentation Control

Three fields in the datagram header, *IDENTIFICATION*, *FLAGS*, and *FRAGMENT OFFSET*, control fragmentation and reassembly of datagrams. Field *IDENTIFICATION* contains a unique integer that identifies the datagram. Recall that when a gateway fragments a datagram, it copies most of the fields in the datagram header into each fragment. The *IDENTIFICATION* field must be copied. Its primary purpose is to allow the destination to know which arriving fragments belong to which datagrams. As a fragment arrives, the destination uses the *IDENTIFICATION* field along with the datagram source address to identify the datagram. Computers sending IP datagrams must generate a unique value for the *IDENTIFICATION* field for each unique datagram†. One technique used by IP software keeps a global counter in memory, increments it each time a new datagram is created, and assigns the result as the datagram's *IDENTIFICATION* field.

Recall that each fragment has exactly the same format as a complete datagram. For a fragment, field *FRAGMENT OFFSET* specifies the offset in the original datagram of the data being carried in the fragment, measured in units of 8 octets‡, starting at offset zero. To reassemble the datagram, the destination must obtain all fragments starting with the fragment that has offset *0* through the fragment with highest offset. Fragments do not necessarily arrive in order, and there is no communication between the gateway that fragmented the datagram and the destination trying to reassemble it.

The low-order 2 bits of the 3-bit *FLAGS* field controls fragmentation. Usually, application software using TCP/IP does not care about fragmentation because both fragmentation and reassembly are automatic procedures that occur at a low level in the operating system, invisible to end users. However, to test internet software or debug operational problems, it may be important to test sizes of datagrams for which fragmentation occurs. The first control bit aids in such testing by specifying whether the datagram may be fragmented. It is called the *do not fragment* bit because setting it to *1* specifies that the datagram should not be fragmented. An application may choose to disallow fragmentation when only the entire datagram is useful. For example, consider a computer bootstrap sequence in which a machine begins executing a small program in ROM that uses the internet to request an initial bootstrap, and another machine sends back a memory image. If the software has been designed so it needs the entire image or none of it, the datagram should have the *do not fragment* bit set. Whenever a gateway needs to fragment a datagram that has the *do not fragment* bit set, the gateway discards the datagram and sends an error message back to the source.

---

†In theory, retransmissions of a datagram carry the same *IDENTIFICATION* field as the original; in practice, higher-level protocols usually perform retransmission, resulting in a new datagram with its own *IDEN-TIFICATION*.

‡Offsets are measured in multiples of 8 octets to save space in the header.

The low order bit in the *FLAGS* field specifies whether the fragment contains data from the middle of the original datagram or from the end. It is called the *more fragments* bit. To see why such a bit is needed, consider the IP software at the ultimate destination attempting to reassemble a datagram. It will receive fragments (possibly out of order) and needs to know when it has received all fragments for a datagram. When a fragment arrives, the *TOTAL LENGTH* field in the header refers to the size of the fragment and not to the size of the original datagram, so the destination cannot use the *TOTAL LENGTH* field to tell whether it has collected all fragments. The *more fragments* bit solves the problem easily: once the destination receives a fragment with the *more fragments* bit turned off, it knows this fragment carries data from the tail of the original datagram. From the *FRAGMENT OFFSET* and *TOTAL LENGTH* fields, it can compute the length of the original datagram. By examining the *FRAGMENT OFFSET* and *TOTAL LENGTH* of all fragments that have arrived, a receiver can tell whether the fragments on hand contain all the data needed to reassemble the entire original datagram.

7.7.7 Time to Live (TTL)

Field *TIME TO LIVE* specifies how long, in seconds, the datagram is allowed to remain in the internet system. The idea is both simple and important: whenever a machine injects a datagram into the internet, it sets a maximum time that the datagram should survive. Gateways and hosts that process datagrams must decrement the *TIME TO LIVE* field as time passes and remove the datagram from the internet when its time expires.

Estimating exact times is difficult because gateways do not usually know the transit time for physical networks. A few rules simplify processing and make it easy to handle datagrams without synchronized clocks. First, each gateway along the path from source to destination is required to decrement the *TIME TO LIVE* field by *1* when it processes the datagram header. Furthermore, to handle cases of overloaded gateways that introduce long delays, each gateway records the local time when the datagram arrives, and decrements the *TIME TO LIVE* by the number of seconds the datagram remained inside the gateway waiting for service.

Whenever a *TIME TO LIVE* field reaches zero, the gateway discards the datagram and sends an error message back to the source. The idea of keeping a timer for datagrams is interesting because it guarantees that datagrams cannot travel around an internet forever, even if routing tables become corrupt and gateways route datagrams in a circle.

7.7.8 Other Datagram Header Fields

Field *PROTOCOL* is analogous to the type field in an Ethernet frame. The value in the *PROTOCOL* field specifies which high-level protocol was used to create the message being carried in the *DATA* area of a datagram. In essence, the value of *PROTOCOL* specifies the format of the *DATA* area. The mapping between a high level protocol and the integer value used in the *PROTOCOL* field must be administered by a central authority to guarantee agreement across the entire Internet.

Field *HEADER CHECKSUM* ensures integrity of header values. The IP checksum is formed by treating the header as a sequence of 16-bit integers (in network byte order), adding them together using one's complement arithmetic, and then taking the one's complement of the result. For purposes of computing the checksum, field *HEADER CHECKSUM* is assumed to contain zero.

It is important to note that the checksum only applies to values in the IP header and not to the data. Separating the checksum for headers and data has advantages and disadvantages. Because the header usually occupies fewer octets than the data, having a separate checksum reduces processing time at gateways which only need to compute header checksums. The separation also allows higher level protocols to choose their own checksum scheme for the data. The chief disadvantage is that higher level protocols are forced to add their own checksum or risk having corrupted data go undetected.

Fields *SOURCE IP ADDRESS* and *DESTINATION IP ADDRESS* contain the 32-bit IP addresses of the datagram's sender and intended recipient. Although the datagram may be routed through many intermediate gateways, the source and destination fields never change; they specify the IP addresses of the original source and ultimate destination.

The field labeled *DATA* in Figure 7.3 shows the beginning of the data area of the datagram. Its length depends, of course, on what is being sent in the datagram.

The *IP OPTIONS* field, discussed below, is variable length. The field labeled *PADDING*, depends on the options selected. It represents bits containing zero that may be needed to ensure the datagram header extends to an exact multiple of 32 bits (recall that the header length field is specified in units of 32-bit words).

7.8 Internet Datagram Options

The *IP OPTIONS* field following the destination address is not required in every datagram; options are included primarily for network testing or debugging. Options processing is an integral part of the IP protocol, however, so all standard implementations must include it.

The length of the *IP OPTIONS* field varies depending on which options are selected. Some options are one octet long; they consist of a single octet *option code*. Other options are variable length. When options are present in a datagram, they appear contiguously, with no special separators between them. Each option consists of a single octet option code, which may be followed by a single octet length and a set of data octets for that option. The option code octet is divided into three fields as Figure 7.8 shows.

Figure 7.8 The division of the option code octet into three fields of length 1, 2, and 5 bits.

The fields consist of a 1-bit *COPY* flag, a 2-bit *OPTION CLASS*, and the 5-bit *OPTION NUMBER*. The *COPY* flag controls how gateways treat options during fragmentation. When the *COPY* bit is set to *1*, it specifies that the option should be copied into all fragments. When set to *0*, the *COPY* bit means that the option should only be copied into the first fragment and not into all fragments.

The *OPTION CLASS* and *OPTION NUMBER* bits specify the general class of the option and give a specific option in that class. The table in Figure 7.9 shows how classes are assigned.

Option Class	Meaning
0	Datagram or network control
1	Reserved for future use
2	Debugging and measurement
3	Reserved for future use

Figure 7.9 Classes of IP options as encoded in the *OPTION CLASS* bits of an option code octet.

The table in Figure 7.10 lists the possible options that can accompany an IP datagram and gives their *OPTION CLASS* and *OPTION NUMBER* values. As the list shows, most options are used for control purposes.

Option Class	Option Number	Length	Description
0	0	-	End of option list. Used if options do not end at end of header (also see header padding field).
0	1	-	No operation (used to align octets in a list of options).
0	2	11	Security and handling restrictions (for military applications).
0	3	var	Loose source routing. Used to route a datagram along a specified path.
0	7	var	Record route. Used to trace a route.
0	8	4	Stream identifier. Used to carry a SATNET stream identifier (Obsolete).
0	9	var	Strict source routing. Used to route a datagram along a specified path.
2	4	var	Internet timestamp. Used to record timestamps along the route.

Figure 7.10 The eight possible IP options with their numeric class and number codes. The value *var* in the length column stands for *variable*.

7.8.1 Record Route Option

The routing and timestamp options are the most interesting because they provide a way to monitor or control how internet gateways route datagrams. The *record route* option allows the source to create an empty list of IP addresses and arrange for each gateway that handles the datagram to add its IP address to the list. Figure 7.11 shows the format of the record route option.

As described above, the *CODE* field contains the option number and option class (*7* for record route). The *LENGTH* field specifies the total length of the option as it appears in the IP datagram, including the first three octets. The fields starting with one labeled *FIRST IP ADDRESS* comprise the area reserved for recording internet addresses. The *POINTER* field specifies the offset within the option of the next available slot.

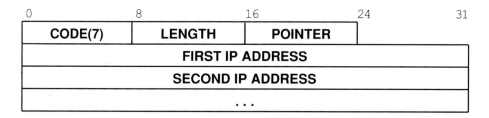

Figure 7.11 The format of the record route option in an IP datagram.

Whenever a machine handles a datagram that has the record route option set, the machine adds its address to the record route list (enough space must be allocated in the option by the original source to hold all entries that will be needed). To add itself to the list, a machine first compares the pointer and length fields. If the pointer is greater than the length, the list is full, so the machine forwards the datagram without inserting its entry. If the list is not full, the machine inserts its 4-octet IP address at the position specified by the *POINTER*, and increments the *POINTER* by four.

When the datagram arrives, the destination machine must extract and process the list of IP addresses. If the destination handles the datagram as usual, it will ignore the recorded route. Note that the source must agree to enable the record route option and the destination must agree to process the resultant list; a single machine will not receive information about recorded routes automatically just because it turns on the record route option.

7.8.2 Source Route Options

Another idea that network builders find interesting is the *source route* option. The idea behind source routing is that it provides a way for the sender to dictate a path through the internet. For example, to test the throughput over a particular physical network, *N*, system administrators can use source routing to force IP datagrams to traverse network *N* even if gateways would normally choose a path that did not include it. The ability to make such tests is especially important in a production environment, because it gives the network manager freedom to route users' datagrams over networks that are known to operate correctly while simultaneously testing other networks. Of course, such routing is only useful to people who understand the network topology; the average user has no need to know or use it.

IP supports two forms of source routing. One form, called *strict source routing*, specifies a routing path by including a sequence of IP addresses in the option as figure 7.12 shows.

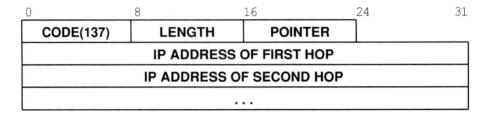

Figure 7.12 The strict source route option specifies an exact route by giving a list of IP addresses the datagram must follow.

Strict source routing means that the addresses specify the exact path the datagram must follow to reach its destination. The path between two successive addresses in the list must consist of a single physical network; an error results if a gateway cannot follow a strict source route. The other form, called *loose source routing*, also includes a sequence of IP addresses. It specifies that the datagram must follow the sequence of IP addresses, but allows multiple network hops between successive addresses on the list.

Both source route options require gateways along the path to overwrite items in the address list with their local network addresses. Thus, when the datagram arrives at its destination, it contains a list of all addresses visited, exactly like the list produced by the record route option.

The format of a source route option resembles that of the record route option shown above. Each gateway examines the *POINTER* and *LENGTH* fields to see if the list has been exhausted. If it has, the pointer is greater than the length, and the gateway routes the datagram to its destination as usual. If the list is not exhausted, the gateway follows the pointer, picks up the IP address, replaces it with the gateway's address†, and routes the datagram using the address it obtained from the list.

7.8.3 Timestamp Option

The *timestamp option* works like the record route option in that the timestamp option contains an initially empty list, and each gateway along the path from source to destination fills in one item in the list. Each entry in the list contains two 32-bit items: the IP address of the gateway that supplied the entry, and a 32-bit integer timestamp. Figure 7.13 shows the format of the timestamp option.

---

†A gateway has one address for each interface; it records the address that corresponds to the network over which it routes the datagram.

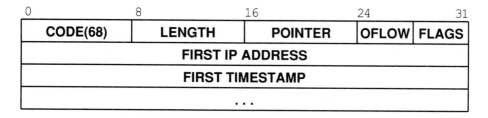

Figure 7.13 The format of the timestamp option. Bits in the FLAG field control the exact format and rules gateways use to process this option.

In the figure, the *LENGTH* and *POINTER* fields are used to specify the length of the space reserved for the option and the location of the next unused slot (exactly as in the record route option). The 4-bit *OFLOW* field contains an integer count of gateways that could not supply a timestamp because the option was too small.

The value in the 4-bit *FLAGS* field controls the exact format of the option and tells how gateways should supply timestamps. The values are:

Flags value	Meaning
0	Record timestamps only; omit IP addresses.
1	Precede each timestamp by an IP address (this is the format shown in Figure 7.13).
3	IP addresses are specified by sender; a gateway only records a timestamp if the next IP address in the list matches the gateway's IP address.

Figure 7.14 The interpretation of values in the FLAGS field of a timestamp option.

Timestamps give the time and date at which a gateway handles the datagram, expressed as milliseconds since midnight, Universal Time†. If the standard representation for time is unavailable, the gateway can use any representation of local time provided it turns on the high-order bit in the timestamp field. Of course, timestamps issued by independent computers are not always consistent even if represented in universal time; each machine reports time according to its local clock, and clocks may differ. Thus, timestamp entries should always be treated as estimates, independent of the representation.

It may seem odd that the timestamp option includes a mechanism to have gateways record their IP addresses along with timestamps because the record route option already provides that capability. However, recording IP addresses with timestamps eliminates

---

† Universal Time was formerly called Greenwich Mean Time; it is the time of day at the prime meridian.

ambiguity. Having the route recorded along with timestamps is also useful because it allows the receiver to know exactly which path the datagram followed.

7.8.4 Processing Options During Fragmentation

The idea behind the *COPY* bit in the option *CODE* field should now be clear. When fragmenting a datagram, a gateway replicates some IP options in all fragments while it places others in only one fragment. For example, consider the option used to record the datagram route. We said that each fragment will be handled as an independent datagram, so there is no guarantee that all fragments follow the same path to the destination. If all fragments contained the record route option, the destination might receive a different list of routes from each fragment. It could not produce a single, meaningful list of routes for the reassembled datagram. Therefore, the IP standard specifies that the record route option should only be copied into one of the fragments.

Not all IP options can be restricted to one fragment. Consider the source route option, for example, that specifies how a datagram should travel through the internet. Source routing information must be replicated in all fragment headers, or fragments will not follow the specified route. Thus, the code field for source route specifies that the option must be copied into all fragments.

7.9 Summary

The fundamental service provided by TCP/IP internet software is a connectionless, unreliable, best-effort packet delivery system. The Internet Protocol (IP) formally specifies the format of internet packets, called *datagrams*, and informally embodies the ideas of connectionless delivery. This chapter concentrated on datagram formats; later chapters will discuss IP routing and error handling.

Analogous to a physical frame, the IP datagram is divided into header and data areas. Among other information, the datagram header contains the source and destination IP addresses, fragmentation control, precedence, and a checksum used to catch transmission errors. Besides fixed-length fields, each datagram header can contain an options field. The options field is variable length, depending on the number and type of options used as well as the size of the data area allocated for each option. Intended to help monitor and control the internet, options allow one to specify or record routing information, or to gather timestamps as the datagram traverses an internet.

FOR FURTHER STUDY

Postel [1980] discusses possible ways to approach internet protocols, addressing, and routing. In later publications, Postel [RFC 791] gives the standard for the Internet Protocol, and Hornig [RFC 894] specifies the standard for the transmission of IP datagrams across an Ethernet. Clark [RFC 815] describes efficient reassembly of fragments. In addition to the packet format, Internet authorities also specify many constants needed in the network protocols. These values can be found in Reynolds and Postel [RFC 1010]. Kent and Mogul [1987] discuss the disadvantages of fragmentation.

An alternative internet protocol suite known as *xns*, is given in Xerox [1981]. Boggs *et. al.* [1980] describe the PARC Universal Packet (PUP) protocol, an abstraction from xns closely related to the IP datagram.

EXERCISES

7.1   What is the single greatest advantage of having the IP checksum cover only the datagram header and not the data? What is the disadvantage?

7.2   Is it ever necessary to use an IP checksum when sending packets over an Ethernet?

7.3   What is the MTU size for the MILNET? NSFNET? X25NET? Hyperchannel?

7.4   Do you expect high-speed local area networks to have larger or smaller MTU size than slower, long-haul networks?

7.5   Argue that fragments should have small, nonstandard headers.

7.6   Find out when the IP protocol version last changed. Is having a protocol version number really useful?

7.7   Can you imagine why a one's complement checksum was chosen for IP instead of a cyclic redundancy check?

7.8   What are the advantages of doing reassembly at the ultimate destination instead of doing it after the datagram travels across one network?

7.9   What is the minimum network MTU required to send an IP datagram that contains at least one octet of data?

7.10 Suppose you are hired to implement IP datagram processing in hardware. Is there any rearrangement of fields in the header that would have made your hardware more efficient? Easier to build?

7.11 If you have access to an implementation of IP, revise it and test your locally available implementations of IP to see if they reject IP datagrams with an out-of-date version number.

8

Internet Protocol: Routing IP Datagrams

8.1 Introduction

We have seen that all internet services build on an unreliable, connectionless packet delivery system, and that the basic unit of transfer in a TCP/IP internet is the IP datagram. This chapter adds to the description of connectionless service by describing how gateways route IP datagrams and deliver them to their final destinations. We think of the datagram format from Chapter 7 as characterizing the static aspects of the Internet Protocol. The description of routing in this chapter characterizes the operational aspects. The next chapter concludes our presentation of IP by describing how errors are handled; later chapters show how other protocols use it to provide higher-level services.

8.2 Routing In An Internet

In a packet switching system, *routing* refers to the process of choosing a path over which to send packets, and *router* refers to any computer making such a choice.

Routing occurs at several levels. For example, within a wide area network that has multiple physical connections between packet switches, the network itself is responsible for routing packets from the time they enter until they leave. Such internal routing is completely self-contained inside the wide area network. Machines on the outside can not participate in decisions; they merely view the network as an entity that delivers packets.

Remember that the goal of TCP/IP is to provide a virtual network that offers a connectionless IP datagram delivery service. Thus, we will focus on *internet routing* or *IP routing*. Analogous to routing within a physical network, IP routing chooses a path over which a datagram should be sent. The IP routing algorithm must choose how to send a datagram across multiple physical networks.

Routing in an internet can be difficult, especially between machines with multiple physical network connections. Ideally, the routing software would examine such things as network load, datagram length, or the type of service specified in the datagram header, when selecting the best path. Most internet routing software is much less sophisticated, however, and selects routes based on fixed assumptions about shortest paths.

To understand IP routing completely, we must go back and look at the architecture of a TCP/IP internet. First, recall that an internet is composed of multiple physical networks interconnected by computers called *gateways*. Each gateway has direct connections to two or more networks. Unlike a gateway, a host usually connects directly to one physical network. We know that it is possible, however, to have multi-homed hosts that connect directly to multiple networks.

Both hosts and gateways participate in IP routing. When an application program on a host attempts to communicate, the TCP/IP protocols eventually generate one or more IP datagrams. The host must make a routing decision when it chooses where to send the datagrams. As figure 8.1 shows, hosts must make routing decisions even if they have only one network connection.

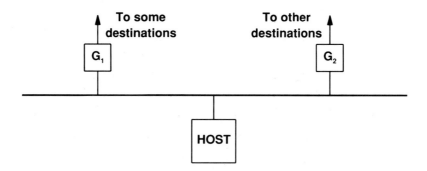

Figure 8.1 An example of a singly-homed host that must route datagrams. It must choose to send the datagram either to gateway G_1 or to gateway G_2 because no single gateway provides the best path to all destinations.

Of course, gateways make IP routing decisions (that is their primary purpose and the motivation for calling them *routers*). What about multi-homed hosts? Any computer with multiple network connections can act as a gateway, and as we will see, multi-homed hosts running TCP/IP have all the software needed for routing. Furthermore, sites that cannot afford separate gateway computers often do use general-purpose timesharing machines as both hosts and gateways (the practice is especially widespread among university sites). However, the TCP/IP standards draw a sharp distinction between the functions of a host and those of a gateway, and sites that try to mix host and gateway functions on a single machine sometimes find that their multi-homed hosts engage in unexpected interactions. For now, we will distinguish hosts from gateways and assume that hosts do not perform the gateway function of transferring packets from one network to another.

8.3 Direct And Indirect Delivery

Loosely speaking, we can divide routing into two forms: *direct routing* and *indirect routing*. Direct routing, the transmission of a datagram from one machine directly to another, is the basis on which all internet communication rests. Two machines can engage in direct routing only if they both attach directly to an underlying physical transmission system (e.g., a single Ethernet). *Indirect routing* occurs when the destination is not on a directly attached network, forcing the sender to pass the datagram to a gateway for delivery.

8.3.1 Datagram Delivery Over A Single Network

We know that one machine on a given physical network can send a physical frame directly to another machine on the same network. To transfer an IP datagram, the sender encapsulates the datagram in a physical frame, maps the destination IP address into a physical address, and uses the network hardware to deliver it. Chapter 5 presented two possible mechanisms for address resolution, including using the ARP protocol for dynamic address binding on Ethernet-like networks. Chapter 7 discussed datagram encapsulation. Thus, we have reviewed all the pieces needed to understand direct delivery. To summarize:

> *Transmission of an IP datagram between two machines on a single physical network does not involve gateways. The sender encapsulates the datagram in a physical frame, binds the destination IP address to a physical hardware address, and sends the resulting frame directly to the destination.*

How does the sender know whether the destination lies on a directly connected network? The test is straightforward. We know that IP addresses are divided into a network-specific prefix and a host-specific suffix. To see if a destination lies on one of the directly connected networks, the sender extracts the network portion of the destination IP address and compares it to the network portion of its own IP address(es). A match means the datagram can be sent directly. Here we see one of the advantages of the Internet address scheme, namely:

Because the internet addresses of all machines on a single network include a common network id, and because extracting that id can be done in a few instructions, testing whether a machine can be reached directly is extremely efficient.

From the internet perspective, it is easiest to think of direct routing as *datagram delivery*. Delivery is the final step in any datagram transmission, even if the datagram traverses many networks and intermediate gateways. The final gateway along the path between the datagram source and its destination will connect directly to the same physical network as the destination. Thus, the final gateway will deliver the datagram using direct routing. We can think of direct routing between the source and destination as a special case of general purpose routing – in a direct route the datagram does not happen to pass through any intervening gateways.

8.3.2 Indirect Routing

Indirect routing is more difficult than direct routing because the sender must identify a gateway to which the datagram can be sent. The gateway must then forward the datagram on toward its destination network.

To visualize how indirect routing works, imagine a large internet with many networks interconnected by gateways but with only two hosts at the far ends. When one host wants to send to the other, it encapsulates the datagram and sends it to the nearest gateway. We know that it can reach a gateway because all physical networks are interconnected, so there must be a gateway attached to each one. Thus, the originating host can reach a gateway using a single physical network. Once the frame reaches the gateway, software extracts the encapsulated datagram, and the IP routing routines select the next gateway along the path towards the destination. The datagram is again placed in a frame and sent over the next physical network to a second gateway, and so on, until it can be delivered directly. These ideas can be summarized:

Gateways in a TCP/IP internet form a cooperative, interconnected structure. Datagrams pass from gateway to gateway until they reach a gateway that can deliver the datagram directly.

How can a gateway know where to send each datagram? How can a host know which gateway to use for a given destination? The two questions are related because they both involve IP routing. We will answer them in two stages, considering the basic table-driven routing algorithm in this chapter and postponing a discussion of how gateways learn new routes until later.

8.4 Table-Driven IP Routing

The usual IP routing algorithm employs an *Internet routing table* (sometimes called an *IP routing table*) on each machine that stores information about possible destinations and how to reach them. Because both hosts and gateways route datagrams, both have IP routing tables. Whenever the IP routing software in a host or gateway needs to transmit a datagram, it consults the routing table to decide where to send the datagram.

What information should be kept in routing tables? If every routing table contained information about every possible destination address, it would be impossible to keep the tables current. Furthermore, because the number of possible destinations is large, machines would have insufficient space to store the information.

Conceptually, we would like to use the principle of information hiding and allow machines to make routing decisions with minimal information. For example, we would like to isolate information about specific hosts to the local environment in which they exist and arrange for machines that are far away to route packets to them without knowing such details. Fortunately, the IP address scheme helps achieve this goal. Recall that IP addresses are assigned to make all machines connected to a given physical network share a common prefix (the network portion of the address). We have already seen that such an assignment makes the test for direct delivery efficient. It also means that routing tables only need to contain network prefixes and not full IP addresses.

Using the network portion of a destination address instead of the complete host address makes routing efficient and keeps routing tables small. More important, it helps hide information, keeping the details of specific hosts confined to the local environment in which those hosts operate. Typically, a routing table contains pairs (N, G), where N is the IP address of a destination *network*, and G is the IP address of the "next" gateway along the path to network N. Thus, the routing table in a gateway G only specifies one step along the path from G to a destination network – the gateway does not know the complete path to a destination.

It is important to understand that the routing table always points to gateways that can be reached across a single network. That is, all gateways listed in machine M's routing table must lie on networks to which M connects directly. When a datagram is ready to leave M, IP software locates the destination IP address and extracts the network portion. M then uses the network id to make a routing decision, selecting a gateway that can be reached directly.

In practice, we apply the principle of information hiding to hosts as well. We insist that although hosts have IP routing tables, they must keep minimal information in their tables. The idea is to force hosts to rely on gateways for most routing.

Figure 8.2 shows a concrete example that helps explain routing tables. The example internet consists of four networks connected by three gateways. In the figure, the routing table gives the routes that gateway G uses. Because G connects directly to networks 20.0.0.0 and 30.0.0.0, it can reach any host on those networks directly (possibly using ARP to find physical addresses). Given a datagram destined for a host on network 40.0.0.0, G routes it to address 30.0.0.7, the address of gateway H. H will then deliver the datagram directly. G can reach address 30.0.0.7 because both G and H attach directly to network 30.0.0.0.

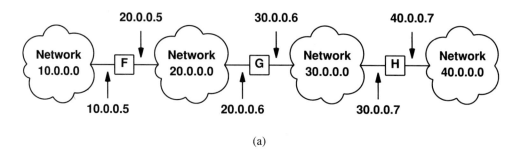

(a)

TO REACH HOSTS ON NETWORK	ROUTE TO THIS ADDRESS
20.0.0.0	DELIVER DIRECTLY
30.0.0.0	DELIVER DIRECTLY
10.0.0.0	20.0.0.5
40.0.0.0	30.0.0.7

(b)

Figure 8.2 (a) An example internet with 4 networks and 3 gateways, and (b) the routing table for gateway *G*.

As Figure 8.2 demonstrates, the size of the routing table depends on the number of networks in the internet; it only grows when new networks are added. However, the table size and contents are independent of the number of individual hosts connected to the networks. We can summarize the underlying principle:

> *To hide information, keep routing tables small, and make routing decisions efficient, IP routing software only keeps information about destination network addresses, not about individual host addresses.*

Choosing routes based on the destination network id alone has several consequences. First, in most implementations, it means that all traffic headed for a given network takes the same path. As a result, even when multiple paths exist, they may not be used concurrently. Also, all types of traffic follow the same path without regard to the delay or throughput of physical networks. Second, because only the final gateway along the path attempts to communicate with the destination host, only it can determine if the host exists or is operational. Thus, we need to arrange a way for that gateway to send reports of delivery problems back to the original source. Third, because each gateway routes traffic independently, datagrams traveling from host *A* to host *B* may follow an entirely different path than datagrams traveling from host *B* back to host A. We need to ensure that gateways cooperate to guarantee that two-way communication is always possible.

8.5 Default Routes

Another technique used to hide information and keep routing table sizes small consolidates multiple entries into a default case. The idea is to have the IP routing software first look in the routing table for the destination network. If no route appears in the table, the routing routines send the datagram to a *default gateway*.

Default routing is especially useful when a site has a small set of local addresses and only one connection to the rest of the internet. For example, default routes work well in host machines that attach to a single physical network and reach only one gateway leading to the remainder of the internet. The entire routing decision consists of two tests: one for the local net, and a default that points to the only possible gateway. Even if the site contains a few local networks, the routing is simple because it consists of a few tests for the local networks plus a default for all other destinations.

8.6 Host-Specific Routes

Although we said that all routing is based on networks and not on individual hosts, most IP routing software allows per-host routes to be specified as a special case. Having per-host routes gives the local network administrator more control over network use and can also be used to control access for security purposes. When debugging network connections or routing tables, the ability to specify a special route to one individual machine turns out to be especially useful.

8.7 The Final Algorithm

Taking into account everything we have said, the IP routing algorithm becomes:

Algorithm:

Route_IP_Datagram (datagram, routing_table)

Extract destination IP address, I_D, from datagram
Compute IP address of destination network, I_N
if I_N matches any directly connected network address
      send datagram to destination over that network;
      (This involves resolving I_D to a physical address,
      encapsulating datagram, and sending the frame.)
else if I_D appears as a host-specific route
      route datagram as specified in the table;
else if I_N appears in routing table
      route datagram as specified in the table;
else if a default route has been specified
      route datagram to the default gateway;
else declare a routing error;

Figure 8.3 The IP routing algorithm. Given an IP datagram and a routing table, this algorithm selects the next machine to which the datagram should be sent. Routing tables always specify a next machine that lies on a directly connected network.

8.8 Routing With IP Addresses

It is important to understand that IP routing does not alter the original datagram. In particular, the datagram source and destination addresses remain unaltered; they always specify the IP address of the original source and the IP address of the ultimate destination. When IP executes the routing algorithm it computes a new address, the IP address of the machine to which the datagram should be sent next. The new address is most likely the address of a gateway. However, if the datagram can be delivered directly, the new address will be the same as the address of the ultimate destination.

The IP address computed by the IP routing algorithm is known as the *next hop* address because it tells where the datagram must be sent next (even though it may not be the ultimate destination). Where does IP store the next hop address? Not in the datagram; no place is reserved for it. In fact, IP does not ''store'' the next hop address at all. After executing the routing algorithm, IP passes the datagram and the next hop address to the network interface software responsible for the physical network over which the datagram must be sent. The network interface software binds the next hop address to a physical address, forms a frame using that physical address, places the datagram in the data portion of the frame, and sends the result. After using the next hop address to find a physical address, the network interface software discards the next hop address.

It may seem odd that routing tables store the IP address of a next hop for each destination network when those addresses must be translated into corresponding physical addresses before the datagram can be sent. If we imagine a host sending a sequence of datagrams to the same destination address, the use of IP addresses will appear incredibly inefficient. IP dutifully extracts the destination address in each datagram and uses the routing table to produce a next hop address. It then passes the datagram and next hop address to the network interface, which recomputes the binding to a physical address. If the routing table used physical addresses, the binding between the next hop's IP address and physical address could be performed once, saving unneeded computation.

Why does IP software avoid using physical addresses when storing and computing routes? As Figure 8.4 shows, there are two important reasons.

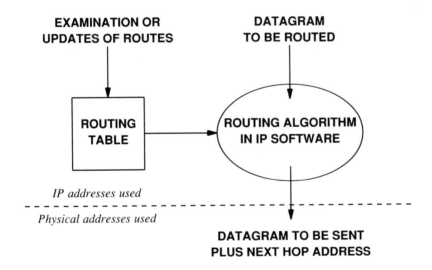

Figure 8.4 IP software and the routing table it uses reside above the address boundary. Using only IP addresses makes routes easy to examine or change and hides the details of physical addresses at the lowest possible level.

First, the routing table provides an especially clean interface between IP software that routes datagrams and high-level software that manipulates routes. To debug routing problems, network managers often need to examine the routing tables. Using only IP addresses in the routing table makes it easy for managers to understand and easy to see whether software has updated the routes correctly. Second, the whole point of the Internet Protocol is to build an abstraction that hides the details of underlying networks.

Figure 8.4 shows the *address boundary*, the important conceptual division between low-level software that understands physical addresses and internet software that only uses high-level addresses. Above this boundary, all software can be written to communicate using internet addresses; knowledge of physical addresses is relegated to a few small, low-level routines. We will see that observing the boundary also helps keep the implementation of remaining TCP/IP protocols easy to understand, test, and modify.

8.9 Handling Incoming Datagrams

So far, we have discussed IP routing by describing how decisions are made about outgoing packets. It should be clear, however, that IP software must process incoming datagrams as well.

When an IP datagram arrives at a host, the network interface software delivers it to the IP software for processing. If the datagram's destination address matches the host's IP address, IP software on the host accepts the datagram and passes it to the appropriate higher-level protocol software for further processing. If the destination IP address does not match, a host is required to discard the datagram (i.e., hosts are forbidden from attempting to forward datagrams that are accidentally routed to the wrong machine).

Unlike hosts, gateways perform forwarding. When an IP datagram arrives at a gateway it is delivered to the IP software. Again, two cases arise: the datagram could have reached its final destination, or it may need to travel further. As with hosts, if the datagram destination IP address matches the gateway's own IP address, the IP software passes the datagram to higher-level protocol software for processing†. If the datagram has not reached its final destination, IP routes the datagram using the standard algorithm and the information in the local routing table.

Determining whether an IP datagram has reached its final destination is not quite as trivial as it seems. Remember that even a host may have multiple physical connections, each with its own IP address. When an IP datagram arrives, the machine must compare the destination internet address to the IP address for each of its network connections. If any match, it keeps the datagram and processes it. A machine must also accept datagrams that were broadcast on the physical network if their destination IP address is the limited IP broadcast address or the directed IP broadcast address for that network. As we will see in Chapters 16 and 17, subnet and multicast addresses make address recognition even more complex. In any case, if the address does not match any of the local machine's addresses, IP decrements the time-to-live field in the datagram header, discarding the datagram if the count reaches zero, or computing a new checksum and routing the datagram if the count remains positive.

Should every machine route the IP datagrams it receives? Obviously, gateways must route incoming datagrams because that is their main function. We have also said that some multi-homed hosts act like gateways even though they are really general

---

†Usually, the only datagrams destined for a gateway are those used to test connectivity or those that carry gateway management commands.

purpose computing systems. While using a host as a gateway is not usually a good idea, if one chooses to use that arrangement, the host must be configured to route datagrams just as a gateway does. But what about other hosts, those that are not intended to be gateways? The answer is that hosts not designated to be gateways should *not* route datagrams that they receive; they should discard them.

There are four reasons why a host not designated to serve as a gateway should refrain from performing any gateway functions. First, when such a host receives a datagram intended for some other machine, something has gone wrong with internet addressing, routing, or delivery. The problem may not be revealed if the host takes corrective action by routing the datagram. Second, routing will cause unnecessary network traffic (and may steal CPU time from legitimate uses of the host). Third, simple errors can cause chaos. Suppose that every host routes traffic and imagine what happens if one machine accidentally broadcasts a datagram that is destined for some host, *H*. Every host on the network receives a copy of the datagram from the broadcast, and every machine routes its copy to *H*, which will be bombarded with many copies. Fourth, as later chapters show, gateways do more than merely route traffic. As the next chapter shows, gateways use a special protocol to report errors, while hosts do not (again, to avoid having multiple error reports bombard a source). Gateways also propagate routing information to ensure that their routing tables are consistent. If hosts route datagrams without participating fully in all gateway functions, unexpected anomalies may arise.

8.10 Establishing Routing Tables

We have discussed how IP routes datagrams based on the contents of routing tables, without saying how systems initialize their routing tables or update them as the network changes. Later chapters deal with these questions and discuss protocols that allow gateways to keep routes consistent. For now, it is only important to understand that IP bases all routing decisions on tables, so changing those tables will change the routes datagrams follow.

8.11 Summary

IP routing consists of deciding where to send a datagram based on its destination IP address. The route is direct if the destination machine lies on a network to which the sending machine attaches; we think of this as the final delivery step in datagram transmission. The route is indirect if the datagram must be sent to a gateway for delivery. The general paradigm is that hosts send indirectly routed datagrams to the nearest gateway; the datagrams travel through the internet from gateway to gateway until they can be delivered directly across one physical network.

IP routing produces the IP address of the next machine (i.e., the address of the next hop) to which the datagram should be sent; IP passes the datagram and next hop address to network interface software. Transmission of a datagram from one machine to the next always involves encapsulating the datagram in a physical frame, mapping the next hop internet address to a physical address, and sending the frame using the underlying hardware.

The internet routing algorithm is table driven and uses only IP addresses. It bases routing decisions on the destination network address instead of the destination host address, keeping routing tables small. Default routes also help keep tables small, especially for hosts that can access only one gateway.

FOR FURTHER STUDY

Routing is an important topic. Frank and Chou [1971] and Schwartz and Stern [1980] discuss routing in general; Postel [1980] discusses internet routing. Braden and Postel [RFC 1009] provides a summary of how Internet gateways handle IP datagrams. Narten [1989] contains a survey of Internet routing. Fultz and Kleinrock [1971] analyze adaptive routing schemes; and McQuillan, Richer, and Rosen [1980] describe the ARPANET adaptive routing algorithm.

The idea of using policy statements to formulate rules about routing has been considered often. Leiner [RFC 1124] considers policies for interconnected networks. Braun [RFC 1104] discusses models of policy routing for internets, Rekhter [RFC 1092] relates policy routing to the second NSFNET backbone, and Clark [RFC 1102] describes using policy routing with IP.

EXERCISES

8.1 Complete routing tables for all gateways in Figure 8.1. Which benefit most from default routes?

8.2 Examine the routing algorithm used in 4.3 BSD UNIX. Are all the cases mentioned here covered? Does the algorithm allow anything not mentioned?

8.3 What does a gateway do with the *time to live* value in an IP header?

8.4 Consider a machine with two physical network connections and two IP addresses I_1 and I_2. Is it possible for that machine to receive a datagram destined for I_2 over the network with address I_1? Explain.

8.5 Consider two hosts, *A* and *B*, that both attach to a common physical network, *N*. Is it ever possible, when using our routing algorithm, for *A* to receive a datagram destined for *B*? Explain.

8.6 Modify the routing algorithm to accommodate the IP source route options discussed in Chapter 7.

8.7   An IP gateway must perform a computation that takes time proportional to the length of the datagram header each time it processes a datagram. Explain.

8.8   A network administrator argues that to make monitoring and debugging his local network easier, he wants to rewrite the routing algorithm so it tests host-specific routes *before* it tests for direct delivery. Can you imagine how he could use the revised algorithm to build a network monitor?

8.9   Is it possible to address a datagram to a gateway's IP address? Does it make sense to do so?

8.10 Consider a modified routing algorithm that examines host-specific routes testing for delivery on directly connected networks. Under what circumstances might such an algorithm be desirable?

8.11 Play detective: after monitoring IP traffic on a local area network for 10 minutes one evening, someone notices that all frames destined for machine *A* carry IP datagrams that have destination equal to *A*'s IP address, while all frames destined for machine *B* carry IP datagrams with destination *not* equal to *B*'s IP address. Explain.

8.12 How could you change the IP datagram format to support high-speed packet switching at gateways? Hint: a gateway must recompute a header checksum after decrementing the time-to-live field.

8.13 Compare the ISO connectionless delivery protocol (ISO standard 8473) with IP. How well will the ISO protocol support high-speed switching? Hint: variable length fields are expensive.

9

Internet Protocol: Error and Control Messages (ICMP)

9.1 Introduction

We have seen that the Internet Protocol provides an unreliable, connectionless datagram delivery service, and that a datagram travels from gateway to gateway until it reaches one that can deliver it directly to its final destination. If a gateway cannot route or deliver a datagram, or if the gateway detects an unusual condition, like network congestion, that affects its ability to forward the datagram, it needs to instruct the original source to take action to avoid or correct the problem. This chapter discusses a mechanism that gateways and hosts use to communicate such control or error information. We will see how gateways use the mechanism to report delivery problems, and how hosts use it to test whether destinations are reachable.

9.2 The Internet Control Message Protocol

In the connectionless system we have described so far, each gateway operates autonomously, routing or delivering datagrams that arrive without coordinating with the original sender. The system works well if all machines operate correctly and agree on routing, but no system works correctly all the time. Besides failures of communication lines and processors, IP fails to deliver datagrams when the destination machine is temporarily or permanently disconnected from the network, when the time-to-live counter expires, or when intermediate gateways become so congested that they cannot process the incoming traffic. The important difference between having a real, hardware network and a software-based internet is that in the former, the designer can often rely on network hardware to inform machines when such problems arise. In an internet, which has no such hardware mechanism, a sender cannot tell whether a delivery failure resulted from a local malfunction or a remote one. Debugging becomes extremely difficult. The IP protocol itself contains nothing to help the sender test connectivity or learn about such failures.

To allow gateways in an internet to report errors or provide information about unexpected circumstances, the designers added a special-purpose message mechanism to the TCP/IP protocols. The mechanism, known as the *Internet Control Message Protocol* (*ICMP*), is considered a required part of IP and must be included in every IP implementation.

Like all other traffic, ICMP messages travel across the internet in the data portion of IP datagrams. The ultimate destination of an ICMP message is not an application program or user on the destination machine, however, but the Internet Protocol software on that machine. That is, when an ICMP error message arrives, the ICMP software module handles it. Of course, if ICMP determines that a particular higher-level protocol or application program has caused a problem, it will inform the appropriate module. We can summarize:

> *The Internet Control Message Protocol allows gateways to send error or control messages to other gateways or hosts; ICMP provides communication between the Internet Protocol software on one machine and the Internet Protocol software on another.*

Initially designed to allow gateways to report the cause of delivery errors to hosts, ICMP is not restricted to gateways. Although guidelines restrict the use of some ICMP messages, an arbitrary machine can send an ICMP message to any other machine. Thus, a host can use ICMP to correspond with a gateway or another host. The chief advantage of allowing hosts to use ICMP is that it provides a single mechanism used for all control and information messages.

9.3 Error Reporting vs. Error Correction

Technically, ICMP is an *error reporting mechanism*. It provides a way for gateways that encounter an error to report the error to the original source. Although the protocol specification outlines intended uses of ICMP and suggests possible actions to take in response to error reports, ICMP does not fully specify the action to be taken for each possible error. In short,

> *ICMP only reports error conditions to the original source; the source must relate errors to individual application programs and take action to correct the problem.*

Most errors stem from the original source, but others do not. Because ICMP reports problems to the original source, however, it cannot be used to inform intermediate gateways about problems. For example, suppose a datagram follows a route through a set of gateways, G_1, G_2, ..., G_k. If G_k has incorrect routing information and mistakenly routes the datagram to gateway G_E, G_E can only report the error back to the datagram's original source. Unfortunately, the source has no responsibility for the problem or control over the misbehaving gateway. In fact, the source may not be able to determine which gateway caused the problem.

Why restrict ICMP to communication with the original source? The answer should be clear from our discussion of datagram formats and routing in the previous chapters. The datagram only contains fields that specify the original source and the ultimate destination; it does not contain a complete record of its trip through the internet (except for unusual cases where the record route option is used). Furthermore, because gateways can establish and change their own routing tables, there is no global knowledge of routes. Thus, when a datagram reaches a given gateway, it is impossible to know the route it has taken to arrive there. If the gateway detects a problem, it cannot know the set of intermediate machines that processed the datagram, so it cannot inform them of the problem. Instead of silently discarding the datagram, the gateway uses ICMP to inform the original source that a problem has occurred, and trusts that host administrators will cooperate with network administrators to locate and repair the problem.

9.4 ICMP Message Delivery

ICMP messages require two levels of encapsulation as Figure 9.1 shows. Each ICMP message travels across the internet in the data portion of an IP datagram, which itself travels across each physical network in the data portion of a frame. Datagrams carrying ICMP messages are routed exactly like datagrams carrying information for users; there is no additional reliability or priority. Thus, error messages themselves may be lost or discarded. Furthermore, in an already congested network, the error message may cause additional congestion. An exception is made to the error handling procedures if an IP datagram carrying an ICMP message causes an error. The exception, established to avoid the problem of having error messages about error messages, specifies that ICMP messages are not generated for errors that result from datagrams carrying ICMP error messages.

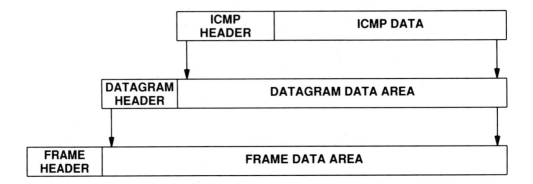

Figure 9.1 Two levels of ICMP encapsulation. The ICMP message is encapsulated in an IP datagram, which is further encapsulated in a
frame for transmission. To identify ICMP, the datagram protocol
field contains the value *1*.

It is important to keep in mind that even though ICMP messages are encapsulated
and sent using IP, ICMP is not considered a higher level protocol – it is a required part
of IP. The reason for using IP to deliver ICMP messages is that they may need to travel across several physical networks to reach their final destination. Thus, they cannot
be delivered by the physical transport alone.

9.5 ICMP Message Format

Although each ICMP message has its own format, they all begin with the same
three fields: an 8-bit integer message *TYPE* field that identifies the message, an 8-bit
CODE field that provides further information about the message type, and a 16-bit
CHECKSUM field (ICMP uses the same additive checksum algorithm as IP, but the
ICMP checksum only covers the ICMP message). In addition, ICMP messages that report errors always include the header and first 64 data bits of the datagram causing the
problem.

The reason for returning more than the datagram header alone is to allow the receiver to determine more precisely which protocol(s) and which application program
were responsible for the datagram. As we will see later, higher-level protocols in the
TCP/IP suite are designed so that crucial information is encoded in the first 64 bits.

The ICMP *TYPE* field defines the meaning of the message as well as its format.
The types include:

Type Field	ICMP Message Type
0	Echo Reply
3	Destination Unreachable
4	Source Quench
5	Redirect (change a route)
8	Echo Request
11	Time Exceeded for a Datagram
12	Parameter Problem on a Datagram
13	Timestamp Request
14	Timestamp Reply
15	Information Request (obsolete)
16	Information Reply (obsolete)
17	Address Mask Request
18	Address Mask Reply

The next sections describe each of these messages, giving details of the message format and its meaning.

9.6 Testing Destination Reachability And Status

TCP/IP protocols provide facilities to help network managers or users identify network problems. One of the most frequently used debugging tools invokes the ICMP *echo request* and *echo reply* messages. A host or gateway sends an ICMP echo request message to a specified destination. Any machine that receives an echo request formulates an echo reply and returns it to the original sender. The request contains an optional data area; the reply contains a copy of the data sent in the request. The echo request and associated reply can be used to test whether a destination is reachable and responding. Because both the request and reply travel in IP datagrams, successful receipt of a reply verifies that major pieces of the transport system work. First, IP software on the source machine must route the datagram. Second, intermediate gateways between the source and destination must be operating and must route the datagram correctly. Third, the destination machine must be running (at least it must respond to interrupts), and both ICMP and IP software must be working. Finally, routes in gateways along the return path must be correct.

On many systems, the command users invoke to send ICMP echo requests is named *ping*. Sophisticated versions of ping send a series of ICMP echo requests, capture responses, and provide statistics about datagram loss. They allow the user to specify the length of the data being sent and the interval between requests. Less sophisticated versions merely send one ICMP echo request and await a reply.

9.7 Echo Request And Reply Message Format

Figure 9.2 shows the format of echo request and reply messages.

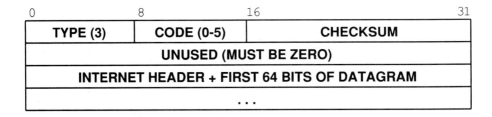

Figure 9.2 ICMP echo request or reply message format.

The field listed as *OPTIONAL DATA* is a variable length field that contains data to be returned to the sender. An echo reply always returns exactly the same data as was received in the request. Fields *IDENTIFIER* and *SEQUENCE NUMBER* are used by the sender to match replies to requests. The value of the *TYPE* field specifies whether the message is a request (*8*) or a reply (*0*).

9.8 Reports Of Unreachable Destinations

When a gateway cannot deliver an IP datagram, it sends a *destination unreachable* message back to the original source, using the format shown in Figure 9.3.

0	8	16	31
TYPE (3)	CODE (0-5)	CHECKSUM	
UNUSED (MUST BE ZERO)			
INTERNET HEADER + FIRST 64 BITS OF DATAGRAM			
. . .			

Figure 9.3 ICMP destination unreachable message format.

The *CODE* field in a destination unreachable message contains an integer that further describes the problem. Possible values are:

Code Value	Meaning
0	Network Unreachable
1	Host Unreachable
2	Protocol Unreachable
3	Port Unreachable
4	Fragmentation Needed and DF set
5	Source Route Failed
6	Destination network unknown
7	Destination host unknown
8	Source host isolated
9	Communication with destination network administratively prohibited
10	Communication with destination host Administratively prohibited
11	Network unreachable for type of service
12	Host unreachable for type of service

Although IP is a best-effort delivery mechanism, discarding datagrams should not be taken lightly. Whenever an error prevents a gateway from routing or delivering a datagram, the gateway sends a destination unreachable message back to the source and then *drops* (i.e., discards) the datagram. Network unreachable errors usually imply routing failures; host unreachable errors imply delivery failures†. Because the message contains a short prefix of the datagram that caused the problem, the source will know exactly which address is unreachable.

Destinations may be unreachable because hardware is temporarily out of service, because the sender specified a nonexistent destination address, or (in rare circumstances) because the gateway does not have a route to the destination network. Note that although gateways report failures they encounter, they may not know of all delivery failures. For example, if the destination machine connects to an Ethernet network, the network hardware does not provide acknowledgements. Therefore, a gateway can continue to send packets to a destination after the destination is powered down without receiving any indication that the packets are not being delivered. To summarize:

> *Although gateways send destination unreachable messages if they cannot route or deliver datagrams, not all such errors can be detected.*

The meaning of protocol and port unreachable messages will become clear when we study how higher level protocols use abstract destination points called *ports*. Most of the remaining messages are self explanatory. If the datagram contains the source route option with an incorrect route, it may trigger a *source route* failure message. If a gateway needs to fragment a datagram but the "don't fragment" bit is set, the gateway sends a *fragmentation needed* message back to the source.

---

†An exception occurs for gateways using the subnet addressing scheme of Chapter 16. They report subnet routing failures with ICMP host unreachable messages.

9.9 Congestion And Datagram Flow Control

Because IP is connectionless, gateways cannot reserve memory or communication resources in advance of receiving datagrams. As a result, gateways can be overrun with traffic, a condition known as *congestion*. It is important to understand that congestion can arise for two entirely different reasons. First, a high-speed computer may be able to generate traffic faster than a network can transfer it. For example, imagine a supercomputer generating internet traffic. The datagrams may eventually need to cross a slow-speed wide area network (WAN) even though the supercomputer itself attaches to a high-speed local area net. Congestion will occur in the gateway that attaches to the WAN because datagrams arrive faster than they can be sent. Second, if many computers simultaneously need to send datagrams through a single gateway, the gateway can experience congestion, even though no single source causes the problem.

When datagrams arrive too quickly for a host or gateway to process, it enqueues them in memory temporarily. If the datagrams are part of a small burst, such buffering solves the problem. If the traffic continues, the host or gateway eventually exhausts memory and must discard additional datagrams that arrive. A machine uses ICMP *source quench* messages to relieve congestion. A source quench message is a request for the source to reduce its current rate of datagram transmission. Usually, congested gateways send one source quench message for every datagram that they discard. Gateways may also use more sophisticated congestion control techniques. Some monitor incoming traffic and quench sources that have the highest datagram transmission rates. Others attempt to avoid congestion altogether by arranging to send quench requests as their queues start to become long but before they overflow.

There is no ICMP message to reverse the effect of a source quench. Instead, a host that receives source quench messages from some machine, M, lowers the rate at which it sends datagrams to M until it stops receiving source quench messages; it then gradually increases the rate as long as no further source quench requests are received.

9.10 Source Quench Format

In addition to the usual ICMP *TYPE*, *CODE*, *CHECKSUM* fields, and an unused 32-bit field, source quench messages have a field that contains a datagram prefix. Figure 9.4 illustrates the format. As with most ICMP messages that report an error, the datagram prefix field contains a prefix of the datagram that triggered the source quench request.

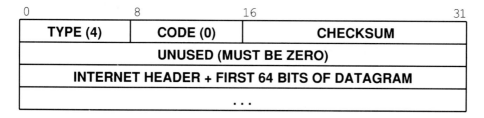

0	8	16	31
TYPE (4)	CODE (0)	\multicolumn{2}{c}{CHECKSUM}	
\multicolumn{4}{c}{UNUSED (MUST BE ZERO)}			
\multicolumn{4}{c}{INTERNET HEADER + FIRST 64 BITS OF DATAGRAM}			
\multicolumn{4}{c}{. . .}			

Figure 9.4 ICMP source quench message format. Congested gateways send one source quench message each time they discard a datagram; the datagram prefix identifies the datagram that was dropped.

9.11 Route Change Requests From Gateways

Internet routing tables usually remain static over long periods of time. Hosts initialize them from a configuration file at system startup, and system administrators seldom make routing changes during normal operations. If network topology changes, routing tables in a gateway or host may become incorrect. A change can be temporary (e.g., when hardware needs to be repaired) or permanent (e.g., when a new network is added to the internet). As we will see in later chapters, gateways exchange routing information periodically to accommodate network changes and keep their routes up-to-date. Thus, as a general rule:

> *Gateways are assumed to know correct routes; hosts begin with minimal routing information and learn new routes from gateways.*

To help follow this rule and to avoid duplicating routing information in the configuration file on each host, the initial host route configuration specifies the minimum possible routing information needed to communicate (e.g., the address of a single gateway). Thus, the host begins with minimal information and relies on gateways to update its routing table. In one special case, when a gateway detects a host using a nonoptimal route, it sends the host an ICMP message, called a *redirect*, requesting that the host change its routes. The gateway also forwards the original datagram on to its destination.

The advantage of the ICMP redirect scheme is simplicity: it allows a host to boot knowing the address of only one gateway on the local network. The initial gateway returns ICMP redirect messages whenever a host sends a datagram for which there is a better route. The host routing table remains small but still contains optimal routes for all destinations in use.

Redirect messages do not solve the problem of propagating routes in a general way, however, because they are limited to interactions between a gateway and a host on a directly connected network. Figure 9.5 illustrates the problem. In the Figure, assume source S sends a datagram to destination D. Assume that gateway G_1 incorrectly routes the datagram through gateway G_2 instead of through gateway G_4 (i.e., G_1 incorrectly chooses a longer path then necessary). When gateway G_5 receives the datagram it cannot send an ICMP redirect message to G_1 because it does not know G_1's address. Later chapters explore the problem of how to propagate routes across multiple networks.

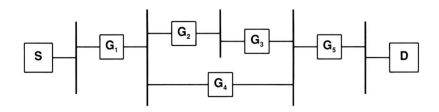

Figure 9.5 ICMP redirect messages do not provide routing among gateways. In this example, Gateway G_5 cannot redirect G_1 to use the shorter path for datagrams from S to D.

In addition to the requisite *TYPE, CODE,* and *CHECKSUM* fields, each redirect message contains a 32-bit *GATEWAY INTERNET ADDRESS* field and a *DATAGRAM PREFIX* field, as Figure 9.6 shows.

0	8	16	31
TYPE (5)	CODE (0 to 3)	CHECKSUM	
GATEWAY INTERNET ADDRESS			
INTERNET HEADER + FIRST 64 BITS OF DATAGRAM			
. . .			

Figure 9.6 ICMP redirect message format.

The *GATEWAY INTERNET ADDRESS* field contains the address of a gateway that the host is to use to reach the destination mentioned in the datagram header. The *INTERNET HEADER* field contains the IP header plus the next 64 bits of the datagram that triggered the message. Thus, a host receiving an ICMP redirect examines the datagram prefix to determine the datagram's destination address. The *CODE* field of an ICMP redirect message further specifies how to interpret the destination address, based on values assigned as follows:

Code Value	Meaning
0	Redirect datagrams for the Net (now obsolete)
1	Redirect datagrams for the Host
2	Redirect datagrams for the Type of Service† and Net
3	Redirect datagrams for the Type of Service and Host

As a general rule, gateways only send ICMP redirect requests to hosts and not to other gateways. We will see in later chapters that gateways use other protocols to exchange routing information.

9.12 Detecting Circular Or Excessively Long Routes

Because internet gateways compute a next hop using local tables, errors in routing tables can produce a *routing cycle* for some destination, *D*. A routing cycle can consist of two gateways that each route a datagram for destination *D* to the other, or it can consist of several gateways. When several form a routing cycle they each route a datagram for destination *D* to the next gateway in the cycle. If a datagram enters a routing cycle, it will pass around the cycle endlessly. As mentioned previously, to prevent datagrams from circling forever in a TCP/IP internet, each IP datagram contains a time-to-live counter, sometimes called a *hop count*. A gateway decrements the time-to-live counter whenever it processes the datagram and discards the datagram when the count reaches zero.

Whenever a gateway discards a datagram because its hop count has reached zero or because a timeout occurred while waiting for fragments of a datagram, it sends an ICMP *time exceeded* message back to the datagram's source, using the format shown in Figure 9.7.

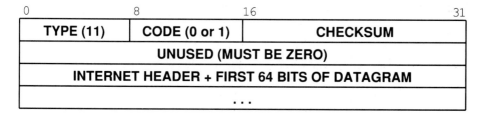

Figure 9.7 ICMP time exceeded message format. A gateway sends this message whenever a datagram is discarded because the time-to-live field in the datagram header has reached zero or because its reassembly timer expired while waiting for fragments.

The *CODE* field explains the nature of the timeout:

†Recall that each IP header specifies a type of service used for routing.

Code Value	Meaning
0	Time-to-live count exceeded
1	Fragment reassembly time exceeded

Fragment reassembly refers to the task of collecting all the fragments from a datagram. When the first fragment of a datagram arrives, the receiving host starts a timer and considers it an error if the timer expires before all the pieces of the datagram arrive. Code value *1* is used to report such errors to the sender; one message is sent for each such error.

9.13 Reporting Other Problems

When a gateway or host finds problems with a datagram not covered by previous ICMP error messages (e.g., an incorrect datagram header), it sends a *parameter problem* message to the original source. One possible cause of such problems occurs when arguments to an option are incorrect. The message, formatted as shown in Figure 9.8, is only sent when the problem is so severe that the datagram must be discarded.

```
0                 8                16                              31
┌─────────────────┬─────────────────┬─────────────────────────────┐
│   TYPE (12)     │  CODE (0 or 1)  │          CHECKSUM           │
├─────────────────┼─────────────────┴─────────────────────────────┤
│    POINTER      │          UNUSED (MUST BE ZERO)                │
├─────────────────┴───────────────────────────────────────────────┤
│        INTERNET HEADER + FIRST 64 BITS OF DATAGRAM              │
├─────────────────────────────────────────────────────────────────┤
│                              . . .                              │
└─────────────────────────────────────────────────────────────────┘
```

Figure 9.8 ICMP parameter problem message format. Such messages are only sent when the problem causes the datagram to be dropped.

To make the message unambiguous, the sender uses the *POINTER* field in the message header to identify the octet in the datagram that caused the problem. Code *1* is used to report that a required option is missing (e.g., a security option in the military community); the *POINTER* field is not used for code *1*.

9.14 Clock Synchronization And Transit Time Estimation

Although machines on an internet can communicate, they usually operate independently, with each machine maintaining its own notion of the current time. Clocks that differ widely can confuse users of distributed systems software. The TCP/IP protocol suite includes several protocols that can be used to synchronize clocks. One of the simplest techniques uses an ICMP message to obtain the time from another machine. A requesting machine sends an ICMP *timestamp request* message to another machine, asking that the second machine return its current value for the time of day. The receiving machine returns a *timestamp reply* back to the machine making the request. Figure 9.9 shows the format of timestamp request and reply messages.

0	8	16	31
TYPE (13 or 14)	CODE (0)	CHECKSUM	
IDENTIFIER		SEQUENCE NUMBER	
ORIGINATE TIMESTAMP			
RECEIVE TIMESTAMP			
TRANSMIT TIMESTAMP			

Figure 9.9 ICMP timestamp request or reply message format.

The *TYPE* field identifies the message as a request (*13*) or a reply (*14*); the *IDENTIFIER* and *SEQUENCE NUMBER* fields are used by the source to associate replies with requests. Remaining fields specify times, given in milliseconds since midnight, Universal Time†. The *ORIGINATE TIMESTAMP* field is filled in by the original sender just before the packet is transmitted, the *RECEIVE TIMESTAMP* field is filled immediately upon receipt of a request, and the *TRANSMIT TIMESTAMP* field is filled immediately before the reply is transmitted.

Hosts use the three timestamp fields to compute estimates of the delay time between them and to synchronize their clocks. Because the reply includes the *ORIGINATE TIMESTAMP* field, a host can compute the total time required for a request to travel to a destination, be transformed into a reply, and return. Because the reply carries both the time at which the request entered the remote machine, as well as the time at which the reply left, the host can compute the network transit time, and from that, estimate the differences in remote and local clocks.

In practice, accurate estimation of round-trip delay can be difficult and substantially restricts the utility of ICMP timestamp messages. Of course, to obtain an accurate estimate of round trip delay one must take many measurements and average them. However, the round-trip delay between a pair of machines that connect to a large internet can vary dramatically, even over short periods of time. Furthermore, recall that because IP is a best-effort technology, datagrams can be dropped, delayed, or delivered out of order. Thus, merely taking many measurements may not guarantee consistency; sophisticated statistical analysis may be needed to produce precise estimates.

---

† Universal Time was formerly called Greenwich Mean Time; it is the time of day at the prime meridian.

9.15 Information Request And Reply Messages

The ICMP *information request* and *information reply* messages (types *15* and *16*) are now considered obsolete and should not be used. It was originally intended to allow hosts to discover their internet address at system startup. The current protocols for address determination are RARP, described in Chapter 6, and BOOTP, described in Chapter 19.

9.16 Obtaining A Subnet Mask

Chapter 16 discusses the motivation for subnet addressing as well as the details of how subnets operate. For now, it is only important to understand that when hosts use subnet addressing, some bits in the hostid portion of their IP address identify a physical network. To participate in subnet addressing, hosts need to know which bits of the 32-bit internet address correspond to the physical network and which correspond to host identifiers. The information needed to interpret the address is represented in a 32-bit quantity called the *subnet mask*.

To learn the subnet mask used for the local network, a machine can send an *address mask request* message to a gateway and receive an *address mask reply*. The machine making the request can either send the message directly, if it knows the gateway's address, or broadcast the message if it does not. Figure 9.10 shows the format of address mask messages.

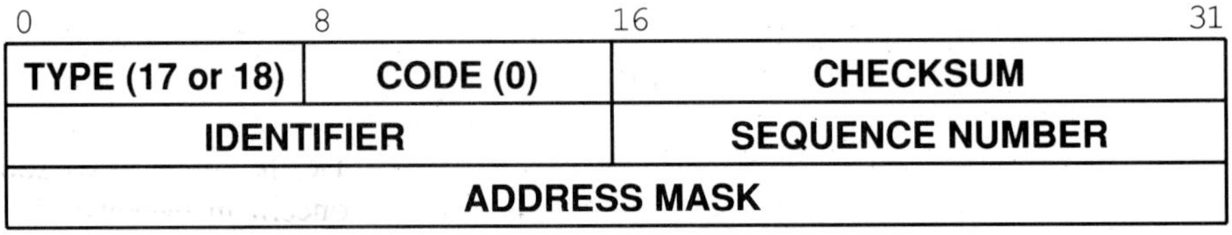

0	8	16	31
TYPE (17 or 18)	CODE (0)	CHECKSUM	
IDENTIFIER		SEQUENCE NUMBER	
ADDRESS MASK			

Figure 9.10 ICMP address mask request or reply message format. Usually, hosts broadcast a request without knowing which specific gateway will respond.

The *TYPE* field in an address mask message specifies whether the message is a request (*17*) or a reply (*18*). A reply contains the network's subnet address mask in the *ADDRESS MASK* field. As usual, the *IDENTIFIER* and *SEQUENCE NUMBER* fields allow a machine to associate replies with requests.

9.17 Summary

Normal communication across an internet involves sending messages from a user process on one host to a user process on another host. Gateways may need to communicate directly with the network software on a particular host to report abnormal conditions or to send the host new routing information.

The Internet Control Message Protocol provides for extranormal communication among gateways and hosts; it is an integral, required part of IP. ICMP includes *source quench* messages that retard the rate of transmission, *redirect* messages that request a host to change its routing tables, and *echo request/reply* messages that hosts can use to determine whether a destination can be reached. An ICMP message travels in the data area of an IP datagram and has three fixed-length fields at the beginning of the message: an ICMP message *type* field, a *code* field, and an ICMP *checksum* field. The message type determines the format of the rest of the message as well as its meaning.

FOR FURTHER STUDY

Both Tanenbaum [1981] and Stallings [1985] discuss control messages in general and relate them to various network protocols. The central issue is not how to send control messages but when. Grange and Gien [1979], as well as Driver, Hopewell, and Iaquinto [1979], concentrate on a problem for which control messages are essential, namely, flow control. Gerla and Kleinrock [1980] compare flow control strategies analytically.

The Internet Control Message Protocol described here is a TCP/IP standard defined by Postel [RFC 792]. Nagle [RFC 896] discusses ICMP source quench messages and shows how gateways should use them to handle congestion control. Prue and Postel [RFC 1016] discusses a more recent technique gateways use in response to source quench. Nagle [1987] argues that congestion is always a concern in packet switched networks. Mogul and Postel [RFC 950] discusses subnet mask request and reply messages. Finally, Jain, Ramakrishnan and Chiu [1987] discusses how gateways and transport protocols could cooperate to avoid congestion.

For a discussion of clock synchronization protocols see Mills [RFCs 956, 957, and 958].

EXERCISES

9.1 Devise an experiment to record how many of each ICMP message type appear on your local network during a day.

9.2 Experiment to see if you can send packets through a gateway fast enough to trigger an ICMP source quench message.

9.3   Devise an algorithm that synchronizes clocks using ICMP timestamp messages.

9.4   See if your local operating system contains a *ping* command. Does it allow you to build one?

9.5   Assume that the operating system sends ICMP time-exceeded messages to application programs, and use them to build a *traceroute* command that reports the list of gateways between the source and a particular destination.

9.6   If you connect to the Internet, try to ping host 128.10.2.1 (a machine at Purdue).

9.7   Should a gateway give ICMP messages priority over normal traffic? Why or why not?

9.8   Consider an Ethernet that has one conventional host, *H*, and 12 gateways connected to it. Find a single (slightly illegal) frame carrying an IP packet that, when sent by host *H*, causes *H* to receive exactly 24 packets.

9.9   Compare ICMP source quench packets with Jain's 1-bit scheme. Which is a more effective strategy for dealing with congestion? Why?

9.10 There is no ICMP message that allows a machine to inform the source that transmission errors are causing datagrams to arrive corrupted. Under what circumstances might such a message be useful?

9.11 Should ICMP error messages contain a timestamp that specifies when they are sent? Why or why not?

10

Protocol Layering

10.1 Introduction

Previous chapters have reviewed the architectural foundations of internetworking, described how gateways route Internet datagrams among themselves or to hosts, and presented mechanisms used to map IP addresses to physical network addresses. This chapter considers the general structure of software found in gateways and hosts that carries out network communication. It presents the general principle of layering, shows how layering makes Internet Protocol software easier to understand and build, and traces the path of datagrams through the protocol software they encounter when traversing a TCP/IP internet.

10.2 The Need For Multiple Protocols

We have said that protocols allow one to specify or understand communication without knowing the details of a particular vendor's network hardware. They are to computer communication what programming languages are to computation. It should be apparent by now how closely the analogy fits. Like assembler language, some protocols describe communication across a physical network. For example, the details of the Ethernet frame format, network access policy, and frame error handling comprise a protocol that describes communication on an Ethernet. Similarly, the details of IP addresses, the datagram format, and the concept of unreliable, connectionless delivery comprise the Internet Protocol.

Complex data communication systems do not use a single protocol to handle all transmission tasks. Instead, they require a set of cooperative protocols, sometimes called a *protocol family* or *protocol suite*. To understand why, think of the problems that arise when machines communicate over a data network:

• *Hardware failure*. A host or gateway may fail either because the hardware fails or because the operating system crashes. A network transmission link may fail or accidentally be disconnected. The protocol software needs to detect such failures and recover from them if possible.

• *Network congestion*. Even when all hardware and software operates correctly, networks have finite capacity which can be exceeded. The protocol software needs to arrange ways that a congested machine can suppress further traffic.

• *Packet delay or loss*. Sometimes, packets experience extremely long delays or are lost. The protocol software needs to learn about failures or adapt to long delays.

• *Data corruption*. Electrical or magnetic interference or hardware failures can cause transmission errors that corrupt the contents of transmitted data. Protocol software needs to detect and recover from such errors.

• *Data duplication or sequence errors*. Networks that offer multiple routes may deliver data out of sequence or may deliver duplicates of packets. The protocol software needs to reorder packets and remove any duplicates.

Taken together, all these problems seem overwhelming. It is difficult to understand how to write a single protocol that will handle them all. From the analogy with programming languages, we can see how to conquer the complexity. Program translation has been partitioned into four conceptual subproblems identified with the software that handles each subproblem: compiler, assembler, link editor, and loader. The division makes it possible for the designer to concentrate on one subproblem at a time, and for the implementor to build and test each piece of software independently.

Two final observations about our programming language analogy will help clarify the organization of protocols. First, it should be clear that pieces of translation software must agree on the exact format of data passed between them. For example, the data passed from the compiler to the assembler consists of a program defined by the assembly programming language. Thus, we see how the translation process involves multiple programming languages. The analogy will hold for communication software, where we will see that multiple protocols define the interfaces between the modules of communication software. Second, the four parts of the translator form a linear sequence in which output from the compiler becomes input to the assembler, and so on. Protocol software also uses a linear sequence.

10.3 The Conceptual Layers Of Protocol Software

Think of the modules of protocol software on each machine as being stacked vertically into *layers*, as in Figure 10.1. Each layer takes responsibility for handling one part of the problem.

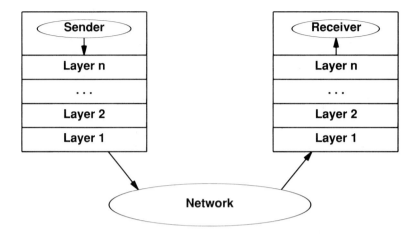

Figure 10.1 The conceptual organization of protocol software in layers.

Conceptually, sending a message from an application program on one machine to an application program on another means transferring the message down through successive layers of protocol software on the sender's machine, transferring the message across the network, and transferring the message up through successive layers of protocol software on the receiver's machine.

In practice, the protocol software is much more complex than the simple model of Figure 10.1 indicates. Each layer makes decisions about the correctness of the message and chooses an appropriate action based on the message type or destination address. For example, one layer on the receiving machine must decide whether to keep the message or forward it to another machine. Another layer must decide which application program should receive the message.

To understand the difference between the conceptual organization of protocol software and the implementation details, consider the comparison shown in Figure 10.2. The conceptual diagram in Figure 10.2a shows an Internet layer between a high level protocol layer and a network interface layer. The realistic diagram in Figure 10.2b shows that the IP software may communicate with multiple high-level protocol modules and with multiple network interfaces.

Although a diagram of conceptual protocol layering does not show all details, it does help explain the general ideas. For example, Figure 10.3 shows the layers of protocol software used by a message that traverses three networks. The diagram shows only the network interface and Internet Protocol layers in gateways because only those layers are needed to receive, route, and then send datagrams. We understand that any machine attached to two networks must have two network interface modules, even though the conceptual layering diagram shows only a single network interface layer in each machine.

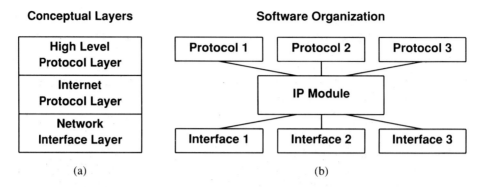

Figure 10.2 A comparison of (a) conceptual protocol layering and (b) a realistic view of software organization showing multiple network interfaces below IP and multiple protocols above it.

As Figure 10.3 shows, a sender on the original machine transmits a message which the
IP layer places in a datagram and sends across network *1*. On intermediate machines
the datagram passes up to the IP layer which routes it back out again (on a different network). Only when it reaches the final destination machine does IP extract the message
and pass it up to higher layers of protocol software.

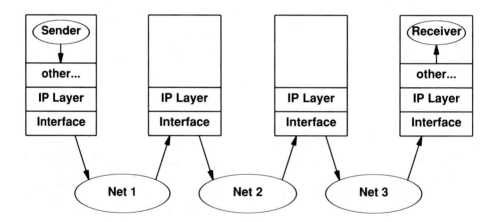

Figure 10.3 The path of a message traversing the Internet from the sender
through two intermediate machines to the receiver. Intermediate
machines only send the datagram to the IP software layer.

10.4 Functionality Of The Layers

Once the decision has been made to partition the communication problem into sub-problems and organize the protocol software into modules that each handle one sub-problem, the question arises: "what functionality should reside in each module?" The question is not easy to answer for several reasons. First, given a set of goals and constraints governing a particular communication problem, it is possible to choose an organization that will optimize protocol software for that problem. Second, even when considering general network-level services such as reliable transport, it is possible to choose from among fundamentally distinct approaches to solving the problem. Third, the design of network (or internet) architecture and the organization of the protocol software are interrelated; one cannot be designed without the other.

10.4.1 ISO 7-Layer Reference Model

Two ideas about protocol layering dominate the field. The first, based on work done by the *International Organization for Standardization (ISO)*, is known as the ISO *Reference Model of Open System Interconnection*, often referred to as the *ISO model*. The ISO model contains 7 conceptual layers organized as Figure 10.4 shows.

Layer	Functionality
7	Application
6	Presentation
5	Session
4	Transport
3	Network
2	Data Link (Hardware Interface)
1	Physical Hardware Connection

Figure 10.4 The ISO 7-layer reference model for protocol software.

The ISO model, built to describe protocols for a single network, does not contain a specific level for internetwork routing in the same way TCP/IP protocols do.

10.5 CCITT X.25 And Its Relation To The ISO Model

Although it was designed to provide a conceptual model and not an implementation guide, the ISO layering scheme has been the basis for several protocol implementations. Among the protocols commonly associated with the ISO model, the set of protocols known as X.25 is probably the best known and most widely used. X.25 was established as a recommendation of the *Consultative Committee on International Telephony and Telegraphy* (CCITT), an international organization that recommends standards for international telephone services. X.25 has been adopted by public data networks throughout the United States and Europe.

In the X.25 view, a network operates much like a telephone system. Like the AR-PANET described in Chapter 2, an X.25 network is assumed to consist of complex packet switches that contain the intelligence needed to route packets. Hosts do not attach directly to communication wires of the network. Instead each host attaches to one of the packet switches using a serial communication line. In one sense the connection between a host and an X.25 packet switch is a miniature network consisting of one serial link. The host must follow a complicated procedure to transfer packets onto the network.

• *Physical Layer.* X.25 specifies a standard for the physical interconnection between host computers and network packet switches, as well as the procedures used to transfer packets from one machine to another. In the reference model, level *1* specifies the physical interconnection including electrical characteristics of voltage and current. A corresponding protocol, X.21, gives the details used by public data networks.

• *Data Link Layer.* The level *2* portion of the X.25 protocol specifies how data travels between a host and the packet switch to which it connects. X.25 uses the term *frame* to refer to a unit of data as it passes between a host and a packet switch (it is important to understand that the X.25 definition of *frame* differs from the way we have used it). Because raw hardware delivers only a stream of bits, the level *2* protocol must define the format of frames and specify how the two machines recognize frame boundaries. Because transmission errors can destroy data, the level *2* protocol includes error detection (e.g., a frame checksum). Finally, because transmission is unreliable, the level *2* protocol specifies an exchange of acknowledgements that allows the two machines to know when a frame has been transferred successfully.

One commonly used level *2* protocol, named the *High Level Data Link Communication*, is best known by its acronym, *HDLC*. Several versions of HDLC exist, with the most recent known as *HDLC/LAPB*. It is important to remember that successful transfer at level *2* means a frame has been passed to the network packet switch for delivery; it does not guarantee that the packet switch accepted the packet or was able to route it.

• *Network Layer.* The ISO reference model specifies that the third level contains functionality that completes the definition of the interaction between host and network. Called the *network* or *communication subnet* layer, this level defines the basic unit of transfer across the network and includes the concepts of destination addressing and routing. Remember that in the X.25 world, communication between host and packet switch is conceptually isolated from the traffic that is being passed. Thus, the network might allow packets defined by level 3 protocols to be larger than the size of frames that can be transferred at level *2*. The level 3 software assembles a packet in the form the network expects and uses level *2* to transfer it (possibly in pieces) to the packet switch. Level 3 must also respond to network congestion problems.

• *Transport Layer.* Level 4 provides end-to-end reliability by having the destination host communicate with the source host. The idea here is that even though lower layers of protocols provide reliable checks at each transfer, the end-to-end layer double checks to make sure that no machine in the middle failed.

• *Session Layer.* Higher levels of the ISO model describe how protocol software can be organized to handle all the functionality needed by application programs. The ISO committee considered the problem of remote terminal access so fundamental that they assigned layer 5 to handle it. In fact, the central service offered by many public data networks consists of terminal to host interconnection. The carrier provides a special purpose host computer called a *Packet Assembler And Disassembler* (*PAD*) on the network with dialup access. Subscribers, usually travelers who carry their own terminal and modem, dial up the local PAD, make a network connection to the host with which they wish to communicate, and log in. Using the network for long distance communication is less expensive than direct dialup.

• *Presentation Layer.* ISO layer 6 is intended to include functions that many application programs need when using the network. Typical examples include standard routines that compress text or convert graphics images into bit streams for transmission across a network. Although it is not completely understood, much work has been expended on this layer in recent years. The ISO draft standard, known as *Abstract Syntax Notation 1* (*ASN.1*), provides a representation of data that application program use.

• *Application Layer.* Finally, ISO layer 7 includes application programs that use the network. Examples include electronic mail or file transfer programs. In particular, the CCITT has devised a protocol for electronic mail called the *X.400* or *X.400(1988)* standard. In fact, the CCITT and ISO worked jointly on message handling systems; the ISO version is called *MOTIS*.

10.5.1 The TCP/IP Internet Layering Model

The second major layering model did not arise from a standards committee, but came instead from research that led to the TCP/IP protocol suite. With a little work, the ISO model can be stretched to describe the TCP/IP layering scheme, but the underlying assumptions are different enough to warrant distinguishing the two.

Broadly speaking, TCP/IP software is organized into four conceptual layers that build on a fifth layer of hardware. Figure 10.5 shows the conceptual layers as well as the form of data as it passes between them.

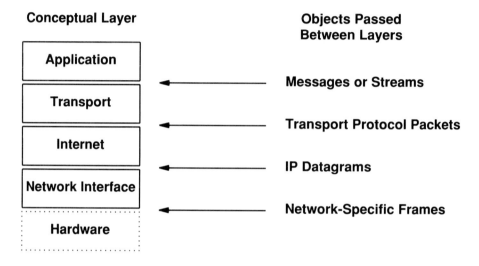

Figure 10.5 The 4 conceptual layers of TCP/IP software and the form of objects passed between layers. The layer labeled *network interface* is sometimes called the *data link* layer.

• *Application Layer*. At the highest level, users invoke application programs that access services available across a TCP/IP internet. An application interacts with the transport level protocol(s) to send or receive data. Each application program chooses the style of transport needed, which can be either a sequence of individual messages or a continuous stream of bytes. The application program passes data in the required form to the transport level for delivery.

• *Transport Layer*. The primary duty of the *transport layer* is to provide communication from one application program to another. Such communication is often called *end-to-end*. The transport layer may regulate flow of information. It may also provide reliable transport, ensuring that data arrives without error and in sequence. To do so, it arranges to have the receiving side send back acknowledgements, and it retransmits lost packets. The transport software divides the stream of data being transmitted into small pieces (called *packets* in the ISO terminology) and passes each packet along with a destination address to the next layer for transmission.

Although Figure 10.5 uses a single block to represent the application layer, a general purpose computer can have multiple application programs accessing the internet at one time. The transport layer must accept data from several user programs and send it to the next lower layer. To do so, it adds additional information to each packet, including codes that identify which application program sent it and which application program should receive it, as well as a checksum. The receiving machine uses the checksum to verify that the packet arrived intact, and uses the destination code to identify the application program to which it should be delivered.

• *Internet Layer.* As we have already seen, the Internet layer handles communication from one machine to another. It accepts a request to send a packet from the transport layer along with an identification of the machine to which the packet should be sent. It encapsulates the packet in an IP datagram, fills in the datagram header, uses the routing algorithm to determine whether to deliver the datagram directly or send it to a gateway, and passes the datagram to the appropriate network interface for transmission. The Internet layer also handles incoming datagrams, checking their validity, and using the routing algorithm to decide whether the datagram should be processed locally or forwarded. For datagrams addressed to the local machine, software in the internet layer deletes the datagram header and chooses from among several transport protocols the one that will handle the packet. Finally, the Internet layer sends ICMP error and control messages as needed and handles all incoming ICMP messages.

• *Network Interface Layer.* The lowest level TCP/IP software comprises a network interface layer, responsible for accepting IP datagrams and transmitting them over a specific network. A network interface may consist of a device driver (e.g., when the network is a local area network to which the machine attaches directly) or a complex subsystem that uses its own data link protocol (e.g., when the network consists of packet switches that communicate with hosts using HDLC).

10.6 Differences Between X.25 And Internet Layering

There are two subtle and important differences between the TCP/IP layering scheme and the X.25 scheme. The first difference revolves around the focus of attention on reliability, while the second involves the location of intelligence in the overall system.

10.6.1 Link-Level vs. End-To-End Reliability

One major difference between the TCP/IP protocols and the X.25 protocols lies in their approaches to providing reliable data transfer services. In the X.25 model, protocol software detects and handles errors at all levels. At the link level, complex protocols guarantee that the transfer between a host and the packet switch to which it connects will be correct. Checksums accompany each piece of data transferred, and the receiver acknowledges each piece of data received. The link level protocol includes timeout and retransmission algorithms that prevent data loss and provide automatic recovery after hardware fails and restarts.

Successive levels of X.25 provide reliability of their own. At level *3*, X.25 also provides error detection and recovery for packets transferred onto the network, using checksums as well as timeout and retransmission techniques. Finally, level *4* must provide end-to-end reliability, having the source correspond with the ultimate destination to verify delivery.

In contrast to such a scheme, TCP/IP bases its protocol layering on the idea that reliability is an end-to-end problem. The architectural philosophy is simple: construct the internet so it can handle the expected load, but allow individual links or machines to lose data or corrupt it without trying to repeatedly recover. In fact, there is little or no reliability in most TCP/IP network interface layer software. Instead, the transport layer handles most error detection and recovery problems.

The resulting freedom from interface layer verification makes TCP/IP software much easier to understand and implement correctly. Intermediate gateways can discard datagrams that become corrupted because of transmission errors. They can discard any datagrams that cannot be delivered. They can discard datagrams when the arrival rate exceeds machine capacity. They can reroute datagrams through paths with shorter or longer delay without informing the source or destination.

Having unreliable links means that some datagrams do not arrive. Detection and recovery of datagram loss is carried out between the source host and the ultimate destination and is, therefore, called *end-to-end* verification. The end-to-end software located in the transport layer uses checksums, acknowledgements, and timeouts to control transmission. Thus, unlike the connection-oriented X.25 protocol layering, the TCP/IP software focuses most of its reliability control in one layer.

10.6.2 Locus of Intelligence and Decision Making

Another difference between the X.25 model and the TCP/IP model emerges when one considers the locus of authority and control. As a general rule, networks using X.25 adhere to the idea that a network is a utility that provides a transport service. The vendor that offers the service controls network access and monitors traffic to keep records for accounting and billing. The network vendor handles problems like routing, flow control, and acknowledgements internally, making transfers reliable. This view leaves little that the hosts can (or need to) do. In short, the network is a complex, independent system to which one can attach relatively simple host computers; the hosts themselves participate in the network operation very little.

By contrast, TCP/IP requires hosts to participate in almost all of the network protocols. We have already mentioned that hosts actively implement end-to-end error detection and recovery. They also participate in routing because they must choose a gateway when sending datagrams, and they participate in network control because they must handle ICMP control messages. Thus, when compared to an X.25 network, a TCP/IP internet can be viewed as a relatively simple packet delivery system to which intelligent hosts attach.

10.7 The Protocol Layering Principle

Independent of the particular layering scheme used, or the functions of the layers, the operation of layered protocols is based on a fundamental idea. The idea, called the *layering principle*, can be summarized succinctly:

> *Layered protocols are designed so that layer* n *at the destination receives exactly the same object sent by layer* n *at the source.*

The layering principle explains why layering is such a powerful idea. It allows the protocol designer to focus attention on one layer at a time, without worrying about how lower layers perform. For example, when building a file transfer application, the designer thinks only of two copies of the application program executing on two machines and concentrates on the messages they need to exchange for file transfer. The designer assumes that the application on one host receives exactly what the application on the other host sends.

Figure 10.6 illustrates how the layering principle works:

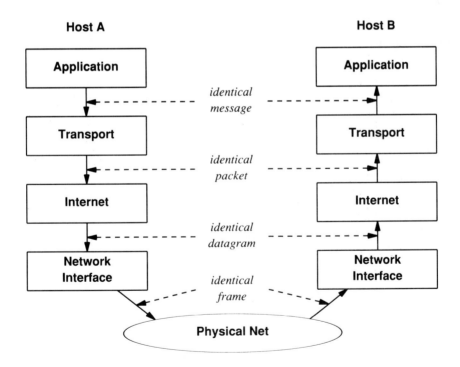

Figure 10.6 The path of a message as it passes from an application on one host to an application on another. Layer *n* on host *B* receives exactly the same object that layer *n* sent on host *A*.

10.7.1 Layering in a TCP/IP Internet Environment

Our statement of the layering principle is somewhat vague, and the illustration in Figure 10.6 skims over an important issue because it fails to distinguish between transfers from source to ultimate destination and transfers across multiple networks. Figure 10.7 illustrates the distinction, showing the path of a message sent from an application program on one host to an application on another through a gateway.

As the figure shows, message delivery uses two separate network frames, one for the transmission from host *A* to gateway *G*, and another from gateway *G* to host *B*. The network layering principle states that the frame delivered to *G* is identical to the frame sent by host *A*. By contrast, the application and transport layers deal with end-to-end issues and are designed so the software at the source communicates with its peer at the ultimate destination. Thus, the layering principle states that the packet received by the transport layer at the ultimate destination is identical to the packet sent by the transport layer at the original source.

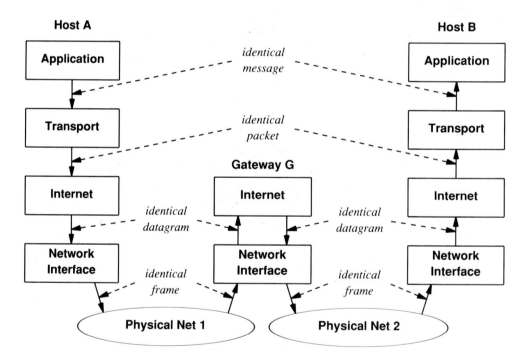

Figure 10.7 The layering principle when a gateway is used. The frame delivered to gateway *G* is exactly the frame sent from host *A*, but differs from the frame sent between *G* and *B*.

It is easy to understand that in higher layers, the layering principle applies across end-to-end transfers, and that at the lowest layer it applies to a single machine transfer. It is not as easy to see how the layering principle applies to the Internet layer. On one hand, we have said that hosts attached to an internet should view it as a large, virtual network, with the IP datagram taking the place of a network frame. In this view, datagrams travel from original source to ultimate destination, and the layering principle guarantees that the ultimate destination receives exactly the datagram that the original source sent. On the other hand, we know that the datagram header contains fields, like a *time to live* counter, that change every time the datagram passes through a gateway. Thus, the ultimate destination will not receive exactly the same datagram as the source sent. We conclude that although most of the datagram stays intact as it passes across an internet, the layering principle only applies to datagrams across single machine transfers. To be accurate, we should not view the Internet layer as providing end-to-end service.

10.8 Layering In The Presence Of Network Substructure

Recall from Chapter 2 that some wide area networks contain multiple packet switches. For example, the Cypress network consists of gateways that connect to an Ethernet local area network as well as to other Cypress gateways over leased serial lines. Cypress transfers IP datagrams but uses its own internal packet protocol when transferring them across serial lines. The Cypress serial line protocol software must be merged with other protocols, and the question arises: "How do the Cypress protocols fit into the TCP/IP layering scheme?" The answer depends on how the designer views the serial line interconnections.

From the perspective of IP, the set of point-to-point connections among gateways can either function like a set of independent physical networks, or they can function collectively like a single physical network. In the first case, each physical link is treated exactly like any other network in the internet. It is assigned a unique (class C) network number, and the two hosts that share the link each have a unique IP address assigned for their connection. Routes are added to the IP routing table as they would be for any other network. A new software module is added at the network interface layer to control the new link hardware, but no substantial changes are made to the layering scheme. The main disadvantage of the independent network approach is that it proliferates network numbers (one for each connection between two machines), causing routing tables to be larger than necessary.

The second approach to accommodating point-to-point connections avoids assigning multiple IP addresses to the physical wires. Instead, it treats all the connections collectively as a single, independent IP network with its own frame format, hardware addressing scheme, and data link protocols. Cypress uses the single network approach and has only one network number for all point-to-point connections.

Using the single network approach means extending the protocol layering scheme to add a new intranetwork routing layer between the network interface layer and the hardware devices. For machines with only one point-to-point connection, an additional layer seems unnecessary. To see why it is needed, consider a machine with several physical point-to-point connections, and recall from Figure 10.2 how the network interface layer is divided into multiple software modules that each control one network. We need to add one new network interface for the new point-to-point network, but the new interface must control multiple hardware devices. Furthermore, given a datagram to send, the new interface must choose the correct link over which the datagram should be sent. Figure 10.8 shows the organization.

The Internet layer passes to the network interface all datagrams that should be sent out on any of the point-to-point connections. The interface passes them to the intranet routing layer that must further distinguish among multiple physical connections and route the datagram across the correct one.

The programmer who designs the intranet routing software determines exactly how the software chooses a physical link. Usually, the algorithm relies on an intranet routing table. The intranet routing table is analogous to the internet routing table in that it specifies a mapping of destination address to route. It contains pairs of entries, (D, L), where D is a destination host address and L specifies one of the physical lines used to reach that destination.

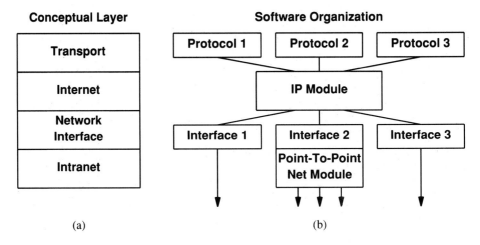

Figure 10.8 (a) conceptual position of an intranet protocol for point-to-point connections when IP treats them as a single IP network, and (b) detailed diagram of corresponding software modules. Each arrow corresponds to one physical device.

The difference between the internet routing table and the intranet routing table is that intranet routing tables are quite small. They only contain routing information for hosts directly attached to the point-to-point network. The reason is simple: the Internet layer maps an arbitrary destination address to a specific gateway address before passing the datagram to a network interface. Thus, the intranet layer is only asked to distinguish among machines on a single point-to-point network.

10.9 Two Important Boundaries In The TCP/IP Model

The conceptual protocol layering includes two boundaries that may not be obvious: a protocol address boundary that separates high-level and low-level addressing, and an operating system boundary that separates the system from application programs.

10.9.1 High-Level Protocol Address Boundary

Now that we have seen the layering of TCP/IP software, we can be precise about an idea introduced in Chapter 8: a conceptual boundary partitions software that uses low-level (physical) addresses from software that uses high-level (IP) addresses. As Figure 10.9 shows, the boundary occurs between the network interface layer and the Internet layer. That is,

> Application programs as well as all protocol software from the Internet layer upward use only IP addresses; the network interface layer handles physical addresses.

Thus, protocols like ARP belong in the network interface layer. They are not part of IP.

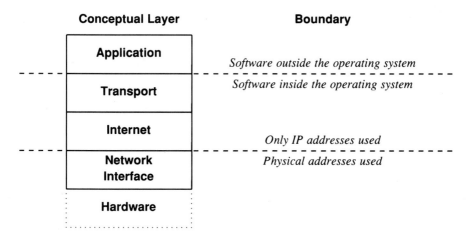

Figure 10.9 The relationship between conceptual layering and the boundaries for operating system and high-level protocol addresses.

10.9.2 Operating System Boundary

Figure 10.9 shows another important boundary as well, the division between software that is generally considered part of the operating system and software that is not. While each implementation of TCP/IP chooses how to make the distinction, many follow the scheme shown. Because they lie inside the operating system, passing data between lower layers of protocol software is much less expensive than passing it between an application program and a transport layer. Chapter 21 discusses the problem in more detail and describes an example of the interface an operating system might provide.

10.10 The Disadvantage Of Layering

We have said that layering is a fundamental idea that provides the basis for protocol design. It allows the designer to divide a complicated problem into subproblems and solve each one independently. Unfortunately, the software that results from strict layering can be extremely inefficient. As an example, consider the job of the transport layer. It must accept a stream of bytes from an application program, divide the stream into packets, and send each packet across the internet. To optimize transfer, the transport layer should choose the largest possible packet size that will allow one packet to travel in one network frame. In particular, if the destination machine attaches directly to one of the same networks as the source, only one physical net will be involved in the transfer, so the sender can optimize packet size for that network. If the software preserves strict layering, however, the transport layer cannot know how the Internet module will route traffic or which networks attach directly. Furthermore, the transport layer will not understand the datagram or frame formats nor will it be able to determine how many octets of header will be added to a packet. Thus, strict layering will prevent the transport layer from optimizing transfers.

Usually, implementors relax the strict layering scheme when building protocol software. They allow information like route selection and network MTU to propagate upward. When allocating buffers, they often leave space for headers that will be added by lower layer protocols and may retain headers on incoming frames when passing them to higher layer protocols. Such optimizations can make dramatic improvements in efficiency while retaining the basic layered structure.

10.11 The Basic Idea Behind Multiplexing And Demultiplexing

Communication protocols use a technique called *multiplexing* and *demultiplexing* throughout the layered hierarchy. When sending a message, the source computer includes extra bits that encode the message type, originating program, and protocols used.

Eventually, all messages are placed into network frames for transfer and combined into a stream of packets. At the receiving end, the destination machine uses the extra information to guide processing.

Consider an example of demultiplexing shown in Figure 10.10.

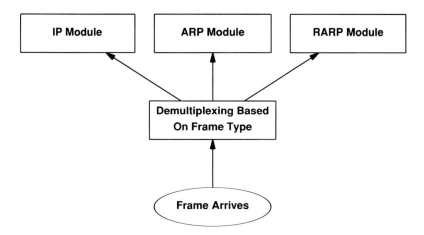

Figure 10.10 Demultiplexing of incoming packets based on the protocol type found in the packet header.

The figure illustrates how software in the network interface layer uses the frame type to choose a procedure that handles the incoming frame. We say that the network interface *demultiplexes* the frame based on its type. To make such a choice possible, software in the source machine must set the frame type field before transmission. Thus, each software module that sends frames uses the type field to specify frame contents.

Multiplexing and demultiplexing occur at almost every protocol layer. For example, after the network interface demultiplexes frames and passes those frames that contain IP datagrams to the IP module, the IP software extracts the datagram and demultiplexes further based on the transport protocol. Figure 10.11 demonstrates demultiplexing at the Internet layer.

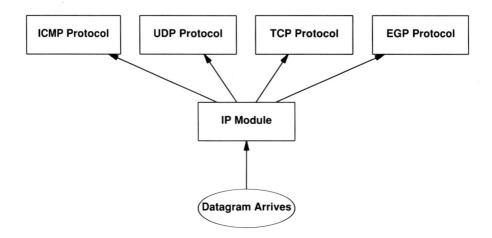

Figure 10.11 Demultiplexing at the Internet layer. IP software chooses an appropriate procedure to handle a datagram based on the type field in the datagram header.

To decide how to handle a datagram, internet software examines the header of a datagram and selects a protocol handler based on the datagram type. In the example, the possible datagram types are: *ICMP*, which we have already examined, and *UDP*, *TCP*, and *EGP*, which we will examine in later chapters.

10.12 ISO's OSI Protocols

The International Organization for Standardization has an effort underway to develop a set of protocols that follow the 7-layer reference model. There are currently five transport standards, known as *TP-0*, *TP-1*, *TP-2*, *TP-3*, and *TP-4*. They range in sophistication from simple to complex and are intended for use in a variety of environments. The simplest of the protocols, *TP-0*, provides little in the way of flow control or reliability. It is meant for use in an environment like the one provided by X.25 where the underlying network offers a reliable, stream oriented delivery service.

In some ways, the most complex of the OSI transport protocols, *TP-4*, resembles TCP. It assumes that the underlying environment only provides connectionless, unreliable packet delivery. Thus, it handles the problems of lost data, flow control, window management, and data that arrives out of sequence.

The future of ISO's OSI protocols is unclear. Many people believe that once ISO eventually finishes the design of its OSI protocols and makes them international standards, vendors will begin to build and test serious implementations. Past experience with protocol design has shown that implementations will reveal flaws and inefficiencies in the standards, and the design will be modified to solve these problems. Once the design stabilizes, TP-4 may attain the same level of performance as TCP and may begin to take over the market because it is an internationally accepted standard. Others believe that the future for OSI is not as bright. They think the OSI technology will always lag behind TCP/IP and that users who are installing TCP/IP now will be unwilling to pay for conversion to OSI protocols later.

10.13 Summary

Protocols are the standards that specify how data is represented when being transferred from one machine to another. Protocols specify how the transfer occurs, how errors are detected, and how acknowledgements are passed. To simplify protocol design and implementation, communication problems are segregated into subproblems that can be solved independently. Each subproblem is assigned a separate protocol.

The idea of layering is fundamental in protocol design because it provides a conceptual framework for protocol design. In a layered model, each layer handles one part of the communication problem and usually corresponds to one protocol. Protocols follow the layering principle, which states that the software implementing layer n on the destination machine receives exactly what the software implementing layer n on the source machine sends.

We examined the 4-layer Internet reference model as well as the ISO 7-layer reference model. In both cases, the layering model provides only a conceptual framework for protocol software. The CCITT X.25 protocols follow the ISO reference model and provide an example of reliable communication service offered by a commercial utility, while the TCP/IP protocols provide an example of a different layering scheme.

In practice, protocol software uses multiplexing and demultiplexing to distinguish among multiple protocols within a given layer, making protocol software more complex than the layering model suggests.

FOR FURTHER STUDY

Postel [RFC 791] provides a sketch of the Internet Protocol layering scheme and Clark [RFC 817] discusses the effect of layering on implementations. Saltzer, Reed, and Clark [1984] argues that end-to-end verification is important. Chesson [1987] makes the controversial argument that layering produces intolerably bad network throughput. Comer [1987] shows an example implementation that achieves efficiency by compromising strict layering and passing pointers between layers.

A description of the ISO protocols TP-0 through TP-4 can be found in the International Organization for Standardization documents [1986a] and [1986b]. The ISO protocol documents [1987a] and [1987b] describe ASN.1 in detail. Sun [RFC 1014] describes XDR, an example of what might be called a TCP/IP presentation protocol. Clark discusses passing information upward through layers [Clark 1985].

EXERCISES

10.1   Study the ISO layering model in more detail. How well does a local area network like the Ethernet fit it?

10.2   Build a case that TCP/IP is moving toward a five-level protocol architecture that includes a presentation layer. (hint: various programs use the XDR protocol, Courier, and ASN.1.)

10.3   Do you think any single presentation protocol will eventually emerge that replaces all others? Why or why not?

10.4   Compare and contrast the tagged data format used by the ASN.1 presentation scheme with the untagged format used by XDR. Characterize situations in which one is better than the other.

10.5   Find out how BSD UNIX uses the *mbuf* structure to make layered protocol software efficient.

10.6   Read about the AT&T *streams* mechanism. How does it help make protocol implementation easier?

11

User Datagram Protocol

11.1 Introduction

Previous chapters described a TCP/IP internet capable of transferring IP datagrams among host computers, where each datagram is routed through the internet based on the destination's IP address. At the Internet Protocol layer, a destination address identifies a host computer; no further distinction is made regarding which user or which application program will receive the datagram. This chapter extends the TCP/IP protocol suite by adding a mechanism that distinguishes among multiple destinations within a given host, allowing multiple application programs executing on a given computer to send and receive datagrams independently.

11.2 Identifying The Ultimate Destination

The operating systems in most computers support multiprogramming, which means they permit multiple application programs to execute simultaneously. Using operating system jargon, we refer to each executing program as a *process*, *task*, *application program*, or a *user level process*; and the systems are called multiprocessing systems. It may seem natural to say that a process is the ultimate destination for a message. However, specifying that a particular process on a particular machine is the ultimate destination for a datagram is somewhat misleading. First, because processes are created and destroyed dynamically, senders seldom know enough to identify a process on another machine. Second, we would like to be able to replace processes that receive datagrams without informing all senders (e.g., rebooting a machine can change all the processes, but senders should not be required to know about the new processes). Third, we need to identify destinations based on the functions they implement without knowing the process that implements the function (e.g., to allow a sender to contact a file server without knowing which process on the destination machine implements the file server function). More important, in systems that allow a single process to handle two or more functions, it is essential that we arrange a way for a process to decide exactly which function the sender desires.

Instead of thinking of a process as the ultimate destination, we will imagine that each machine contains a set of abstract destination points called *protocol ports*. Each protocol port is identified by a positive integer. The local operating system provides an interface mechanism that processes use to specify a port or access it.

Most operating systems provide synchronous access to ports. From a particular process' point of view, synchronous access means the computation stops during a port access operation. For example, if a process attempts to extract data from a port before any data arrives, the operating system stops (blocks) the process until data arrives. Once the data arrives, the operating system passes the data to the process and restarts it. In general, ports are *buffered*, so data that arrives before a process is ready to accept it will not be lost. To achieve buffering, the protocol software located inside the operating system places packets that arrive for a particular protocol port in a (finite) queue until a process extracts them.

To communicate with a foreign port, a sender needs to know both the IP address of the destination machine and the protocol port number of the destination within that machine. Each message carries both a *destination port* number on the foreign machine to which the message is sent, as well as a *source port* number on the source machine to which replies should be addressed. Thus, it is possible for any process that receives a message to reply to the sender.

11.3 The User Datagram Protocol

In the TCP/IP protocol suite, the *User Datagram Protocol* or *UDP* provides the primary mechanism that application programs use to send datagrams to other application programs. UDP provides protocol ports used to distinguish among multiple programs executing on a single machine. That is, in addition to the data sent, each UDP message contains both a destination port number and a source port number, making it possible for the UDP software on the destination to deliver the message to the correct recipient and for the recipient to send a reply.

UDP uses the underlying Internet Protocol to transport a message from one machine to another, and provides the same unreliable, connectionless datagram delivery semantics as IP. It does not use acknowledgements to make sure messages arrive, it does not order incoming messages, and it does not provide feedback to control the rate at which information flows between the machines. Thus, UDP messages can be lost, duplicated, or arrive out of order. Furthermore, packets can arrive faster than the recipient can process them. We can summarize:

> *The User Datagram Protocol (UDP) provides unreliable connection-less delivery service using IP to transport messages between machines. It adds the ability to distinguish among multiple destinations within a given host computer.*

An application program that uses UDP accepts full responsibility for handling the problem of reliability, including message loss, duplication, delay, out-of-order delivery, and loss of connectivity. Unfortunately, application programmers often ignore these problems when designing software. Furthermore, because programmers often test network software using highly reliable, low-delay local area networks, testing may not expose potential failures. Thus, many application programs that rely on UDP work well in a local environment but fail in dramatic ways when used in a larger TCP/IP internet.

11.4 Format Of UDP Messages

Each UDP message is called a *user datagram*. Conceptually, the user datagram consists of two parts, a UDP header and UDP data area. As Figure 11.1 shows, the header is divided into four 16-bit fields that specify the port from which the message was sent, the port to which the message is destined, the message length, and a UDP checksum.

0   16   31

UDP SOURCE PORT	UDP DESTINATION PORT
UDP MESSAGE LENGTH	UDP CHECKSUM
DATA	
. . .	

Figure 11.1   The format of fields in a UDP datagram.

The *SOURCE PORT* and *DESTINATION PORT* fields contain the 16-bit UDP protocol port numbers used to demultiplex datagrams among the processes waiting to receive them. The *SOURCE PORT* is optional. When used, it specifies the port to which replies should be sent; if not used, it should be zero.

The *LENGTH* field contains a count of octets in the UDP datagram, including the UDP header and the user data. Thus, the minimum value for *LENGTH* is eight, the length of the header alone.

The UDP checksum is optional and need not be used at all; a value of zero in the *CHECKSUM* field means that the checksum has not been computed. The designers chose to make the checksum optional to allow implementations to operate with little computational overhead when using UDP across a highly reliable local area network. Recall, however, that IP does not compute a checksum on the data portion of an IP datagram. Thus, the UDP checksum provides the only way to guarantee that data has arrived intact and should be used.

Beginners often wonder what happens to UDP messages for which the computed checksum is zero. A computed value of zero is possible because UDP uses the same checksum algorithm as IP: it divides the data into 16-bit quantities and computes the one's complement of their one's complement sum. Surprisingly, zero is not a problem because one's complement arithmetic has two representations for zero: all bits set to zero or all bits set to one. When the computed checksum is zero, UDP uses the representation with all bits set to one.

11.5 UDP Pseudo-Header

The UDP checksum covers more information than is present in the UDP datagram alone. To compute the checksum, UDP prepends a *pseudo-header* to the UDP datagram, appends an octet of zeros to pad the datagram to an exact multiple of 16 bits, and computes the checksum over the entire object. The octet used for padding and the pseudo-header are *not* transmitted with the UDP datagram, nor are they included in the length. To compute a checksum, the software first stores zero in the *CHECKSUM* field, then accumulates a 16-bit one's complement sum of the entire object, including the pseudo-header, UDP header, and user data.

The purpose of using a pseudo-header is to verify that the UDP datagram has reached its correct destination. The key to understanding the pseudo-header lies in realizing that the correct destination consists of a specific machine and a specific protocol port within that machine. The UDP header itself specifies only the protocol port number. Thus, to verify the destination, UDP on the sending machine computes a checksum that covers the destination IP address as well as the UDP datagram. At the ultimate destination, UDP software verifies the checksum using the destination IP address obtained from the header of the IP datagram that carried the UDP message. If the checksums agree, then it must be true that the datagram has reached the intended destination host as well as the correct protocol port within that host.

The pseudo-header used in the UDP checksum computation consists of 12 octets of data arranged as Figure 11.2 shows. The fields of the pseudo-header labeled *SOURCE IP ADDRESS* and *DESTINATION IP ADDRESS* contain the source and destination IP addresses that will be used when sending the UDP message. Field *PROTO* contains the IP protocol type code (*17* for UDP), and the field labeled *UDP LENGTH* contains the length of the UDP datagram (not including the pseudo-header). To verify the checksum, the receiver must extract these fields from the IP header, assemble them into the pseudo-header format, and recompute the checksum.

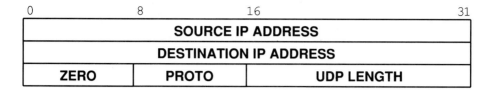

0	8	16	31
SOURCE IP ADDRESS			
DESTINATION IP ADDRESS			
ZERO	PROTO	UDP LENGTH	

Figure 11.2 The 12 octets of the pseudo-header used during UDP checksum
computation.

11.6 UDP Encapsulation And Protocol Layering

UDP provides our first example of a transport protocol. In the layering model of
Chapter 10, UDP lies in the layer above the Internet Protocol layer. Conceptually, application programs access UDP, which uses IP to send and receive datagrams as Figure
11.3 shows.

Conceptual Layering

Application
User Datagram (UDP)
Internet (IP)
Network Interface

Figure 11.3 The conceptual layering of UDP between applications programs
and IP.

Layering UDP above IP means that a complete UDP message, including the UDP
header and data, is encapsulated in an IP datagram as it travels across an internet as Figure 11.4 shows.

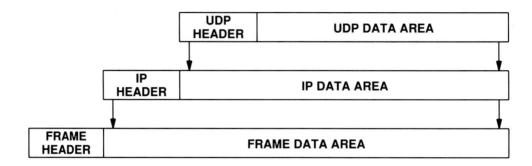

Figure 11.4 A UDP datagram encapsulated in an IP datagram for transmission across an internet. The datagram is further encapsulated in a frame each time it travels across a single network.

For the protocols we have examined, encapsulation means that UDP prepends a header to the data that a user sends and passes it to IP. The IP layer prepends a header to what it receives from UDP. Finally, the network interface layer embeds the datagram in a frame before sending it from one machine to another. The format of the frame depends on the underlying network technology. Usually, network frames include an additional header.

On input, a packet arrives at the lowest layer of network software and begins its ascent through successively higher layers. Each layer removes one header before passing the message on, so that by the time the highest level passes data to the receiving process, all headers have been removed. Thus, the outermost header corresponds to the lowest layer of protocol, while the innermost header corresponds to the highest protocol layer. When considering how headers are inserted and removed, it is important to keep in mind the layering principle. In particular, observe that the layering principle applies to UDP, so the UDP datagram received from IP on the destination machine is identical to the datagram that UDP passed to IP on the source machine. Also, the data that UDP delivers to a user process on the receiving machine will be exactly the data that a user process passed to UDP on the sending machine.

The division of duties among various protocol layers is rigid and clear:

> *The IP layer is responsible only for transferring data between a pair of hosts on an internet, while the UDP layer is responsible only for differentiating among multiple sources or destinations within one host.*

Thus, only the IP header identifies the source and destination hosts; only the UDP layer identifies the source or destination ports within a host.

11.7 Layering And The UDP Checksum Computation

Observant readers will have noticed a seeming contradiction between the layering rules and the UDP checksum computation. Recall that the UDP checksum includes a pseudo-header that has fields for the source and destination IP address. It can be argued that the destination IP address must be known to the user when sending a UDP datagram, and the user must pass it to the UDP layer. Thus, the UDP layer can obtain the destination IP address without interacting with the IP layer. However, the source IP address depends on the route IP chooses for the datagram, because the IP source address identifies the network interface over which the datagram is transmitted. Thus, UDP cannot know a source IP address unless it interacts with the IP layer.

We assume that UDP software asks the IP layer to compute the source and (possibly) destination IP addresses, uses them to construct a pseudo-header, computes the checksum, discards the pseudo-header, and then passes the UDP datagram to IP for transmission. An alternative approach that produces greater efficiency arranges to have the UDP layer encapsulate the UDP datagram in an IP datagram, fill in the source and destination IP header fields, compute the UDP checksum, and then pass the IP datagram to the IP layer, which fills in the remaining IP header fields.

Does the strong interaction between UDP and IP violate our basic premise that layering reflects separation of functionality? Yes. UDP has been tightly integrated with the IP protocol. It is clearly a compromise of the pure separation, made for entirely practical reasons. We are willing to overlook the layering violation because it is impossible to fully identify a destination application program without specifying the destination machine, and we want to make the mapping between addresses used by UDP and those used by IP efficient. One of the exercises examines this issue from a different point of view, asking the reader to consider whether UDP should be separated from IP.

11.8 UDP Multiplexing, Demultiplexing, And Ports

We have seen in Chapter 10 that software throughout the layers of a protocol hierarchy must multiplex or demultiplex among multiple objects at the next layer. UDP software provides another example of multiplexing and demultiplexing. It accepts UDP datagrams from many application programs and passes them to IP for transmission, and it accepts arriving UDP datagrams from IP and passes them to the appropriate application program.

Conceptually, all multiplexing and demultiplexing between UDP software and application programs occur through the port mechanism. In practice, each application program must negotiate with the operating system to obtain a protocol port and an associated port number before it can send a UDP datagram†. Once the port has been assigned, any datagram the application program sends through that port will have that port number in its UDP *SOURCE PORT* field.

---

†For now, we will describe ports abstractly; Chapter 21 provides an example of the operating system primitives used to create and use ports.

While processing input, UDP accepts incoming datagrams from the IP software and demultiplexes based on the UDP destination port, as Figure 11.5 shows.

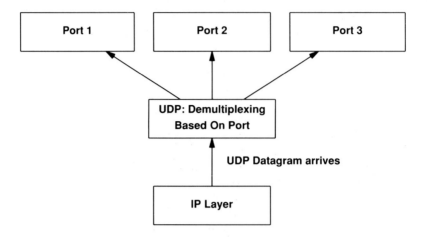

Figure 11.5 Example of demultiplexing one layer above IP. UDP uses the
UDP destination port number to select an appropriate destination
port for incoming datagrams.

The easiest way to think of a UDP port is as a queue. In most implementations, when an application program negotiates with the operating system to use a given port, the operating system creates an internal queue that can hold arriving messages. Often, the application can specify or change the queue size. When UDP receives a datagram, it checks to see that the destination port number matches one of the ports currently in use. If not, it sends an ICMP *port unreachable* error message and discards the datagram. If a match is found, UDP enqueues the new datagram at the port where an application program can access it. Of course, an error occurs if the port is full, and UDP discards the new datagram.

11.9 Reserved And Available UDP Port Numbers

How should protocol port numbers be assigned? The problem is important because two computers need to agree on port numbers before they can interoperate. For example, when computer *A* wants to obtain a file from computer *B*, it needs to know what port the file transfer program on computer *B* uses. There are two fundamental approaches to port assignment. The first approach uses central authority. Everyone agrees to allow a central authority to assign port numbers as needed and to publish the list of all assignments. Then all software is built according to the list. This approach is sometimes called *universal assignment* and the port assignments specified by the authority are called *well-known port assignments*.

The second approach to port assignment uses dynamic binding. In the dynamic binding approach, ports are not globally known. Instead, whenever a program needs a port the network software assigns one. To learn about the current port assignment on another computer, it is necessary to send a request that asks a question like, "How do I reach the file transfer service." The target machine replies by giving the correct port number to use.

The TCP/IP designers adopted a hybrid approach that assigns a few port numbers a priori, but leaves most available for local sites or application programs. The assigned port numbers begin at low values and extend upward, leaving large integer values available for dynamic assignment. The table in Figure 11.6 lists some of the currently assigned UDP port numbers. The second column contains Internet standard assigned keywords, while the third contains keywords used on most UNIX systems.

Decimal	Keyword	UNIX Keyword	Description
0	-	-	Reserved
7	ECHO	echo	Echo
9	DISCARD	discard	Discard
11	USERS	systat	Active Users
13	DAYTIME	daytime	Daytime
15	-	netstat	Who is up or NETSTAT
17	QUOTE	qotd	Quote of the Day
19	CHARGEN	chargen	Character Generator
37	TIME	time	Time
42	NAMESERVER	name	Host Name Server
43	NICNAME	whois	Who Is
53	DOMAIN	nameserver	Domain Name Server
67	BOOTPS	bootps	Bootstrap Protocol Server
68	BOOTPC	bootpc	Bootstrap Protocol Client
69	TFTP	tftp	Trivial File Transfer
111	SUNRPC	sunrpc	Sun Microsystems RPC
123	NTP	ntp	Network Time Protocol
161	-	snmp	SNMP net monitor
162	-	snmp-trap	SNMP traps
512	-	biff	UNIX comsat
513	-	who	UNIX rwho daemon
514	-	syslog	system log
525	-	timed	Time daemon

Figure 11.6 An illustrative sample of currently assigned UDP ports showing the standard keyword and the UNIX equivalent; the list is not exhaustive. To the extent possible, other transport protocols that offer identical services use the same port numbers as UDP.

11.10 Summary

Most computer systems permit multiple application programs to execute simultaneously. Using operating system jargon, we refer to each executing program as a *process*.
The User Datagram Protocol, UDP, distinguishes among multiple processes within a
given machine by allowing senders and receivers to add two 16-bit integers called protocol port numbers to each UDP message. The port numbers identify the source and
destination. Some UDP port numbers, called *well known*, are permanently assigned and
honored throughout the Internet (e.g., port *69* is reserved for use by the trivial file
transfer protocol *TFTP* described in Chapter 23). Other port numbers are available for
arbitrary application programs to use.

UDP is a thin protocol in the sense that it does not add significantly to the semantics of IP. It merely provides application programs with the ability to communicate using the unreliable connectionless packet delivery service. Thus, UDP messages can be
lost, duplicated, delayed, or delivered out of order; the application program using UDP
must handle these problems. Many programs that use UDP do not work correctly
across an internet because they fail to accommodate these conditions.

In the protocol layering scheme, UDP lies in the Transport layer, above the Internet
Protocol layer and below the Application layer. Conceptually, the transport layer is independent of the Internet layer, but in practice they interact strongly. The UDP checksum includes IP source and destination addresses, meaning that UDP software must interact with IP software to find addresses before sending datagrams.

FOR FURTHER STUDY

Tanenbaum [1981] contains a tutorial comparison of the datagram and virtual circuit models of communication. Ball *et. al.* [1979] describes message-based systems
without discussing the message protocol. The UDP protocol described here is a standard for TCP/IP and is defined by Postel [RFC 768].

EXERCISES

11.1 Try UDP in your local environment. Measure the average transfer speed with messages
of 128, 256, 512, 1024, 2048, and 4096 bytes. Can you explain the results (hint: what is
your network MTU)?

11.2 Why is the UDP checksum separate from the IP checksum? Would you object to a protocol that used a single checksum for the complete IP datagram including the UDP message?

11.3 Not using checksums can be dangerous. Explain how a single corrupted ARP packet broadcast by machine *P* can make it impossible to reach another machine, *Q*.

11.4 Should the notion of multiple destinations identified by protocol ports have been built into IP? Why, or why not?

11.5 *Name Registry.* Suppose you want to allow arbitrary pairs of application programs to establish communication with UDP, but you do not wish to assign them fixed UDP port numbers. Instead, you would like potential correspondents to be identified by a character string of 64 or fewer characters. Thus, a program on machine *A* might want to communicate with the "funny-special-long-id" program on machine *B* (you can assume that a process always knows the IP address of the host with which it wants to communicate). Meanwhile, a process on machine *C* wants to communicate with the "comer's-own-program-id" on machine *A*. Show that you only need to assign one UDP port to make such communication possible by designing software on each machine that allows (a) a local process to pick an unused UDP port id over which it will communicate, (b) a local process to register the 64-character name to which it responds, and (c) a foreign process to use UDP to establish communication using only the 64-character name and destination internet address.

11.6 Implement name registry software from the previous exercise.

11.7 What is the chief advantage of using preassigned UDP port numbers? The chief disadvantage?

11.8 What is the chief advantage of using protocol ports instead of process identifiers to specify the destination within a machine?

11.9 UDP provides unreliable datagram communication because it does not guarantee delivery of the message. Devise a reliable datagram protocol that uses timeouts and acknowledgements to guarantee delivery. How much does reliability cost?

12

Reliable Stream Transport Service (TCP)

12.1 Introduction

Previous chapters have explored the unreliable connectionless packet delivery service that forms the basis for all internet communication and the IP protocol that defines it. This chapter introduces the second most important and well known internet service, reliable stream delivery, and the *Transmission Control Protocol* (*TCP*) that defines it. We will see that TCP adds substantial functionality to the protocols already discussed, but that its implementation is also substantially more complex.

Although TCP is presented here as part of the TCP/IP Internet protocol suite, it is an independent, general purpose protocol that can be adapted for use with other delivery systems. For example, because TCP makes very few assumptions about the underlying network, it is possible to use it over a single network like an Ethernet, as well as over a complex internet. In fact, TCP has been so popular that one of the International Organization for Standardization's open systems protocols, TP-4, has been derived from it.

12.2 The Need For Stream Delivery

At the lowest level, computer communication networks provide unreliable packet delivery. Packets can be lost or destroyed when transmission errors interfere with data, when network hardware fails, or when networks become too heavily loaded to accommodate the load presented. Networks that route packets dynamically can deliver them out of order, delivery them after a substantial delay, or deliver duplicates. Furthermore,

171

underlying network technologies may dictate an optimal packet size or pose other constraints needed to achieve efficient transfer rates.

At the highest level, application programs often need to send large volumes of data from one computer to another. Using an unreliable connectionless delivery system for large volume transfers becomes tedious and annoying, and it requires programmers to build error detection and recovery into each application program. Because it is difficult to design, understand, or modify software that correctly provides reliability, few application programmers have the necessary technical background. As a consequence, one goal of network protocol research has been to find general purpose solutions to the problems of providing reliable stream delivery, making it possible for experts to build a single instance of stream protocol software that all application programs use. Having a single general purpose protocol helps isolate application programs from the details of networking, and makes it possible to define a uniform interface for the stream transfer service.

12.3 Properties Of The Reliable Delivery Service

The interface between application programs and the TPC/IP reliable delivery service can be characterized by 5 features:

• *Stream Orientation.* When two application programs (user processes) transfer large volumes of data, we think of the data as a *stream* of bits, divided into 8-bit *octets* or *bytes*. The stream delivery service on the destination machine passes to the receiver exactly the same sequence of octets that the sender passes to it on the source machine.

• *Virtual Circuit Connection.* Making a stream transfer is analogous to placing a telephone call. Before transfer can start, both the sending and receiving application programs interact with their respective operating systems, informing them of the desire for a stream transfer. Conceptually, one machine places a "call" which must be accepted by the other. Protocol software modules in the two operating systems communicate by sending messages across an internet, verifying that the transfer is authorized, and that both sides are ready. Once all details have been settled, the protocol modules inform the application programs that a *connection* has been established and that transfer can begin. During transfer, protocol software on the two machines continue to communicate to verify that data is received correctly. If the communication fails for any reason (e.g., because network hardware along the path between the machines fails), both machines detect the failure and report it to the appropriate application programs. We use the term *virtual circuit* to describe such connections because although application programs view the connection as a dedicated hardware circuit, the reliability is an illusion provided by the stream delivery service.

• *Buffered Transfer.* Application programs send a data stream across the virtual circuit by repeatedly passing data octets to the protocol software. When transferring data, each application uses whatever size pieces it finds convenient, which can be as small as a single octet. At the receiving end, the protocol software delivers octets from the data stream in exactly the same order they were sent, making them available to the receiving application program as soon as they have been received and verified. The protocol software is free to divide the stream into packets independent of the pieces the application program transfers. To make transfer more efficient and to minimize network traffic, implementations usually collect enough data from a stream to fill a reasonably large datagram before transmitting it across an internet. Thus, even if the application program generates the stream one octet at a time, transfer across an internet may be quite efficient. Similarly, if the application program chooses to generate extremely large blocks of data, the protocol software can choose to divide each block into smaller pieces for transmission.

For those applications where data should be delivered even though it does not fill a buffer, the stream service provides a *push* mechanism that applications use to force a transfer. At the sending side, a push forces protocol software to transfer all data that has been generated without waiting to fill a buffer. When it reaches the receiving side, the push causes TCP to make the data available to the application without delay. The reader should note, however, that the push function only guarantees that all data will be transferred; it does not provide record boundaries. Thus, even when delivery is forced, the protocol software may choose to divide the stream in unexpected ways.

• *Unstructured Stream.* It is important to understand that the TCP/IP stream service does not honor structured data streams. For example, there is no way for a payroll application to have the stream service mark boundaries between employee records, or to identify the contents of the stream as being payroll data. Application programs using the stream service must understand stream content and agree on stream format before they initiate a connection.

• *Full Duplex Connection.* Connections provided by the TCP/IP stream service allow concurrent transfer in both directions. Such connections are called *full duplex*. From the point of view of an application process, a full duplex connection consists of two independent streams flowing in opposite directions, with no apparent interaction. The stream service allows an application process to terminate flow in one direction while data continues to flow in the other direction, making the connection *half duplex*. The advantage of a full duplex connection is that the underlying protocol software can send control information for one stream back to the source in datagrams carrying data in the opposite direction. Such *piggybacking* reduces network traffic.

12.4 Providing Reliability

We have said that the reliable stream delivery service guarantees to deliver a stream of data sent from one machine to another without duplication or data loss. The question arises: "How can protocol software provide reliable transfer if the underlying communication system offers only unreliable packet delivery?" The answer is complicated, but most reliable protocols use a single fundamental technique known as *positive acknowledgement with retransmission*. The technique requires a recipient to communicate with the source, sending back an *acknowledgement* message as it receives data. The sender keeps a record of each packet it sends and waits for an acknowledgement before sending the next packet. The sender also starts a timer when it sends a packet and *retransmits* a packet if the timer expires before an acknowledgement arrives.

Figure 12.1 shows how the simplest positive acknowledgement protocol transfers data.

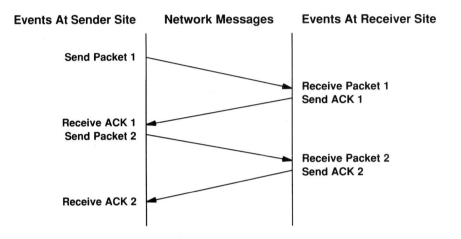

Figure 12.1 A protocol using positive acknowledgement with retransmission in which the sender awaits an acknowledgement for each packet sent. Vertical distance down the figure represents increasing time and diagonal lines across the middle represent network packet transmission.

In the figure, events at the sender and receiver are shown on the left and right. Each diagonal line crossing the middle shows the transfer of one message across the network.

Figure 12.2 uses the same format diagram as Figure 12.1 to show what happens when a packet is lost or corrupted. The sender starts a timer after transmitting a packet. When the timer expires, the sender assumes the packet was lost and retransmits it.

The final reliability problem arises when an underlying packet delivery system duplicates packets. Duplicates can also arise when networks experience high delays that cause premature retransmission. Solving duplication requires careful thought because both packets and acknowledgements can be duplicated. Usually, reliable protocols detect duplicate packets by assigning each packet a sequence number and requiring the receiver to remember which sequence numbers it has received. To avoid confusion caused by delayed or duplicated acknowledgements, positive acknowledgement protocols send sequence numbers back in acknowledgements, so the receiver can correctly associate acknowledgements with packets.

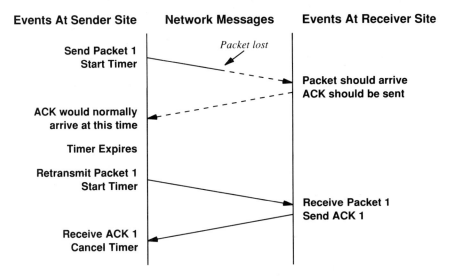

Figure 12.2 Timeout and retransmission that occurs when a packet is lost. The dotted lines show the time that would be taken by the transmission of a packet and its acknowledgement, if the packet was not lost.

12.5 The Idea Behind Sliding Windows

Before examining the TCP stream service, we need to explore an additional concept that underlies stream transmission. The concept, known as a *sliding window*, makes stream transmission efficient. To understand the motivation for sliding windows, recall the sequence of events that Figure 12.1 depicts. To achieve reliability, the sender transmits a packet and then waits for an acknowledgement before transmitting another. As Figure 12.1 shows, data only flows between the machines in one direction at any time, even if the network is capable of simultaneous communication in both directions. The network will be completely idle during times that machines delay responses (e.g., while machines compute routes or checksums). If we imagine a network with high transmission delays, the problem becomes clear:

> *A simple positive acknowledgement protocol wastes a substantial amount of network bandwidth because it must delay sending a new packet until it receives an acknowledgement for the previous packet.*

The sliding window technique is a more complex form of positive acknowledgement and retransmission than the simple method discussed above. Sliding window protocols use network bandwidth better because they allow the sender to transmit multiple

packets before waiting for an acknowledgement. The easiest way to envision sliding
window operation is to think of a sequence of packets to be transmitted as Figure 12.3
shows. The protocol places a small *window* on the sequence and transmits all packets
that lie inside the window.

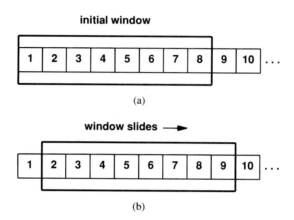

Figure 12.3 (a) A sliding window protocol with eight packets in the window,
and (b) The window sliding so that packet *9* can be sent when
an acknowledgement has been received for packet *1*. Only
unacknowledged packets are retransmitted.

We say that a packet is *unacknowledged* if it has been transmitted but no acknowledgement has been received. Technically, the number of packets that can be unacknowledged at any given time is constrained by the *window size* and is limited to a
small, fixed number. For example, in a sliding window protocol with window size *8*,
the sender is permitted to transmit *8* packets before it receives an acknowledgement.

As Figure 12.3 shows, once the sender receives an acknowledgement for the first
packet inside the window, it "slides" the window along and sends the next packet. The
window continues to slide as long as acknowledgements are received.

The performance of sliding window protocols depends on the window size and the
speed at which the network accepts packets. Figure 12.4 shows an example of the
operation of a sliding window protocol when sending three packets. Note that the
sender transmits all three packets before receiving any acknowledgements.

With a window size of *1*, a sliding window protocol is exactly the same as our
simple positive acknowledgement protocol. By increasing the window size, it is possible to eliminate network idle time completely. That is, in the steady state, the sender
can transmit packets as fast as the network can transfer them. The main point is:

> *Because a well tuned sliding window protocol keeps the network com-*
> *pletely saturated with packets, it obtains substantially higher*
> *throughput than a simple positive acknowledgement protocol.*

Conceptually, a sliding window protocol always remembers which packets have been acknowledged and keeps a separate timer for each unacknowledged packet. If a packet is lost, the timer expires and the sender retransmits that packet. When the sender slides its window, it moves past all acknowledged packets. At the receiving end, the protocol software keeps an analogous window, accepting and acknowledging packets as they arrive. Thus, the window partitions the sequence of packets into three sets: those packets to the left of the window have been successfully transmitted, received, and acknowledged; those packets to the right have not yet been transmitted; and those packets that lie in the window are being transmitted. The lowest numbered packet in the window is the first packet in the sequence that has not been acknowledged.

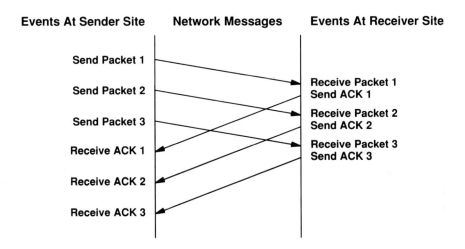

Figure 12.4 An example of three packets transmitted using a sliding window protocol. The key concept is that the sender can transmit all packets in the window without waiting for an acknowledgement.

12.6 The Transmission Control Protocol

Now that we understand the principle of sliding windows, we can examine the reliable stream service provided by the TCP/IP Internet protocol suite. The service is defined by the *Transmission Control Protocol*, or *TCP*. The reliable stream service is so important that the entire protocol suite is often referred to as TCP/IP. It is important to understand that:

TCP is a communication protocol, not a piece of software.

The difference between a protocol and the software that implements it is analogous to the difference between the definition of a programming language and a compiler. As in the programming language world, the distinction between definition and implementation sometimes becomes blurred. People encounter TCP software much more frequently than they encounter the protocol specification, so it is natural to think of a particular implementation as the standard. Nevertheless, the reader should try to distinguish between the two.

Exactly what does TCP provide? TCP is complex, so there is no simple answer. The protocol specifies the format of the data and acknowledgements that two computers exchange to achieve a reliable transfer, as well as the procedures the computers use to ensure that the data arrives correctly. It specifies how TCP software distinguishes among multiple destinations on a given machine, and how communicating machines recover from errors like lost or duplicated packets. The protocol also specifies how two computers initiate a TCP stream transfer and how they agree when it is complete.

It is also important to understand what the protocol does not include. Although the TCP specification describes how application programs use TCP in general terms, it does not dictate the details of the interface between an application program and TCP. That is, the protocol documentation only discusses the operations TCP supplies; it does not specify the exact procedures application programs invoke to access these operations. The reason for leaving the application program interface unspecified is flexibility. In particular, because programmers usually implement TCP in the computer's operating system, they need to employ whatever interface the operating system supplies. Allowing the implementor flexibility makes it possible to have a single specification for TCP that can be used to build software for a variety of machines.

Because TCP assumes little about the underlying communication system, TCP can be used with a variety of packet delivery systems, including the IP datagram delivery service. For example, TCP can be implemented to use dialup telephone lines, a local area network, a high speed fiber optic network, or a lower speed long haul network. In fact, the large variety of delivery systems TCP can use is one of its strengths.

12.7 Ports, Connections, And Endpoints

Like the User Datagram Protocol (UDP) presented in Chapter 11, TCP resides above IP in the protocol layering scheme. Figure 12.5 shows the conceptual organization. TCP allows multiple application programs on a given machine to communicate concurrently, and it demultiplexes incoming TCP traffic among application programs. Like the User Datagram Protocol, TCP uses *protocol port* numbers to identify the ultimate destination within a machine. Each port is assigned a small integer used to identify it†.

---

†Both TCP and UDP use integer port identifiers starting at *1* to identify ports. There is no confusion between them because an incoming IP datagram identifies the protocol being used as well as the port number.

Conceptual Layering

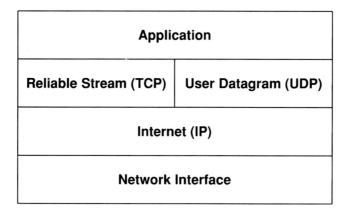

Application	
Reliable Stream (TCP)	**User Datagram (UDP)**
Internet (IP)	
Network Interface	

Figure 12.5 The conceptual layering of UDP and TCP above IP. TCP provides a reliable stream service, while UDP provides an unreliable datagram delivery service. Application programs use both.

When we discussed UDP ports, we said to think of each port as a queue into which protocol software places arriving datagrams. TCP ports are much more complex because a given port number does not correspond to a single object. Instead, TCP has been built on the *connection abstraction*, in which the objects to be identified are virtual circuit connections, not individual ports. Understanding that TCP uses the notion of connections is crucial because it helps explain the meaning and use of TCP port numbers:

> *TCP uses the connection, not the protocol port, as its fundamental abstraction; connections are identified by a pair of endpoints.*

Exactly what are the "endpoints" of a connection? We have said that a connection consists of a virtual circuit between two application programs, so it might be natural to assume that an application program serves as the connection "endpoint." It is not. Instead, TCP defines an endpoint to be a pair of integers (*host, port*), where *host* is the IP address for a host and *port* is a TCP port on that host. For example, the endpoint (*128.10.2.3, 25*) specifies TCP port *25* on the machine with IP address *128.10.2.3*.

Now that we have defined endpoints, it will be easy to understand connections. Recall that a connection is defined by its two endpoints. Thus, if there is a connection from machine (*18.26.0.36*) at MIT to machine (*128.10.2.3*) at Purdue University, it might be defined by the endpoints:

(*18.26.0.36, 1069*) and (*128.10.2.3, 25*).

Meanwhile, another connection might be in progress from machine (*128.9.0.32*) at the Information Sciences Institute to the same machine at Purdue, identified by its endpoints:

(*128.9.0.32, 1184*) and (*128.10.2.3, 53*).

So far, our examples of connections have been straightforward because the ports used at all endpoints have been unique. However, the connection abstraction allows multiple connections to share an endpoint. For example, we could add another connection to the two listed above from machine (*128.2.254.139*) at CMU to the machine at Purdue:

(*128.2.254.139, 1184*) and (*128.10.2.3, 53*).

It might seem strange that two connections can use the TCP port *53* on machine 128.10.2.3 simultaneously, but there is no ambiguity. Because TCP associates incoming messages with a connection instead of a protocol port, it uses both endpoints to identify the appropriate connection. The important idea to remember is:

> *Because TCP identifies a connection by a pair of endpoints, a given TCP port number can be shared by multiple connections on the same machine.*

From a programmer's point of view, the connection abstraction is significant. It means a programmer can devise a program that provides concurrent service to multiple connections simultaneously without needing unique local port numbers for each connection. For example, most systems provide concurrent access to their electronic mail service, allowing multiple computers to send them electronic mail concurrently. Because the program that accepts incoming mail uses TCP to communicate, it only needs to use one local TCP port even though it allows multiple connections to proceed concurrently.

12.8 Passive And Active Opens

Unlike UDP, TCP is a connection oriented protocol that requires both endpoints to agree to participate. That is, before TCP traffic can pass across an internet, application programs at both ends of the connection must agree that the connection is desired. To do so, the application program on one end performs a *passive open* function by contacting its operating system and indicating that it will accept an incoming connection. At that time, the operating system assigns a TCP port number for its end of the connection. The application program at the other end must then contact its operating system using an *active open* request to establish a connection. The two TCP software modules communicate to establish and verify a connection. Once a connection has been created, application programs can begin to pass data; the TCP software modules at each end exchange messages that guarantee reliable delivery. We will return to the details of establishing connections after examining the TCP message format.

12.9 Segments, Streams, And Sequence Numbers

TCP views the data stream as a sequence of octets or bytes that it divides into *segments* for transmission. Usually, each segment travels across an internet in a single IP datagram.

TCP uses a specialized sliding window mechanism to solve two important problems: efficient transmission and flow control. Like the sliding window protocol described earlier, the TCP window mechanism makes it possible to send multiple segments before an acknowledgement arrives. Doing so increases total throughput because it keeps the network busy. The TCP form of a sliding window protocol also solves the end-to-end *flow control* problem, by allowing the receiver to restrict transmission until it has sufficient buffer space to accommodate more data.

The TCP sliding window mechanism operates at the octet level, not at the segment or packet level. Octets of the data stream are numbered sequentially, and a sender keeps three pointers associated with every connection. The pointers define a sliding window as Figure 12.6 illustrates. The first pointer marks the left of the sliding window, separating octets that have been sent and acknowledged from octets yet to be sent. A second pointer marks the right of the sliding window and defines the highest octet in the sequence that can be sent before more acknowledgements are received. The third pointer marks the boundary inside the window that separates those octets that have already been sent from those octets that have not been sent. The protocol software sends all octets in the window without delay, so the boundary inside the window usually moves from left to right quickly.

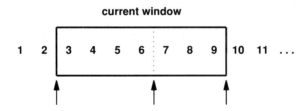

Figure 12.6 An example of the TCP sliding window. Octets through 2 have been sent and acknowledged, octets 3 through 6 have been sent but not acknowledged, octets 7 though 9 have not been sent but will be sent without delay, and octets 10 and higher cannot be sent until the window moves.

We have described how the sender's TCP window slides along and mentioned that the receiver must maintain a similar window to piece the stream together again. It is important to understand, however, that because TCP connections are full duplex, two transfers proceed simultaneously over each connection, one in each direction. We think of the transfers as completely independent because at any time data can flow across the connection in one direction, or in both directions. Thus, TCP software at each end maintains two windows per connection (for a total of four), one slides along the data stream being sent, while the other slides along as data is received.

12.10 Variable Window Size And Flow Control

One difference between the TCP sliding window protocol and the simplified sliding window protocol presented earlier occurs because TCP allows the window size to vary over time. Each acknowledgement, which specifies how many octets have been received, contains a *window advertisement* that specifies how many additional octets of data the receiver is prepared to accept. We think of the window advertisement as specifying the receiver's current buffer size. In response to an increased window advertisement, the sender increases the size of its sliding window and proceeds to send octets that have not been acknowledged. In response to a decreased window advertisement, the sender decreases the size of its window and stops sending octets beyond the boundary. TCP software should not contradict previous advertisements by shrinking the window past previously acceptable positions in the octet stream. Instead, smaller advertisements accompany acknowledgements, so the window size changes at the time it slides forward.

The advantage of using a variable size window is that it provides flow control as well as reliable transfer. If the receiver's buffers begin to become full, it cannot tolerate more packets, so it sends a smaller window advertisement. In the extreme case, the receiver advertises a window size of zero to stop all transmissions. Later, when buffer space becomes available, the receiver advertises a nonzero window size to trigger the flow of data again†.

Having a mechanism for flow control is essential in an internet environment, where machines of various speeds and sizes communicate through networks and gateways of various speeds and capacities. There are really two independent flow problems. First, internet protocols need end-to-end flow control between the source and ultimate destination. For example, when a minicomputer communicates with a large mainframe, the minicomputer needs to regulate the influx of data, or protocol software would be overrun quickly. Thus, TCP must implement end-to-end flow control to guarantee reliable delivery. Second, internet protocols need a flow control mechanism that allows intermediate systems (i.e., gateways) to control a source that sends more traffic than the machine can tolerate.

When intermediate machines become overloaded, the condition is called *congestion*, and mechanisms to solve the problem are called *congestion control* mechanisms. TCP uses its sliding window scheme to solve the end-to-end flow control problem; it does not have an explicit mechanism for congestion control. We will see later, however, that a carefully programmed TCP implementation can detect and recover from congestion while a poor implementation can make it worse. In particular, a carefully chosen retransmission scheme can help avoid congestion while a poor one can exacerbate it.

---

†There are two exceptions to transmission when the window size is zero. First, a sender is allowed to transmit a segment with the urgent bit set to inform the receiver that urgent data is available. Second, to avoid a potential deadlock that can arise if a nonzero advertisement is lost after the window size reaches zero, the sender probes a zero-sized window periodically.

12.11 TCP Segment Format

The unit of transfer between the TCP software on two machines is called a *segment*. Segments are exchanged to establish connections, to transfer data, to send acknowledgements, to advertise window sizes, and to close connections. Because TCP uses piggybacking, an acknowledgement traveling from machine *A* to machine *B* may travel in the same segment as data traveling from machine *A* to machine *B*, even though the acknowledgement refers to data sent from *B* to *A*†. Figure 12.7 shows the TCP segment format.

0	4	10	16	24	31
SOURCE PORT			DESTINATION PORT		
SEQUENCE NUMBER					
ACKNOWLEDGEMENT NUMBER					
HLEN	RESERVED	CODE BITS	WINDOW		
CHECKSUM			URGENT POINTER		
OPTIONS (IF ANY)				PADDING	
DATA					
. . .					

Figure 12.7 The format of a TCP segment with a TCP header followed by data. Segments are used to establish connections as well as to carry data and acknowledgements.

Each segment is divided into two parts, a header followed by data. The header, known as the *TCP header*, carries the expected identification and control information. Fields *SOURCE PORT* and *DESTINATION PORT* contain the TCP port numbers that identify the application programs at the ends of the connection. The *SEQUENCE NUMBER* field identifies the position in the sender's byte stream of the data in the segment. The *ACKNOWLEDGEMENT NUMBER* field identifies the number of the octet that the source expects to receive next. Note that the sequence number refers to the stream flowing in the same direction as the segment, while the acknowledgement number refers to the stream flowing in the opposite direction as the segment.

The *HLEN*‡ field contains an integer that specifies the length of the segment header measured in 32-bit multiples. It is needed because the *OPTIONS* field varies in length, depending on which options have been included. Thus, the size of the TCP header varies depending on the options selected. The 6-bit field marked *RESERVED* is reserved for future use.

---

†In practice, piggybacking does not usually occur unless the recipient delays acknowledgements.
‡The specification says the field is the *offset* of the data area within the segment.

Some segments carry only an acknowledgement while some carry data. Others carry requests to establish or close a connection. TCP software uses the 6-bit field labeled *CODE BITS* to determine the purpose and contents of the segment. The six bits tell how to interpret other fields in the header according to the table in Figure 12.8.

Bit (left to right)	Meaning if bit set to 1
URG	Urgent pointer field is valid
ACK	Acknowledgement field is valid
PSH	This segment requests a push
RST	Reset the connection
SYN	Synchronize sequence numbers
FIN	Sender has reached end of its byte stream

Figure 12.8 Bits of the CODE field in the TCP header.

TCP software advertises how much data it is willing to accept every time it sends a segment by specifying its buffer size in the *WINDOW* field. The field contains a 32-bit unsigned integer in network-standard byte order. Window advertisements provide another example of piggybacking because they accompany all segments, including those carrying data as well as those carrying only an acknowledgement.

12.12 Out Of Band Data

Although TCP is a stream-oriented protocol, it is sometimes important for the program at one end of a connection to send data *out of band*, without waiting for the program at the other end of the connection to consume octets already in the stream. For example, when TCP is used for a remote login session, the user may decide to send a keyboard sequence that *interrupts* or *aborts* the program at the other end. Such signals are most often needed when a program on the remote machine fails to operate correctly. The signals must be sent without waiting for the program to read octets already in the TCP stream (or one would not be able to abort programs that stop reading input).

To accommodate out of band signaling, TCP allows the sender to specify data as *urgent*, meaning that the receiving program should be notified of its arrival as quickly as possible, regardless of its position in the stream. The protocol specifies that when urgent data is found, the receiving TCP should notify whatever application program is associated with the connection to go into "urgent mode." After all urgent data has been consumed, TCP tells the application program to return to normal operation.

The exact details of how TCP informs the application program about urgent data depend on the computer's operating system, of course. The mechanism used to mark urgent data when transmitting it in a segment consists of the URG code bit and the *UR-*

GENT POINTER field. When the URG bit is set, the urgent pointer specifies the position in the window where urgent data ends.

12.13 Maximum Segment Size Option

Not all segments sent across a connection will be of the same size. However, both ends need to agree on a maximum segment they will transfer. TCP software uses the *OPTIONS* field to negotiate with the TCP software at the other end of the connection; one of the options allows TCP software to specify the *maximum segment size*(MSS) that it is willing to receive. For example, when a small personal computer that only has a few hundred bytes of buffer space connects to a large supercomputer, it can negotiate a MSS that restricts segments so they fit in the buffer. It is especially important for computers connected by high-speed local area networks to choose a maximum segment size that fills packets or they will not make good use of the bandwidth. Therefore, if the two endpoints lie on the same physical network, TCP usually computes a maximum segment size such that the resulting IP datagrams will match the network MTU. If the endpoints do not lie on the same physical network, the current specification suggests using a maximum segment size of *536* (the default size of an IP datagram, *576*, minus the standard size of IP and TCP headers).

In a general internet environment, choosing a good maximum segment size can be difficult because performance can be poor for either extremely large segment sizes or extremely small sizes. On one hand, when the segment size is small, network utilization remains low. To see why, recall that TCP segments travel encapsulated in IP datagrams which are encapsulated in physical network frames. Thus, each segment has at least 40 octets of TCP and IP headers in addition to the data. Therefore, datagrams carrying only one octet of data use at most 1/41 of the underlying network bandwidth for user data; in practice, minimum interpacket gaps and network hardware framing bits make the ratio even smaller.

On the other hand, extremely large segment sizes can also produce poor performance. Large segments result in large IP datagrams. When such datagrams travel across a network with small MTU, IP must fragment them. Unlike datagrams, fragments are not independent messages; all fragments must arrive or the entire datagram must be retransmitted. Because the probability of losing a given fragment is nonzero, increasing segment size above the fragmentation threshold decreases the probability the datagram will arrive, which decreases throughput.

In theory, the optimum segment size, S, occurs when the IP datagrams carrying the segments are as large as possible without requiring fragmentation anywhere along the path from the source to the destination. In practice, finding S is difficult for several reasons. First, TCP does not include a mechanism for doing so. Second, because gateways in an internet can change routes dynamically, the path datagrams follow between a pair of communicating computers can change dynamically and so can the size at which datagrams must be fragmented. Third, the optimum size depends on lower-level protocol headers (e.g., the segment size must be reduced to accommodate IP options).

Several research projects are exploring ways to find optimum segment size, but no standard currently exists.

12.14 TCP Checksum Computation

The *CHECKSUM* field in the TCP header contains a 16-bit integer checksum used to verify the integrity of the data as well as the TCP header. To compute the checksum, TCP software on the sending machine follows a procedure like the one described in Chapter 11 for UDP. It prepends a *pseudo header* to the segment, appends enough bytes containing zero to pad the segment to a multiple of 16 bits, and computes the 16-bit checksum over the entire result. TCP does not count the padded zeros in the segment length, nor does it transmit them. Also, it assumes the checksum field itself is zero for purposes of the checksum computation. As with other checksums, TCP uses 16-bit arithmetic and takes the one's complement of the one's complement sum. At the receiving site, TCP software performs the same computation to verify that the segment arrived intact.

The purpose of using a pseudo header is exactly the same as in UDP. It allows the receiver to verify that the segment has reached its correct destination, which includes both a host IP address as well as a protocol port number. Both the source and destination IP addresses are important to TCP because it must use them to identify a connection to which the segment belongs. Therefore, whenever a datagram arrives carrying a TCP segment, IP must pass to TCP the source and destination IP addresses from the datagram as well as the segment itself. Figure 12.9 shows the format of the pseudo header used in the checksum computation.

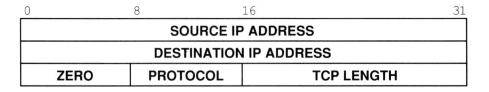

0	8	16	31
SOURCE IP ADDRESS			
DESTINATION IP ADDRESS			
ZERO	PROTOCOL	TCP LENGTH	

Figure 12.9 The format of the pseudo header used in TCP checksum computations. At the receiving site, this information is extracted from the IP datagram that carried the segment.

The sending TCP assigns field *PROTOCOL* the value that the underlying delivery system will use in its protocol type field. For IP datagrams carrying TCP, the value is 6. The *TCP LENGTH* field specifies the total length of the TCP segment including the TCP header. At the receiving end, information used in the pseudo header is extracted from the IP datagram that carried the segment and included in the checksum to verify that the segment arrived at the correct destination intact.

12.15 Acknowledgements And Retransmission

Because TCP sends data in variable length segments, and because retransmitted segments can include more data than the original, acknowledgements cannot easily refer to datagrams or segments. Instead, they refer to a position in the stream using the stream sequence numbers. The receiver collects data octets from arriving segments and reconstructs an exact copy of the stream being sent. Because segments travel in IP datagrams, they can be lost or delivered out of order; the receiver uses the sequence numbers to reorder segments. At any time, the receiver will have reconstructed zero or more octets contiguously from the beginning of the stream, but may have additional pieces of the stream from datagrams that arrived out of order. The receiver always acknowledges the longest contiguous prefix of the stream that has been received correctly. Each acknowledgement specifies a sequence value one greater than the highest octet position in the contiguous prefix it received. Thus, the sender receives continuous feedback from the receiver as it progresses through the stream. We can summarize this important idea:

> *Acknowledgements always specify the sequence number of the next octet that the receiver expects to receive.*

The TCP acknowledgement scheme is called *cumulative* because it reports how much of the stream has accumulated. Cumulative acknowledgements have both advantages and disadvantages. One advantage is that acknowledgements are both easy to generate and unambiguous. Another advantage is that lost acknowledgements do not necessarily force retransmission. A major disadvantage is that the sender does not receive information about all successful transmissions, but only about a single position in the stream that has been received.

To understand why lack of information about all successful transmissions makes the protocol less efficient, think of a window that spans *5000* octets starting at position *101* in the stream, and suppose the sender has transmitted all data in the window by sending five segments. Suppose further that the first segment is lost, but all others arrive intact. The receiver continues to send acknowledgements, but they all specify octet *101*, the next highest contiguous octet it expects to receive. There is no way for the receiver to tell the sender that most of the data for the current window has arrived.

When a timeout occurs at the sender's side, the sender must choose between two potentially inefficient schemes. It may choose to retransmit all five segments instead of the one missing segment. Of course, when the retransmitted segment arrives, the receiver will have correctly received all data from the window, and will acknowledge that it expects octet *5101* next. However, that acknowledgement may not reach the sender quickly enough to prevent the unnecessary retransmission of other segments from the window. If the sender follows accepted implementation policy and retransmits only the first unacknowledged segment, it must wait for the acknowledgement before it can decide what and how much to send. Thus, it reverts to a simple positive acknowledgement protocol and may lose the advantages of having a large window.

12.16 Timeout And Retransmission

One of the most important and complex ideas in TCP is embedded in the way it handles timeout and retransmission. Like other reliable protocols, TCP expects the destination to send acknowledgements whenever it successfully receives new octets from the data stream. Every time it sends a segment, TCP starts a timer and waits for an acknowledgement. If the timer expires before data in the segment has been acknowledged, TCP assumes that the segment was lost or corrupted and retransmits it.

To understand why the TCP retransmission algorithm differs from the algorithm used in many network protocols, we need to remember that TCP is intended for use in an internet environment. In an internet, a segment traveling between a pair of machines may traverse a single, low-delay network (e.g., a high-speed LAN), or it may wind across multiple intermediate networks through multiple gateways. Thus, it is impossible to know *a priori* how quickly acknowledgements will return to the source. Furthermore, the delay at each gateway depends on traffic, so the total time required for a segment to travel to the destination and an acknowledgement to return to the source varies dramatically from one instant to another. Figure 12.10, which shows measurements of round trip times across the connected Internet for 100 consecutive packets, illustrates the problem. TCP software must accommodate both the vast differences in the time required to reach various destinations and the changes in time require to reach a given destination as traffic load varies.

TCP accommodates varying internet delays by using an *adaptive retransmission algorithm*. In essence, TCP monitors the performance of each connection and deduces reasonable values for timeouts. As the performance of a connection changes, TCP revises its timeout value (i.e., it adapts to the change).

To collect the data needed for an adaptive algorithm, TCP records the time at which each segment is sent, and the time at which an acknowledgement arrives for the data in that segment. From the two times, TCP computes an elapsed time known as a *sample round trip time* or *round trip sample*. Whenever it obtains a new round trip sample, TCP adjusts its notion of the average round trip time for the connection. Usually, TCP software stores the estimated round trip time, *RTT*, as a weighted average and uses new round trip samples to change the average slowly. For example, when computing a new weighted average, one early averaging technique used a constant weighting factor, α, where $0 \leq \alpha < 1$, to weight the old average against the latest round trip sample:

$$RTT = (\alpha * Old\_RTT) + ((1-\alpha) * New\_Round\_Trip\_Sample)$$

Choosing a value for α close to *1* makes the weighted average immune to changes that last a short time (e.g., a single segment that encounters long delay). Choosing a value for α close to *0* makes the weighted average respond to changes in delay very quickly.

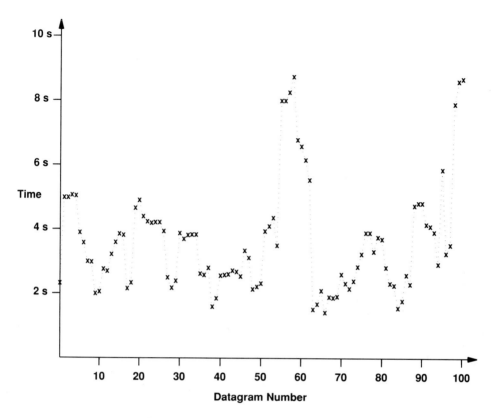

Figure 12.10 A plot of Internet round trip times as measured for 100 successive IP datagrams.

When it sends a packet, TCP computes a timeout value as a function of the current round trip estimate. Again, early implementations used a constant weighting factor, β ($\beta > 1$), and made the timeout greater than the current round trip estimate:

$$\text{Timeout} = \beta * \text{RTT}$$

Choosing a value for β can be difficult. On one hand, to detect packet loss quickly, the timeout value should be close to the current round trip time (i.e., β should be close to *1*). Detecting packet loss quickly improves throughput because TCP will not wait an unnecessarily long time before retransmitting. On the other hand, if $\beta = 1$, TCP is overly eager – any small delay will cause an unnecessary retransmission, which wastes network bandwidth. The original specification recommended setting $\beta = 2$; more recent work described below has produced better techniques for adjusting timeout.

We can summarize the ideas presented so far:

> *To accommodate the varying delays encountered in an internet environment, TCP uses an adaptive retransmission algorithm that monitors delays on each connection and adjusts its timeout parameter accordingly.*

12.17 Accurate Measurement Of Round Trip Samples

In theory, measuring a round trip sample is trivial – it consists of subtracting the time at which the segment is sent from the time at which the acknowledgement arrives. However, complications arise because TCP uses a cumulative acknowledgement scheme in which an acknowledgement refers to data received, and not to the instance of a specific datagram that carried the data. Consider a retransmission. TCP forms a segment, places it in a datagram and sends it, the timer expires, and TCP sends the segment again in a second datagram. Because both datagrams carry exactly the same data, the sender has no way of knowing whether an acknowledgement corresponds to the original or retransmitted datagram. This phenomenon has been called *acknowledgement ambiguity*, and TCP acknowledgements are said to be *ambiguous*.

Should TCP assume acknowledgements belong with the earliest (i.e., original) transmission or the latest (i.e., the most recent retransmission)? Surprisingly, neither assumption works. Associating the acknowledgement with the original transmission can make the estimated round trip time grow without bound in cases where an internet loses datagrams†. If an acknowledgement arrives after one or more retransmissions, TCP will measure the round trip sample from the original transmission, and compute a new RTT using the excessively long sample. Thus, RTT will grow slightly. The next time TCP sends a segment, the larger RTT will result in slightly longer timeouts, so if an acknowledgement arrives after one or more retransmissions, the next sample round trip time will be even larger, and so on.

Associating the acknowledgement with the most recent retransmission can also fail. Consider what happens when the end-to-end delay suddenly increases. When TCP sends a segment, it uses the old round trip estimate to compute a timeout, which is now too small. The segment arrives and an acknowledgement starts back, but the increase in delay means the timer expires before the acknowledgement arrives, and TCP retransmits the segment. Shortly after TCP retransmits, the first acknowledgement arrives and is associated with the retransmission. The round trip sample will be much too small and will result in a slight decrease of the estimated round trip time, RTT. Unfortunately, lowering the estimated round trip time guarantees that TCP will set the timeout too small for the next segment. Ultimately, the estimated round trip estimate can stablize at a value, T, such that the correct round trip time is slightly longer than some multiple of T. Implementations of TCP that associate acknowledgements with the most recent retransmission have been observed in a stable state with RTT slightly less than one-half

---

†The estimate can only grow arbitrarily large if every segment is lost at least once.

of the correct value (i.e., TCP sends each segment exactly twice even though no loss occurs).

12.18 Karn's Algorithm And Timer Backoff

If the original transmission and the most recent transmission both fail to provide accurate round trip times, what should TCP do? The accepted answer is simple: TCP should not update the round trip estimate for retransmitted segments. This idea, known as *Karn's Algorithm*, avoids the problem of ambiguous acknowledgements altogether by only adjusting the estimated round trip for unambiguous acknowledgements (acknowledgements that arrive for segments that have only been transmitted once).

Of course, a simplistic implementation of Karn's algorithm, one that merely ignores times from retransmitted segments, can lead to failure as well. Consider what happens when TCP sends a segment after a sharp increase in delay. TCP computes a timeout using the existing round trip estimate. The timeout will be too small for the new delay and will force retransmission. If TCP ignores acknowledgements from retransmitted segments, it will never update the estimate and the cycle will continue.

To accommodate such failures, Karn's algorithm requires the sender to combine retransmission timeouts with a *timer backoff* strategy. The backoff technique computes an initial timeout using a formula like the one shown above. However, if the timer expires and causes a retransmission, TCP increases the timeout. In fact, each time it must retransmit a segment, TCP increases the timeout (to keep timeouts from becoming ridiculously long, most implementations limit increases to an upper bound that is larger than the delay along any path in the internet).

Implementations use a variety of techniques to compute backoff. Most choose a multiplicative factor, and set the new value to:

$$new\_timeout = \gamma * timeout$$

Typically, γ is *2*. (It has been argued that values of γ less than 2 lead to instabilities). Other implementations use a table of multiplicative factors, allowing arbitrary backoff at each step[†].

Karn's algorithm combines the backoff technique with round trip estimation to solve the problem of never increasing round trip estimates:

> *Karn's algorithm: When computing the round trip estimate, ignore samples that correspond to retransmitted segments, but use a backoff strategy, and retain the timeout value from a retransmitted packet for subsequent packets until a valid sample is obtained.*

Generally speaking, when an internet misbehaves, Karn's algorithm separates computation of the timeout value from the current round trip estimate. It uses the round trip estimate to compute an initial timeout value, but then backs off the timeout on each re-

---

[†]Berkeley UNIX is the most notable system that uses a table of factors, but current values in the table are equivalent to using $\gamma=2$.

transmission until it can successfully transfer a segment. When it sends subsequent segments, it retains the timeout value that results from backoff. Finally, when an acknowledgement arrives corresponding to a segment that did not require retransmission, TCP recomputes the round trip estimate and resets the timeout accordingly. Experience shows that Karn's algorithm works well even in networks with high packet loss‡.

12.19 Responding To High Variance In Delay

Recent research into round trip estimation has shown that the computations described above do not adapt to a wide range of variation in delay. Queueing theory suggests that the variation in round trip time, σ, varies proportional to $1/(1-L)$, where L is the current network load, $0 \le L \le 1$. If an internet is running at 50% of capacity, we expect the round trip delay to vary by a factor of $\pm 2\sigma$, or 4. When the load reaches 80%, we expect a variation of 16. The original TCP standard specified the technique for estimating round trip time that we described earlier. Using that technique and limiting β to the suggested value of 2 means the round trip estimation can adapt to loads of at most 30%.

The 1989 specification for TCP requires implementations to estimate both the average round trip time and the variance, and to use the estimated variance in place of the constant β. As a result, new implementations of TCP can adapt to a wider range of variation in delay and yield substantially higher throughput. Fortunately, the approximations require little computation; extremely efficient programs can be derived from the following simple equations:

$$DIFF = SAMPLE - Old\_RTT$$

$$RTT = Old\_RTT - \delta * DIFF$$

$$DEV = Old\_DEV + \delta(|DIFF| - Old\_DEV)$$

where DEV is the estimated mean deviation, and δ is a fraction between 0 and 1 that controls how quickly the new sample affects the weighted average. To make the computation efficient, TCP chooses δ to be $1/2^n$, scales the computation by 2^n, and uses integer arithmetic. Research suggests a value of $n=3$ will work well.

12.20 Response To Congestion

It may seem that TCP software could be designed by considering the interaction between the two endpoints of a connection and the communication delays between those endpoints. In practice, however, TCP must also react to *congestion* in the internet. Congestion is a condition of severe delay caused by an overload of datagrams at one or more switching points (e.g., at gateways). When congestion occurs, delays increase and the gateway begins to enqueue datagrams until it can route them. We must

---

‡Phil Karn is an amateur radio enthusiast who developed this algorithm to allow TCP communication across a high-loss packet radio connection.

remember that each gateway has finite storage capacity and that datagrams compete for that storage (i.e., in a datagram based internet, there is no preallocation of resources to individual TCP connections). In the worst case, the total number of datagrams arriving at the congested gateway grows until the gateway reaches capacity and starts to drop datagrams.

Endpoints do not usually know the details of where congestion has occurred or why. To them, congestion simply means increased delay. Unfortunately, most transport protocols use timeout and retransmission, so they respond to increased delay by retransmitting datagrams. Retransmissions aggravate congestion instead of alleviating it. If unchecked, the increased traffic will produce increased delay, leading to increased traffic, and so on, until the network becomes useless. The condition is known as *congestion collapse*.

To avoid congestion collapse, TCP must reduce transmission rates when congestion occurs. Gateways watch queue lengths and use techniques like ICMP source quench to inform hosts that congestion has occurred†, but transport protocols like TCP can help avoid congestion by reducing transmission rates automatically whenever delays occur. Of course, algorithms to avoid congestion must be constructed carefully because even under normal operating conditions an internet will exhibit wide variation in round trip delays.

To avoid congestion, the TCP standard now recommends using two techniques: *slow start* and *multiplicative decrease*. They are related and can be implemented easily. We said that for each connection, TCP must remember the size of the receiver's window (i.e., the buffer size advertised in acknowledgements). To control congestion TCP maintains a second limit, called the *congestion window limit* or *congestion window*. At any time, TCP acts as if the window size is:

Allowed_window = min(receiver_advertisement, congestion_window)

In the steady state on a non-congested connection, the congestion window is the same size as the receiver's window. Reducing the congestion window reduces the traffic TCP will inject into the connection. To estimate congestion window size, TCP assumes that most datagram loss comes from congestion and uses the following strategy:

> *Multiplicative Decrease Congestion Avoidance: Upon loss of a segment, reduce the congestion window by half (down to a minimum of at least one segment). For those segments that remain in the allowed window, backoff the retransmission timer exponentially.*

Because TCP reduces the congestion window by half for *every* loss, it decreases the window exponentially if loss continues. In other words, if congestion is likely, TCP reduces the volume of traffic exponentially and the rate of retransmission exponentially. If loss continues, TCP eventually limits transmission to a single datagram and continues to double timeout values before retransmitting. The idea is to provide quick and significant traffic reduction to allow gateways enough time to clear the datagrams already in their queues.

---

†In a congested network, queue lengths grow exponentially for a significant time.

How can TCP recover when congestion ends? You might suspect that TCP should reverse the multiplicative decrease and double the congestion window when traffic begins to flow again. However, doing so produces an unstable system that oscillates wildly between no traffic and congestion. Instead, TCP uses a technique called *slow-start*† to scale up transmission:

> *Slow-Start (Additive) Recovery: Whenever starting traffic on a new connection or increasing traffic after a period of congestion, start the congestion window at the size of a single segment and increase the congestion window by one segment each time an acknowledgement arrives.*

Slow-start avoids swamping the internet with additional traffic immediately after congestion clears or when new connections suddenly start.

The term *slow-start* may be a misnomer because under ideal conditions, the start is not very slow. TCP initializes the congestion window to *1*, sends an initial segment, and waits. When the acknowledgement arrives, it increases the congestion to *2*, sends two segments, and waits. When the two acknowledgements arrive they each increase the congestion window by *1*, so TCP can send *4* segments. Acknowledgements for those will increase the congestion window to *8*. Within four round-trip times, TCP can send *16* segments, often enough to reach the receiver's window limit. Even for extremely large windows, it takes only $\log_2 N$ round trips before TCP can send *N* segments.

To avoid increasing the window size too quickly and causing additional congestion, TCP adds one additional restriction. Once the congestion window reaches one half of its original size, TCP enters a *congestion avoidance* phase and slows down the rate of increment. During congestion avoidance, it increases the congestion window by *1* only if all segments in the window have been acknowledged.

Taken together, the slow-start increase, multiplicative decrease, congestion avoidance, measurement of variation, and exponential timer backoff improve the performance of TCP dramatically without adding any significant computational overhead to the protocol software. Versions of TCP that use these techniques have improved the performance of previous versions by factors of *2* to *10*.

12.21 Establishing A TCP Connection

To establish a connection, TCP uses a three-way handshake. In the simplest case, the handshake proceeds as Figure 12.11 shows.

---

†The term *slow-start* is attributed to John Nagle; the technique was originally called *soft-start*.

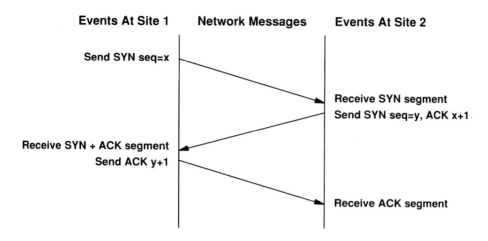

Figure 12.11 The sequence of messages in a three-way handshake. Time proceeds down the page; diagonal lines represent segments sent between sites. SYN segments carry initial sequence number information.

The first segment of a handshake can be identified because it has the SYN† bit set in the code field. The second message has both the SYN bit and ACK bits set, indicating that it acknowledges the first SYN segment as well as continuing the handshake. The final handshake message is only an acknowledgement and is merely used to inform the destination that both sides agree that a connection has been established.

Usually, the TCP software on one machine waits passively for the handshake, and the TCP software on another machine initiates it. However, the handshake is carefully designed to work even if both machines attempt to initiate a connection simultaneously. Thus, a connection can be established from either end or from both ends simultaneously. Once the connection has been established, data can flow in both directions equally well. There is no master or slave.

The three-way handshake is both necessary and sufficient for correct synchronization between the two ends of the connection. To understand why, remember that TCP builds on an unreliable packet delivery service, so messages can be lost, delayed, duplicated, or delivered out of order. Thus, the protocol must use a timeout mechanism and retransmit lost requests. Trouble arises if retransmitted and original requests arrive while the connection is being established, or if retransmitted requests are delayed until after a connection has been established, used, and terminated. A three-way handshake (plus the rule that TCP ignores additional requests for connection after a connection has been established) solves these problems.

---

†SYN stands for *synchronization*; it is pronounced ''sin''.

12.22 Initial Sequence Numbers

The three-way handshake accomplishes two important functions. İt guarantees that both sides are ready to transfer data (and that they know they are both ready), and it allows both sides to agree on initial sequence numbers. Sequence numbers are sent and acknowledged during the handshake. Each machine must choose an initial sequence number at random that it will use to identify bytes in the stream it is sending. Sequence numbers cannot always start at the same value. In particular, TCP cannot merely choose sequence *1* every time it creates a connection (one of the exercises examines problems that can arise if it does). Of course, it is important that both sides agree on an initial number, so octet numbers used in acknowledgements agree with those used in data segments.

To see how machines can agree on sequence numbers for two streams after only three messages, recall that each segment contains both a sequence number field and an acknowledgement field. The machine that initiates a handshake, call it *A*, passes its initial sequence number, *x*, in the sequence field of the first SYN segment in the three-way handshake. The second machine, *B*, receives the SYN, records the sequence number, and replies by sending its initial sequence number in the sequence field as well as an acknowledgement that specifies *B* expects octet *x+1*. In the final message of the handshake, *A* "acknowledges" receiving from *B* all octets through *y*. In all cases, acknowledgements follow the convention of using the number of the *next* octet expected.

We have described how TCP usually carries out the three-way handshake by exchanging segments that contain a minimum amount of information. Because of the protocol design, it is possible to send data along with the initial sequence numbers in the handshake segments. In such cases, the TCP software must hold the data until the handshake completes. Once a connection has been established, the TCP software can release data being held and deliver it to a waiting application program quickly. The reader is referred to the protocol specification for the details.

12.23 Closing a TCP Connection

Two programs that use TCP to communicate can terminate the conversation gracefully using the *close* operation. Internally, TCP uses a modified three-way handshake to close connections. Recall that TCP connections are full duplex and that we view them as containing two independent stream transfers, one going in each direction. When an application program tells TCP that it has no more data to send, TCP will close the connection *in one direction*. To close its half of a connection, the sending TCP finishes transmitting the remaining data, waits for the receiver to acknowledge it, and then sends a segment with the FIN bit set. The receiving TCP acknowledges the FIN segment and informs the application program on its end that no more data is available (e.g., using the operating system's end-of-file mechanism).

Once a connection has been closed in a given direction, TCP refuses to accept more data for that direction. Meanwhile, data can continue to flow in the opposite direction until the sender closes it. Of course, acknowledgements continue to flow back to the sender even after a connection has been closed. When both directions have been closed, the TCP software at each endpoint deletes its record of the connection.

The details of closing a connection are even more subtle than suggested above because TCP uses a modified three-way handshake to close a connection. Figure 12.12 illustrates the procedure.

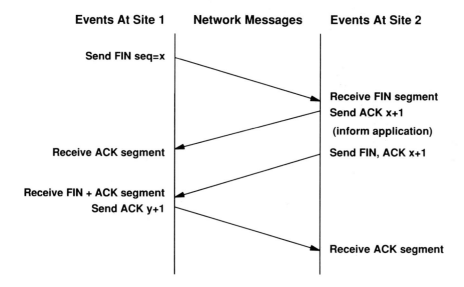

Figure 12.12 The modified three-way handshake used to close connections. The site that receives the first FIN segment acknowledges it immediately and then delays before sending the second FIN segment.

The difference between three-way handshakes used to establish and break connections occurs after a machine receives the initial FIN segment. Instead of generating a second FIN segment immediately, TCP sends an acknowledgement and then informs the application of the request to shut down. Informing the application program of the request and obtaining a response may take considerable time (e.g., it may involve human interaction). The acknowledgement prevents retransmission of the initial FIN segment during the wait. Finally, when the application program instructs TCP to shut down the connection completely, TCP sends the second FIN segment and the original site replies with the third message, an ACK.

12.24 TCP Connection Reset

Normally, an application program uses the close operation to shut down a connection when it finishes using it. Thus, closing connections is considered a normal part of use, analogous to closing files. Sometimes abnormal conditions arise that force an application program or the network software to break a connection. TCP provides a reset facility for such abnormal disconnections.

To reset a connection, one side initiates termination by sending a segment with the RST bit in the *CODE* field set. The other side responds to a reset segment immediately by aborting the connection. TCP also informs the application program that a reset occurred. A reset is an instantaneous abort that means that transfer in both directions ceases immediately, and resources such as buffers are released.

12.25 TCP State Machine

Like most protocols, the operation of TCP can best be explained with a theoretical model called a *finite state machine*. Figure 12.13 shows the TCP finite state machine, with circles representing states and arrows representing transitions between them. The label on each transition shows what TCP receives to cause the transition and what it sends in response. For example, the TCP software at each endpoint begins in the *CLOSED* state. Application programs must issue either a *passive open* command (to wait for a connection from another machine), or an *active open* command (to initiate a connection). An active open command forces a transition from the *CLOSED* state to the *SYN SENT* state. When TCP follows the transition, it emits a SYN segment. When the other end returns a segment that contains a SYN plus ACK, TCP moves to the *ESTABLISHED* state and begins data transfer.

The *TIMED WAIT* state reveals how TCP handles some of the problems incurred with unreliable delivery. TCP keeps a notion of *maximum segment lifetime*, the maximum time an old segment can remain alive in an internet. To avoid having segments from a previous connection interfere with a current one, TCP moves to the *TIMED WAIT* state after closing a connection. It remains in that state for twice the maximum segment lifetime before deleting its record of the connection. If any duplicate segments happen to arrive for the connection during the timeout interval, TCP will reject them. However, to handle cases where the last acknowledgement was lost it acknowledges valid segments and restarts the timer. Because the timer allows TCP to distinguish old connections from new ones, it prevents TCP from responding with a *RST* (reset) if the other end retransmits a *FIN* request.

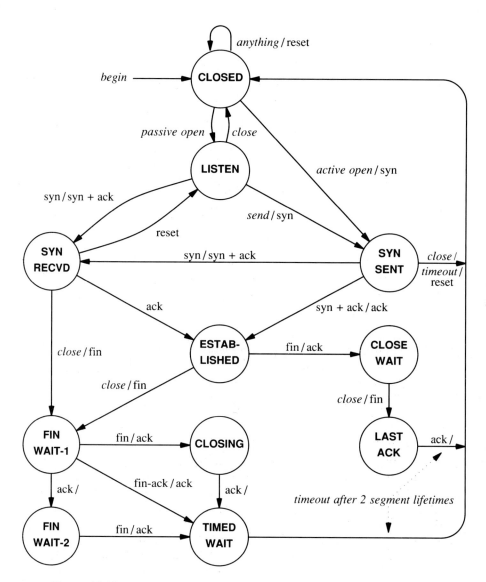

Figure 12.13 The TCP finite state machine. Each endpoint begins in the *closed* state. Labels on transitions show the input that caused the transition followed by the output if any.

12.26 Forcing Data Delivery

We have said that TCP is free to divide the stream of data into segments for transmission without regard to the size of transfer application programs use. The chief advantage of allowing TCP to choose a division is efficiency. It can accumulate enough octets in a buffer to make segments reasonably long, reducing the high overhead that occurs when segments contain only a few data octets.

Although buffering improves network throughput, it can interfere with some applications. Consider using a TCP connection to pass characters from an interactive terminal to a remote machine. The user expects instant response to each keystroke. If the sending TCP buffers the data, response may be delayed, perhaps for hundreds of keystrokes. Similarly, because the receiving TCP may buffer data before making it available to the application program on its end, forcing the sender to transmit data may not be sufficient to guarantee delivery.

To accommodate interactive users, TCP provides a *push* operation that an application program can use to force delivery of octets currently in the stream without waiting for the buffer to fill. The push operation does more than force TCP to send a segment. It also requests TCP to set the *PSH* bit in the segment code field, so the data will be delivered to the application program on the receiving end. Thus, when sending data from an interactive terminal, the application uses the push function after each keystroke. Similarly, application programs can force output to be sent and displayed on the terminal promptly by calling the push function after writing a character or line.

12.27 Reserved TCP Port Numbers

Like UDP, TCP combines static and dynamic port binding, using a set of *well-known port assignments* for commonly invoked programs (e.g., electronic mail), but leaving most port numbers available for the operating system to allocate as programs need them. The specification states that only port numbers less than *256* will be used for well-known ports; the remainder are available for arbitrary applications. Figure 12.14 lists some of the currently assigned TCP ports. It should be pointed out that although TCP and UDP port numbers are independent, the designers have chosen to use the same integer port numbers for any service that is accessible from both UDP and TCP. For example, a domain name server can be accessed either with TCP or with UDP. In either protocol, port number *53* has been reserved for servers in the domain name system.

12.28 TCP Performance

As we have seen, TCP is a complex protocol that handles communication over a wide variety of underlying network technologies. Many people assume that because TCP tackles a much more complex task than other transport protocols, the code must be cumbersome and inefficient. Surprisingly, the generality we discussed does not seem to hinder TCP performance. Experiments at Berkeley have shown that the same TCP that operates efficiently over the connected Internet can deliver 8 Mbps of sustained throughput between two workstations on a 10 Mbps Ethernet. At Cray Research, Inc., researchers have demonstrated TCP throughput of over 600 Mbps.

Decimal	Keyword	UNIX Keyword	Description
0			Reserved
1	TCPMUX	-	TCP Multiplexor
5	RJE	-	Remote Job Entry
7	ECHO	echo	Echo
9	DISCARD	discard	Discard
11	USERS	systat	Active Users
13	DAYTIME	daytime	Daytime
15	-	netstat	Network status program
17	QUOTE	qotd	Quote of the Day
19	CHARGEN	chargen	Character Generator
20	FTP-DATA	ftp-data	File Transfer Protocol (data)
21	FTP	ftp	File Transfer Protocol
23	TELNET	telnet	Terminal Connection
25	SMTP	smtp	Simple Mail Transport Protocol
37	TIME	time	Time
42	NAMESERVER	name	Host Name Server
43	NICNAME	whois	Who Is
53	DOMAIN	nameserver	Domain Name Server
77	-	rje	any private RJE service
79	FINGER	finger	Finger
93	DCP	-	Device Control Protocol
95	SUPDUP	supdup	SUPDUP Protocol
101	HOSTNAME	hostnames	NIC Host Name Server
102	ISO-TSAP	iso-tsap	ISO-TSAP
103	X400	x400	X.400 Mail Service
104	X400-SND	x400-snd	X.400 Mail Sending
111	SUNRPC	sunrpc	SUN Remote Procedure Call
113	AUTH	auth	Authentication Service
117	UUCP-PATH	uucp-path	UUCP Path Service
119	NNTP	nntp	USENET News Transfer Protocol
129	PWDGEN	-	Password Generator Protocol
139	NETBIOS-SSN	-	NETBIOS Session Service
160-223	Reserved		

Figure 12.14 Examples of currently assigned TCP port numbers. To the extent possible, protocols like UDP use the same numbers.

12.29 Summary

The Transmission Control Protocol, TCP, defines a key service provided by an internet, namely, reliable stream delivery. TCP provides a full duplex connection between two machines, allowing them to exchange large volumes of data efficiently.

Because it uses a sliding window protocol, TCP can make efficient use of a network. Because it makes few assumptions about the underlying delivery system, TCP is flexible enough to operate over a large variety of delivery systems. Because it provides flow control, TCP allows systems of widely varying speeds to communicate.

The basic unit of transfer used by TCP is a segment. Segments are used to pass control information (e.g., to allow TCP software on two machines to establish connections or break them) or data. The segment format permits a machine to piggyback acknowledgements for data flowing in one direction by including them in the segment headers of data flowing in the opposite direction.

TCP implements flow control by having the receiver advertise the amount of data it is willing to accept. It also supports out-of-band messages using an urgent data facility and forced delivery using a push mechanism.

The current TCP standard specifies exponential backoff for retransmission timers and congestion avoidance algorithms like slow-start, multiplicative decrease, and additive increase.

FOR FURTHER STUDY

The standard for TCP can be found in Postel [RFC 793]; Braden [RFC 1122] contains an update that clarifies several points. Clark [RFC 813] describes TCP window management, Clark [RFC 816] describes fault isolation and recovery, and Postel [RFC 879] reports on TCP maximum segment sizes. Nagle [RFC 896] comments on congestion in TCP/IP networks. Karn and Partridge [1987] discusses estimation of round-trip times and presents Karn's algorithm. Jacobson [1988] gives the congestion control algorithms that are now a required part of the standard. Tomlinson [1975] considers the three-way handshake in more detail. Mills [RFC 889] reports measurements of Internet round-trip delays. Jain [1986] describes timer-based congestion control in a sliding window environment. Borman [April 1989] summarizes experiments with high-speed TCP on Cray computers.

EXERCISES

12.1   TCP uses a finite field to contain stream sequence numbers. Study the protocol specification to find out how it allows an arbitrary length stream to pass from one machine to another.

12.2   The text notes that one of the TCP options permits a receiver to specify the maximum segment size it is willing to accept. Why does TCP support an option to specify maximum segment size when it also has a window advertisement mechanism?

12.3   Under what conditions of delay, bandwidth, load, and packet loss will TCP retransmit significant volumes of data unnecessarily?

12.4   Lost TCP acknowledgements do not necessarily force retransmissions. Explain why.

12.5   Experiment with local machines to determine how TCP handles machine restart. Establish a connection (e.g., a remote login) and leave it idle. Wait for the destination machine to crash and restart, and then force the local machine to send a TCP segment (e.g., by typing characters to the remote login).

12.6   Imagine an implementation of TCP that discards segments that arrive out of order, even if they fall in the current window. That is, the imagined version only accepts segments that extend the byte stream it has already received. Does it work? How does it compare to a standard TCP implementation?

12.7   Consider computation of a TCP checksum. Assume that although the checksum field in the segment has *not* been set to zero, the result of computing the checksum *is* zero. What can you conclude?

12.8   What are the arguments for and against automatically closing idle connections?

12.9   If two application programs use TCP to send data but only send one character per segment (e.g., by using the PUSH operation), what is the maximum percent of the network bandwidth they will have for their data?

12.10 Suppose an implementation of TCP uses initial sequence number *1* when it creates a connection. Explain how a system crash and restart can confuse a remote system into believing that the old connection remained open.

12.11 Look at the round-trip time estimation algorithm suggested in the ISO TP-4 protocol specification and compare it to the TCP algorithm discussed in this chapter. Which would you prefer to use?

12.12 Find out how implementations of TCP must solve the *overlapping segment problem*. The problem arises because the receiver must receive only one copy of all bytes from the data stream even if the sender transmits two segments that partially overlap one another (e.g., the first segment carries bytes 100 through 200 and the second carries bytes 150 through 250).

12.13 Trace the TCP finite state machine transitions for two sites that execute a passive and active open and step through the three-way handshake.

12.14 Read the TCP specification to find out the exact conditions under which TCP can make the transition from *FIN WAIT-1* to *TIMED WAIT*.

12.15 Trace the TCP state transitions for two machines that agree to close a connection gracefully.

12.16 Assume TCP is sending segments using a maximum window size (64 Kbytes) on a channel that has infinite bandwidth and an average roundtrip time of 20 milliseconds. What is the maximum throughput? How does throughput change if the roundtrip time increases to 40 milliseconds (while bandwidth remains infinite)?

12.17 Can you derive and equation that expresses the maximum possible TCP throughput as a function of the network bandwidth, the network delay, and the time to process a segment and generate an acknowledgement. Hint: consider the previous exercise.

13

Routing: Cores, Peers, and Algorithms (GGP)

13.1 Introduction

Previous chapters have concentrated on the network level services TCP/IP offers and the details of the protocols in hosts and gateways that provide those services. We assumed that gateways always contained correct routes, and we said that gateways can ask directly connected hosts to change routes with the ICMP redirect mechanism.

This chapter considers two broad questions: "what values should gateway routing tables contain?" and "how can those values be obtained?" To answer the first question, we will consider the relationship between internet architecture and routing. In particular, we will discuss internets structured around a backbone and those composed of multiple peer networks, and consider their consequences for routing. While many of our examples are drawn from the connected Internet, the ideas apply equally well to smaller corporate internets. To answer the second question, we will consider the two basic types of route propagation algorithms and see how each supplies routing information automatically.

We begin by discussing routing in general. Later sections concentrate on internet architecture and describe the type of protocols gateways use to exchange routing information. Chapters 14 and 15 continue to expand our discussion of routing. They explore protocols that gateways owned by two independent administrative groups use to exchange information, and protocols that a single group uses among all its gateways.

13.2 The Origin Of Gateway Routing Tables

Recall from Chapter 3 that IP gateways provide active interconnections among networks. Each gateway attaches to two or more physical networks and routes IP datagrams among them, accepting datagrams that arrive over one network interface, and routing them out over another interface. Except for destinations on directly attached networks, hosts pass all IP traffic to gateways which route the datagrams on toward their final destinations. A datagram travels from gateway to gateway until it reaches a gateway that attaches directly to the same network as the final destination. Thus, the gateway system forms the architectural basis of an internet and handles all traffic except for direct delivery from one host to another.

Chapter 8 described the IP routing algorithm that hosts and gateways follow and showed how it uses a table to make routing decisions. Each entry in the routing table specifies the network portion of a destination address and gives the address of the next machine along a path used to reach that network. Like hosts, gateways directly deliver datagrams to destinations on networks to which the gateway directly attaches.

Although we have seen the basics of routing, we have not said how hosts or gateways obtain the information for their routing tables. The issue has two aspects: *what* values should be placed in the tables, and *how* gateways obtain those values. Both choices depend on the architectural complexity and size of the internet as well as administrative policies.

In general, establishing routes involves initialization and update. Each gateway must establish an initial set of routes when it starts, and it must update the table as routes change (e.g., when a network interface fails). Initialization depends on the operating system. In some systems, the gateway reads an initial routing table from secondary storage at startup, keeping it resident in main memory. In others, the operating system begins with an empty table which must be filled in by executing explicit commands (e.g., commands found in a startup command script). Finally, some operating systems start by deducing an initial set of routes from the set of addresses for the networks to which the machine attaches and contacting a neighboring machine to ask for additional routes.

Once an initial routing table has been built, a gateway must accommodate changes in routes. In small, slowly changing internets, managers can establish and modify gateway routes by hand. In rapidly changing environments like the Internet, however, manual update is impossibly slow. Automated methods are needed.

Before we can understand the automatic routing table update protocols used in IP gateways, we need to review several underlying ideas. The next sections do so, providing the necessary conceptual foundation for routing. Later sections discuss internet architecture and the protocols gateways use to exchange routing information.

13.3 Routing With Partial Information

The principal difference between gateways and typical hosts is that hosts usually know little about the structure of the internet to which they connect. Hosts do not have complete knowledge of all possible destination addresses, or even of all possible destination networks. They depend on default entries in their routing tables to send to a nearby gateway all datagrams for which they have no specific route. The point is that:

Hosts can route datagrams successfully even if they only have partial routing information because they can rely on gateways.

Can gateways also route datagrams with only partial information? Yes, but only under certain circumstances. To understand the criteria, imagine an internet to be a foreign country crisscrossed with dirt roads that have directional signs posted at intersections. Imagine that you have no map, cannot ask directions because you cannot speak the local language, have no ideas about visible landmarks, but you need to travel to a village named *Sussex*. You leave on your journey, following the only road out of town and begin to look for directional signs. The first sign reads:

Norfolk to the left; Hammond to the right; others straight ahead.†

Because the destination you seek is not listed explicitly, you continue straight ahead. In routing jargon, we call this the *default route*. After several more signs, you finally find one that reads:

Essex to the left; Sussex to the right; others straight ahead.

You turn to the right, follow several more signs, and emerge on a road that leads to Sussex.

Our imagined travel is analogous to a datagram traversing an internet, and the road signs are analogous to gateway routing tables. Without a map or other navigational aids, travel is completely dependent on road signs, just as datagram routing in an internet depends entirely on routing tables. Clearly, it is possible to navigate even though each road sign contains only partial information.

A central question concerns correctness. As a traveler, you might ask, "How can I be sure that following signs will lead to my final destination?" You also might ask, "How can I be sure that following the signs will lead me to my destination along a shortest path?" These questions may seem especially troublesome if you pass many signs without finding your destination listed explicitly. Of course, the answers depend on the topology of the road system and the contents of the signs, but the fundamental idea is that when taken as a whole, the information on the signs is both consistent and complete. Looking at this another way, we see that it is not necessary for each intersection to have a sign for every destination. The signs can list default paths as long as all explicit signs point along a shortest path, and the turns for shortest paths to all destina-

---

†Fortunately, signs are printed in English.

tions are marked. A few examples will explain some ways that consistency can be achieved.

At one extreme, consider a simple star-shaped topology of roads in which each village has exactly one road leading to it, and all those roads meet at a central point. To guarantee consistency, the sign at the central intersection must contain information about all possible destinations. At the other extreme, imagine an arbitrary set of roads with signs at all intersections listing all possible destinations. To guarantee consistency, it must be true that at any intersection if the sign for destination D points to road R, no road other than R leads to a shorter path to D.

Neither of these architectural extremes works well for an internet gateway system. On one hand, the central intersection approach fails because no machine is fast enough to serve as a central switch through which all traffic passes. On the other hand, having information about all possible destinations in all gateways is impractical because it requires propagating large volumes of information whenever a change occurs or whenever administrators need to check consistency. Thus, we seek a solution that allows groups to manage local gateways autonomously, adding new network interconnections and routes without changing distant gateways.

To help explain some of the architecture described later, consider a third topology in which half the cities lie in the eastern part of the country and half lie in the western part. Suppose a single bridge spans the river that separates east from west. Assume that people living in the eastern part do not like westerners, so they are willing to allow road signs that list destinations in the east but none in the west. Assume that people living in the west do the opposite. Routing will be consistent if every road sign in the east lists all eastern destinations explicitly and points the default path to the bridge, while every road sign in the west lists all western destinations explicitly and points the default path to the bridge.

13.4 Original Internet Architecture And Cores

Much of our knowledge of routing and route propagation protocols has been derived from experience with the connected Internet. When TCP/IP was first developed, participating research sites were connected to the ARPANET and they used it as the national backbone of the Internet. During initial experiments, each site managed routing tables and installed routes to other destinations by hand. As the fledgling Internet began to grow, it became apparent that manual maintenance of routes was impractical; automated mechanisms were needed.

The Internet designers selected a gateway architecture that consisted of a small, central set of gateways that kept complete information about all possible destinations, and a larger set of outlying gateways that kept partial information. In terms of our analogy, it is like designating a small set of centrally located intersections to have signs that list all destinations, and allowing the outlying intersections to list only local destinations. As long as the default route at each outlying intersection points to one of the central intersections, travelers will eventually reach their destination. The advantage of using partial information in outlying gateways is that it permitted local administrators to manage local structural changes without affecting other parts of the Internet. The disadvantage is that it introduced the potential for inconsistency. In the worst case, an error in an outlying gateway can make distant routes unreachable.

We can summarize these ideas:

> *The routing tables in a given gateway contain partial information about possible destinations. Routing that uses partial information allows sites autonomy in making local routing changes but introduces the possibility of inconsistencies that may make some destinations unreachable from some sources.*

In gateways, routing inconsistencies usually arise from errors in the algorithms that compute routing tables, incorrect data supplied to those algorithms, or from errors that occur while transmitting the results to other gateways. Protocol designers look for ways to limit the impact of errors, with the objective being to keep all routes consistent at all times. If routes become inconsistent for some reason, the protocols gateways use should be robust enough to detect and correct the errors quickly. Most important, the protocols should be designed to constrain the effect of errors.

13.5 Core Gateways

Loosely speaking, early Internet gateways could be partitioned into two groups, a small set of *core gateways* controlled by the Internet Network Operations Center (INOC), and a larger set of *noncore gateways*† controlled by individual groups. The core system was designed to provide reliable, consistent, authoritative routes for all possible destinations; it was the glue that held the Internet together and made universal interconnection possible. By fiat, each site assigned an Internet network address had to arrange to advertise that address to the core system. The core gateways communicated among themselves, so they could guarantee that the information they shared was consistent. Because a central authority monitored and controlled the core gateways, they were highly reliable.

To fully understand the core gateway system, it is necessary to recall that the Internet evolved with a wide-area network, the ARPANET, already in place. When the Internet experiments began, designers thought of the ARPANET as a main backbone on which to build. Thus, a large part of the motivation for the core gateway system came from the desire to connect local networks to the ARPANET. Figure 13.1 illustrates this view.

---

†The terms *stub gateway* and *nonrouting gateway* have also been applied to gateways that connect local area networks to the ARPANET.

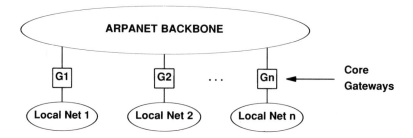

Figure 13.1 The Internet core gateway system viewed as a set of routers that connect local area networks to the ARPANET. Hosts on the local networks pass all nonlocal traffic to the closest core gateway.

To understand why such an architecture does not lend itself to routing with partial information, suppose that a large internet consists entirely of local area networks attached to a backbone network through gateways. Assume that a gateway at each site connects the local network at that site to the backbone, and imagine that the gateways rely on default routes. Now consider the path a datagram follows. At the source site, the local gateway checks to see if it has an explicit route to the destination and, if not, sends the datagram along the path specified by its default route. All datagrams for which the gateway has no route follow the same default path regardless of their ultimate destination. The next gateway along the path diverts datagrams for which it has an explicit route, and sends the rest along its default route. To insure global consistency, the chain of default routes must reach every gateway in a giant cycle as Figure 13.2 shows. Thus, the architecture requires all local sites to coordinate their default routes. In addition, depending on default routes can be inefficient even when it is consistent. As Figure 13.2 shows, in the worst case a datagram will pass through all *n* gateways as it travels from source to destination instead of going directly across the backbone.

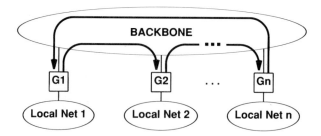

Figure 13.2 A set of gateways connected to a backbone network with default routes shown. Routing is inefficient even though it is consistent.

To avoid the inefficiencies default routes cause, Internet designers arranged for all core gateways to exchange routing information so that each would have complete information about optimal routes to all possible destinations. Because each core gateway knew routes to all possible destinations, it did not need a default route. If the destination address on a datagram was not in a core gateway's routing table, the gateway would generate an ICMP destination unreachable message and drop the datagram. In essence, the core design avoided inefficiency by eliminating default routes.

Figure 13.3 depicts the conceptual basis of a core routing architecture. The figure shows a central core system consisting of one or more core gateways, and a set of outlying gateways at local sites. Outlying gateways keep information about local destinations and use a default route that sends datagrams destined for other sites to the core.

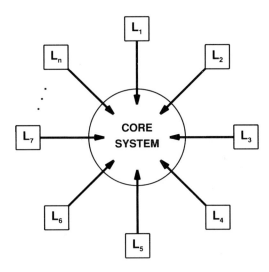

Figure 13.3 The routing architecture of a simplistic core system showing default routes. Core gateways do not use default routes; outlying gateways, labeled L_i, each have a default route that points to the core.

Although the simplistic core architecture illustrated in Figure 13.3 is easy to understand, it became impractical for three reasons. First, the Internet outgrew a single, centrally managed long-haul backbone. The topology became complex and the protocols needed to maintain consistency among core gateways became nontrivial. Second, not every site could have a core gateway connected to the backbone, so additional routing structure and protocols were needed. Third, because core gateways all interacted to ensure consistent routing information, the core architecture did not scale to large size. We will return to this last problem in Chapter 14 after we examine the protocols that the core system used to exchange routing information.

13.6 Beyond The Core Architecture To Peer Backbones

The introduction of the NSFNET backbone into the Internet added new complexity to the routing structure. From the core system point of view, the connection to NSFNET was initially no different than the connection to any other site. NSFNET attached to the ARPANET backbone through a single gateway in Pittsburgh. The core had explicit routes to all destinations in NSFNET. Gateways inside NSFNET knew about destinations in NSFNET and used a default route to send all non-NSFNET traffic to the core via the Pittsburgh gateway.

As NSFNET grew to become a major part of the Internet, it became apparent that the core routing architecture would not suffice. The most important conceptual change occurred when multiple connections were added between the ARPANET backbone and the NSFNET backbone. We say that the two became *peer backbone networks* or simply *peers*. Figure 13.4 illustrates the resulting peer topology.

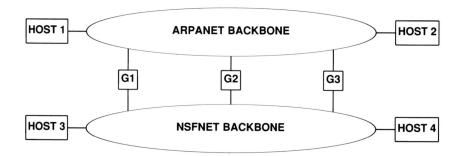

Figure 13.4 An example of peer backbones interconnected through multiple gateways. The diagram illustrates the architecture of the Internet in 1989.

To understand the difficulties of IP routing among peer backbones, consider routes from host *3* to host *2* in Figure 13.4. Assume for the moment that the figure shows geographic orientation, so host *3* is on the West Coast attached to the NSFNET backbone while host *2* is on the East Coast attached to the ARPANET backbone. When establishing routes between hosts *3* and *2*, the managers must decide whether to (a) route the traffic from host *3* through the West Coast gateway, *G1*, and then across the ARPANET backbone, or (b) route the traffic from host *3* across the NSFNET backbone, through the Midwest gateway, *G2*, and then across the ARPANET backbone to host *2*, or (c) route the traffic across the NSFNET backbone, through the East Coast gateway, *G3*, and then to host *2*. A more circuitous route is possible as well: traffic could flow from host *3* through the West Coast gateway, across the ARPANET backbone to the Midwest gateway, back onto the NSFNET backbone to the East Coast gateway, and finally across the ARPANET backbone to host *2*. Such a route may or may not be advisable, depending on the policies for network use and the capacity of various gateways and backbones.

For most peer backbone configurations, traffic between a pair of geographically close hosts should take a shortest path, independent of the routes chosen for cross-country traffic. For example, traffic from host *3* to host *1* should flow through the West Coast gateway because it minimizes distance on both backbones.

All these statements sound simple enough, but they are complex to implement for two reasons. First, although the standard IP routing algorithm uses the network portion of an IP address to choose a route, optimal routing in a peer backbone architecture requires individual routes for individual hosts. For our example above, the routing table in host *3* needs different routes for host *1* and host *2*, even though both hosts *1* and *2* attach to the ARPANET backbone. Second, managers of the two backbones must agree to keep routes consistent among all gateways or *routing loops* can develop (a routing loop occurs when routes in a set of gateways point in a circle).

It is important to distinguish network topology from routing architecture. It is possible, for example, to have a single core system that spans multiple backbone networks. The core machines can be programmed to hide the underlying architectural details and to compute shortest routes among themselves. It is not possible, however, to partition the core system into subsets that each keep partial information without losing functionality. Figure 13.5 illustrates the problem.

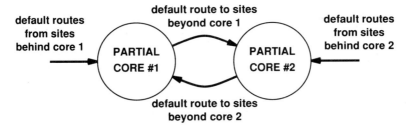

Figure 13.5 An attempt to partition a core routing architecture into two sets of gateways that keep partial information and use default routes. Such an architecture results in a routing loop for datagrams that have an illegal (nonexistent) destination.

As the figure shows, outlying gateways have default routes to one side of the partitioned core. Each side of the partition has information about destinations on its side of the world and a default route for information on the other side of the world. In such an architecture, any datagram sent to an illegal address will cycle between the two partitions in a routing loop until its time to live counter reaches zero.

We can summarize as follows:

A core routing architecture assumes a centralized set of gateways serves as the repository of information about all possible destinations in an internet. Core systems work best for internets that have a single, centrally managed backbone. Expanding the topology to multiple backbones makes routing complex; attempting to partition the core architecture so that all gateways use default routes introduces potential routing loops.

13.7 Automatic Route Propagation

We said that the original Internet core system avoided default routes because it propagated complete information about all possible destinations to every core gateway. The next sections discuss two basic types of distributed algorithms that compute and propagate routing information, and use the original core gateway routing protocol to illustrate one of them.

It may seem that automatic route propagation mechanisms are not needed, especially on small internets. However, internets are not static. Connections fail and are later replaced. Networks can become overloaded at one moment and underutilized at the next. The purpose of routing propagation mechanisms is not merely to find a set of routes, but to continually update the information. Humans simply cannot respond to changes fast enough; computers must be used. Thus, when we think about route propagation, it is important to consider the dynamic behavior of protocols and algorithms.

13.8 Vector Distance (Bellman-Ford) Routing

The term *vector-distance*† refers to a class of algorithms gateways use to propagate routing information. The idea behind vector-distance algorithms is quite simple. We assume that each gateway begins with a set of routes for those networks to which it attaches. It keeps the list of routes in a table, where each entry identifies a destination network and gives the distance to that network measured in hops.

Destination	Distance
Net 1	0
Net 2	0

Figure 13.6 An initial vector-distance routing table with an entry for each directly connected network. Entries contain the IP address of a network and an integer distance to that network.

---

†The names *Ford Fulkerson*, *Bellman-Ford*, and *Bellman* are synonymous with *vector-distance*; they are taken from the names of researchers who first published the idea.

Periodically, each gateway sends a copy of its routing table to any other gateway it can reach directly. When a report arrives at gateway K from gateway J, K examines the set of destinations reported and the distance to each. If J knows a shorter way to reach a destination, or if J lists a destination that K does not have in its table, or if K currently routes to a destination through J and J's distance to that destination changes, K replaces its table entry. For example, Figure 13.7 shows an existing table in a gateway, K, and an update message from another gateway, J.

Destination	Distance	Route
Net 1	0	direct
Net 2	0	direct
Net 4	8	Gate. L
Net 17	5	Gate. M
Net 24	6	Gate. J
Net 30	2	Gate. Q
Net 42	2	Gate. J

(a)

Destination	Distance
Net 1	2
➤ Net 4	3
Net 17	6
➤ Net 21	4
Net 24	5
Net 30	10
➤ Net 42	3

(b)

Figure 13.7 (a) An existing route table for a gateway K, and (b) an incoming routing update message from gateway J. The marked entries will be used to update existing entries or add new entries to K's table.

Note that if J reports distance N, an updated entry in K will have distance $N+1$ (the distance to reach the destination from J plus the distance to reach J). Of course, the routing table entries contain a third column that specifies a route. Initial entries are all marked *direct delivery*. When gateway K adds or updates an entry in response to a message from gateway J, it assigns gateway J as the route for that entry.

The term *vector-distance* comes from the information sent in the periodic messages. A message contains a list of pairs (V, D), where V identifies a destination (called the *vector*), and D is the distance to that destination. Note that vector-distance algorithms report routes in the first person (i.e., we think of a gateway advertising, "I can reach destination V at distance D"). In such a design, all gateways must participate in the vector-distance exchange for the routes to be efficient and consistent.

Although vector-distance algorithms are easy to implement, they have disadvantages. In a completely static environment, vector-distance algorithms propagate routes to all destinations. When routes change rapidly, however, the computations may not stabilize. When a route changes (i.e, a new connection appears or an old one fails), the information propagates slowly from one gateway to another. Meanwhile, some gateways may have incorrect routing information.

For now, we will examine a protocol that uses the vector-distance algorithm without discussing all the shortcomings. Chapter 15 completes the discussion by showing another vector-distance protocol, the problems that can arise, and the heuristics used to solve the most serious of them.

13.9 Gateway-To-Gateway Protocol (GGP)

The original core gateways used a vector-distance protocol known as the *Gateway-to-Gateway Protocol (GGP)* to exchange routing information. While GGP is no longer a key part of the TCP/IP suite, it does provide a concrete example of vector-distance routing. GGP was designed to travel in IP datagrams like UDP user datagrams or TCP segments. Each GGP message has a fixed format header that identifies the message type and the format of the remaining fields. Because only core gateways participated in GGP, and because core gateways were controlled by the INOC, outsiders could not interfere with the exchange.

The original core system was arranged to permit new core gateways to be added without modifying existing gateways. When a new gateway was added to the core system, it was assigned one or more core *neighbors* with which it communicated. The neighbors, already members of the core, already propagated routing information among themselves. Thus, the new gateway only needed to inform its neighbors about networks it could reach; they updated their routing tables and propagated this new information further.

GGP is a true vector-distance protocol. The routing information gateways exchange with GGP consists of a set of pairs, (N, D), where N is an IP network address, and D is a distance measured in hops. We say that a gateway using GGP *advertises* the networks it can reach and its cost for reaching them.

GGP measures distance in *gateway hops*, where a gateway is defined to be zero hops from directly connected networks, one hop from networks that are reachable through one other gateway, and so on. Thus, the *number of hops* or the *hop count* along a path from a given source to a given destination refers to the number of gateways that a datagram encounters along that path. It should be obvious that using hop counts to calculate shortest paths does not always produce desirable results. For example, a path with hop count *3* that crosses three Ethernets may be substantially faster than a path with hop count *2* that crosses two slow speed serial lines. Many gateways use artificially high hop counts for routes across slow networks.

13.10 GGP Message Formats

There are four types of GGP messages, each with its own format. The first octet contains a code that identifies the message *type*. Figure 13.8 shows the format of one GGP message type, the message gateways exchange to learn about routes. Recall that the information consists of pairs of IP network and distance values. To keep messages small, networks are grouped together by distance, and the message consists of a sequence of sets, where each set contains a distance value followed by a list of all networks at that distance.

The value *12* in the field labeled *TYPE* specifies that this message is a *routing update* message, distinguishing it from other GGP message types. The 16-bit *SEQUENCE NUMBER* is used to validate a GGP message; both sender and receiver must agree on the sequence number before the receiver will accept the message. The field labeled *UPDATE* is a binary value that specifies whether the sender needs an update from the receiver. Because GGP groups networks by distance, the field labeled *NUM. DISTANCES* specifies how many distance groups are present in this update.

The last part of a GGP routing update message contains sets of networks grouped by distance. Each set starts with two 8-bit fields that specify a distance value and a count of networks at that distance. If the count specifies *n* networks at a given distance, exactly *n* network IP addresses must occur before the next set header. To conserve space, only the network portion of the IP address is included, so network numbers may be 1, 2, or 3 octets long. The receiver must look at the first bits of the network identifier to determine its length.

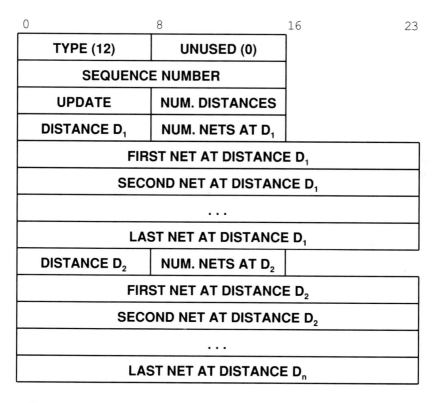

Figure 13.8 The format of a GGP routing update message. A gateway sends such a message to advertise destination networks it knows how to reach. Network numbers contain either 1, 2, or 3 octets, depending on whether the network is class *A*, *B*, or *C*.

When a gateway receives a GGP routing update message, it sends a GGP *ack-nowledgement* message back to the sender, using a positive acknowledgement if the routing update was acceptable, and a negative acknowledgement if an error was detected. Figure 13.9 illustrates the format of GGP acknowledgements:

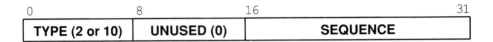

Figure 13.9 The format of a GGP acknowledgement message. Type *2* identifies the message as a positive acknowledgement, while type *10* identifies the message as a negative acknowledgement.

In positive acknowledgement messages, the field labeled *SEQUENCE* specifies a sequence number that the receiver is acknowledging. In negative acknowledgements, the *SEQUENCE* field gives the sequence number that the receiver last received correctly.

In addition to routing update messages, the GGP protocol includes messages that allow one gateway to test whether another is responding. A gateway sends an *echo request* message to a neighbor, which requests that the recipient respond by sending back an *echo reply* message. Figure 13.10 shows the echo message formats.

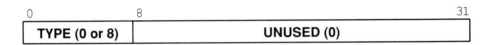

Figure 13.10 The format of a GGP echo request or reply message. Type *8* identifies the message as an echo request, while type *0* identifies the message as an echo reply.

13.11 Link-State (SPF) Routing

The main disadvantage of vector-distance algorithms is that they do not scale well. Besides the problem of slow response to change mentioned earlier, the algorithm requires large message exchanges. Because routing update messages contain an entry for every possible network, message size is proportional to the total number of networks in an internet. Furthermore, because a vector-distance protocol requires every gateway to participate, the volume of information exchanged can be enormous.

The primary alternative to vector-distance schemes is a class of algorithms known as *link-state*, *Shortest Path First*, or *SPF*†. SPF algorithms require each participating gateway to have complete topology information. The easiest way to think of the topology information is to imagine that every gateway has a map that shows all other gate-

---

†The name "shortest path first" is an unfortunate misnomer because most route computations choose shortest paths. However, it seems to have gained wide acceptance.

ways and the networks to which they connect. In abstract terms, the gateways correspond to nodes in a graph and networks that connect gateways correspond to edges. There is an edge (link) between two nodes if and only if the corresponding gateways can communicate directly.

Instead of sending messages that contain lists of destinations, a gateway participating in an SPF algorithm performs two tasks. First, it actively tests the status of all neighbor gateways. In terms of the graph, two gateways are neighbors if they share a link; in network terms, two neighbors connect to a common network. Second, it periodically propagates the link status information to all other gateways.

To test the status of a directly connected neighbor, a gateway periodically exchanges short messages that ask whether the neighbor is alive and reachable. If the neighbor replies, the link between them is said to be 'up'. Otherwise, the link is said to be 'down'. (In practice, to prevent oscillations between the up and down states, most protocols use a *k-out-of-n rule* to test liveness, meaning that the link remains up until a significant percentage of requests have no reply, and then it remains down until a significant percentage of messages receive a reply.)

To inform all other gateways, each gateway periodically broadcasts a message that lists the status (state) of each of its links. The status message does not specify routes – it simply reports whether communication is possible between pairs of gateways. Protocol software in the gateways arranges to deliver a copy of each link status message to all participating gateways (if the underlying networks do not support broadcast, delivery is done by forwarding individual copies of the message point-to-point).

Whenever a link status message arrives, a gateway uses the information to update its map of the internet, by marking links 'up' or 'down'. Whenever link status changes, the gateway recomputes routes by applying the well-known *Dijkstra shortest path algorithm* to the resulting graph. Dijkstra's algorithm computes the shortest paths to all destinations from a single source.

One of the chief advantages of SPF algorithms is that each gateway computes routes independently using the same original status data; they do not depend on the computation of intermediate machines. Because link status messages propagate unchanged, it is easy to debug problems. Because gateways perform the route computation locally, it is guaranteed to converge. Finally, because link status messages only carry information about the direct connections from a single gateway, the size does not depend on the number of networks in the internet. Thus, SPF algorithms scale better than vector-distance algorithms.

13.12 SPF Protocols

Besides proprietary protocols offered by vendors, only a few SPF protocols are currently used in the Internet. One of the first examples of SPF comes from the ARPANET, which had used an SPF algorithm internally for approximately ten years. At the other extreme, Chapter 15 discusses a general purpose SPF protocol proposed in the late 1980s, but not widely used as of this writing.

By 1988, the Internet core system had switched from early LSI-11 computers running GGP to *Butterfly* processors† that use a Shortest Path First algorithm. The exact protocol, known as *SPREAD* has not been documented in the RFC literature.

13.13 Summary

To insure that all networks remain reachable with high reliability, an internet must provide globally consistent routing. Hosts and most gateways contain only partial routing information; they depend on default routes to send datagrams to distant destinations. The connected Internet solves the routing problem by using a core gateway architecture in which a small set of core gateways contain complete information about all networks. The core gateways exchange routing information periodically so once a single core gateway learns about a route, all core gateways learn about it. To prevent routing loops, the core is forbidden from using default routes.

A single, centrally managed core system works well for an internet architecture built on a single backbone network. However, when an internet has multiple, separately managed peer backbones that interconnect at multiple places, the core architecture does not suffice.

When gateways exchange routing information they usually use one of two basic algorithms, vector-distance or SPF. We examined the details of GGP, the vector-distance protocol originally used to propagate routing update information throughout the core. Each GGP routing update can be viewed as an advertisement that lists a set of networks along with the gateway's cost to reach those network.

The chief disadvantage of vector-distance algorithms is that they perform a distributed shortest path computation that may not converge. Another disadvantage is that routing update messages grow large as the number of networks increases.

FOR FURTHER STUDY

The definition of the core gateway system and GGP protocol in this chapter comes from Hinden and Sheltzer [RFC 823]. Braden and Postel [RFC 1009] contains further specifications for Internet gateways. Braun [RFC 1093] and Rekhter [RFC 1092] discusses routing in the NSFNET backbone. Clark [RFC 1102] and Braun [RFC 1104] both discusses policy-based routing. The next two chapters present protocols used for propagating routing information between separate sites and within a single site. Rekhter [RFC 1074] considers the SPF algorithm used on the second NSFNET backbone.

---

†The butterfly is a multiprocessor computer that has a special purpose, high speed interconnection among processors, designed to support packet switching. It is manufactured by Bolt, Beranek, and Newman, Inc.

EXERCISES

13.1 Suppose a gateway discovers it is about to route an IP datagram back over the same network interface on which the datagram arrived. What should it do? Why?

13.2 After reading RFC 823 and RFC 1009, explain what an Internet core gateway does in the situation described in the previous question.

13.3 How could core gateways use default routes to send all illegal datagrams to a specific machine?

13.4 Imagine students experimenting with a gateway that attaches a local area network to the Internet. They want to advertise their network to the core gateway system, but if they accidentally advertise zero length routes to arbitrary networks (e.g., the ARPANET), real Internet traffic would be diverted to their gateway. How can the core protect itself from illegal data while still accepting updates from such 'untrusted' gateways?

13.5 Which ICMP messages does a gateway generate?

13.6 How did the original Internet core gateways determine whether a designated neighbor was 'up' or 'down'? Hint: consult RFC 823.

13.7 Suppose two core gateways each advertise the same cost, k, to reach a given network, N. Describe the circumstances under which routing through one of them may take fewer hops than routing through the other one.

13.8 How can a gateway know whether an incoming datagram carries a GGP message?

13.9 Consider the vector-distance update shown in Figure 13.7 carefully. Give three reasons why the gateway will update its table with the three items shown.

14

Routing: Autonomous Systems (EGP)

14.1 Introduction

The previous chapter introduced the idea of route propagation and examined one protocol gateways use to exchange routing information. This chapter extends our understanding of internet gateway architecture. It discusses the concept of autonomous systems and shows the protocol that a group of networks and gateways operating under one administrative authority use to propagate network reachability information to other groups.

14.2 Adding Complexity To The Architectural Model

As we said, the original core gateway system evolved at a time when the Internet had a single backbone (the ARPANET), and part of the motivation for a core architecture was to provide connections between local area networks and the backbone (see Figure 13.1). If an internet consists of only a single backbone plus a set of attached local area networks, no further structure is needed. Each gateway knows the single local network to which it attaches and can learn about all other networks by exchanging messages with other gateways across the backbone. Unfortunately, most internets are not nearly this simple. First, even if each internet site has only one local network, a core architecture is inadequate because it cannot grow to accommodate an arbitrary number of sites. Second, most sites have multiple local area networks and multiple gateways interconnecting them. Because a core gateway connects to a single network at each site,

223

the core only knows about one network at that site. Third, large internets connect networks managed by independent groups. The routing architecture must provide a way for each group to independently control routing and access. After examining the consequences of each of these ideas, we will learn how a single protocol mechanism allows construction of an internet that spans multiple sites while allowing autonomy at each site.

14.3 A Fundamental Idea: Extra Hops

So far, we have discussed an internet architecture consisting of one or more backbone networks surrounded by a core gateway system. We have been thinking of the core system as a central routing mechanism to which noncore gateways can send datagrams for delivery. We also said that it is impossible to expand a single backbone arbitrarily. Having fewer core gateways than networks in the internet means that we must change our view of core architecture or routing will be suboptimal. To see why, consider the example in Figure 14.1

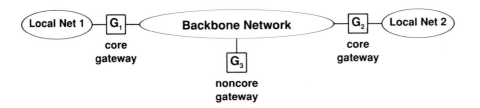

Figure 14.1 The extra hop problem. Noncore gateways connected to the backbone must learn routes from core gateways to have optimal routing.

In the figure, core gateways G_1 and G_2 connect to local area networks 1 and 2, respectively. Because they exchange routing information, they both know how to reach both networks. Suppose noncore gateway G_3 thinks of the core as a delivery system and chooses one of the core gateways, say G_1, to deliver all datagrams destined for networks to which it has no direct connection. G_3 sends datagrams for network 2 across the backbone to its chosen core gateway, G_1, which must then send them back across the backbone to gateway G_2. The optimal route, of course, requires G_3 to send datagrams destined for network 2 directly to G_2. Notice that the choice of core gateway makes no difference. Only destinations that lie beyond the chosen gateway have optimal routes; all paths that go through other backbone gateways require an extra hop. Also notice that the core gateways cannot use ICMP redirect messages to inform G_3 that it has incorrect routes because ICMP redirect messages can only be sent to the original source and not to intermediate gateways.

We call the routing anomaly illustrated in Figure 14.1 the *extra hop problem.* Solving it requires us to change our view of a core architecture:

> *Treating a core system as a central router introduces an extra hop for most traffic. A mechanism is needed that allows noncore gateways to learn routes from core gateways so they can choose optimal backbone routes.*

Allowing sites to have multiple networks and gateways means that the core does not attach to all networks directly, so an additional mechanism is needed to allow the core system to learn about them. Consider, for example, the set of networks and gateways shown in Figure 14.2. We might imagine such an interconnection on a corporate or university campus, where each network corresponds to a single building or to a single department.

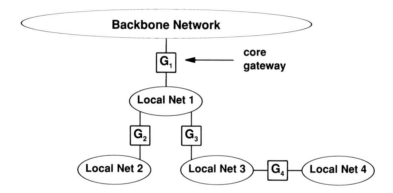

Figure 14.2 An example of multiple networks and gateways with a single backbone connection. A mechanism is needed to pass reachability information about additional local networks to the core system.

Suppose the site has just installed local network *4* and has obtained an internet address for it. Also assume that the gateways G_2, G_3, and G_4 have routes for all four local networks as well as default routes that pass other traffic to the core gateway, G_1. Hosts directly attached to local network *4* can communicate with one another, and any machine on that network can route packets out to other backbone sites. However, because gateway G_1 attaches only to local network *1*, it does not know about local network *4*. We say that, from the point of view of the core system, local network *4* is *hidden* behind local network *1*. The important point is:

Because individual sites can have an arbitrarily complex structure, a core system will not attach directly to all networks. A mechanism is needed that allows noncore gateways to inform the core about hidden networks.

Keep in mind that in addition to providing the core with information about hidden networks, we need a mechanism that allows noncore gateways to obtain routing information from the core. Ideally, a single mechanism should solve both problems. Building such a mechanism can be tricky. The subtle issues are responsibility and capability. Exactly where does responsibility for informing the core reside? If we decide that one of the gateways should inform the core, which one is capable of doing it? Look again at the example. Gateway G_4 is the gateway most closely associated with local network *4*, but it lies *2* hops away from the nearest core gateway. Thus, G_4 must depend on gateway G_3 to route packets to network *4*. The point is that G_4 cannot guarantee reachability of local network *4* on its own. Gateway G_3 lies one hop from the core and can guarantee to pass packets, but it does not directly attach to local network *4*. So, it seems incorrect to grant G_3 responsibility for network *4*. Solving this dilemma will require us to introduce a new concept. The next sections discuss the concept and a protocol built around it.

14.4 Autonomous System Concept

The puzzle over which gateway should communicate reachability information to the core system arises because we have only considered the mechanics of an internet routing architecture and not the administrative issues. Interconnections, like those in the example of Figure 14.2, that arise when a backbone site has a complex local structure, should not be thought of as multiple independent networks connected to an internet, but as a single site that has multiple networks under its control. Because the networks and gateways fall under a single administrative authority, that authority can guarantee that internal routes remain consistent and viable. Furthermore, the administrative authority can choose one of its machines to serve as the machine that will apprise the outside world of network reachability. In the example from Figure 14.2, because gateways G_2, G_3, and G_4 fall under control of one administrative authority, that authority can arrange to have G_3 advertise reachability for networks *2*, *3*, and *4* (we assume the core system already knows about network *1* because a core gateway attaches directly to it).

For purposes of routing, a group of networks and gateways controlled by a single administrative authority is called an *autonomous system*. Gateways within an autonomous system are free to choose their own mechanisms for discovering, propagating, validating, and checking the consistency of routes. Note that, under this definition, the core gateways themselves form an autonomous system. We said that the original Internet core gateways used GGP to communicate among themselves and that the current Internet core uses SPREAD. The next chapter reviews other protocols autonomous systems use to propagate routing information.

Conceptually, the autonomous system idea is a straightforward and natural generalization of the architecture, depicted by Figure 14.2, with autonomous systems replacing local area networks. Figure 14.3 illustrates the idea.

To make networks that are hidden inside autonomous systems reachable throughout the Internet, each autonomous system must agree to advertise network reachability information to other autonomous systems. Although advertisements can be sent to any autonomous system, in a core architecture, it is crucial that each autonomous system propagate information to a core gateway. Usually, one gateway in an autonomous system takes responsibility for advertising routes and interacts directly with one of the core gateways. It is possible, however, to have several gateways each advertise a subset of the networks.

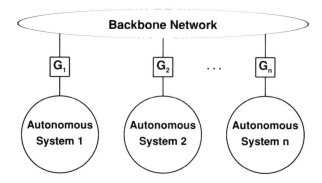

Figure 14.3 Architecture of an internet with autonomous systems at backbone sites. Each autonomous system consists of multiple networks and gateways under a single administrative authority.

It may seem that our definition of an autonomous system is vague, but in practice the boundaries between autonomous systems must be precise to allow automated algorithms to make routing decisions. For example, an autonomous system owned by a corporation may choose not to route packets through an autonomous system owned by another even though they connect directly. To make it possible for automated routing algorithms to distinguish among autonomous systems, each is assigned an *autonomous system number* by the same central authority that is charged with assigning all Internet network addresses. When two gateways exchange network reachability information, the messages carry the autonomous system identifier that the gateway represents.

We can summarize these ideas:

*A large TCP/IP internet has additional structure to accommodate ad-
ministrative boundaries: each collection of networks and gateways
managed by one administrative authority is considered to be a single
autonomous system. An autonomous system is free to choose an internal routing architecture, but must collect information about all its networks and designate one or more gateways that will pass the reachability information to other autonomous systems. Because the connected Internet uses a core architecture, every autonomous system must
pass reachability information to Internet core gateways.*

The next section presents the details of the protocol gateways use to advertise network
reachability. Later sections return to architectural questions to discuss an important restriction the protocol imposes on routing. They also show how the Internet model can be
extended.

14.5 Exterior Gateway Protocol (EGP)

Two gateways that exchange routing information are said to be *exterior neighbors*
if they belong to two different autonomous systems, and *interior neighbors* if they belong to the same autonomous system. The protocol exterior neighbors use to advertise
reachability information to other autonomous systems is called the *exterior gateway
protocol* or *EGP*, and the gateways using it are called *exterior gateways*. In the connected Internet, EGP is especially important because autonomous systems use it to advertise reachability information to the core system.

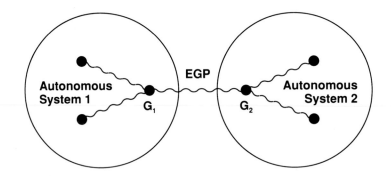

Figure 14.4 Conceptual illustration of two exterior gateways, G_1 and G_2, using EGP to advertise networks in their autonomous systems after
collecting the information. As the name implies, *exterior* gateways are usually close to the outer ''edge'' of an autonomous
system.

Figure 14.4 illustrates two exterior neighbors using EGP. Gateway G_1 gathers information about networks in autonomous system *1* and reports that information to gateway G_2 using EGP, while gateway G_2 reports information from autonomous system *2*.

EGP has three main features. First, it supports a *neighbor acquisition* mechanism that allows one gateway to request another to agree that the two should communicate reachability information. We say that a gateway *acquires* an *EGP peer* or an *EGP neighbor*. EGP peers are neighbors only in the sense that they will exchange routing information; there is no notion of geographic proximity. Second, a gateway continually tests whether its EGP neighbors are responding. Third, EGP neighbors periodically exchange network reachability information by passing *routing update messages*.

14.6 EGP Message Header

To accommodate the three basic functions, EGP defines nine message types as the following table shows:

EGP Message Type	Description
Acquisition Request	Requests gateway become a neighbor (peer)
Acquisition Confirm	Positive response to acquisition request
Acquisition Refuse	Negative response to acquisition request
Cease Request	Requests termination of neighbor relationship
Cease Confirm	Confirmation response to cease request
Hello	Requests neighbor to respond if alive
I Heard You	Response to hello message
Poll Request	Requests network routing update
Routing Update	Network reachability information
Error	Response to incorrect message

All EGP messages begin with a fixed header that identifies the message type. Figure 14.5 shows the EGP header format.

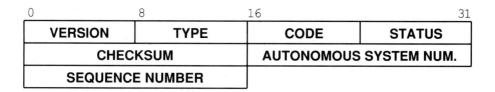

Figure 14.5 The fixed header that precedes every EGP message.

The header field labeled *VERSION* contains an integer that identifies the version of EGP used to format the message. Receivers check the version number to verify that their software is using the same version of the protocol. Field *TYPE* identifies the type of the message, with the *CODE* field used to distinguish among subtypes. The *STATUS* field contains message-dependent status information.

EGP uses a checksum to verify that the message arrives intact. It uses the same checksum algorithm as IP, treating the entire EGP message as a sequence of 16-bit integers, and taking the one's complement of the one's complement sum. When performing the computation, field *CHECKSUM* is assumed to contain zeros, and the message is padded to a multiple of 16 bits by adding zeros.

The field labeled *AUTONOMOUS SYSTEM NUM.* gives the assigned number of the autonomous system of the gateway sending the message, and the *SEQUENCE NUMBER* field contains a number that the sender uses to synchronize messages and replies. A gateway establishes an initial sequence value when acquiring a neighbor and increments the sequence number each time it sends a message. The neighbor replies with the last sequence number it received, allowing the sender to match responses to transmissions.

14.7 EGP Neighbor Acquisition Messages

A gateway sends *neighbor acquisition* messages to establish EGP communication with another gateway. Note that EGP does not specify why or how one gateway chooses another gateway as its neighbor. We assume that such choices are made by the organizations responsible for administering the gateways and not by the protocol software.

In addition to the standard header with a sequence number, neighbor acquisition messages contain initial values for a time interval to be used for testing whether the neighbor is alive (called a *hello interval*), and a *polling interval* that controls the maximum frequency of routing updates. The sender supplies a polling interval of n to specify that the receiver should not poll more often than every n seconds†. The original sender can change the polling interval dynamically as time passes. Furthermore, the polling intervals that peers use can be asymmetric, allowing one peer to poll more frequently than another. Figure 14.6 shows the format of acquisition messages and responses.

---

†In practice, most implementations use the polling interval as the exact frequency at which they send poll requests.

```
0                  8                 16                24                31
| VERSION      | TYPE (3)     | CODE (0 to 4)   | STATUS          |
| CHECKSUM                    | AUTONOMOUS SYSTEMS NUM.            |
| SEQUENCE NUMBER             | HELLO INTERVAL                    |
| POLL INTERVAL               |
```

Figure 14.6 EGP neighbor acquisition message format. Fields beyond the header specify initial parameters used by the protocol.

The *CODE* field identifies the specific message as the following table shows:

Code	Meaning
0	Acquisition Request
1	Acquisition Confirm
2	Acquisition Refuse
3	Cease Request
4	Cease Confirm

14.8 EGP Neighbor Reachability Messages

EGP permits two forms of testing whether a neighbor is alive. In active mode, gateways test neighbors by periodically sending *Hello* messages along with *poll* messages and waiting for responses. In passive mode, a gateway depends on its neighbor to periodically send *hello* or *poll* messages. A gateway operating in passive mode uses information from the *status field* of a reachability message (see below) to deduce whether the peer is alive and whether the peer knows it is alive. Usually both gateways in a pair operate in active mode.

Separating the calculation of neighbor reachability from routing information exchanges is important because it leads to lower network overhead. Because network routing information does not change as frequently as the status of individual gateway machines, it need not be passed frequently. Furthermore, neighbor reachability messages are small and require little computational overhead, while routing exchange messages are large and require much computation. Thus, by separating the two tests, neighbors can be tested frequently with minimal computational and communication overhead. Figure 14.7 shows that neighbor reachability requests consist of only the EGP message header.

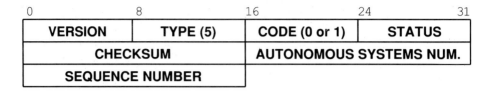

Figure 14.7 EGP neighbor reachability message format. Code *0* specifies a *Hello* request message, while code *1* specifies an *I Heard You* response.

Because it is possible for *Hello* messages or *I Heard You* responses to be lost in transit, EGP uses a form of the *k-out-of-n rule* to determine whether a peer has changed from 'up' to 'down'. The best way to think of the algorithm is to imagine a gateway sending a continuous sequence of *Hello* messages and receiving *I Heard You* responses, and think of a window spanning the last n exchanges. At least k of the last n exchanges must fail for the gateway to declare its neighbor down, and at least j must succeed for the gateway to declare that the neighbor is up, once it has been declared down. The protocol standard suggests values for j and k that imply two successive messages must be lost (received) before EGP will declare the peer down (up).

The hysteresis introduced by j and k have an important effect on the overall performance of EGP. As with any routing algorithm, EGP should not propagate unnecessary changes. The reason is simple: changes do not stop after a gateway propagates them to its EGP peer. The peer may propagate them on to other gateways as well. Minimizing rapid route changes is especially crucial when an EGP peer uses a vector-distance algorithm to propagate changes because continual changes can make vector-distance algorithms unstable. Thus, if exterior gateways report changes of reachability whenever a message is lost, they can cause the routing system to remain in continual transition.

14.9 EGP Poll Request Messages

EGP *poll request* and *poll response* messages allow a gateway to obtain network reachability information. Figure 14.8 shows the message format. The field labeled *IP SOURCE NETWORK* specifies a network common to the autonomous systems to which both gateways attach. The response will contain routes that have distances measured with respect to gateways on the specified IP source network.

0	8	16	24	31
VERSION	TYPE (2)	CODE (0 or 1)	STATUS	
CHECKSUM		AUTONOMOUS SYSTEMS NUM.		
SEQUENCE NUMBER		RESERVED		
IP SOURCE NETWORK				

Figure 14.8 EGP poll message format. Code *0* specifies a *Hello* request message, while code *1* specifies an *I Heard You* response.

It may be difficult to understand why EGP chooses to make a polling request specify a source network. There are two reasons. First, recall that a gateway connects to two or more physical networks. If an application on the gateway implements EGP, it may not know over which interface EGP requests arrive. Thus, it may not know to which network the request refers. Second, gateways that run EGP often collect information for an entire autonomous system. When advertising network reachability, the exterior gateway sends neighbors a set of pairs that each specify a destination network in the autonomous system and the gateway used to reach that destination. Of course, the gateway used to reach a destination depends on where traffic enters the autonomous system. The source network mentioned in the polling request specifies the point at which packets will enter the autonomous system. Figure 14.9 illustrates the idea of a common network used as a base for network reachability information.

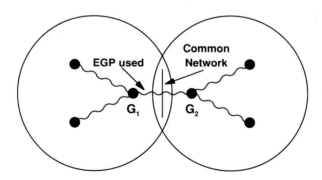

Figure 14.9 Gateways in two autonomous systems using EGP to communicate network reachability information. A reachability message specifies gateways on a network common to both systems and destinations reachable via those gateways.

14.10 EGP Routing Update Messages

An exterior gateway sends a *routing update* message to convey information about reachable networks to its EGP neighbor. Usually, the gateway has collected the information and is making that information available to a gateway in another autonomous system. In principle, a gateway running EGP could report two types of reachability to a peer. The first type consists of destination networks that are reachable entirely within the gateway's autonomous system. The second type consists of destination networks that the gateway has learned about, but which lie beyond the gateway's autonomous system boundary.

It is important to understand that EGP does not permit an arbitrary gateway to advertise reachability to an arbitrary destination network. The restriction limits gateways to advertising only those destinations for which it is an authority. That is:

> *EGP restricts a (noncore) gateway to advertise only those networks reachable entirely from within its autonomous system.*

This rule, sometimes called the *EGP third party restriction* is intended to control the propagation of information and allow each autonomous system to choose exactly how it advertises reachability. For example, if each university campus forms an autonomous system, a gateway on a given university campus might collect information about networks on that campus and advertise them to the Internet core, but it would not advertise routes to networks on other campuses. Naturally, the restriction does not apply to the core system.

Figure 14.10 illustrates the format of a routing update message. The fields labeled *# INT. GWYS* and *# EXT. GWYS* give the number of interior and exterior gateways appearing in the message. Distinguishing between interior and exterior gateways allows the recipient to know whether distances are comparable. Unfortunately, it is impossible to make such a distinction based on gateway addresses alone, and there is no provision in the message for such a distinction. In practice, EGP implementations overcome the problem by sending separate update messages for interior and exterior gateways. The field labeled *IP SOURCE NETWORK* gives the network from which all reachability is measured.

In a sense, EGP routing update messages are a generalization of GGP routing update messages because they accommodate multiple gateways instead of a single gateway. Thus, the fields of the routing update message following the *IP SOURCE NETWORK* form a sequence of blocks, where each block gives reachability information for one of the gateways on the source network. A block begins with the IP address of a gateway. The networks reachable from that gateway are listed along with their distance. Like GGP, EGP groups networks into sets based on "distance." For each distance, there is a count of networks at that distance followed by the list of network addresses. After the list of all networks at a given distance, the pattern is repeated for all distance values.

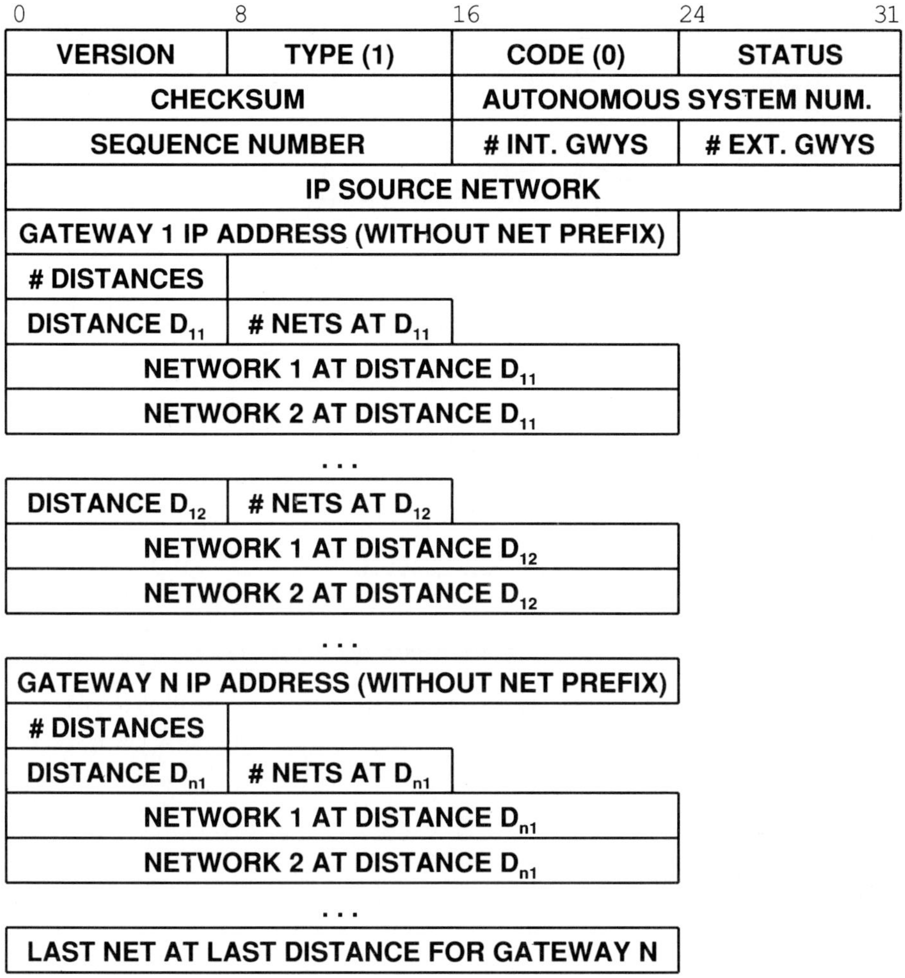

VERSION	TYPE (1)	CODE (0)	STATUS
CHECKSUM		AUTONOMOUS SYSTEM NUM.	
SEQUENCE NUMBER		# INT. GWYS	# EXT. GWYS
IP SOURCE NETWORK			

```
GATEWAY 1 IP ADDRESS (WITHOUT NET PREFIX)
# DISTANCES
DISTANCE D₁₁  | # NETS AT D₁₁
NETWORK 1 AT DISTANCE D₁₁
NETWORK 2 AT DISTANCE D₁₁
```

GATEWAY 1 IP ADDRESS (WITHOUT NET PREFIX)

DISTANCES

$\text{DISTANCE } D_{11}$ | $\text{\# NETS AT } D_{11}$

NETWORK 1 AT DISTANCE D_{11}

NETWORK 2 AT DISTANCE D_{11}

. . .

$\text{DISTANCE } D_{12}$ | $\text{\# NETS AT } D_{12}$

NETWORK 1 AT DISTANCE D_{12}

NETWORK 2 AT DISTANCE D_{12}

. . .

GATEWAY N IP ADDRESS (WITHOUT NET PREFIX)

DISTANCES

$\text{DISTANCE } D_{n1}$ | $\text{\# NETS AT } D_{n1}$

NETWORK 1 AT DISTANCE D_{n1}

NETWORK 2 AT DISTANCE D_{n1}

. . .

LAST NET AT LAST DISTANCE FOR GATEWAY N

Figure 14.10 EGP routing update message format. All routes are given relative to a specified network. The message lists gateways on that network and the distance of destinations through each. Network addresses contain *1*, *2*, or *3* octets.

14.11 Measuring From The Receiver's Perspective

Unlike most protocols that propagate routing information, EGP does not report its own costs for reaching destination networks. Instead, it measures distances from the common source network so all distances are correct from the peer's perspective. Figure 14.11 illustrates the idea.

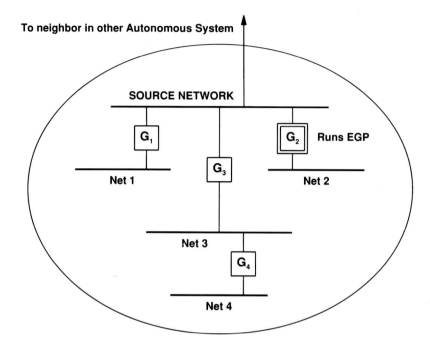

Figure 14.11 Example of an autonomous system. Gateway G_2 runs EGP and
reports distances to all networks measured from the source network, not from its own routing table.

In the example of Figure 14.11, gateway G_2 has been designated to run EGP on
behalf of the autonomous system. It must report reachability to networks *1* through *4*.
It reports network *1* as reachable through gateway G_1, networks *3* and *4* as reachable
through gateway G_3, and network *2* as reachable through G_2. From G_2's perspective,
network *2* lies at distance *0*. However, it reports network *2* at distance *1*, its distance
from the source network.

14.12 The Key Restriction Of EGP

We have already seen that EGP restricts gateways, allowing them to advertise only
those destination networks reachable entirely within the gateway's autonomous system.
However, there is a more fundamental limitation imposed by EGP:

*EGP does not interpret any of the distance metrics that appear in
routing update messages.*

The rules specify that a value of *255* means the network is unreachable, but other values
are only comparable if they refer to gateways in the same autonomous system. In
essence, EGP uses the distance field to specify whether a path exists; the value cannot
be used to compute the shorter of two routes unless those routes are both contained
within a single autonomous system.

We can now see why a gateway in one autonomous system should not advertise
reachability to networks in another autonomous system (i.e., why the third party rule exists). The essential observation is this: when a gateway learns of a network in another
autonomous system, it does not obtain a universally accepted measure of distance.
Therefore, it should not pass that measure on. Advertising reachability with EGP is
equivalent to saying, "My autonomous system provides *the* path to this network."
There is no way for the gateway to say, "My autonomous system provides one possible
path to this network."

Looking at interpretation of distances another way allows us to realize that EGP
cannot be used as a routing algorithm. In particular, even if a gateway learns about two
different routes to the same network, it cannot know which is shorter. Without routing
information, we must be careful to advertise only the route we want traffic to follow.
As a result, there is only one path from the core to any network. We can summarize:

> *Because EGP only propagates reachability information, it restricts the
> topology of any internet using EGP to a tree structure in which a core
> system forms the root; there are no loops among other autonomous
> systems connected to it.*

The key point here is that the current Internet architecture uses a tree-shaped topology,
and it cannot change until EGP changes.

The restriction on EGP that produces a tree structure results partially from the historical evolution of the Internet centered around the ARPANET. Although it may seem
innocuous, the restriction has some surprising consequences:

1. Universal connectivity fails if the core gateway system fails. Of course, it is
    unlikely the entire Internet core will fail simultaneously, but there have been
    interesting examples of minor failures. In particular, on several occasions
    the rapid growth of the Internet resulted in table overflows in core gateways,
    preventing EGP from successfully installing routes to new networks. Those
    network addresses that could not be installed in the core tables were un-
    reachable from many parts of the Internet.

2. EGP can only advertise one path to a given network. That is, at any given
    instant, all traffic routed from one autonomous system to a network in
    another will traverse one path, even if multiple physical connections are

present. Also note that an outside autonomous system will only use one return path even if the source system divides outgoing traffic among two or
more paths. As a result, delay and throughput between a pair of machines
can be asymmetric, making an internet difficult to monitor or debug.

3. EGP does not support load sharing on gateways between arbitrary auto-
    nomous systems. If two autonomous systems have multiple gateways con-
    necting them, one would like to balance the traffic equally between all gate-
    ways. EGP allows autonomous systems to divide the load by network (e.g.,
    to partition themselves into multiple subsets and have multiple gateways ad-
    vertise partitions), but it does not support more general load sharing.

4. As a special case of point 3, EGP is inadequate for optimal routing in an ar-
    chitecture that has multiple backbone networks interconnected at multiple
    points. For example, the NSFNET and DDN backbone interconnection
    described in Chapter 13 cannot use EGP alone to exchange routing informa-
    tion if routes are to be optimal. Instead, managers manually divide the set
    of NSFNET networks and advertise some of them to one exterior gateway
    and others to a different gateway.

5. It is difficult to switch to alternate physical paths if one fails, especially
    when the paths cross two or more autonomous systems. Because EGP does
    not interpret distances, third parties cannot advertise routes and rely on the
    receiver to switch to an alternate route if one fails. Instead, responsibility
    for selecting the least cost route falls to the exterior gateways that advertise
    reachability.

14.13 Technical Problems

EGP has several weaknesses, many of which are trivial technicalities. The
weaknesses must be repaired before EGP can support the rapidly expanding Internet environment. The latest attempt to fix some of these problems has concentrated on the
most pressing: reducing the size of update messages. Recall from Figure 14.10 that update messages contain long lists of networks. For large autonomous systems with many
gateways and networks, the size of a single EGP routing update message can exceed
gateway or network capacity. In the past, not all gateways handled fragmentation and
reassembly, so it was sometimes impossible to transfer routing update messages. A
new version of the protocol is needed that will allow the sender to divide routing updates into multiple messages.

Although many technical problems have been identified, several attempts to produce a new version of EGP have failed. The efforts called *EGP2* and *EGP3* were both
dropped after participants were unable to agree on approaches and details. While exploring possibilities, the working groups discussed EGP replacements and decided that
because so many fundamental changes were needed, simple improvements would be
inadequate. Consequently, EGP remains in use unchanged.

14.14 Decentralization Of The Internet Architecture

Two important architecture questions remain unanswered. The first focuses on centralization: how can an internet architecture be modified to further remove dependence on a (centralized) core gateway system? The second concerns levels of trust: can an internet architecture be expanded to allow closer cooperation (trust) between some autonomous systems than among others?

Removing all dependence on a core system will not be easy. Although TCP/IP architectures continue to evolve, centralized roots are evident in many protocols. As more software is built using existing protocols, inertia increases and change becomes more difficult and expensive. More important, because the connected Internet core system is reliable, supported by a professional staff, and uses automated mechanisms to update routing information, there is little motivation for change. Finally, as the size of an internet grows, so does the volume of routing information that gateways must keep. A mechanism must be found to limit the information needed by each node, or the update traffic will inundate the network.

14.15 Beyond Autonomous Systems

Extending the notions of trust between autonomous systems is complex. The easiest step is to group autonomous systems hierarchically. Imagine, for example, three autonomous systems in three separate academic departments on a large university campus. It is natural to group these three together because they share administrative ties. The motivation for hierarchical grouping comes primarily from the notion of trust. Gateways within a group trust one another with a high level of confidence.

Grouping autonomous systems requires only minor changes to EGP. New versions of EGP must agree to use an artificial scaling factor when reporting hop counts, allowing counts to be increased when passed across the boundary from one group to another. The technique, loosely called *metric transformation*, partitions distance values into three categories. For example, suppose gateways within an autonomous system use distance values less than 128. We could make the rule that when passing distance information across an autonomous system boundary within a single group, the distances must be transformed into the range of 128 to 191. Finally, we could make the rule that when passing distance values across the boundary between two groups, the values must be transformed into the range of 192 to 254†. The effect of such transformations is obvious: for any given destination network, any path that lies entirely within the autonomous system is guaranteed to have lower cost than a path that strays outside the autonomous system. Furthermore, among all paths that stray outside the autonomous system, those that remain within the group have lower cost than those that cross group boundaries. The key advantage of metric transformations is that they use an extant protocol, EGP. Transformations allow an autonomous system manager freedom to choose internal distance metrics, yet make it possible for other systems to compare routing costs.

---

†The term *autonomous confederation* has been used to describe a group of autonomous systems; boundaries of autonomous confederations correspond to transformations beyond 191.

14.16 Summary

The Internet is composed of a set of autonomous systems, where each autonomous system consists of gateways and networks under one administrative authority. Autonomous systems use the Exterior Gateway Protocol to advertise routes to other autonomous systems. Specifically, an autonomous system must advertise reachability of its networks to another system before its networks are reachable from sources within that system. We saw that EGP supports three basic functions: neighbor (peer) acquisition, testing neighbor reachability, and advertising reachability to neighbors.

The connected Internet architecture consists of a central, connected piece (built around the ARPANET and NSFNET backbone), with autonomous systems connected to the center in a tree structure topology. The Internet core gateway system is part of the central piece, while the ''fringe'' consists of local area networks that have only a single connection to the rest of the Internet. Moving from a centralized architecture to a completely distributed one requires substantial changes in protocols like EGP.

FOR FURTHER STUDY

Mills [RFC 904] contains the formal EGP protocol specification. An early version of EGP is given in Rosen [RFC 827], which also discusses the restriction to tree structured topologies. Additional background can be found in the early gateway documents by Seamonson and Rosen [RFC 888], and Mills [RFC 975]. Braden and Postel [RFC 1009] discusses requirements for Internet gateways and outlines some of the problems with EGP (also see the predecessor, in RFC 985). Lougheed and Rekhter [RFC 1105] presents *BGP*, the EGP-like protocol used between NSFNET mid-level networks and the backbone. Finally, Kirton [RFC 911] describes the widely used implementation of EGP that runs under Berkeley 4.3 BSD UNIX.

EXERCISES

14.1 If your site connects to the Internet, find out if any gateways advertise routes to the core gateway system.

14.2 Implementations of EGP use a ''hold down'' mechanism that causes the protocol to delay accepting an *acquisition request* from a neighbor for a fixed time following the receipt of a *cease request* message from that neighbor. Read the protocol specification to find out why.

14.3 For the networks in Figure 14.2, which machine(s) should run EGP? Why?

14.4 The formal specification of EGP includes a finite state machine that explains how EGP operates. Why does a *confirm* message take the EGP finite state machine from the *acquisition* state to the *down* state, instead of from the *acquisition* state to the *up* state?

14.5   What happens if a gateway in an autonomous system sends EGP routing update messages to a gateway in another autonomous system, claiming to have reachability for every possible internet destination?

14.6   Can two autonomous systems establish a routing loop by sending EGP updates messages to one another? Explain.

14.7   Should gateways treat EGP separately from their own routing tables? For example, should a gateway ever advertise reachability if it has not installed a route to that network in its routing table? Why or why not?

14.8   Read RFC 1105 and compare BGP to EGP.

15

Routing: Interior Gateway Protocols (RIP, OSPF, HELLO)

15.1 Introduction

The previous chapter introduced the autonomous system concept and examined the Exterior Gateway Protocol that a gateway uses to advertise networks within its system to other autonomous systems. This chapter completes our overview of internet gateway routing by examining how a gateway in an autonomous system learns about other networks within its autonomous system.

15.2 Static Vs. Dynamic Interior Routes

Two gateways within an autonomous system are said to be *interior* to one another. For example, two Internet core gateways are interior to one another because the core forms a single autonomous system. Two gateways on a university campus are considered interior to one another as long as machines on the campus are collected into a single autonomous system.

How can gateways in an autonomous system learn about networks within the autonomous system? In small, slowly changing internets, managers can establish and modify gateway routes by hand. The administrator keeps a table of networks and updates the table whenever a new network is added to, or deleted from, the autonomous system. For example, consider the small corporate internet shown in Figure 15.1. Routing for such an internet is trivial because only one path exists between any two points. The manager can manually configure routes in all hosts and gateways. If the internet changes (e.g., a new network is added), the manager must reconfigure the routes in all machines.

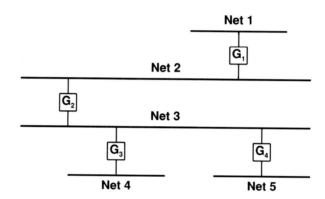

Figure 15.1 An example of a small internet consisting of 5 Ethernets and 4 gateways at a single site. Only one possible route exists between any two hosts in this internet.

The disadvantages of a manual system are obvious; manual systems cannot accommodate rapid growth or rapid change. In large, rapidly changing environments like the Internet, humans simply cannot respond to changes fast enough to handle problems and automated methods must be used. Automated methods can also help improve robustness and response to failure in small internets that have alternate routes. To see how, consider what happens if we add one additional gateway to the internet in Figure 15.1, producing the internet shown in Figure 15.2.

In internet architectures that have multiple physical paths, managers usually choose one to be the primary path. If the gateways along the primary path fail, routes must be changed to send traffic along an alternate path. Changing routes manually is both time consuming and error-prone. Thus, even in small internets, an automated system should be used to change routes quickly and reliably.

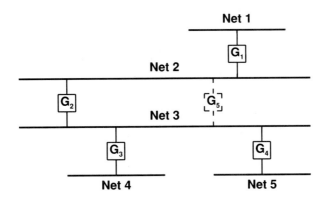

Figure 15.2 The addition of gateway G_5 introduces an alternate path between networks *2* and *3*. Routing software can quickly adapt to failure of one gateway and automatically switch routes to the alternate path.

To automate the task of keeping network reachability information accurate, interior gateways usually communicate with one another, exchanging either network reachability data or network routing information from which reachability can be deduced. Once the reachability information for an entire autonomous system has been assembled, one of the gateways in the system can advertise it to other autonomous systems using EGP.

Unlike exterior gateway communication, for which EGP provides a widely accepted standard, no single protocol has emerged for use within an autonomous system. Part of the reason for diversity comes from varied topologies and technologies used in autonomous systems. Another part of the reason stems from the lack of an early standard that was both functionally adequate and well-defined. As a result, a handful of protocols have become popular; most autonomous systems use one of them exclusively to propagate routing information internally.

Because there is no single standard, we use the term *interior gateway protocol* or *IGP* as a generic description that refers to any algorithm that interior gateways use when they exchange network reachability and routing information. For example, the Butterfly core gateways form a somewhat specialized autonomous system that uses SPREAD as its Interior Gateway Protocol. Some autonomous systems use EGP as their IGP, although this seldom makes sense for small autonomous systems that span local area networks with broadcast capability.

Figure 15.3 illustrates an autonomous system using an IGP to propagate reachability among interior gateways.

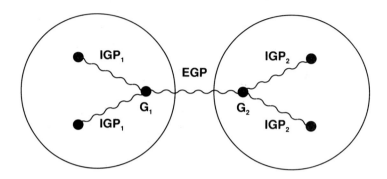

Figure 15.3 Conceptual view of two autonomous systems each using its own IGP internally but using EGP to communicate between an exterior gateway and the other system.

In the figure, *IGP₁* refers to the interior gateway protocol used within autonomous system *1*, and *IGP₂* refers to the protocol used within autonomous system *2*. The figure also illustrates an important idea:

> *A single gateway may use two different routing protocols simultaneously, one for communication outside its autonomous system and another for communication within its autonomous system.*

In particular, gateways that run EGP to advertise reachability usually also need to run an IGP to obtain information from within their autonomous system.

15.3 Routing Information Protocol (RIP)

One of the most widely used IGPs is the *Routing Information Protocol* (RIP), also known by the name of a program that implements it, *routed†*. The *routed* software was originally designed at the University of California at Berkeley to provide consistent routing and reachability information among machines on their local networks. It relies on physical network broadcast to make routing exchanges quickly. It was never intended to be used on large, long haul networks (although it now is).

Based on earlier internetworking research done at Xerox Corporation's Palo Alto Research Center (PARC), *routed* implements a protocol derived from the Xerox *NS Routing Information Protocol* (*RIP*), but generalizes it to cover multiple families of networks.

Despite minor improvements over its predecessors, the popularity of RIP as an IGP does not arise from its technical merits. Instead, it is the result of Berkeley distributing *routed* software along with their popular 4BSD UNIX systems. Thus, many TCP/IP

---

†The name comes from the UNIX convention of attaching ''d'' to the names of daemon processes; it is pronounced ''route-d''.

sites adopted and installed *routed* and started using RIP without even considering its technical merits or limitations. Once installed and running, it became the basis for local routing, and research groups adopted it for larger networks. For example, the Cypress network, described in Chapter 2, uses RIP to propagate network reachability among all its machines.

Perhaps the most startling fact about RIP is that it was built and widely adopted before a formal standard was written. Most implementations were derived from the Berkeley code, with interoperability among them limited by the programmer's understanding of undocumented details and subtleties. As new versions appeared, more problems arose. An RFC standard finally appeared in June 1988.

The underlying RIP protocol is a straightforward implementation of vector-distance routing for local networks. It partitions participants into *active* and *passive* (*silent*) machines. Active gateways advertise their routes to others; passive machines listen and update their routes based on advertisements, but do not advertise. Typically, gateways run RIP in active mode, while hosts use passive mode.

A gateway running RIP in active mode broadcasts a message every 30 seconds. The message contains information taken from the gateway's current routing database. Each message consists of pairs, where each pair contains an IP network address and an integer distance to that network. RIP uses a *hop count metric* to measure the distance to a destination. In the RIP metric, a gateway is defined to be one hop† from directly connected networks, two hops from networks that are reachable through one other gateway, and so on. Thus, the *number of hops* or the *hop count* along a path from a given source to a given destination refers to the number of gateways that a datagram encounters along that path. It should be obvious that using hop counts to calculate shortest paths does not always produce optimal results. For example, a path with hop count *3* that crosses three Ethernets may be substantially faster than a path with hop count *2* that crosses two slow speed serial lines. To compensate for differences in technologies, many RIP implementations use artificially high hop counts when advertising connections to slow networks.

Both active and passive RIP participants listen to all broadcast messages and update their tables according to the vector-distance algorithm described earlier. For example, in the internet of Figure 15.2, gateway G_1 will broadcast a message on network *2* that contains the pair (*1*,*1*), meaning that it can reach network *1* at cost *1*. Gateways G_2 and G_5 will receive the broadcast and install a route to network *1* through G_1 (at cost *2*). Later, gateways G_2 and G_5 will include the pair (*1*,*2*) when they broadcast their RIP messages on network *3*. Eventually, all gateways and hosts will install a route to network *1*.

RIP specifies a few rules to improve performance and reliability. For example, once a gateway learns a route from another gateway, it must keep that route until it learns of a better one. In our example, if gateways G_2 and G_5 both advertise network *1* at cost *2*, gateways G_3 and G_4 will install a route through the one that happens to advertise first. We can summarize:

---

†RIP is somewhat unusual: many other protocols define direct connections to have cost zero.

To prevent routes from oscillating between two or more equal cost paths, RIP specifies that existing routes should be retained until a new route has strictly lower cost.

What happens if the first gateway to advertise a route fails (e.g., if it crashes)? RIP specifies that all listeners must timeout routes they learn via RIP. When a gateway installs a route in its table, it starts a timer for that route. The timer must be restarted whenever the gateway receives another RIP message advertising the route. The route becomes invalid if 180 seconds pass without the route being advertised again.

RIP must handle three kinds of errors caused by the underlying algorithm. First, because the algorithm does not explicitly detect routing loops, RIP must either assume participants can be trusted or take precautions to prevent such loops. Second, to prevent instabilities RIP must use a low value for the maximum possible distance (RIP uses *16*). Thus, managers must use an alternative protocol for internets in which legitimate hop counts approach *16*. (Indeed, the small limit on hop counts makes RIP unsuitable for the largest corporate internets.) Third, the vector-distance algorithm used by RIP creates a *slow convergence* or *count to infinity* problem in which inconsistencies arise, because routing update messages propagate slowly across the network. Choosing a small infinity (*16*) helps limit slow convergence, but does not eliminate it.

Routing table inconsistency is not unique to RIP. It is a fundamental problem that occurs with any vector-distance protocol in which update messages carry only pairs of destination network and distance to that network. To understand the problem consider the set of gateways shown in Figure 15.4. The figure depicts routes to network *1* for the internet shown in Figure 15.2.

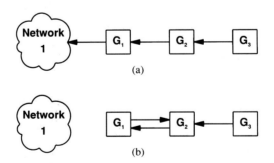

Figure 15.4 The slow convergence problem. In (a) three gateways each have a route to network *1*. In (b) the connection to network *1* has vanished, but G_2 causes a loop by advertising it.

As the figure shows, gateway G_1 has a direct connection to network *1*, so it has a route in its table with distance *1*; it includes the route in its periodic broadcasts. Gateway G_2 has learned the route from G_1, installed the route in its routing table, and advertises the route at distance *2*. Finally, G_3 has learned the route from G_2 and advertises it at distance *3*.

Now suppose that G_1's connection to network *1* fails. G_1 will update its routing table immediately to make the distance *16* (infinity). In the next broadcast, G_1 will report the higher cost route. However, unless the protocol includes extra mechanisms to prevent it, some other gateway could broadcast its routes before G_1. In particular, suppose G_2 happens to advertise routes just after G_1's connection fails. If so, G_1 will receive G_2's message and follow the usual vector-distance algorithm: it notices that G_2 has advertised a route to network *1* at lower cost, calculates that it now takes *3* hops to reach network *1* (*2* for G_2 to reach network *1* plus *1* to reach G_2), *and installs a new route through G_2*. Figure 15.4b depicts the result. At this point, if either G_1 or G_2 receives a datagram destined for network *1*, they will route the datagram back and forth until its time-to-live counter expires.

Subsequent RIP broadcasts by the two gateways do not solve the problem quickly. In the next round of routing exchanges, G_1 broadcasts its routing table entries. When G_2 learns that G_1's route to network *1* has length *3*, it calculates a new length for its route, making it *4*. In the third round, G_1 receives a report of the increase from G_2 and increases the distance in its table to *5*. They continue counting to RIP infinity.

15.3.1 Solving The Slow Convergence Problem

For the example in Figure 15.4, it is possible to solve the slow convergence problem by using a technique known as *split horizon update*. When using split horizons, a gateway records the interface over which it received a particular route and does not propagate its information about that route back over the same interface. In the example, gateway G_2 would not advertise its length *2* route back to gateway G_1, so when G_1 loses connectivity to network *1*, it would stop advertising a route. After a few rounds of routing updates, all machines would agree that the network is unreachable. However, splitting the horizon does not cover all topologies as one of the exercises suggests.

Another way to think of the slow convergence problem is in terms of information flow. If a gateway advertises a short route to some network, all receiving gateways respond quickly to install that route. If a gateway stops advertising a route, the protocol must depend on a timeout mechanism before it considers the route unreachable. Once the timeout occurs, the gateway finds an alternative route and starts propagating that information. Unfortunately, a gateway cannot know if the alternate route depended on the route that just disappeared. Thus, negative information does not always propagate quickly. A short epigram captures the idea and explains the phenomenon:

Good news travels quickly; bad news travels slowly.

Another technique used to solve the slow convergence problem employs *hold down*. Hold down forces a participating gateway to ignore information about a network for a fixed period of time following receipt of a message that claims the network is unreachable. Typically, the hold down period is set to 60 seconds. The idea is to wait long enough to ensure that all machines receive the bad news and not to mistakenly accept a message that is out of date. It should be noted that all machines participating in a RIP exchange need to use identical notions of hold down, or routing loops can occur. The disadvantage of a hold down technique is that if routing loops occur, they will be preserved for the duration of the hold down period. More important, the hold down technique preserves all incorrect routes during the hold down period, even when alternatives exist.

A final technique for solving the slow convergence problem is called *poison reverse*. Once a connection disappears, the gateway advertising the connection retains the entry for several update periods, and includes an infinite cost in its broadcasts. To make poison reverse most effective, it must be combined with *triggered updates*. Triggered updates force a gateway to send an immediate broadcast when receiving bad news, instead of waiting for the next periodic broadcast. By sending an update immediately, a gateway minimizes the time it is vulnerable to believing good news.

Unfortunately, while triggered updates, poison reverse, hold down, and split horizon techniques all solve some problems, they introduce others. For example, consider what happens with triggered updates when many gateways share a common network. A single broadcast may change all their routing tables, triggering a new round of broadcasts. If the second round of broadcasts changes tables, it will trigger even more broadcasts. A broadcast avalanche can result.

The use of broadcast, potential for routing loops, and use of hold down to prevent slow convergence can make RIP extremely inefficient in a wide area network. Broadcasting always takes substantial bandwidth. Even if no avalanche problems occur, having all machines broadcast periodically means that the traffic increases as the number of gateways increases. The potential for routing loops can also be deadly when line capacity is limited. Once lines become saturated by looping packets, it may be difficult or impossible for gateways to exchange the routing messages needed to break these loops. Also, in a wide area network, hold down periods are so long that the timers used by higher level protocols can expire and lead to broken connections. Despite these well known problems, many groups continue to use RIP as an IGP in wide area networks.

15.3.2 RIP Message Format

RIP messages can be broadly classified into two types: routing information messages and messages used to request information. Both use the same format which consists of a fixed header followed by an optional list of network and distance pairs. Figure 15.5 shows the message format:

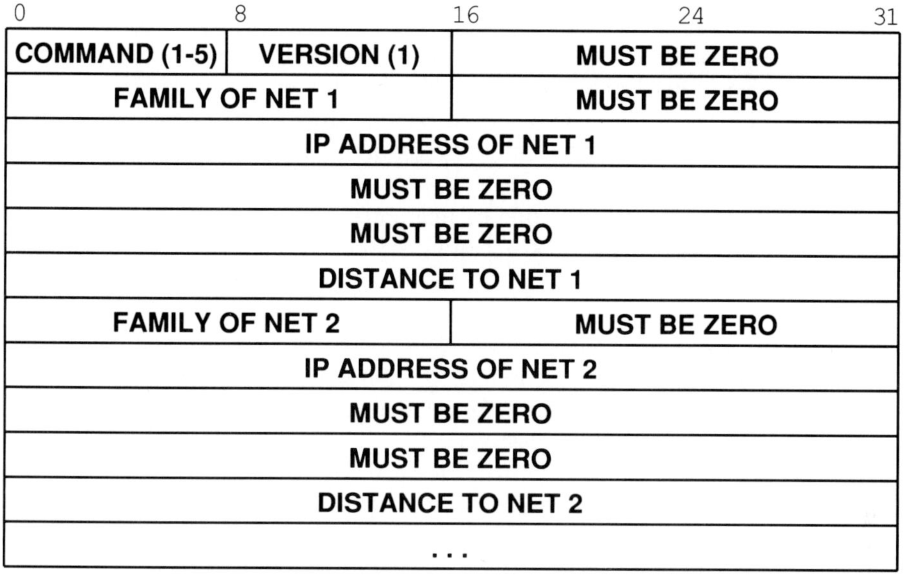

COMMAND (1-5)	VERSION (1)	MUST BE ZERO	
FAMILY OF NET 1		MUST BE ZERO	
IP ADDRESS OF NET 1			
MUST BE ZERO			
MUST BE ZERO			
DISTANCE TO NET 1			
FAMILY OF NET 2		MUST BE ZERO	
IP ADDRESS OF NET 2			
MUST BE ZERO			
MUST BE ZERO			
DISTANCE TO NET 2			
. . .			

Figure 15.5 The format of a RIP message. After the 32-bit header, the message contains a sequence of pairs, where each pair consists of a network IP address and an integer distance to that network.

In the figure, field *COMMAND* specifies an operation according to the following table:

Command	Meaning
1	Request for partial or full routing information
2	Response containing network-distance pairs from sender's routing table
3	Turn on trace mode (obsolete)
4	Turn off trace mode (obsolete)
5	Reserved for Sun Microsystems internal use

A gateway or host can ask another gateway for routing information by sending a *request* command. Gateways reply to requests using the *response* command. In most cases, however, gateways broadcast unsolicited response messages periodically.

Field *VERSION* contains the protocol version number (currently *1*), and is used by the receiver to verify it will interpret the message correctly.

15.3.3 RIP Addressing conventions

The generality of RIP is also evident in the way it transmits network addresses. The address format is not limited to use by TCP/IP; it can be used with multiple network protocol suites. As Figure 15.5 shows, each network address reported by RIP can have an address of up to 14 octets. Of course, IP addresses need only 4, so the remaining octets are zero. The field labeled *FAMILY OF NET i* identifies the protocol family under which the network address should be interpreted. RIP uses values assigned to address families under the 4BSD UNIX operating system (IP addresses are assigned value *2*).

In addition to normal IP addresses, RIP uses the convention that address *0.0.0.0* denotes a *default route*. RIP attaches a distance metric to every route it advertises, including default routes. Thus, it is possible to arrange for two gateways to advertise a default route (i.e., a route to the rest of the internet) at different metrics, making one of them a primary path and the other a backup.

The final field of each entry in a RIP message, *DISTANCE TO NET i*, contains an integer count of the distance to the specified network. Distances are measured in gateway hops, but values are limited to the range *1* through *15*, with distance *16* used to signify infinity (i.e., no route exists).

15.3.4 Transmitting RIP Messages

RIP messages do not contain an explicit length field. Instead, RIP assumes that the underlying delivery mechanism will tell the receiver the length of an incoming message. In particular, when used with TCP/IP, RIP messages rely on UDP to tell the receiver the message length. RIP operates on UDP port *520*. Although a RIP request can originate at other UDP ports, the destination UDP port for requests is always *520*, as is the source port from which RIP broadcast messages originate.

Using RIP as an interior gateway protocol limits routing to a metric based on hop counts. Often, hop counts provide only a crude measure of network response or capacity that does not produce optimal routes. Furthermore, computing routes on the basis of minimum hop counts has the severe disadvantage that it makes routing relatively static because routes cannot respond to changes in network load.

15.4 The Hello Protocol

The HELLO protocol provides an example of an IGP that uses a routing metric based on network delay instead of hop count. HELLO is significant in the history of the Internet because it was the IGP used among the original NSFNET backbone "fuzzball" gateways. It is significant to us because it provides an example of a vector-distance algorithm that does not use hop counts.

HELLO provides two functions: it synchronizes the clocks among a set of machines, and it allows each machine to compute shortest delay paths to destinations. Thus, HELLO messages carry timestamp information as well as routing information. The basic idea behind HELLO is simple: each machine participating in the HELLO exchange maintains a table of its best estimate of the clock in neighboring machines. Before transmitting a packet, a machine adds its timestamp by copying the current clock value into the packet. When a packet arrives, the receiver computes the current delay on the link. To do so, the receiver subtracts the timestamp on the incoming packet from its estimate for the current clock in the neighbor. Periodically, machines poll their neighbors to reestablish estimates for clocks.

HELLO messages also allow participating machines to compute new routes. The algorithm works much like RIP, but uses delays instead of hop count. Each machine periodically sends its neighbor a table of estimated delays for all other machines. Suppose machine A sends machine B a routing table that specifies destinations and delays. B examines each entry in the table. If B's current delay to reach a given destination, D, is greater than the delay from A to D plus the delay from B to A, B changes its route and sends traffic to D via A. That is, B routes traffic to A as long as taking that path shortens the delay.

As in any routing algorithm, HELLO cannot change routes too rapidly, or it would become unstable. Instabilities in routing algorithms produce a two-stage oscillation effect in which traffic switches back and forth between alternate paths. In the first stage, the machines find a lightly loaded path and abruptly switch their traffic onto it, only to find that it becomes completely overloaded. In the second stage, the machines switch traffic away from the overloaded path, only to find that it becomes the least loaded path, and the cycle continues. Such oscillations do occur. To avoid them, implementations of HELLO choose to change routes only when the difference in delays is large.

Figure 15.6 shows the HELLO message format. The protocol is more complex than the message format shows because it distinguishes local network connections from those multiple hops away, times out stale entries in its routing tables, and uses local identifiers for hosts instead of full IP addresses.

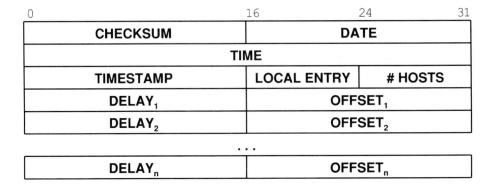

Figure 15.6 The format of HELLO messages. Each message carries an entry
for the date and time as well as a timestamp that the protocol
uses to estimate network delays.

Field *CHECKSUM* contains a checksum over the message, field *DATE* contains
the local date of the sender, and field *TIME* contains the local time according to the
sender's clock. The *TIMESTAMP* field is used in round trip computation.

The field labeled *# HOSTS* specifies how many entries follow in the list of hosts
and the field labeled *LOCAL ENTRY* points into the list to mark the block of entries
used for the local network. Each entry contains two fields, *DELAY* and *OFFSET*, that
give the delay to reach a host, and the sender's current estimate of the offset between
the host's clock and the sender's clock.

15.5 Combining RIP, Hello, And EGP

We have already observed that a single gateway may use both an IGP to gather
routing information within its autonomous system and EGP to advertise routes to other
autonomous systems. In principle, it should be easy to construct a single piece of
software that combines the two protocols, making it possible to gather routes and advertise them without human intervention. In practice, technical and political obstacles
make doing so complex.

Technically, IGP protocols, like RIP and Hello, are routing protocols. A gateway
uses such protocols to update its routing table based on information it acquires from
other gateways inside its autonomous system. Unlike interior gateway protocols, EGP
works in addition to a gateway's usual routing table. A gateway uses EGP to communicate reachability information to other autonomous systems independent of the gateway's
own routing table. Thus, *routed*, the UNIX program that implements RIP, advertises information from the local routing table and changes the local routing table when it receives updates. It trusts those machines that use RIP to pass correct data. In contrast

the program that implements EGP does not advertise routes from the local routing table; it keeps a separate database of network reachability.

A gateway using EGP to advertise reachability must take care to propagate only those routes it is authorized to advertise, or it may affect other parts of the internet. For example, if a gateway in an autonomous system happens to propagate a distance *0* route to Purdue University when it has no such route, RIP will install the route in other machines and start passing Purdue traffic to the gateway that made the error. As a result, it may be impossible for machines in that autonomous system to reach Purdue. If EGP propagates such errors outside the autonomous system, it may become impossible to reach Purdue from some parts of the internet.

Written at Cornell University, the UNIX program *gated*† combines RIP, Hello, and EGP along with a set of rules that constrains how it advertises routes to exterior gateways. *Gated* accepts RIP or Hello messages and modifies the local machine routing tables just like the *routed* program, and it advertises routes from within its autonomous system using EGP. The rules allow a system administrator to specify exactly which networks *gated* may and may not advertise and how to report distances to those networks. Thus, although *gated* is not an IGP, it plays an important role in gateway routing because it demonstrates that it is feasible to build an automated mechanism linking an IGP with EGP without sacrificing protection.

Gated performs another useful task by implementing metric transformations. Recall from Chapter 14 that extensions to EGP allow autonomous systems to make intelligent routing decisions as long as all gateways using EGP agree to a loose interpretation of distance metrics. In particular, the gateways within an autonomous system must agree to use distance values below a fixed threshold, say 128. Whenever an exterior gateway advertises reachability outside its autonomous system but inside its autonomous confederation, it must transform the distance metrics into a higher range, say 128-191. The transformation tends to keep traffic within an autonomous system by artificially raising the cost to route outside. Finally, gateways transform distances into an even higher range, say 192-254, when passing them across an autonomous confederation boundary to encourage traffic to remain within the autonomous confederation. Because *gated* provides the interface between its autonomous system and other autonomous systems, it can implement such transformations easily.

15.6 The Open SPF Protocol (OSPF)

We said that the SPF route propagation algorithm scales better than vector-distance algorithms. Recently, a working group of the Internet Engineering Task Force has proposed a new interior gateway protocol that uses the SPF algorithm. Called the *Open SPF protocol (OSPF)*, the new protocol tackles several ambitious goals.

• The specification is available in the published literature, making it an open standard that anyone can implement without paying license fees. The specification authors hope many vendors will support OSPF and make it a popular standard that replaces proprietary protocols.

---

† pronounced "gate d" from "gate daemon"

• OSPF includes *type of service routing*. Managers can install multiple routes to a given destination, one for each type of service (e.g., low delay or high throughput). When routing a datagram, a gateway running OSPF uses both the destination address and type of service fields in an IP header to choose a route. OSPF is among the first TCP/IP protocols to use type of service routing.

• OSPF provides *load balancing*. If a manager specifies multiple routes to a given destination at the same cost, OSPF distributes traffic over all routes equally. Again, OSPF is among the first open IGPs to offer load balancing; protocols like RIP compute a single route to each destination.

• To permit growth and make the networks at a site easier to manage, OSPF allows a site to partition its networks and gateways into subsets called *areas*. Each area is self-contained; knowledge of an area's topology remains hidden from other areas. Thus, multiple groups within a given site can cooperate in the use of OSPF for routing even though each group retains the ability to change its internal network topology independently.

• The OSPF protocol specifies that all exchanges between gateways are *authenticated*. OSPF allows a variety of authentication schemes, and even allows one area to choose a different scheme than another area. The idea behind authentication is to guarantee that only trusted gateways propagate routing information. To understand why this might be a problem, consider what can happen when using RIP, which has no authentication. If a malicious person uses a personal computer to propagate RIP messages advertising low-cost routes, other gateways and hosts running RIP will change their routes and start sending datagrams to the personal computer.

• OSPF supports host-specific routes as well as network-specific routes. (It also supports subnet routes, a topic we will discuss in Chapter 16.)

• To accommodate multi-access networks like Ethernet, OSPF extends the SPF algorithm described above. We described the algorithm using a point-to-point graph and said that each gateway running SPF would periodically broadcast link status messages about each reachable neighbor. If K gateways attach to an Ethernet, they will broadcast K^2 reachability messages. OSPF minimizes broadcasts by allowing a more complex graph topology in which every multi-access network has a *designated gateway* (*designated router*) that sends link-status messages on behalf of all gateways on the net. It also uses hardware broadcast capabilities, where they exist, to deliver link status messages.

• To permit maximum flexibility, OSPF allows managers to describe a virtual network topology that abstracts away from details of physical connections. For example, a manager can configure a virtual link between two gateways in the routing graph even if the physical connection between the two gateways requires communication across a transit network.

• OSPF allows gateways to exchange routing information learned from other (external) sites. Basically, one or more gateways with connections to other sites learn information about those sites and include it when sending update messages. The message format distinguishes between information acquired from external sources and information acquired from gateways interior to the site, so there is no ambiguity about the source or reliability of routes.

15.6.1 OSPF Message Format

Each OSPF message begins with a fixed, 24-octet header as Figure 15.7 shows:

0	8	16	24	31
VERSION (1)	TYPE	MESSAGE LENGTH		
SOURCE GATEWAY IP ADDRESS				
AREA ID				
CHECKSUM		AUTHENTICATION TYPE		
AUTHENTICATION (octets 0-3)				
AUTHENTICATION (octets 4-7)				

Figure 15.7 The fixed 24-octet OSPF message header.

Field *VERSION* specifies the version of the protocol. Field *TYPE* identifies the message type as one of:

Type	Meaning
1	Hello (used to test reachability)
2	Database description (topology)
3	Link status request
4	Link status update
5	Link status acknowledgement

The field labeled *SOURCE GATEWAY IP ADDRESS* gives the address of the sender, and the field labeled *AREA ID* gives the 32-bit identification number for the area.

Because each message can include authentication, field *AUTHENTICATION TYPE* specifies which authentication scheme is used (currently, *0* means no authentication and *1* means a simple password is used).

15.6.2 OSPF Hello Message Format

OSPF sends *hello* messages on each link periodically to establish and test neighbor reachability. Figure 15.8 shows the format.

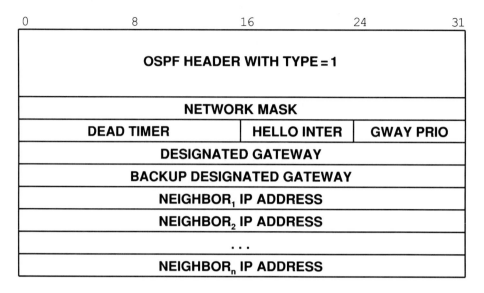

Figure 15.8 OSPF ''hello'' message format. A pair of neighbor gateways exchange these messages periodically to test reachability.

Field *NETWORK MASK* contains a network mask for the network over which the message has been sent (see Chapter 16 for details about masks). Field *DEAD TIMER* gives a time in seconds after which a nonresponding neighbor is considered dead. Field *HELLO INTER* is the normal period, in seconds, between hello messages. Field *GWAY PRIO* is the integer priority of this gateway used in selecting a backup designated gateway. The fields labeled *DESIGNATED GATEWAY* and *BACKUP DESIGNATED GATEWAY* contain IP addresses that give the sender's view of the designated gateway and backup designated gateway for the network over which the message is sent. Finally, fields labeled *NEIGHBOR$_i$ IP ADDRESS* give the IP addresses of all neighbors from which the sender has recently received hello messages.

15.6.3 OSPF Database Description Message Format

Gateways exchange OSPF database description messages to initialize their network topology database. In the exchange, one gateway serves as a master, while the other is a slave. The slave acknowledges each database description message with a response. Figure 15.9 shows the format.

Because the topology database can be large, it may be broken into several messages using the *I* and *M* bits. Bit *I* is set to *1* in the initial message; bit *M* is set to *1* if additional messages follow. Bit *S* determines if the message was sent by a master (*1*) or a slave (*0*). Field *DATABASE SEQUENCE NUMBER* numbers messages sequentially so the receiver can tell if one is missing. The initial message contains a random integer *R*; subsequent messages contain sequential integers starting at *R*.

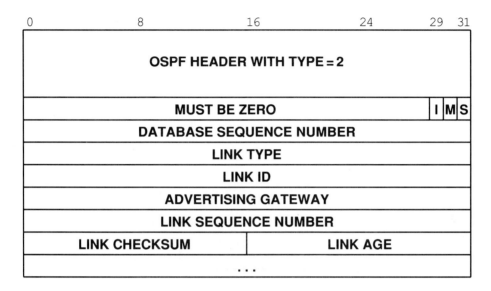

Figure 15.9 OSPF Database Description message format. The fields starting at *LINK TYPE* are repeated for each link being specified.

The fields from *LINK TYPE* through *LINK AGE* describe one link in the network topology; they are repeated for each link. The *LINK TYPE* describes a link according to the following table.

Link Type	Meaning
1	Gateway link
2	Network link
3	Summary link (IP network)
4	Summary link (link to border gateway)
5	External link (link to another site)

Field *LINK ID* gives an identification for the link (which can be the IP address of a gateway or a network, depending on the link type).

Field *ADVERTISING GATEWAY* specifies the address of the gateway advertising this link, and *LINK SEQUENCE NUMBER* contains an integer generated by that gateway to insure that messages are not missed or received out of order. Field *LINK*

CHECKSUM provides further insurance that the link information has not been corrupt-ed. Finally, field *LINK AGE* also helps order messages – it gives the time in seconds since the link was established.

15.6.4 OSPF Link Status Request Message Format

After exchanging database description messages with a neighbor, a gateway may discover that parts of its database are out of date. To request that the neighbor supply updated information, the gateway sends a request message. The message lists specific links as shown in Figure 15.10. The neighbor responds with the most current informa-tion it has about those links. The three fields shown are repeated for each link about which status is requested. More than one request message may be needed if the list of requests is long.

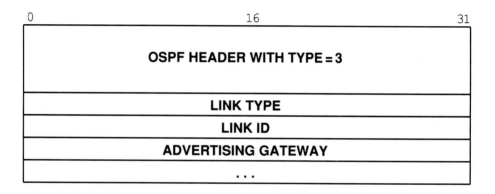

Figure 15.10 OSPF Link Status request message format. A gateway sends this message to a neighbor to request current information about a specific set of links.

15.6.5 OSPF Link Status Update Message Format

Gateways broadcast the status of links with an update message. Each update con-sists of a list of advertisements, as Figure 15.11 shows.

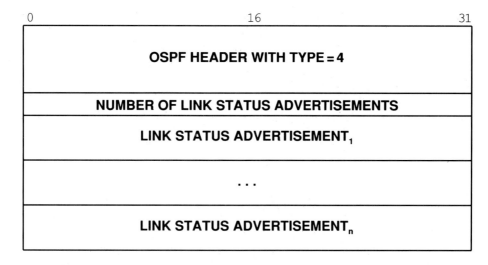

Figure 15.11 OSPF Link Status update message format. A gateway sends such a message to broadcast information about its directly connected links to all other gateways.

Each link status advertisement has a header format as shown in Figure 15.12. The values used in each field are the same as in the database description message.

0		16		31
LINK AGE			LINK TYPE	
LINK ID				
ADVERTISING GATEWAY				
LINK SEQUENCE NUMBER				
LINK CHECKSUM			LENGTH	

Figure 15.12 The format of the header used for all link status advertisements.

Following the link status header comes one of four possible formats to describe the links from a gateway to a given area, the links from a gateway to a specific network, the links from a gateway to the physical networks that comprise a single IP network (see Chapter 16), or the links from a gateway to networks at other sites. In all cases, the *LINK TYPE* field in the link status header specifies which of the formats has been used. Thus, a gateway that receives a link status update message knows exactly which of the described destinations lie inside the site and which are external.

15.7 Routing With Partial Information

We began our discussion of internet gateway architecture and routing by discussing the concept of partial information. Hosts can route with only partial information because they rely on gateways. It should now be clear that not all gateways have complete information. Most autonomous systems have a single gateway that forms a bridge, connecting the autonomous system to other autonomous systems. If the site connects to the Internet, at least one gateway must have a connection that leads from the site to a national backbone. Gateways within the autonomous system know about destinations within that autonomous system, but they route all other traffic to the bridge.

How to do routing with partial information becomes obvious if we examine a gateway's routing tables. Gateways in the core system have a complete set of routes to all possible destinations; they do not use default routing. In fact, if a destination network address does not appear in the core tables, only two possibilities exist: either the address is not a valid destination IP address, or the address is valid but currently unreachable (e.g., because the only gateways leading to that address have failed). Noncore gateways do not usually have a complete set of routes; they rely on a default route to handle network addresses they do not understand.

Using default routes for most noncore gateways has two consequences. First, it means that local routing errors can go undetected. For example, if a machine in an autonomous system incorrectly routes a packet to a core gateway instead of a local gateway, the core will route it back to the autonomous system (perhaps sending an ICMP redirect message to the original source). Thus, connectivity may appear to be preserved even if routing is incorrect. The problem may not seem severe for small autonomous systems that have high speed interconnections, but in a wide area network with relatively low speed lines, incorrect routes can be disastrous. Second, on the positive side, having default routes means that the IGP routing update messages will be much smaller than the routing updates the core system uses.

15.8 Summary

Managers must choose how to pass routing information among the local gateways within an autonomous system. Manual maintenance of routing information suffices only for small, slowly changing internets that have minimal interconnection; most require automated procedures that discover and update routes automatically. Two gateways under the control of a single manager run Interior Gateway Protocols, IGPs, to exchange routing information.

Usually an IGP implements either the vector-distance or SPF algorithm. We examined three specific IGPs: RIP, HELLO, and OSPF. RIP, a vector-distance protocol implemented by the UNIX program *routed*, is the most popular. It uses split horizon, hold-down, and poison reverse techniques to help eliminate routing loops and the problem of counting to infinity. Hello is interesting because it illustrates a vector-distance protocol that uses delay instead of a hop count as a distance metric. Finally, OSPF is a proposed new protocol that implements the link-status algorithm.

Also, we saw that the *gated* program provides an interface between an interior gateway protocol like RIP and the Exterior Gateway Protocol, EGP, automating the process of gathering routes from within an autonomous system and advertising them to another autonomous system.

FOR FURTHER STUDY

Hedrick [RFC 1058] discusses algorithms for exchanging routing information in general and contains the standard specification for RIP. The HELLO protocol is documented in Mills [RFC 891]. Mills and Braun [1987] considers the problems of converting between delay and hop-count metrics. Moy [RFC 1131] contains the lengthy specification of OSPF as well as a discussion of the motivation behind it. Fedor [June 1988] describes *gated*.

EXERCISES

15.1   What possible network families does RIP support? Hint: read the networking section of the 4.3 BSD UNIX Programmer's Manual.

15.2   Consider a large autonomous system using an interior gateway protocol like HELLO that bases routes on delay. What difficulty does this autonomous system have if a subgroup decides to use RIP on its gateways?

15.3   An autonomous system can be as small as a single local area network or as large as multiple long haul networks. Why does the variation in size make it difficult to find a standard IGP?

15.4   Characterize the circumstances under which the split horizon technique will prevent slow convergence.

15.5   Consider an internet composed of many local area networks running RIP as an IGP. Find an example that shows how a routing loop can result even if the code uses ''hold down'' after receiving information that a network is unreachable.

15.6   Should a host ever run RIP in active mode?

15.7   Under what circumstances will a hop count metric produce better routes than a metric that uses delay?

15.8   Can you imagine a situation in which an autonomous system chooses *not* to advertise all its networks? Hint: think of a university.

15.9   In broad terms, we could say that RIP distributes its own routing table, while EGP distributes a table of known networks and gateways used to reach them (i.e., a gateway can send an EGP advertisement for a network without installing a route to that network in its own routing table). What are the advantages of each approach?

15.10   Consider a function used to convert between delay and hop-count metrics. Can you find properties of such functions that are sufficient to prevent routing loops. Are your properties necessary as well? (Hint: look at the paper by Mills and Braun.)

15.11   Are there circumstances under which an SPF protocol can form routing loops? Hint: think of best-effort delivery.

15.12   Build an application program that sends a request to a gateway running RIP and displays the routes the gateway uses.

15.13   Read the OSPF specification carefully. How could a manager use the virtual link facility?

15.14   OSPF allows managers to assign many of their own identifiers, possibly leading to duplication of values at multiple sites. Which identifier(s) may need to change if two sites running OSPF decide to merge?

15.15   Compare the version of OSPF available under 4BSD UNIX to the version of RIP for the same system. What are the differences in source code size? Object code size? Data storage size? What can you conclude?

15.16   Can you use ICMP redirect messages to pass routing information among *interior* gateways? Why or why not?

16

Transparent Gateways And Subnet Addressing

16.1 Introduction

Chapter 4 discussed addressing in an internet and presented the three primary forms of IP addresses. Chapters 12 through 15 showed how gateways acquire reachability and routing information by exchanging addresses. This chapter examines three extensions of the original IP address scheme that allow a site to use a single IP network address for multiple physical networks. It considers the motivation for the address extensions, as well as the details of the subnet scheme that is now part of the TCP/IP standard.

16.2 Review Of Relevant Facts

Chapter 4 discussed addressing in internetworks and presented the fundamentals of the current IP address scheme. We said that the 32-bit addresses are carefully assigned to make the IP addresses of all hosts on a given physical network share a common prefix. In the original IP address scheme, designers thought of the common prefix as defining the network portion of an internet address and the remainder as a host portion. The consequence of importance to us is:

In the original IP addressing scheme, each physical network is assigned a unique network address; hosts on the network have the network address embedded in their individual addresses.

The chief advantage of dividing an IP address into two parts is that it reduces the size of routing tables required in gateways. Instead of keeping one routing entry per destination host, a gateway can keep one entry per network and examine only the network portion of a destination address when making routing decisions.

Recall that TCP/IP accommodates widely diverse network sizes by having three classes of primary addresses. Networks assigned class *A* addresses partition the 32 bits into an 8-bit network portion and a 24-bit host portion. Class *B* addresses partition the 32 bits into 16-bit network and host portions, while class *C* partitions the address into a 24-bit network portion and an 8-bit host portion.

Also recall the internet routing architecture described in Chapters 13, 14, and 15. TCP/IP internets are composed of individual autonomous systems in which each autonomous system is free to choose its own internal routing scheme. In particular, the connected Internet can be thought of as a central core system with a set of autonomous systems attached to it. For routing purposes, topology is restricted to a tree structure. As we consider extensions to the basic address and routing structures in this chapter, it will be important to remember that individual sites have the freedom to modify their addresses and routes as long as the modifications remain invisible to other sites.

16.3 Minimizing Network Numbers

The IP addressing scheme seems to handle all possibilities, but it has a minor weakness. How did the weakness arise? What did the designers fail to envision? The answer is simple: growth. Because they worked in a world of expensive mainframe computers, the designers envisioned an internet with tens of networks and hundreds of hosts. They did not foresee tens of thousands of small networks of personal computers that would suddenly appear a decade later.

Growth has been most apparent in the connected Internet. A large number of trivial networks stresses the entire Internet design because it means (1) immense administrative overhead is required merely to manage network addresses, and (2) the routing tables in gateways are extremely large. The second problem is important because it means that when gateways use vector-distance protocols like GGP or reachability protocols like EGP to exchange information from their routing tables, the load on the network is high, as is the computational effort required in the gateway. So the problem becomes how to minimize the number of assigned network addresses without destroying the original addressing scheme.

To minimize network addresses, the same IP network prefix must be shared by multiple physical networks. Of course, the routing procedures must be modified, and all machines that connect to those networks must understand the conventions used.

The idea of sharing one network address among multiple physical networks is not new and has taken several forms. We will examine three: transparent gateways, proxy ARP, and standard IP subnets.

16.4 Transparent Gateways

The *transparent gateway* scheme is based on the observation that networks which have class *A* IP addresses can be extended through a simple trick illustrated in Figure 16.1.

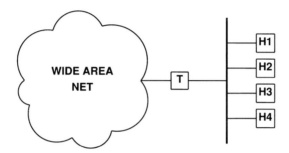

Figure 16.1 Transparent gateway *T* extending a wide area network to multiple hosts at a site. Each host appears to have an IP address on the WAN.

The trick consists of arranging for a wide area network to multiplex several host connections through a single host port. As Figure 16.1 shows, a special purpose gateway, *T*, connects one host port from the wide area net to a local area network. *T* is called a *transparent gateway* because other hosts and gateways on the WAN do not know it exists.

The local area network does not have its own IP prefix; hosts attached to it are assigned addresses as if they connected directly to the WAN. The transparent gateway demultiplexes datagrams that arrive from the WAN by sending them to the appropriate host either by using a table of addresses or by decoding some part of the IP address. The transparent gateway also accepts datagrams from hosts on the local area network and routes them across the WAN toward their destination.

To make demultiplexing efficient, transparent gateways often divide the IP address into multiple parts and encode information in unused parts. For example, assume the WAN is the ARPANET which has class *A* network address *10.0.0.0*. Each packet switch node (PSN) on the ARPANET is assigned a unique integer address. Internally, the ARPANET treats any 4-octet IP address of the form *10.p.u.i* as four separate octets that specify the network (*10*), a specific port on the destination PSN (*p*), and a destination PSN (i). Octet u is uninterpreted. Thus, ARPANET addresses $10.2.5.37$ and $10.2.9.37$ both refer to host 2 on PSN 37. A transparent gateway connected to PSN 37 on port 2 can use octet u to decide which real host should receive the datagram. The ARPANET itself need not be aware of the multiple hosts that lie beyond the PSN.

Transparent gateways have advantages and disadvantages when compared to conventional gateways. The chief advantage is that they require fewer network addresses. Another is that they can support load balancing. That is, if two transparent gateways connect to the same local area network, traffic to hosts on that network can be split between them. By comparison, conventional gateways can only advertise one route to a given network.

One disadvantage of transparent gateways is that they only work with networks that have a large address space from which to choose host addresses. Thus, they work best with class A networks, and they do not work well with class C networks. Another disadvantage is that because they are not conventional gateways, transparent gateways do not provide all the same services as standard gateways. In particular, transparent gateways may not participate fully in ICMP or network management protocols. Therefore, they do not return ICMP echo requests (i.e., one cannot easily "ping" a transparent gateway to determine if it is operating).

16.5 Proxy ARP

The terms *proxy ARP*, *promiscuous ARP*, and *the ARP hack* refer to a second technique used to map a single IP network prefix onto multiple physical addresses. The technique, which only applies to networks that use ARP to bind internet addresses to physical addresses, can best be explained with an example. Figure 16.2 illustrates the situation.

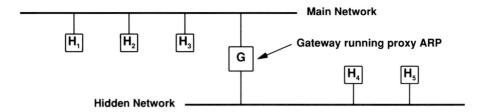

Figure 16.2 Proxy ARP technique (the ARP hack) allows one network address to be shared between two physical nets. Gateway G answers ARP requests on each network for hosts on the other network, giving its hardware address and then routing datagrams correctly when they arrive. In essence, G lies about IP-to-physical address bindings.

In the figure, two networks share a single IP network address. Imagine that the network labeled *main network* was the original network, and that the second, labeled *hidden network*, was added later. The gateway connecting the two networks, G, knows which hosts lie on which physical network and uses ARP to maintain the illusion that only one network exists. To make the illusion work, G keeps the location of hosts completely hidden, allowing all other machines on the network to communicate as if directly connected. In our example, when host H_1 needs to communicate with host H_4, it first invokes ARP to map H_4's IP address into a physical address. Once it has a physical address, H_1 can send the datagram directly to that physical address.

Because G runs proxy ARP software, it captures the broadcast ARP request from H_1, decides that the machine in question lies on the other physical network, and responds to the ARP request by sending its own physical address. H_1 receives the ARP response, installs the mapping in its ARP table, and then uses the mapping to send datagrams destined for H_4 to G. When G receives a datagram, it searches a special routing table to determine how to route the datagram. G must forward datagrams destined for H_4 over the hidden network. To allow hosts on the hidden network to reach hosts on the main network, G performs the proxy ARP service on that network as well.

Gateways using the proxy ARP technique are taking advantage of an important feature of the ARP protocol, namely, trust. ARP is based on the idea that all machines cooperate and that any response is legitimate. Most hosts install mappings obtained through ARP without checking their validity and without maintaining consistency. Thus, it may happen that the ARP table maps several IP addresses to the same physical address, but that does not violate the protocol specification.

Some implementations of ARP are not as lax as others. In particular, ARP implementations designed to alert managers to possible security violations will inform them whenever two distinct IP addresses map to the same physical hardware address. The purpose of alerting the manager is to warn about *spoofing*, a situation in which one machine claims to be another in order to intercept packets. Host implementations of ARP that warn managers of possible spoofing cannot be used on networks that have proxy ARP gateways because the software will generate messages frequently.

The chief advantage of proxy ARP is that it can be added to a single gateway on a network without disturbing the routing tables in other hosts or gateways on that network. Thus, proxy ARP completely hides the details of physical connections.

The chief disadvantage of proxy ARP is that it does not work for networks unless they use ARP for address resolution. Furthermore, it does not generalize to more complex network topology (e.g., multiple gateways interconnecting two physical networks), nor does it support a reasonable form of routing. In fact, most implementations of proxy ARP rely on managers to maintain tables of machines and addresses manually, making it both time consuming and prone to errors.

16.6 Subnet Addresses

The third technique used to allow a single network address to span multiple physical networks is called *subnet addressing, subnet routing*, or *subnetting*. Subnetting is the most widely used of the three techniques because it is the most general and because it has been standardized. In fact, subnetting is now a required part of IP addressing.

The easiest way to understand subnet addressing is to imagine that a site has a single class *B* IP network address assigned to it, but it has two or more physical networks. Only local gateways know that there are multiple physical nets and how to route traffic among them; gateways in other autonomous systems route all traffic as if there were a single physical network. Figure 16.3 shows an example.

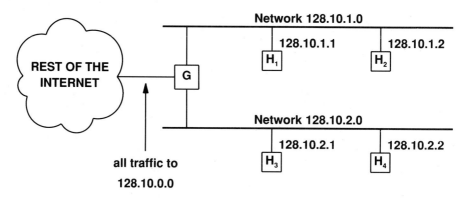

Figure 16.3 A site with two physical networks using subnet addressing to label them with a single class *B* network address. Gateway *G* accepts all traffic for net 128.10.0.0 and chooses a physical network based on the third octet of the address.

In the example, the site is using the single class *B* network address *128.10.0.0* for two networks. Except for gateway *G*, all gateways in the internet route as if there were a single physical net. Once a packet reaches *G*, it must be sent across the correct physical network to its destination. To make the choice of physical network efficient, the local site has chosen to use the third octet of the address to distinguish between the two networks. The manager assigns machines on one physical net addresses of the form *128.10.1.X*, and machines on the other physical net addresses of the form *128.10.2.X*, where *X* represents a small integer used to identify a specific host. To choose a physical network, *G* examines the third octet of the destination address and routes datagrams with value *1* to the network labeled *128.10.1.0* and those with value *2* to the network labeled *128.10.2.0*.

Conceptually, adding subnets only changes the interpretation of IP addresses slightly. Instead of dividing the 32-bit IP address into a network prefix and a host suffix, subnetting divides the address into a *network portion* and a *local portion*. The interpretation of the network portion remains the same as for networks that do not use subnetting. As before, reachability to the network must be advertised to outside autonomous systems; all traffic destined for the network will follow the advertised route. The interpretation of the local portion of an address is left up to the site (within the constraints of the formal standard for subnet addressing). To summarize:

> *We think of a 32-bit IP address as having an internet portion and a local portion, where the internet portion identifies a site, possibly with multiple physical networks, and the local portion identifies a host at that site.*

The example of Figure 16.3 showed subnet addressing with a class *B* address that had a 2-octet internet portion and a 2-octet local portion. To make routing among the physical networks efficient, the site administrator in our example chose to use one octet of the local portion to identify a physical network, and the other octet of the local portion to identify a host on that network, as Figure 16.4 shows.

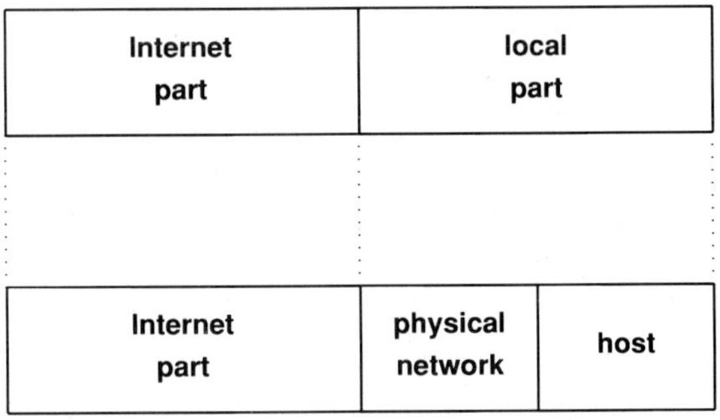

Internet part	local part	

Internet part	physical network	host

Figure 16.4 (a) Conceptual interpretation of a 32-bit IP address in the original IP address scheme, and (b) conceptual interpretation of addresses using the subnet scheme shown in Figure 16.3. The local portion is divided into two parts that identify a physical network and a host on that network.

The result is a form of *hierarchical addressing* that leads to corresponding *hierarchical routing*. The top level of the routing hierarchy (i.e., other autonomous systems in the internet) uses the first two octets when routing, and the next level (e.g., the local site) uses an additional octet. Finally, the lowest level (i.e., delivery across one physical network) uses the entire address.

Hierarchical addressing is not new; many systems have used it before. The best example is the U.S. telephone system, where a 10-digit phone number is divided into a 3-digit area code, 3-digit exchange, and 4-digit connection. The advantage of using hierarchical addressing is that it accommodates large growth because it means a given gateway does not need to know as much detail about distant destinations as it does about local ones. One disadvantage is that choosing a hierarchical structure is difficult, and it often becomes difficult to change a hierarchy once it has been established.

16.7 Flexibility In Subnet Address Assignment

The TCP/IP standard for subnet addressing recognizes that not every site will have the same hierarchical addresses; it allows sites flexibility in choosing how to assign them. To understand why such flexibility is desirable, imagine a site with five networks interconnected, as Figure 16.5 shows. Suppose the site has a single class *B* network address that it wants to use for all physical networks. How should the local part be divided to make routing efficient?

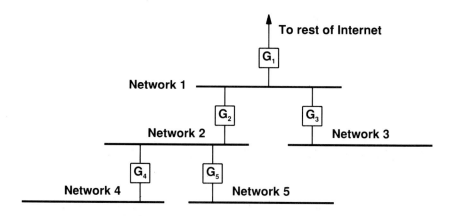

Figure 16.5 A site with five physical networks arranged in three "levels." The simplistic division of addresses into physical net and host parts may not be optimal for such cases.

In our example, the site will choose a partition of the local part of the IP address based on how it expects to grow. Dividing the 16-bit local part into an 8-bit network identifier and an 8-bit host identifier (as shown in Figure 16.4) allows up to 256 networks, with up to 256 hosts per network. Using 3 bits to identify a physical network and 13 bits to identify a host on that network allows up to 8 networks with up to 8192 hosts per network.

No single partition of the local part of the address will work for all sites because some have many networks with few hosts per network, while others have a few networks with many hosts attached to each. Furthermore, it may be that even within one site, some groups have many networks, while others have many hosts on a few networks. To allow maximum autonomy, the TCP/IP subnet standard allows the subnet partition to be selected on a per-network basis. Once a partition has been selected for a particular network, machines attached to that network are expected to use it. If they do not, datagrams can be lost or misrouted. We can summarize:

> *To allow maximum flexibility in choosing how to partition subnet ad-*
> *dresses, the TCP/IP subnet standard permits subnet interpretation to*
> *be chosen independently for each physical network. Once a subnet*
> *partition has been selected, all machines on that network must honor*
> *it.*

16.8 Implementation Of Subnets With Masks

We have implied that choosing a subnet addressing scheme is synonymous with choosing how to partition the local portion of an IP address into physical net and host part. Indeed, most sites that use subnet addresses do exactly that, but subnet addressing allows more complex assignments as well. The standard specifies that a site using sub-net addressing must choose a 32-bit *subnet mask* for each network. Bits in the subnet mask are set to *1* if the network treats the corresponding bit in the IP address as part of the network address, and *0* if it treats the bit as part of the host identifier. For example, the 32-bit subnet mask

11111111   11111111   11111111   00000000

specifies that the first three octets identify the network and the fourth octet identifies a host on that network. It is assumed that the subnet mask has *1*s for all bits that correspond to the net portion of the address (e.g., the subnet mask for a class *B* network will always include the first two octets plus zero or more subnet bits).

The interesting twist in subnet addressing arises because the standard does not res-trict subnet masks to selecting contiguous bits of the address. For example, a network might be assigned the mask

11111111   11111111   00011000   01000000

which selects the first two octets, two bits from the third octet, and one bit from the fourth. Although such flexibility makes it possible to arrange interesting assignments of addresses to machines, it makes assigning host addresses and understanding routing tables tricky. Thus, it is recommended that sites use contiguous subnet masks and that they use the same mask throughout an entire set of physical nets that share an IP ad-dress.

16.9 Subnet Mask Representation

Specifying subnet masks in binary is both awkward and prone to errors. Therefore, most software allows alternative representations. Often, the representation follows whatever conventions the local operating system uses for representation of binary quantities, with hexadecimal being quite popular.

Dotted decimal representation is also used for subnet addresses. It works best when sites choose to align subnetting on octet boundaries. For example, many sites choose to subnet class *B* addresses by using the third octet to identify the physical net and the fourth octet to identify hosts. In such cases, the subnet mask has dotted decimal representation *255.255.255.0*, making it easy to write and understand.

The literature also contains examples of subnet addresses and subnet masks represented in braces as a 3-tuple:

{ <network number>, <subnet number>, <host number> }

In this representation, the value *-1* means "all ones." For example, if the subnet mask for a class *B* network is *255.255.255.0*, it can be written *{-1, -1, 0}*.

The chief disadvantage of the 3-tuple representation is that it does not accurately specify how many bits are used for each part of the address; the advantage is that it abstracts away from the details of bit fields and emphasizes the values of the three parts of the address. To see why values are sometimes more important than bit fields, consider the 3-tuple

{ 128.10 , -1, 0 }

which denotes an address with a network number *128.10*, all ones in the subnet field, and all zeroes in the host field. Expressing the same address value using other representations requires a 32-bit IP address and a 32-bit subnet mask, and forces readers to decode bit fields before they can deduce the values of individual fields. Furthermore, the 3-tuple representation is independent of the IP address class or size of the subnet field. Thus, it can be used to represent sets of addresses or abstract ideas. For example, the 3-tuple

{ <network number>, -1, -1 }

denotes "addresses with a valid network number, a subnet field containing all ones, and a host field containing all ones." We will see additional examples later in this chapter.

16.10 Routing In The Presence Of Subnets

The standard IP routing algorithm must be modified to work with subnet addresses. Obviously, all machines that have a subnet address need to use the modified algorithm, which is called *subnet routing*. What may not be obvious is that unless restrictions are added to the use of subnetting, other hosts and gateways at the site may also need to use subnet routing. To see why, consider the example set of networks shown in Figure 16.6.

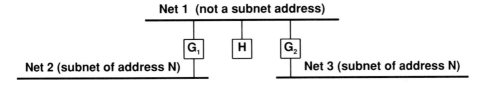

Figure 16.6 An example (illegal) topology with three networks where Nets *2* and *3* are subnets of a single IP network address, *N*. If such topologies were allowed, host *H* would need to use subnet routing even though Net *1* does not have a subnet address.

In the figure, physical networks *2* and *3* have been assigned subnet addresses of a single IP network address, *N*. Although host *H* does not directly attach to a network that has a subnet address, it must use subnet routing to decide whether to send datagrams destined for network *N* to gateway G_1 or gateway G_2. It could be argued that *H* can send to either gateway and let them handle the problem, but that solution means not all traffic will follow a shortest path. In larger examples, the difference between an optimal and nonoptimal path can be significant.

In theory, a simple rule that determines when machines need to use subnet routing is:

> *To achieve optimal routing, a machine* M *must use subnet routing for an IP network address* N, *unless there is a single path* P *that is a shortest path between* M *and every physical network that is a subnet of* N.

Unfortunately, understanding the theoretical restriction does not help much in assigning subnets. First, we know that shortest paths change if hardware fails or if routing algorithms redirect traffic around congestion. Such dynamic changes make it difficult to use the subnet rule except in trivial cases. Second, the subnet rule fails to consider the architectural boundaries of autonomous systems or the difficulties involved in propagating subnet masks. It is impossible to propagate subnet routes beyond the boundary of an autonomous system because network reachability protocols like EGP do not provide for it. Realistically, it becomes extremely difficult to propagate subnet information beyond a given physical network. Therefore, the designers recommend that if a site uses subnet addressing, that site should keep subnetting as simple as possible. In particular, all subnets of a given network IP address must be contiguous, the subnet masks should be uniform across all networks, and all machines should participate in subnet routing.

16.11 The Subnet Routing Algorithm

Like the standard IP routing algorithm, the subnet routing algorithm bases its decisions on a table of routes. Recall that in the standard algorithm, per-host routes and default routes are special cases; the table is used for all others. Each table entry contains a pair of

(network address, next hop address)

where the *network address* field specifies the IP address of a destination network, *N*, and the *next hop address* field specifies the address of a gateway to which datagrams destined for *N* should be sent. The standard routing algorithm compares the network portion of a destination address to the *network address* field of each entry in the routing table until a match is found. Because the *next hop address* field is constrained to specify a machine that is reachable over a directly connected network, only one table lookup is ever needed.

The standard algorithm knows how an address is partitioned into network portion and local portion because the first two bits encode the address type and format (class *A*, *B*, or *C*). With subnets, it is not possible to decide which bits correspond to the network and which to the host from the address alone. Instead, the modified algorithm used with subnets maintains additional information in the routing table. Each table entry contains one additional field that specifies the subnet mask used with the network in that entry:

(subnet mask, network address, next hop address)

When choosing routes, the modified algorithm uses the subnet mask to extract bits of the destination address for comparison with the table entry. That is, it performs a bit-wise Boolean *and* of the full 32-bit destination IP address and the *subnet mask* field from an entry, and it then checks to see if the result equals the value in the *network address* field of that entry. If so, it routes the datagram to the address specified in the *next hop address* field† of the entry.

16.12 Unified Routing Algorithm

Observant readers may have guessed that if we allow arbitrary masks, the subnet routing algorithm can subsume all the special cases of the standard algorithm. It can handle routes to individual hosts, default routes, and routes to directly connected net-

---

†As in the standard routing algorithm, the next hop gateway must be reachable by a directly connected network.

works using the same masking technique it uses for subnets. In addition, masks can handle routes to conventional networks (i.e., networks not using subnet addressing). The flexibility comes from the ability to combine arbitrary 32-bit values in a *subnet mask* field and arbitrary 32-bit addresses in a *network address* field. For example, to install a route for a single host, one uses a mask of all *1*s and network address equal to the host's IP address. To install a default route, one uses a subnet mask of all *0*s and a network address of all *0*s (because any destination address *and* zero equals zero). To install a route to a standard, nonsubnet class *B* network, one specifies a mask with two octets of *1*s and two octets of *0*s. Because the table contains more information, the routing algorithm contains fewer special cases as Figure 16.7 shows.

Algorithm:

Route_IP_Datagram (datagram, routing_table)

Extract destination IP address, I_D, from datagram
Compute IP address of destination network, I_N
if I_N matches any directly connected network address
    send datagram to destination over that network
    (This involves resolving I_D to a physical address,
    encapsulating the datagram, and sending the frame.)
else
    for each entry in routing table do
        Let N be the bitwise-and of I_D and the subnet mask
        If N equals the network address field of the entry then
            route the datagram to the specified next hop address
    endforloop
If no matches were found, declare a routing error

Figure 16.7 The unified IP routing algorithm. Given an IP datagram and a routing table with masks, this algorithm selects a next hop gateway to which the datagram should be sent. The next hop must lie on a directly connected network.

In fact, clever implementations can eliminate the explicit test for destinations on directly connected networks by adding table entries with appropriate values for the mask and network address.

16.13 Maintenance Of Subnet Masks

How do subnet masks get assigned and propagated? Chapter *9* answered the second part of the question by showing that a host can obtain the subnet mask for a given network by sending an ICMP *subnet mask request* to a gateway on that network. The request can be broadcast if the host does not know the specific address of a gateway. However, there is no standard protocol for propagating the information from one gateway to another.

The first part of the question is more difficult to answer. Each site is free to choose subnet masks for its networks. When making assignments, managers attempt to balance sizes of networks, numbers of physical networks, expected growth, and ease of maintenance. Difficulty arises because nonuniform masks give the most flexibility but make possible assignments that lead to ambiguous routes. Or worse, it allows valid assignments that become invalid if more hosts are added to the networks. There are no easy rules, so most sites make conservative choices. Typically, they select contiguous bits from the local portion of an address to identify a network and use the same partition (i.e., the same mask) for all local physical networks at the site. For example, many sites simply use a single subnet octet when subnetting a class *B* address.

16.14 Broadcasting To Subnets

Broadcasting is more difficult in a subnet architecture. Recall that in the original IP addressing scheme, an address with a host portion of all *1*s denotes broadcast to all hosts on the specified network. From the viewpoint of an observer outside a subnetted site, broadcasting to the network address still makes sense. That is, the address:

$$\{ \text{ network, -1, -1 } \}$$

means "deliver a copy to all machines that have *network* as their network addresses, even if they lie on separate physical networks." Operationally, broadcasting to such an address makes sense only if the gateways that interconnect the subnets agree to propagate the datagram to all physical networks.

Within a set of subnetted networks, it becomes possible to broadcast to a specific subnet (i.e., to broadcast to all hosts on a physical network that has been assigned one of the subnet addresses). The subnet address standard uses a host field of all ones to denote subnet broadcast. That is, a subnet broadcast address becomes:

$$\{ \text{ network, subnet, -1 } \}$$

Considering subnet broadcast addresses and subnet broadcasting clarifies the recommendation for using a consistent subnet mask across all networks that share a subnetted IP address. As long as the subnet and host fields are identical, subnet broadcast addresses are unambiguous. More complex subnet address assignments may or may not allow broadcasting to selected subsets of the physical networks that comprise a subnet.

16.15 Summary

The original IP address scheme assigns a unique 32-bit internet address to each physical network and requires gateways to keep routing tables proportional to the number of networks in the internet. We examined three techniques that have been invented to allow sites to share one internet address among multiple physical networks. The first uses transparent gateways to extend the address space of a single network to include hosts on an attached local network. The second, called proxy ARP, arranges for a local gateway to impersonate computers on another physical network by answering ARP messages addressed to them. Proxy ARP is useful only on networks that use ARP for address resolution, and only for ARP implementations that do not complain when multiple internet addresses map to the same hardware address. The third technique, a TCP/IP standard called subnet addressing, allows a site to share a single IP network address among multiple physical networks, as long as all the hosts and gateways on those networks cooperate. Subnetting requires hosts to use a modified routing algorithm in which routing table entries contain a subnet mask. The algorithm can be viewed as a generalization of the original routing algorithm, because it handles special cases like default routes or host-specific routes.

FOR FURTHER STUDY

The standard for subnet addressing comes from Mogul [RFC 950]. Clark [RFC 932], Karels [RFC 936], Gads [RFC 940], and Mogul [RFC 917] all contain early proposals for subnet addressing schemes. Mogul [RFC 922] discusses broadcasting in the presence of subnets. Postel [RFC 925] considers the use of proxy ARP for subnets. Carl-Mitchell and Quarterman [RFC 1027] discusses using proxy ARP to implement transparent subnet gateways.

EXERCISES

16.1 If gateways using proxy ARP use a table of host addresses to decide whether to answer ARP requests, the gateway table must be changed whenever a new host is added to one of the networks. Explain how to assign IP addresses so hosts can be added without changing tables. Hint: think of subnets.

16.2 Can transparent gateways be used with local area networks like the Ethernet?

16.3 Show that proxy ARP can be used with three physical networks that are interconnected by two gateways.

16.4 Consider a fixed subnet partition of a class *B* network number that will accommodate at least 76 networks. How many hosts can be on each network?

16.5   Does it ever make sense to subnet a class *C* network address? Why or why not?

16.6   A site that chose to subnet their class *B* address by using the third octet for the physical net was disappointed that they could not accommodate 255 or 256 networks. Explain.

16.7   Design a subnet address scheme for your organization assuming that you have one class *B* address to use.

16.8   Is it reasonable for a single gateway to use both proxy ARP and subnet addressing? If so, explain how. If not, explain why.

16.9   Argue that any network using proxy ARP is vulnerable to ''spoofing'' (i.e., an arbitrary machine can impersonate any other machine).

16.10   Can you devise a (nonstandard) implementation of ARP that supports normal use, but prohibits proxy ARP?

16.11   One vendor decided to add subnet addressing to its IP software by allocating a single subnet mask used for all IP network addresses. The vendor modified its standard IP routing software to make the subnet check a special case. Find a simple example in which this implementation cannot work correctly.

16.12   Characterize the (restricted) situations in which the subnet implementation discussed in the previous exercise will work correctly.

16.13   Read the standard to find out more about broadcasting in the presence of subnets. Can you characterize subnet address assignments that allow one to specify a broadcast address for all possible subnets?

16.14   The standard allows an arbitrary assignment of subnet masks for networks that comprise a subnetted IP address. Should the standard restrict subnet masks to cover contiguous bits in the address? Why or why not?

16.15   Carefully consider default routing in the presence of subnets. What can happen if a packet arrives destined for a nonexistent subnet?

16.16   Compare architectures that use subnet addressing and gateways to interconnect multiple Ethernets to an architecture that uses bridges as described in Chapter 2. Under what circumstances is one architecture preferable to the other?

16.17   Consider a site that chooses to subnet a class *B* network address, but decides that some physical nets will use *6* bits of the local portion to identify the physical net while others will use *8*. Find an assignment of host addresses that makes destination addresses ambiguous.

16.18   The subnet routing algorithm in Figure 16.7 uses a sequential scan of entries in the routing table, allowing a manager to place host-specific routes before network-specific or subnet-specific routes. Invent a data structure that achieves the same flexibility but uses hashing to make the lookup efficient [This exercise was suggested by Dave Mills].

17

Multicast Addressing (IGMP)

17.1 Introduction

Chapter 4 described the three primary classes of IP addresses and the previous chapter presented subnet addressing, an address extension that permits multiple physical networks to share a single IP network address. This chapter explores a recent addition to the IP addressing scheme that permits efficient multipoint delivery of datagrams. We begin with a brief review of hardware support. Later sections describe the IP address extension that uses multipoint delivery and present an experimental protocol used to propagate special routing information among gateways.

17.2 Hardware Broadcast

Many hardware technologies contain mechanisms to send packets to multiple destinations simultaneously (or nearly simultaneously). Chapter 2 reviewed several technologies and discussed the most common form of multipoint delivery: *broadcasting*. Broadcast delivery means that the network delivers one copy of a packet to each destination. On bus technologies like Ethernet, broadcast delivery can be accomplished with a single packet transmission. On networks composed of switches with point-to-point connections, software must implement broadcasting by forwarding copies of the packet across individual connections until all switches have received a copy.

With most hardware, the user specifies broadcast delivery by sending the packet to a special, reserved destination address called the *broadcast address*. For example, Ethernet hardware addresses consist of 48-bit identifiers, with the all ones address used to denote broadcast. Hardware on each machine recognizes the machine's hardware address as well as the broadcast address, and accepts incoming packets that have either address as their destination.

The chief disadvantage of broadcasting is that every broadcast consumes resources on all machines. For example, it would be possible to design an alternative internet protocol suite that used broadcast to deliver datagrams on a local network and relied on IP software to discard datagrams not intended for the local machine. However, such a scheme would be expensive because all computers on the local network would receive and process all datagrams sent on that network, even though most machines would discard most of the datagrams that arrived. Thus, the designers of TCP/IP used address binding mechanisms like ARP to eliminate broadcast delivery.

17.3 Hardware Multicast

Some hardware technologies support a second, less common form of multi-point delivery called *multicasting*. Unlike broadcasting, multicasting allows each machine to choose whether it wants to participate in a multicast. Typically, a hardware technology reserves a large set of addresses for use with multicast. When a group of machines want to communicate, they choose one particular *multicast address* to use for communication. After configuring their network interface hardware to recognize the selected multicast address, all machines in the group will receive a copy of every packet sent to that multicast address.

Multicast addressing can be viewed as a generalization of all other address forms. For example, we can think of a conventional *unicast address* as a form of multicast addressing in which there is exactly one machine in the multicast group. Similarly, we can think of broadcast addressing as a form of multicasting in which every machine is a member of the multicast group. Other multicast addresses can correspond to arbitrary sets of machines.

Ethernet provides the best example of multicasting in hardware. Ethernet uses the low-order bit of the high-order octet to distinguish conventional unicast addresses (*0*) from multicast addresses (*1*). In dotted hexadecimal notation†, the multicast bit is given by:

$$01.00.00.00.00.00_{16}$$

Initially, the network interface hardware is configured to accept packets destined for the Ethernet broadcast address or the machine's hardware address. However, it can be reconfigured easily to allow it to recognize a small set of multicast addresses as well.

---

†Dotted hexadecimal notation represents each octet as two hexadecimal digits with octets separated by periods; the subscript *16* can be omitted only when the context is unambiguous.

17.4 IP Multicast

IP multicasting is the internet abstraction of hardware multicasting. It allows transmission of an IP datagram to a set of hosts that form a single multicast group. It is possible for members of the group to be spread across separate physical networks. IP multicasting uses the same best-effort delivery semantics as other IP datagram delivery, meaning that multicast datagrams can be lost, delayed, duplicated, or delivered out of order.

Membership in an IP multicast group is dynamic. A host may join or leave a group at any time. Furthermore, a host may be a member of an arbitrary number of multicast groups. Membership in a group determines whether the host will receive datagrams sent to the multicast group; a host may send datagrams to a multicast group without being a member.

Each multicast group has a unique multicast (class *D*) address. Like protocol ports, some IP multicast addresses are assigned by the Internet authority and correspond to groups that always exist even if they have no current members. Such addresses are said to be *well-known*. Other multicast addresses are available for temporary use. They correspond to *transient multicast groups* that are created when needed and discarded when the count of members reaches zero.

IP multicasting may be used on a single physical network or throughout an internet. In the latter case, special *multicast gateways* forward multicast datagrams. However, hosts need not know about multicast gateways explicitly. The host transmits multicast datagrams using the local network multicast capability. If multicast gateways are present, they will receive the datagram and forward it to other networks as needed. Multicast gateways will use the local hardware multicast capability to deliver the datagram on target network(s) that support it. The time-to-live field in a multicast datagram limits propagation through gateways exactly like the time to live field in a unicast datagram limits its propagation. Multicast forwarding may be provided by physically independent gateways or the capability may be added to conventional gateways.

The TCP/IP standard for multicasting defines IP multicast addressing, specifies how hosts send and receive multicast datagrams, and describes the protocol gateways use to determine multicast group membership on a network. The next sections examine each aspect in more detail.

17.5 IP Multicast Addresses

Like hardware multicasting, IP multicasting uses the datagram's destination address to specify multicast delivery. IP multicast uses class *D* addresses of the form shown in Figure 17.1:

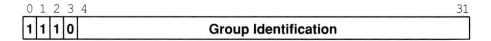

Figure 17.1 The format of class D IP addresses used for IP multicasting. Bits
4 through *31* identify a particular multicast group.

The first *4* bits contain *1110* and identify the address as a multicast. The remaining *28* bits specify a particular multicast group. There is no further structure in the group bits. In particular, the group field does not identify the origin of the group, nor does it contain a network address like class *A*, *B*, and *C* addresses.

When expressed in dotted decimal notation, multicast addresses range from

224.0.0.0   through   239.255.255.255

However, address 224.0.0.0 is reserved; it cannot be assigned to any group. Furthermore, address 224.0.0.1 is permanently assigned to the *all hosts group*, which includes all hosts and gateways participating in IP multicast. In general, the all hosts group address is used to reach all machines that participate in IP multicast on a local network; there is no IP multicast address that refers to all hosts in the internet.

IP multicast addresses can only be used as destination addresses. They can never appear in the source address field of a datagram, nor can they appear in a source route or record route option. Furthermore, no ICMP error messages can be generated about multicast datagrams (e.g., destination unreachable, source quench, echo reply, or time exceeded).

17.6 Mapping IP Multicast To Ethernet Multicast

Although the standard does not cover all types of network hardware, it does specify how to map IP multicast addresses to Ethernet multicast addresses. The mapping is efficient and easy to understand:

> *To map an IP multicast address to the corresponding Ethernet multi-*
> *cast address, place the low-order 23 bits of the IP multicast address*
> *into the low-order 23 bits of the special Ethernet multicast address*
> *01.00.5E.00.00.00$_{16}$.*

For example, IP multicast address 224.0.0.1 becomes Ethernet multicast address 01.00.5E.00.00.01$_{16}$.

Interestingly, the mapping is not unique. Because IP multicast addresses have 28 significant bits that identify the multicast group, more than one group may map onto the same Ethernet multicast address. The designers chose this scheme as a compromise. On one hand, using 23 of the 28 bits for a hardware address means most of the multicast address is included. The set of addresses is large enough so the chances of two groups choosing addresses with all low-order 23 bits identical is small. On the other hand, arranging for IP to use a fixed part of the Ethernet multicast address space makes debugging much easier and eliminates interference between IP and other protocols that share an Ethernet. The consequence of this design is that some multicast datagrams may be received at a host that are not destined for that host. Thus, the IP software must carefully check addresses on all incoming datagrams and discard any unwanted datagrams.

17.7 Extending IP To Handle Multicasting

A host participates in IP multicast at one of three levels as Figure 17.2 shows:

Level	Meaning
0	Host can neither send nor receive IP multicast
1	Host can send but not receive IP multicast
2	Host can both send and receive IP multicast

Figure 17.2 The three levels of participation in IP multicast.

Modifications that allow a machine to send IP multicast are not difficult. The IP software must allow an application program to specify a multicast address as a destination IP address, and the network interface software must be able to map an IP multicast address into the corresponding hardware multicast address (or use broadcast if the hardware does not support multicasting).

Extending host software to receive IP multicast datagrams is more complex. IP software on the host must have an interface that allows an application program to declare that it wants to join or leave a particular multicast group. If multiple application programs join the same group, the IP software must remember to pass each of them a copy of datagrams that arrive destined for that group. If all application programs leave a group, the host must remember that it no longer participates in that group. Furthermore, as we will see in the next section, the host must run a protocol that informs the local multicast gateways of its group membership status. However, much of the complexity comes from a basic idea:

Hosts join specific IP multicast groups on specific networks.

That is, a host with multiple network connections may join a particular multicast group on one network and not on another. To understand the reason for keeping group membership associated with networks, remember that it is possible to use IP multicasting among local sets of machines. The host may want to use a multicast application to interact with machines on one physical net but not with machines on another.

Because group membership is associated with particular networks, the software must keep separate lists of multicast addresses for each network to which the machine attaches. Furthermore, an application program must specify a particular network when it asks to join or leave a multicast group.

17.8 Internet Group Management Protocol

To participate in IP multicast on a local network, a host must have software that allows it to send and receive multicast datagrams. To participate in a multicast that spans multiple networks, the host must inform local multicast gateways. The local gateways contact other multicast gateways, passing on the membership information and establishing routes. The idea is quite similar to conventional route propagation among conventional internet gateways.

Before a multicast gateway can propagate multicast membership information, it must determine that one or more hosts on the local network have decided to join a multicast group. To do so, multicast gateways and hosts that implement multicast must use the *Internet Group Management Protocol* (*IGMP*) to communicate group membership information.

IGMP is analogous to ICMP. Like ICMP, it uses IP datagrams to carry messages. Also like ICMP, it provides a service used by IP. Therefore,

> *Although IGMP uses IP datagrams to carry messages, we think of it as an integral part of IP, not a separate protocol.*

Furthermore, IGMP is a standard for TCP/IP; it is required on all machines that participate in IP multicast at level 2.

Conceptually, IGMP has two phases. Phase 1: When a host joins a new multicast group, it sends an IGMP message to the "all hosts" multicast address declaring its membership. Local multicast gateways receive the message and establish necessary routing by propagating the group membership information to other multicast gateways throughout the internet. Phase 2: Because membership is dynamic, local multicast gateways periodically poll hosts on the local network to determine which hosts remain members of which groups. If no host reports membership in a group after a poll, the multicast gateway assumes that no host on the network remains in that group, and stops advertising group membership to other multicast routers.

17.9 IGMP Implementation

IGMP is carefully designed to avoid congesting a local network. First, all communication between hosts and multicast gateways uses IP multicast. That is, when IGMP messages are encapsulated in an IP datagram for transmission, the IP destination address is the all hosts multicast address. Thus, datagrams carrying IGMP messages are transmitted using hardware multicast if it is available. As a result, on networks that support hardware multicast, hosts not participating in IP multicast never receive IGMP messages. Second, a multicast gateway will not send individual request messages for each multicast group. Instead, it sends a single poll message to request information about membership in all groups. The polling rate is restricted to at most one request per minute. Third, hosts that are members of multiple groups do not send multiple responses at the same time. Instead, after an IGMP request message arrives from a multicast gateway, the host assigns each group in which it has membership a random delay between *0* and *10* seconds, and sends a response for that group after the delay. Thus, a host spaces its responses randomly over *10* seconds. Fourth, hosts listen to responses from other hosts and suppress any of their responses that are unnecessary.

To understand why a response can be unnecessary, recall why multicast gateways send a poll message. Gateways do not need to keep an exact record of group membership because all transmissions to the group will be sent using hardware multicast. Instead, multicast gateways only need to know whether at least one host on the network remains a member of the group. After the multicast gateway sends a poll message, all hosts assign a random delay to their response. When the host with smallest delay sends its response (using multicast), other participating hosts receive a copy. Each host assumes that the multicast gateway also received a copy of the first response and cancels its responses. Thus, in practice, only one host from each group responds to a request message from the multicast gateway.

17.10 Group Membership State Transitions

IGMP must remember the status of each multicast group to which the host belongs. We think of a host as keeping a table in which it records group membership information. Initially, all entries in the table are unused. Whenever an application program on the host joins a new group, IGMP software allocates an entry and fills in information about the group. Among the information, IGMP keeps a group reference counter which it initializes to *1*. If additional applications join the group, IGMP increments the reference counter in the entry. As application programs drop out of the group, IGMP decrements the counter; the host leaves the multicast group when the counter reaches zero.

The actions IGMP takes in response to IGMP messages can best be explained by the state transition diagram in Figure 17.3.

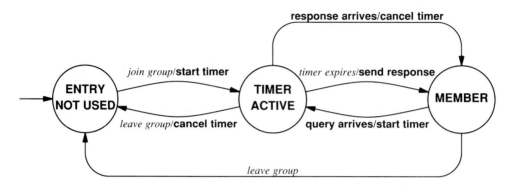

Figure 17.3 The three possible states of an entry in a host's multicast group table and transitions among them. Transitions are caused by the arrival of IGMP messages or events at the host (shown in italic).

As Figure 17.3 shows, a single timer mechanism can be used to generate both the initial response message as well as responses to requests from the multicast gateway. A request to join a group places the entry in the *TIMER ACTIVE* state and sets the timer to a small value. When the timer expires, IGMP generates and sends a response message and moves the entry to the *MEMBER* state.

In the *MEMBER* state, reception of an IGMP query causes the software to choose a timeout value (at random), start a timer for the entry, and move the entry to the *TIMER ACTIVE* state. If another host sends a response for the multicast group before the timer expires, IGMP cancels the timer and moves the entry back to the *MEMBER* state.

17.11 IGMP Message Format

As Figure 17.4 shows, IGMP messages have a simple format.

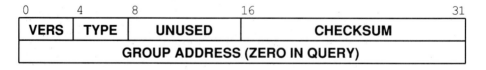

Figure 17.4 The format of IGMP messages.

Field *VERS* gives the protocol version (the current value is *1*). The *TYPE* field identifies the message as a query sent by a multicast gateway (*1*) or a response sent by a host (*2*). The *UNUSED* field must contain zero, and the *CHECKSUM* field contains a checksum for the 8-octet IGMP message (IGMP checksums are computed with the same algorithm used for TCP and IP checksums). Finally, hosts use field *GROUP ADDRESS* to report their membership in a particular multicast group (the field contains zero in a query and has no meaning).

17.12 Multicast Address Assignment

The standard does not specify exactly how groups of machines are assigned multicast addresses, but suggests several possibilities. For example, if the local operating system assigns an integer identifier to a set of processes or to a set of applications, that identifier can be used to form an IP multicast address. Of course, it is possible to have a network manager assign addresses manually. Another possibility is to allow a machine to randomly form multicast addresses until it discovers one that is not in use.

17.13 Propagating Routing Information

Although the IP multicasting described in this chapter is a standard for TCP/IP, no standard exists for the propagation of routing information among multicast gateways. However, the literature describes an experimental protocol called the *Distance Vector Multicast Routing Protocol* (*DVMRP*). Multicast gateways use DVMRP to pass group membership information among themselves. They use the information to establish routes so they can deliver a copy of a multicast datagram to every member of the multicast group.

DVMRP resembles the RIP protocol described in Chapter 15, but incorporates ideas that make it more efficient and robust. In essence, the protocol passes information about current multicast group membership and the cost to route between gateways. For each possible multicast group, the gateways impose a routing tree on top of the graph of physical interconnections. When a gateway receives a datagram destined for an IP multicast address, it sends a copy of the datagram out over the network links that correspond to branches in the routing tree.

DVMRP uses IGMP messages to carry information. It defines new IGMP message types that allow gateways to declare membership in multicast groups, leave a multicast group, and interrogate other gateways. The extensions also provide messages that carry gateway routing information including cost metrics. The protocol has been implemented, but more experimentation is needed before conclusions can be drawn about its performance.

17.14 Summary

IP Multicasting is an abstraction of hardware multicasting. It allows efficient delivery of a datagram to multiple destinations. IP uses class *D* addresses to specify multicast delivery; actual transmission uses hardware multicast if it is available.

IP multicast groups are dynamic: a host can join or leave a group at any time. For local multicast, hosts only need the ability to send and receive multicast datagrams. However, IP multicasting is not limited to a single physical network – multicast gateways propagate membership information and arrange routing so that every member of a multicast group receives a copy of every datagram sent to that group.

Hosts communicate their group membership to multicast gateways using IGMP. IGMP has been designed to be efficient and to avoid using network resources. In most cases, the only traffic IGMP introduces is a periodic message from a multicast gateway and a single reply for each multicast group to which hosts on that network belong.

FOR FURTHER STUDY

Deering [RFC 1112] specifies the standard for IP multicasting described here. Waitzman, Partridge, and Deering [RFC 1075] describes multicast route propagation using a vector-distance protocol similar to RIP. Earlier drafts of these ideas can be found in Deering [RFCs 1054 and 988], and in Deering and Cheriton [RFC 966]. Deering and Cheriton [May 1990] considers modifying various routing algorithms to support wide-area multicasting.

EXERCISES

17.1   The standard suggests using 23 bits of the IP multicast address to form a hardware multicast address. In such a scheme, how many IP multicast addresses map to a single hardware multicast address?

17.2   Argue that IP multicast addresses should use only 23 of the 28 possible bits. Hint: what are the practical limits on the number of groups to which a host can belong and the number of hosts on a single network?

17.3   IP must always check the destination addresses on incoming multicast datagrams and discard datagrams if the host is not in the specified multicast group. Explain how the host might receive a multicast destined for a group to which that host is not a member.

17.4   Is there any advantage in having multicast gateways know the set of hosts on the local network that belong to a given multicast group?

17.5   Find three applications in your environment that can benefit from IP multicast.

17.6   The standard says that IP software must arrange to deliver a copy of any outgoing multicast datagram to application programs on the host that belong to the specified multicast group. Does this design make programming easier or more difficult?

17.7 When the underlying hardware does not support multicast, IP multicast uses hardware broadcast for delivery. How can doing so cause problems?

17.8 Read RFC 1075 on DVMRP. What makes DVMRP more complex than RIP?

17.9 If your local network does not support hardware multicast, IP multicast datagrams will be delivered with hardware broadcast. Is there any advantage to using IP multicast over such networks?

17.10 The all hosts IP multicast address refers only to the local network, while all other IP multicast addresses refer to internet-wide multicast groups. Argue that it would be advantageous to reserve a set of IP multicast addresses for local use only.

17.11 IGMP does not include a strategy for acknowledgment or retransmission, even when used on networks that use best-effort delivery. What can happen if a query is lost? What can happen if a response is lost?

18

Client-Server Model Of Interaction

18.1 Introduction

Early chapters presented the details of TCP/IP technology, including the protocols that provide basic services and the gateway architecture that provides needed routing information. Now that we understand the basic technology, we can examine examples of application programs that profit from the cooperative use of a TCP/IP internet. While the examples are both practical and interesting, they do not comprise the main point. Instead, focus rests on the patterns of interaction among the communicating application programs. The primary pattern of interaction among cooperating applications is known as the *client-server* paradigm. It forms the basis of most network communication. It is fundamental because it helps us understand the foundation on which distributed algorithms are built. This chapter considers the relationship between client and server, paving the way for later chapters that illustrate the client-server pattern with further examples.

18.2 The Client-Server Model

The term *server* applies to any program that offers a service that can be reached over the network. Servers accept requests that arrive over the network, perform their service, and return the result to the requester. For the simplest services, each request arrives in a single IP datagram and the server returns its response in another datagram.

293

An executing program becomes a *client* when it sends a request to a server and waits for a response. Because the client-server model is a convenient and natural extension of interprocess communication on a single machine, it is easy to build programs that use it to interact.

Servers can perform simple or complex tasks. For example, a *time-of-day server* merely returns the current time whenever a client sends it a packet. A *file server* receives requests to perform operations that store or retrieve information from a file; the server performs the operation and returns the result.

Usually, servers are implemented as application level programs†. The advantage of implementing servers as application programs is that they can execute on any computing system that supports TCP/IP communication. Thus, the server for a particular service may execute on a timesharing system along with other programs, or it may execute on a personal computer. Multiple servers may offer the same service, and they may execute on the same machine or on multiple machines. In fact, it is common to replicate copies of a given server onto physically independent machines to increase reliability or improve performance. If a machine's primary purpose is to support a particular server program, the term ''server'' may be applied to the machine as well as to the server program. Thus, one hears statements like ''machine *A* is our file server.''

18.3 A Simple Example: UDP Echo Server

The simplest form of client-server interaction uses unreliable datagram delivery to convey messages from a client to a server and back. Consider, for example, a *UDP echo server*. The mechanics are straightforward as Figure 18.1 shows. At the server site, a UDP *echo server process* begins by negotiating with its operating system for permission to use the UDP port id reserved for the *echo* service. We call this the UDP *echo port*. Once it has obtained permission, the echo server process enters an infinite loop that has three steps: (1) wait for a datagram to arrive at the echo port, (2) reverse the source and destination addresses‡ (including source and destination IP addresses as well as UDP port ids), and (3) return the datagram to its original sender. At some other site, a program becomes a UDP *echo client* when it allocates an unused UDP protocol port, sends a UDP message to the UDP echo server, and awaits the reply. The client expects to receive back exactly the same data as it sent.

The UDP echo service illustrates two important points that are generally true about client-server interaction. The first concerns the difference between the lifetime of servers and clients:

> *A server starts execution before interaction begins and (usually) continues to accept requests and send responses without ever terminating.*
> *A client is any program that makes a request and awaits a response;*
> *it (usually) terminates after using a server a finite number of times.*

---

†The UNIX system refers to application programs as *user processes*.
‡One of the exercises suggests considering this step in more detail.

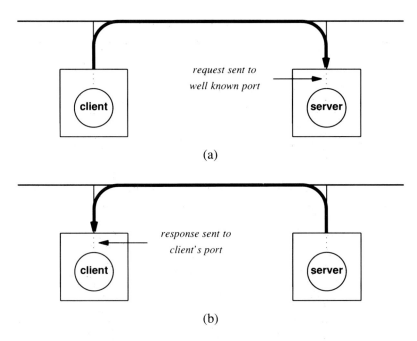

request sent to
well known port

(a)

response sent to
client's port

(b)

Figure 18.1 UDP echo as an example of the client-server model. In (a) the
client sends a request to the server at a known IP address and at
a well-known UDP port, and in (b) the server returns a response.
Clients use any UDP port that is available.

The second point is more technical. It concerns the use of reserved and nonreserved
port identifiers:

> *A server waits for requests at a well-known port that has been*
> *reserved for the service it offers. A client allocates an arbitrary,*
> *unused, nonreserved port for its communication.*

In a client-server interaction, only one of the two ports needs to be reserved. Assigning
a unique port identifier to each service makes it easy to build both clients and servers.

Who would use an echo service? It is not a service that the average user finds interesting. However, programmers who design, implement, measure, or modify network
protocol software, or network managers who test routes and debug communication
problems, often use echo servers in testing. Echo servers can also be used to determine
if it is possible to reach a remote machine.

18.4 Time And Date Service

The echo server is extremely simple, and little code is required to implement either the server or client side (provided that the operating system offers a reasonable way to access the underlying UDP/IP protocols). Our second example, a time server, shows that even simple client-server interaction can provide useful services. The problem it solves is that of setting a computer's time-of-day clock. The time of day clock is the hardware device that maintains the current date and time, making it available to programs. Once set, the time of day clock keeps time as accurately as a wristwatch.

Many systems solve the problem by asking a programmer to type in the time and date when the system boots. The system increments the clock periodically (e.g., every second). When an application program asks for the date or time, the system consults the internal clock and formats the time of day in human readable form. We can use a client-server interaction to set clocks automatically when machines boot. To do so, a manager configures the machine with the most accurate clock to run a time-of-day server. When other machines boot, they contact the server to obtain the current time.

18.4.1 Representation for the Date and Time

How should an operating system maintain the date and time-of-day? One useful representation stores the time and date as the count of seconds since an epoch date. For example, the UNIX operating system uses the zeroth second of January 1, 1970 as its epoch date. The TCP/IP protocols also define an epoch date and report times as seconds past the epoch. For TCP/IP, the epoch is defined to be the zeroth second of January 1, 1900 and times are kept in 32-bit integers, a representation that accommodates all dates in the near future.

Keeping the date as the time in seconds since an epoch makes the representation compact and allows easy comparison. It ties together the date and time of day and makes it possible to measure time by incrementing a single binary integer.

18.4.2 Local and Universal Time

What should we choose as the epoch, and exactly what time zone does the count represent? When two systems communicate across large geographic distances, using the local time zone from one or the other becomes difficult; they must agree on a standard time zone to keep values for date and time comparable. Thus, in addition to defining a representation for the date and choosing an epoch, the TCP/IP time server standard specifies that all values are given with respect to a single time zone. The time zone is Greenwich Mean Time, now called *universal coordinated time*, or *universal time*.

The interaction between a client and a server that offers time service works much like an echo server. At the server side, the server application obtains permission to use the reserved port assigned to time servers, waits for a UDP message directed to that port, and responds by sending a UDP message that contains the current time in a 32-bit integer. We can summarize:

Sending a datagram to a time server is equivalent to making a request for the current time; the server responds by returning a UDP message that contains the current time.

18.5 The Complexity of Servers

In our examples so far, servers are fairly simple because they are sequential. That is, the server processes one request at a time. After accepting a request, the server forms a reply and sends it before going back to see if another request has arrived. We implicitly assume that the operating system will queue requests that arrive for a server while it is busy, and that the queue will not become too long because the server has only a trivial amount of work to do.

In practice, servers are usually much more difficult to build than clients because they need to accommodate multiple concurrent requests, even if a single request takes considerable time to process. For example, consider a file transfer server responsible for copying a file to another machine on request. Typically, servers have two parts: a single master that is responsible for accepting new requests, and a set of slaves that are responsible for handling individual requests. The master server performs the following five steps:

Open port
> The master opens the well-known port at which it can be reached.

Wait for client
> The master waits for a new client to send a request.

Choose port
> If necessary, the master allocates a new local protocol port for this request and informs the client (we will see that this step is unnecessary with TCP).

Start Slave
> The master starts an independent, concurrent slave to handle this request (e.g., in UNIX, it forks a copy of the server process). Note that the slave no longer accepts requests from the well-known server port – it only handles one request and then terminates.

Continue
> The master returns to the *wait* step and continues accepting new requests while the newly created slave handles the previous request concurrently.

Because the master starts a slave for each new request, processing proceeds concurrently. Thus, requests that require little time to complete can finish earlier than requests that take longer, independent of the order in which they are started. For example, suppose the first client that contacts a file server requests a large file transfer that takes many minutes. If a second client contacts the server to request a transfer that takes only a few seconds, the second transfer can start and complete while the first transfer proceeds.

In addition to the complexity that results because servers handle concurrent requests, complexity also arises because servers must enforce authorization and protection rules. Server programs usually need to execute with highest privilege because they must read system files, keep logs, and access protected data. The operating system will not restrict a server program if it attempts to access users' files. Thus, servers cannot blindly honor requests from other sites. Instead, each server takes responsibility for enforcing the system access and protection policies.

Finally, servers must protect themselves against malformed requests or against requests that will cause the server program itself to abort. Often, it is difficult to foresee potential problems. For example, one project at Purdue University designed a file server that allowed student operating systems to access files on a UNIX timesharing system. Students discovered that requesting the server to open a file named */dev/tty* caused the server to abort because UNIX associates that name with the control terminal to which a program is attached. The server, created at system startup, had no such terminal. Once the server program aborted, none of the client machines could access files until a systems programmer restarted it.

A more serious example of server vulnerability became known in the fall of 1988 when a student at Cornell University built a *worm* program that attacked computers on the connected Internet. Once the worm started running on a machine, it searched the Internet for computers with servers that it knew how to exploit, and used them to create more copies of itself. In one of the attacks, the worm used a bug in the UNIX *fingerd* server. Because the server did not check incoming requests, the worm was able to send an illegal string of input that caused the server to overwrite parts of its internal data areas. The server, which executed with highest privilege, then misbehaved, allowing the worm to create copies of itself.

We can summarize our discussion of servers:

> *Servers are usually more difficult to build than clients because, even though they can be implemented with application level programs, servers must enforce all the access and protection policies of the computer system on which they run, and they must protect themselves against all possible errors.*

18.6 RARP Server

So far, all our examples of client-server interaction require the client to know the complete server address. The RARP protocol from Chapter 6 provides an example of client-server interaction with a slightly different twist. Recall that when a diskless machine boots, it uses RARP to find its IP address. Instead of having the client communicate directly with a server, RARP clients broadcast their requests. One or more machines executing RARP server processes respond, each returning a packet that answers the query.

There are two significant differences between a RARP server and a UDP echo or time server. First, RARP packets travel across the physical network in hardware frames, not in IP datagrams. Thus, unlike the UDP echo server which allows a client to contact a server anywhere on an internet, the RARP server requires the client to be on the same physical network. Second, RARP cannot be implemented by an application program. Echo and time servers can be built as application programs because they use UDP. By contrast, a RARP server needs access to raw hardware packets.

18.7 Alternatives To The Client-Server Model

What are the alternatives to client-server interaction, and when might they be attractive? This section gives at least one answer to these questions.

In the client-server model, programs usually act as clients when they need information, but it is sometimes important to minimize such interactions. The ARP protocol from Chapter 5 gives one example. It uses a modified form of client-server interaction to obtain physical address mappings. Machines that use ARP keep a cache of answers to improve the efficiency of later queries. Caching improves the performance of client-server interaction in cases where the recent history of queries is a good indicator of future use.

Although caching improves performance, it does not change the essence of client-server interaction. The essence lies in our assumption that processing must be driven by demand. We have assumed that a program executes until it needs information and then acts as a client to obtain the needed information. Taking a demand-driven view of the world is natural and arises from experience. Caching helps alleviate the cost of obtaining information by lowering the retrieval cost for all except the first process that makes a request.

How can we lower the cost of information retrieval for the first request? In a distributed system, it may be possible to have concurrent background activities that collect and propagate information *before* any particular program requests it, making retrieval costs low even for the initial request. More important, precollecting information can allow a given system to continue executing even though other machines or the networks connecting them fail.

Precollection is the basis for the 4BSD UNIX *ruptime* command. When invoked, *ruptime* reports the CPU load and time since system startup for each machine on the local network. A background program running on each machine uses UDP to broadcast information about the machine periodically. The same program also collects incoming information and places it in a file. Because machines propagate information continuously, each machine has a copy of the latest information on hand; a client seeking information never needs to access the network. Instead, it reads the information from secondary storage and prints it in a readable form.

The chief advantage of having information collected locally before the client needs it is speed. The *ruptime* command responds immediately when invoked without waiting for messages to traverse the network. A secondary benefit occurs because the client can find out something about machines that are no longer operating. In particular, if a machine stops broadcasting information, the client can report the time elapsed since the last broadcast (i.e., it can report how long the machine has been off-line).

Precollection has one major disadvantage: it uses processor time and network bandwidth even when no one cares about the data being collected. For example, the ruptime broadcast and collection continues running throughout the night, even if no one is logged in to read the information. If only a few machines connect to a given network, precollection cost is insignificant. It can be thought of as an innocuous background activity. For networks with many hosts, however, the large volume of broadcast traffic generated by precollection makes it too expensive. In particular, the cost of reading and processing broadcast messages becomes high. Thus, precollection is not among the most popular alternatives to client-server.

18.8 Summary

Processes that use network communication often fall into a pattern of use called the client-server model. Server processes await requests and perform an action based on the request. The action may include sending a response. Clients usually formulate a request, send it to the server, and then await a reply.

We have seen examples of clients and servers and found that some clients send requests directly, while others broadcast requests. Broadcast is especially useful on a local network when a machine does not know the address of a server.

We also noted that if servers use internet protocols like UDP, they can accept and respond to requests across an internet. If they communicate using physical frames and physical hardware addresses, they are restricted to a single physical network.

Finally, we considered an alternative to the client-server paradigm that used precollection of information to avoid delays. An example of precollection came from a machine status service.

FOR FURTHER STUDY

UDP echo service is defined in Postel [RFC 862]. The *UNIX Programmer's Manual* describes the *ruptime* command (also see the related description of *rwho*). Feinler *et. al.* [1985] specifies many standard server protocols not discussed here, including discard, character generation, day and time, active users, and quote of the day. The next chapters consider others.

EXERCISES

18.1   Build a UDP echo client that sends a datagram to a specified echo server, awaits a reply, and compares it to the original message.

18.2   Carefully consider the manipulation of IP addresses in a UDP echo server. Under what conditions is it incorrect to create new IP addresses by reversing the source and destination IP addresses?

18.3   As we have seen, servers can be implemented by separate application programs or by building server code into the protocol software in an operating system. What are the advantages and disadvantages of having an application program (user process) per server?

18.4   Suppose you do not know the IP address of a local machine running a UDP echo server, but you know that it responds to port 7. Is there an IP address you can use to reach it?

18.5   Build a client for the UDP time service.

18.6   Which of the techniques from Chapter 16 allow one to have a RARP server on a separate physical network from its client?

18.7   What is the chief disadvantage of having all machines broadcast their status periodically?

18.8   Examine the format of data broadcast by the servers that implement the 4BSD UNIX *ruptime* command. What information is available to the client in addition to machine status?

19

Bootstrap Protocol (BOOTP)

19.1 Introduction

This chapter contains an example of how the client-server paradigm is used for bootstrapping. We said that each computer attached to a TCP/IP internet needs to know its IP address before it can send or receive datagrams. Chapter 6 described how a diskless machine uses the RARP protocol at system startup to determine its IP address. This chapter discusses an alternative: a bootstrap protocol that allows a diskless machine to determine its IP address without using RARP. Surprisingly, the client and server communicate using UDP, the User Datagram Protocol described in Chapter 11.

What makes the procedure surprising is that UDP relies on IP to transfer messages, and it might seem impossible that a computer could use UDP to find an IP address to use when communicating. Examining the protocol will help us understand how diskless machines use the special IP addresses mentioned in Chapter 4 and the flexibility of the UDP/IP transport mechanism.

19.2 Introduction

Chapter 6 presented the problem diskless computers face during system startup. Such machines usually contain a startup program in nonvolatile storage (e.g., in ROM). To minimize cost and keep parts interchangeable, a vendor places exactly the same program in all machines. Because diskless computers all start from the program, IP addresses cannot be stored in the code. Thus, a diskless machine must learn its IP address from another source. In fact, a diskless computer needs to know much more than its IP address. Usually, the ROM only contains a small startup program, so the diskless computer must also obtain an initial memory image to execute. In addition, each diskless machine must determine the address of a file server on which it can store and retrieve data, and the address of the nearest IP gateway.

The RARP protocol of Chapter 6 has three drawbacks. First, because RARP operates at a low level, using it requires direct access to the network hardware. Thus, it may be difficult or impossible for an application programmer to build a server. Second, although RARP requires a packet exchange between a diskless machine and a computer that answers its request, the reply contains only one small piece of information: the diskless machine's 4-octet IP address. This drawback is especially annoying on networks like an Ethernet that enforce a minimum packet size because additional information could be sent in the response at no additional cost. Third, because RARP uses a computer's hardware address to identify the machine, it cannot be used on networks that dynamically assign hardware addresses.

To overcome some of the drawbacks of RARP, researchers developed the *BOOTstrap Protocol*, *BOOTP*. Because it uses UDP and IP, BOOTP can be implemented with an application program. Like RARP, BOOTP operates in the client-server paradigm and requires only a single packet exchange. However, BOOTP is more efficient because a single BOOTP message specifies many items needed at startup, including the diskless machine's IP address, the address of a gateway, and the address of a server. BOOTP also includes a vendor-specific field in the reply that allows hardware vendors to send additional information used only for their machines. As we will see, the term "vendor-specific" is a misnomer because the current specification also recommends using the vendor-specific area for general purpose information such as subnet masks.

19.3 Using IP To Determine An IP Address

We said that BOOTP uses UDP to carry messages and that UDP messages are encapsulated in IP datagrams for delivery. To understand how BOOTP can use IP before the diskless machine knows its IP address, recall from Chapter 4 that there are several special-case IP addresses. In particular, when used as a destination address, the IP address consisting of all *1*s (255.255.255.255) specifies limited broadcast. IP software can accept and broadcast datagrams that specify the limited broadcast address even before the software has discovered its local IP address information. The point is that:

> *An application program can use the limited broadcast IP address to force IP to broadcast a datagram on the local network even if IP has not yet discovered the IP address of the local network or the machine's IP address.*

Suppose client machine *A* wants to use BOOTP to find bootstrap information (including its IP address) and suppose *B* is the server on the same physical net that will answer the request. Because *A* does not know *B*'s IP address or the IP address of the network, it must broadcast its initial BOOTP request using the IP limited broadcast address. What about the reply? Can *B* send a directed reply? No, not usually. Although it may not be obvious, *B* may need to use the limited broadcast address for its reply, even though it knows *A*'s IP address. To see why, consider what will happen if an application program on *B* attempts to send a datagram using *A*'s IP address. After routing the datagram, IP software on *B* will pass the datagram to the network interface software. This software must map the next hop IP address to a corresponding hardware address, presumably using ARP as described in Chapter 5. However, because *A* has not yet received the BOOTP reply, it does not recognize its IP address, so it cannot answer *B*'s ARP request. Therefore, *B* has only two alternatives: either broadcast the reply or use information from the request packet to manually add an entry to its ARP cache. On systems that do not allow application programs to modify the ARP cache, broadcasting is the only solution.

19.4 The BOOTP Retransmission Policy

BOOTP places all responsibility for reliable communication on the client. We know that because UDP uses IP for delivery, messages can be delayed, lost, delivered out of order, or duplicated. Furthermore, because IP does not provide a checksum for data, the UDP datagram could arrive with some bits corrupted. To guard against corruption, BOOTP requires that UDP use checksums. It also specifies that requests and replies should be sent with the *do not fragment* bit set to accommodate clients that have too little memory to reassemble datagrams. BOOTP is also constructed to allow multiple replies; it accepts and processes the first.

To handle datagram loss, BOOTP uses the conventional technique of *timeout and retransmission*. When the client transmits a request, it starts a timer. If no reply arrives before the timer expires, the client must retransmit the request. Of course, after a power failure all machines on a network will reboot simultaneously, possibly overrunning the BOOTP server(s) with requests. If all clients use exactly the same retransmission timeout, many or all of them will attempt to retransmit simultaneously. To avoid the resulting collisions, the BOOTP specification recommends using a random delay. In addition, the specification recommends starting with a random timeout value between *0* and *4* seconds, and doubling the timer after each retransmission. After the timer reaches a large value, *60* seconds, the client does not increase the timer, but continues to use randomization. Doubling the timeout after each retransmission keeps BOOTP from adding excessive traffic to a congested network; the randomization helps avoid simultaneous transmissions.

19.5 BOOTP Message Format

To keep an implementation as simple as possible, BOOTP messages have fixed-length fields, and replies have the same format as requests. Although we said that clients and servers are programs, the BOOTP protocol uses the terms loosely, referring to the machine that sends a BOOTP request as the *client* and any machine that sends a reply as a *server*. Figure 19.1 shows the BOOTP message format.

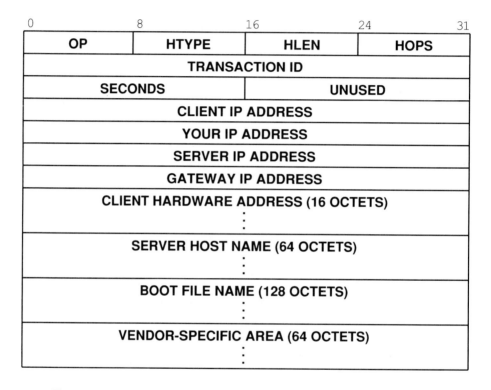

Figure 19.1 The format of BOOTP messages. To keep implementations small enough to fit in ROM, all fields have fixed length.

Field *OP* specifies whether the message is a request (*1*) or a reply (*2*). As in ARP, fields *HTYPE* and *HLEN* specify the network hardware type and length of a hardware address (e.g., Ethernet has type *1* and address length *6*)†. The client places *0* in the *HOPS* field; if a BOOTP server receives the request and decides to pass the request on to another machine (e.g., to allow bootstrapping across multiple gateways), it increments the count. The *TRANSACTION ID* field contains an integer that diskless machines use to match responses with requests. The *SECONDS* field reports the number of seconds since the client started to boot.

---

†Values for the *HTYPE* field can be found in the latest Assigned Numbers RFC.

Fields beginning with *CLIENT IP ADDRESS* contain the most important informa-tion. To allow the greatest flexibility, clients fill in as much information as they know and leave remaining fields set to zero. For example, if a client knows the name or ad-dress of a specific server from which it wants information, it can fill in the *SERVER IP ADDRESS* or *SERVER HOST NAME* fields. If these fields are nonzero, only the server with matching name/address will answer the request; if they are zero, any server that re-ceives the request will reply.

BOOTP can be used from a client that already knows its IP address (e.g., to obtain boot file information). A client that knows its IP address places it in the *CLIENT IP ADDRESS* field; other clients use zero. If the client's IP address is zero in the request, a server returns the client's IP address in the *YOUR IP ADDRESS* field.

19.6 The Two-Step Bootstrap Procedure

BOOTP uses a two-step bootstrap procedure. It does not provide clients with a memory image – it only provides the client with information needed to obtain an image. The client then uses a second protocol (e.g., TFTP from Chapter 23) to obtain the memory image. While the two-step procedure many seem unnecessary, it allows a clean separation of configuration and storage. A BOOTP server does not need to run on the same machine that stores memory images. In fact, the BOOTP server operates from a simple database that only knows the names of memory images.

Keeping configuration separate from storage is important because it allows ad-ministrators to configure sets of machines so they act identically or act independently. The *BOOT FILE NAME* field of a BOOTP illustrates this. Suppose an administrator has several workstations that have different hardware architectures, and suppose that when users boot one of the workstations, they either choose to run UNIX or a local operating system. Because the set of workstations includes multiple hardware architec-tures, no single memory image will operate on all machines. To accommodate such diversity, BOOTP allows the *BOOT FILE NAME* field in a request to contain a generic name like ''unix.'' It means, ''I want to boot the UNIX operating system for this machine.'' The BOOTP server consults its configuration database to map the generic name into a specific file name that contains the UNIX memory image appropriate for the client hardware, and returns the specific (i.e., fully qualified) name in its reply. Of course, the configuration database also allows completely automatic bootstrapping in which the client leaves zeros in the *BOOT FILE NAME* field, and BOOTP selects a memory image for the machine. The advantage of this approach is that it allows users to specify generic names that work on any machine; they do not need to remember specific file names or hardware architectures.

19.7 Vendor-Specific Field

The *VENDOR-SPECIFIC AREA* contains optional information to be passed from the server to the client. Although the syntax is intricate, it is not difficult. The first four octets of the field are called a *magic cookie* and define the format of remaining items; the standard format described here uses a magic cookie value of 99.130.83.99 (dotted decimal notation). A list of items follows the cookie, where each item contains a one-octet *type*, an optional one-octet *length*, and a multi-octet *value*. The standard defines the following types that have predetermined, fixed length values:

Item Type	Item Code	Value Length	Contents of Value
Padding	0	-	Zero - used only for padding
Subnet Mask	1	4	Subnet mask for local net
Time of Day	2	4	Time of day in universal time
End	255	-	End of item list

Figure 19.2 Items in the vendor information. The length field must exist for types *1* and *2*; it must not exist for types *0* and *255*.

Although a computer can obtain subnet mask information with an ICMP request, the standard now recommends that BOOTP servers supply the subnet mask in each reply to eliminate unnecessary ICMP messages.

Additional items in the *VENDOR-SPECIFIC AREA* all have a *type* octet, *length* octet, and *value*, as Figure 19.3 shows.

Item Type	Item Code	Length Octet	Contents of Value
Gateways	3	N	IP addresses of N/4 gateways
Time Server	4	N	IP addresses of N/4 time servers
IEN116 Server	5	N	IP addresses of N/4 IEN116 servers
Domain Server	6	N	IP addresses of N/4 DNS servers
Log Server	7	N	IP addresses of N/4 log servers
Quote Server	8	N	IP addresses of N/4 quote servers
Lpr Servers	9	N	IP addresses of N/4 lpr servers
Impress	10	N	IP addresses of N/4 Impress servers
RLP Server	11	N	IP addresses of N/4 RLP servers
Hostname	12	N	N bytes of client host name
Boot Size	13	2	2-octet integer size of boot file
RESERVED	128-254	-	Reserved for site specific use

Figure 19.3 Types and contents of items in the *VENDOR-SPECIFIC AREA* of a BOOTP reply that have variable lengths.

19.8 Summary

The BOOTstrap Protocol, BOOTP, provides an alternative to RARP for a diskless workstation that needs to determine its IP address. BOOTP is more general than RARP because it uses UDP, making it possible to extend bootstrapping across a gateway. BOOTP also allows a machine to determine a gateway address, a (file) server address, and the subnet mask. Finally, BOOTP allows administrators to establish a configuration database that maps a generic name, like "unix," into the fully qualified file name that contains a memory image appropriate for the client hardware.

BOOTP is designed to be small and simple enough to reside in a bootstrap ROM. The client uses the limited broadcast address to communicate with the server, and takes responsibility for retransmitting requests if the server does not respond. Retransmission uses an exponential backoff policy similar to Ethernet to avoid congestion.

FOR FURTHER STUDY

BOOTP is a standard protocol in the TCP/IP suite. Further details can be found in Croft and Gilmore [RFC 951], which compares BOOTP to RARP and serves as the official standard. Reynolds [RFC 1084] tells how to interpret the vendor-specific area, and Braden [RFC 1123] recommends using the vendor-specific area to pass the subnet mask.

EXERCISES

19.1   BOOTP does not contain an explicit field for returning the time of day from the server to the client, but makes it part of the (optional) vendor-specific information. Should the time be included in the required fields? Why or why not?

19.2   Argue that separation of configuration and storage of memory images is *not* good. (See RFC 951 for hints.)

19.3   The BOOTP message format is inconsistent because it has two fields for client IP address and one for the name of the boot image. If the client leaves its IP address field empty, the server returns the client's IP address in the second field. If the client leaves the boot file name field empty, the server *replaces* it with an explicit name. Why?

19.4   Read the standard to find out how clients and servers use the *HOPS* field.

19.5   When a machine obtains its subnet mask with BOOTP instead of ICMP, it places less load on *other* host computers. Explain.

20

The Domain Name System

20.1 Introduction

So far we have used 32-bit integers called Internet Protocol addresses (IP addresses) to identify machines. Although such addresses provide a convenient, compact representation for specifying the source and destination in packets sent across an internet, users prefer to assign machines pronounceable, easily remembered names.

This chapter considers a scheme for assigning meaningful high-level names to a large set of machines, and it discusses a mechanism that maps between high-level machine names and IP addresses. It considers both the translation from high-level names to IP addresses and the translation from IP addresses to high-level machine names. The naming scheme is interesting for two reasons. First, it has been used to assign machine names throughout the connected Internet. Second, the implementation of the name mapping mechanism provides a large scale example of the client–server paradigm described in Chapter 18, because it uses a geographically distributed set of servers to map names to addresses.

20.2 Names For Machines

The earliest computer systems forced users to understand numeric addresses for objects like system tables and peripheral devices. Timesharing systems advanced computing by allowing users to invent meaningful symbolic names for both physical objects (e.g., peripheral devices) and abstract objects (e.g., files). A similar pattern has emerged in computer networking. Early systems supported point-to-point connections between computers and used low-level hardware addresses to specify machines. Internetworking introduced universal addressing, as well as protocol software to map universal addresses into low-level hardware addresses. Users whose computing environment contains multiple machines want meaningful, symbolic names to identify them.

Early machine names reflected the small environment in which they were chosen. It was quite common for a site with a handful of machines to choose names based on the machines' purposes. For example, machines often had names like *research*, *production*, *accounting*, and *development*. Users find such names preferable to cumbersome hardware addresses.

Although the distinction between *address* and *name* is intuitively appealing, it is artificial. Any *name* is merely an identifier that consists of a sequence of characters chosen from a finite alphabet. Names are only useful if the system can efficiently map them to the object they denote. Thus, we think of an IP address as a *low-level name*, and we say that users prefer *high-level names* for machines.

The form of high-level names is important because it determines how names are translated to lower-level names or bound to objects, as well as how name assignments are authorized. When only a few machines interconnect, choosing names is easy, and any form will suffice. On the Internet, to which over one hundred thousand machines connect, choosing symbolic names becomes difficult. For example, when the Computer Science Department at Purdue University connected to the Internet in 1980, it chose the name *purdue* to identify the connected machine. The list of potential conflicts contained only a few dozen names. By mid 1986, the official list of hosts on the Internet contained 3100 officially registered names and 6500 official aliases. By 1990, the list contained nearly 6400 names†. Although the list was growing rapidly, most sites had additional machines (e.g., personal computers) that were not registered.

20.3 Flat Namespace

The original set of machine names used throughout the Internet formed a *flat namespace* in which each name consisted of a sequence of characters without any further structure. In the original scheme, a central site, the Internet Network Information Center (NIC), administered the namespace and determined whether a new name was appropriate (i.e., it prohibited obscene names or names that conflicted with existing ones).

The chief advantage of a flat namespace is that names are convenient and short; the chief disadvantage of a flat namespace is that it cannot generalize to large sets of machines for both technical and administrative reasons. First, because names are drawn from a single set of identifiers, the potential for conflict increases as the number of sites increases. Second, because authority for adding new names must rest at a single site, the administrative workload at that central site also increases with the number of sites. To understand the severity of the problem, imagine a rapidly growing internet with thousands of sites, each of which has hundreds of individual personal computers and workstations. Every time someone acquires and connects a new personal computer, its name must be approved by the central authority. Third, because the name-to-address bindings change frequently, the cost of maintaining correct copies of the entire list at each site is high and increases as the number of sites increases. Alternatively, if the

---

†In 1990, the list of names maintained by the NIC was obsolete; at that time the Internet domain name system contained more than 137,000 host names.

name database resides at a single site, traffic to that site increases with the number of sites.

20.4 Hierarchical Names

How can a naming system accommodate a large, rapidly expanding set of names without requiring a central site to administer it? The answer lies in decentralizing the naming mechanism by delegating authority for parts of the namespace and distributing responsibility for the mapping between names and addresses. TCP/IP internets now use such a scheme. Before examining the details of the TCP/IP scheme, we will consider the motivation and intuition behind it.

The partitioning of a namespace must be defined in such a way that it supports efficient name mapping and guarantees autonomous control of name assignment. Optimizing only for efficient mapping can lead to solutions that retain a flat namespace and reduce traffic by dividing the names among multiple mapping machines. Optimizing only for administrative ease can lead to solutions that make delegation of authority easy but name mapping expensive or complex.

To understand how the namespace should be divided, think of the internal structure of large organizations. At the top, the chief executive has overall responsibility. Because the chief executive cannot oversee everything, the organization may be partitioned into divisions, with an executive in charge of each division. The chief executive grants each division autonomy within specified limits. More to the point, the executive in charge of a particular division can hire or fire employees, assign offices, and delegate authority, without obtaining direct permission from the chief executive.

Besides making it easy to delegate authority, the hierarchy of a large organization introduces autonomous operation. For example, when office workers need information like telephone numbers of new employees, they begin by asking local clerical workers (who may contact clerical workers in other divisions). The point is that although authority always passes down the corporate hierarchy, information can flow across the hierarchy from one office to another.

20.5 Delegation Of Authority For Names

A hierarchical naming scheme works like the management of a large organization. The namespace is *partitioned* at the top level, and authority for names in the subdivisions is passed to a designated agent. For example, we might choose to partition the namespace based on *site name* and to delegate to each site responsibility for maintaining names within its partition. The topmost level of the hierarchy divides the namespace and delegates authority for each division; it need not be bothered by changes within one division.

The syntax of hierarchically assigned names often reflects the hierarchical delegation of authority used to assign them. As an example, consider a namespace with names of the form:

local . site

where *site* is the site name authorized by the central authority, *local* is the part of a name controlled by the site, and the period† (''.'') is a delimiter used to separate them. When the topmost authority approves adding a new site, *X*, it adds *X* to the list of valid sites and delegates to site *X* authority for all names that end in '*.X*'.

20.6 Subset Authority

In a hierarchical namespace, authority may be further subdivided at each level. In our example of partition by sites, the site itself may consist of several administrative groups, and the site authority may choose to subdivide its namespace among the groups. The idea is to keep subdividing the namespace until each subdivision is small enough to be manageable.

Syntactically, subdividing the namespace introduces another partition of the name. For example, adding a *group* subdivision to names already partitioned by site produces the following name syntax:

local . group . site

Because the topmost level delegates authority, group names do not have to agree among sites. A university site might choose group names like *engineering*, *science*, and *arts*, while a corporate site might choose group names like *production*, *accounting*, and *personnel*.

The U.S. Telephone system provides another example of a hierarchical naming syntax. The 10 digits of a phone number have been partitioned into a 3-digit *area code*, 3-digit *exchange*, and 4-digit *subscriber number* within the exchange. Each exchange has authority for assigning subscriber numbers within its piece of the namespace. Although it is possible to group arbitrary subscribers into exchanges and to group arbitrary exchanges into area codes, the assignment of telephone numbers is not capricious; they are carefully chosen to make it easy to route phone calls across the telephone network.

The telephone example is important because it illustrates a key distinction between the hierarchical naming scheme used in a TCP/IP internet and other hierarchies: partitioning the set of machines owned by an organization along lines of authority does not necessarily imply partitioning by physical location. For example, it could be that at some university, a single building houses the mathematics department, as well as the computer science department. It might even turn out that although the machines from these two groups fall under completely separate administrative domains, they connect to the same physical network. It also may happen that a single group owns machines on

---

†In domain names, the period delimiter is pronounced ''dot.''

several physical networks. For these reasons, the TCP/IP naming scheme allows arbitrary delegation of authority for the hierarchical namespace without regard to physical connections. The concept can be summarized:

> *In a TCP/IP internet, hierarchical machine names are assigned according to the structure of organizations that obtain authority for parts of the namespace, not necessarily according to the structure of the physical network interconnections.*

Of course, at many sites the organizational hierarchy corresponds with the structure of physical network interconnections. At a large university, for example, most departments that have computers also have their own local area network. If the department is assigned part of the naming hierarchy, all machines that have names in its part of the hierarchy will also connect to a single physical network.

20.7 TCP/IP Internet Domain Names

The mechanism that implements a machine name hierarchy for TCP/IP internets is called the *domain name system (DNS)*. It has two, conceptually independent, aspects. The first is abstract: it specifies the name syntax and rules for delegating authority over names. The second is concrete: it specifies the implementation of a distributed computing system that efficiently maps names to addresses. This section considers the name syntax and later sections examine the implementation.

The domain name system uses a hierarchical naming scheme known as *domain names*. As in our earlier examples, a domain name consists of a sequence of subnames separated by a delimiter character, the period. In our examples we said that individual sections of the name might represent sites or groups, but the domain system simply calls each section a *label*. Thus, the domain name

cs.purdue.edu

contains three *labels*: *cs, purdue*, and *edu*. Any suffix of a label in a domain name is also called a *domain*. In the above example the lowest level domain is *cs.purdue.edu*, (the domain name for the Computer Science Department at Purdue University), the second level domain is *purdue.edu* (the domain name for Purdue University), and the top-level domain is *edu* (the domain name for educational institutions). As the example shows, domain names are written with the local label first and the top domain last. As we will see, writing them in this order makes it possible to compress messages that contain multiple domain names.

20.8 Official And Unofficial Internet Domain Names

In theory, the domain name standard specifies an abstract hierarchical namespace with arbitrary values for labels. Because the domain system dictates only the form of names and not their actual values, it is possible for any group that builds an instance of the domain system to choose labels for all parts of its hierarchy. For example, a private company can establish a domain hierarchy in which the top-level labels specify corporate subsidiaries, the next level labels specify corporate divisions, and the lowest level labels specify departments.

However, most users of the domain technology follow the hierarchical labels used by the official Internet domain system. There are two reasons. First, as we will see, the Internet scheme is both comprehensive and flexible. It can accommodate a wide variety of organizations, and allows each group to choose between geographical or organizational naming hierarchies. Second, most sites follow the Internet scheme so they can attach their TCP/IP installations to the connected Internet without changing names. Because the Internet naming scheme dominates almost all uses of the domain name system, examples throughout the remainder of this chapter have labels taken from the Internet naming hierarchy. Readers should remember that, although they are most likely to encounter these particular labels, the domain name system technology can be used with other labels if desired.

The Internet authority has chosen to partition its top level into the domains listed in Figure 20.1.

Domain Name	Meaning
COM	Commercial organizations
EDU	Educational institutions
GOV	Government institutions
MIL	Military groups
NET	Major network support centers
ORG	Organizations other than those above
ARPA	Temporary ARPANET domain (obsolete)
INT	International organizations
country code	Each country (geographic scheme)

Figure 20.1 The top-level Internet domains and their meanings. Although labels are shown in upper case, domain name system comparisons are insensitive to case, so *EDU* is equivalent to *edu*.

Conceptually, the top-level names permit two completely different naming hierarchies: geographic and organizational. The geographic scheme divides the universe of machines by country. Machines in the United States fall under the top-level domain *US*; when foreign countries want to register machines in the domain name system, the central authority assigns the country a new top-level domain with the country's international standard 2-letter identifier as its label. The authority for the US domain has chosen to divide it into one second-level domain per state. For example, the domain for the state of Virginia is

va . us

As an alternative to the geographic hierarchy, the top-level domains also allow organizations to be grouped by organizational type. When an organization wants to participate in the domain naming system, it chooses how it wishes to be registered and requests approval. The central authority reviews the application and assigns the organization a subdomain† under one of the existing top-level domains. For example, it is possible for a university to register itself as a second-level domain under *EDU* (the usual practice), or to register itself under the state and country in which it is located. So far, few organizations have chosen the geographic hierarchy; most prefer to register under *COM, EDU, MIL,* or *GOV*. There are two reasons. First, geographic names are longer and therefore more difficult to type. Second, geographic names are much more difficult to discover or guess. For example, Purdue University is located in West Lafayette, Indiana. While a user could easily guess an organizational name, like *purdue.edu*, a geographic name is often difficult to guess because it is usually an abbreviation, like *laf . in . us*.

Figure 20.2 illustrates a small part of the Internet domain name hierarchy. As the figure shows, Digital Equipment Corporation, a commercial organization, registered as *dec . com*, Purdue University registered as *purdue . edu*, and the National Science Foundation, a government agency, registered as *nsf . gov*. In contrast, the Corporation for National Research Initiatives chose to register under the geographic hierarchy as *nri . reston . va . us*.

---

†The standard does not define the term ''subdomain.'' We have chosen to use it because its analogy to ''subset'' helps clarify the relationship among domains.

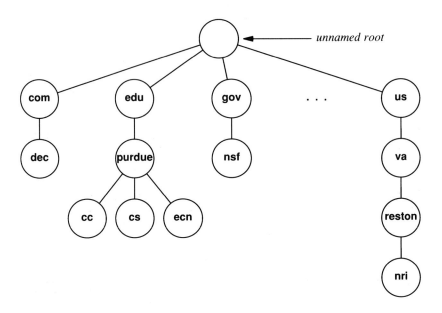

Figure 20.2 A small part of the Internet domain name hierarchy (tree). In practice, the tree is broad and flat; over one hundred thousand host entries appear by the fifth level.

Another example may help clarify the relationship between the naming hierarchy and authority for names. A machine named *xinu* in the Computer Science Department at Purdue University has the official domain name

$$xinu.cs.purdue.edu$$

The machine name was approved and registered by the local network manager in the Computer Science Department. The department manager had previously obtained authority for the subdomain *cs.purdue.edu* from a university network authority, who had obtained permission to manage the subdomain *purdue.edu* from the Internet authority. The Internet authority retains control of the *edu* domain, so new universities can only be added with its permission. Similarly, the university network manager at Purdue University retains authority for the *purdue.edu* subdomain, so new third-level domains may only be added with the manager's permission.

20.9 Items Named And Syntax Of Names

The domain name system is quite general because it allows multiple naming hierarchies to be embedded in one system. To allow clients to distinguish among multiple kinds of entries, each named item stored in the system is assigned a *type* that specifies whether it is the address of a machine, a mailbox, a user, and so on. When a client asks the domain system to resolve a name, it must specify the type of answer desired. For example, when an electronic mail application uses the domain system to resolve a name, it specifies that the answer should be the address of a *mail exchanger*. A remote login application specifies that it seeks a machine's IP address. It is important to understand the following:

> *A given name may map to more than one item in the domain system.*
> *The client specifies the type of object desired when resolving a name,*
> *and the server returns objects of that type.*

In addition to specifying the type of answer sought, the domain system allows the client to specify the protocol family to use. The domain system partitions the entire set of names by *class*, allowing a single database to store mappings for multiple protocol suites†.

The syntax of a name does not determine what type of object it names or the class of protocol suite. In particular, the number of labels in a name does not determine whether the name refers to an individual object (machine) or a domain. Thus, in our example, it is possible to have a machine named

> *gwen*.*purdue*.*edu*

even though

> *cs*.*purdue*.*edu*

names a subdomain. We can summarize this important point:

> *One cannot distinguish the names of subdomains from the names of*
> *individual objects or the type of an object using only the domain name*
> *syntax.*

20.10 Mapping Domain Names To Addresses

In addition to the rules for name syntax and delegation of authority, the domain name scheme includes an efficient, reliable, general purpose, distributed system for mapping names to addresses. The system is distributed in the technical sense, meaning that a set of servers operating at multiple sites cooperatively solve the mapping problem. It is efficient in the sense that most names can be mapped locally; only a few re-

---

†Currently, few domain servers use multiple protocol suites.

quire internet traffic. It is general purpose because it is not restricted to machine names (although we will use that example for now). Finally, it is reliable in that no single machine failure will prevent the system from operating correctly.

The domain mechanism for mapping names to addresses consists of independent, cooperative systems called *name servers*. A name server is a server program that supplies name-to-address translation, mapping from domain names to IP addresses. Often, server software executes on a dedicated processor, and the machine itself is called the name server. The client software, called a *name resolver*, uses one or more name servers when translating a name.

The easiest way to understand how domain servers work is to imagine them arranged in a tree structure that corresponds to the naming hierarchy, as Figure 20.3 illustrates. The root of the tree is a server that recognizes the top-level domains and knows which server resolves each domain. Given a name to resolve, the root can choose the correct server for that name. At the next level, a set of name servers each provide answers for one top-level domain (e.g., *edu*). A server at this level knows which servers can resolve each of the subdomains under its domain. At the third level of the tree, name servers provide answers for subdomains (e.g., *purdue* under *edu*). The conceptual tree continues with one server at each level for which a subdomain has been defined.

Links in the conceptual tree do not indicate physical network connections. Instead, they show which other name servers a given server knows and contacts. The servers themselves may be located at arbitrary locations on an internet. Thus, the tree of servers is an abstraction that uses an internet for communication.

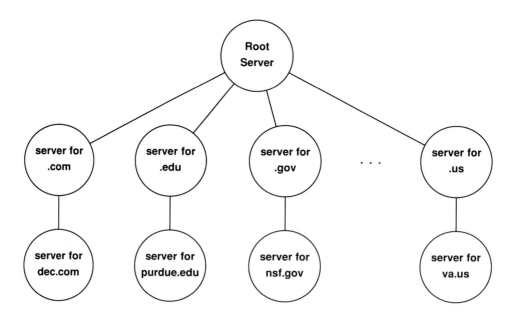

Figure 20.3 The conceptual arrangement of domain name servers in a tree that corresponds to the naming hierarchy. In theory, each server knows the addresses of all lower level servers for all subdomains within the domain it handles.

If servers in the domain system worked exactly as our simplistic model suggests, the relationship between connectivity and authorization would be quite simple. When authority was granted for a subdomain, the organization requesting it would need to establish a domain name server for that subdomain and link it into the tree.

In practice, the relationship between the naming hierarchy and the tree of servers is not as simple as our model implies. The tree of servers has few levels because a single physical server can contain all of the information for large parts of the naming hierarchy. In particular, organizations often collect information from all of their subdomains into a single server. Figure 20.4 shows a more realistic organization of servers for the naming hierarchy of Figure 20.2.

A root server contains information about the root and top-level domains, and each organization uses a single server for its names. Because the tree of servers is shallow, at most two servers need to be contacted to resolve a name like *xinu.cs.purdue.edu*: the root server and the server for domain *purdue.edu* (i.e., the root server knows which server handles *purdue.edu*, and the entire domain information for Purdue resides in its server).

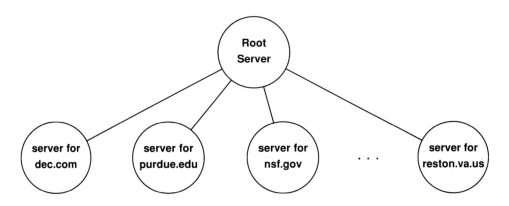

Figure 20.4 A realistic organization of servers for the naming hierarchy of Figure 20.2. Because the tree is broad and flat, few servers need to be contacted when resolving a name.

20.11 Domain Name Resolution

Although the conceptual tree makes understanding the relationship between servers easy, it hides several subtle details. Looking at the name resolution algorithm will help explain them. Conceptually, domain name resolution proceeds top-down, starting with the root name server and proceeding to servers located at the leaves of the tree. There are two ways to use the domain name system: by contacting name servers one at a time or asking the name server system to perform the complete translation. In either case, the client software forms a domain name query that contains the name to be resolved, a declaration of the class of the name, the type of answer desired, and a code that specifies whether the name server should translate the name completely. It sends the query to a name server for resolution.

When a domain name server receives a query, it checks to see if the name lies in the subdomain for which it is an authority. If so, it translates the name to an address according to its database and appends an answer to the query before sending it back to the client. If the name server cannot resolve the name completely, it checks to see what type of interaction the client specified. If the client requested complete translation (*recursive resolution*, in domain name terminology), the server contacts a domain name server that can resolve the name and returns the answer to the client. If the client requested non-recursive resolution (*iterative resolution*), the name server cannot supply an answer. It generates a reply that specifies the name server the client should contact next to resolve the name.

How does a resolver find a name server at which to begin the search? How does a name server find other name servers that can answer questions when it cannot? The answers are simple. A resolver must know how to contact at least one name server. To insure that a domain name server can reach others, the domain system requires that each server know the address of at least one root server†. In addition, a server may know the address of a server for the domain immediately above it (called the *parent*).

Domain name servers use a well-known protocol port for all communication, so clients know how to communicate with a server once they know the IP address of the machine in which the server executes. There is no standard way for hosts to locate a machine in the local environment on which a name server runs; that is left to whomever designs the resolver software‡.

In some systems, the address of the machine that supplies domain name service is bound into application programs at compile time, while in others, the address is configured into the operating system at startup. In others, the administrator places the address of a server in a file on secondary storage.

20.12 Efficient Translation

Although it may seem natural to resolve queries by working down the tree of name servers, it can lead to inefficiencies for three reasons. First, most name resolution refers to local names, those found within the same subdivision of the namespace as the machine from which the request originates. Tracing a path through the hierarchy to contact the local authority would be inefficient. Second, if each name resolution always started by contacting the topmost level of the hierarchy, the machine at that point would become overloaded. Third, failure of machines at the topmost levels of the hierarchy would prevent name resolution, even if the local authority could resolve the name. The telephone number hierarchy mentioned earlier helps explain. Although telephone numbers are assigned hierarchically, they are resolved in a bottom-up fashion. Because the majority of telephone calls are local, they can be resolved by the local exchange

---

†For reliability, there are multiple servers for each node in the domain server tree.
‡See BOOTP in Chapter 19 for one possible approach.

without searching the hierarchy. Furthermore, calls within a given area code can be resolved without contacting sites outside the area code. When applied to domain names, these ideas lead to a two-step name resolution mechanism that preserves the administrative hierarchy but permits efficient translation.

We have said that most queries to name servers refer to local names. In the two-step name resolution process, resolution begins with the local name server. If the local server cannot resolve a name, the query must then be sent to another server in the domain system.

20.13 Caching: The Key To Efficiency

The cost of lookup for nonlocal names can be extremely high if resolvers send each query to the root server. Even if queries could go directly to the server that has authority for the name, name lookup can present a heavy load to an internet. Thus, to improve the overall performance of a name server system, it is necessary to lower the cost of lookup for nonlocal names.

Internet name servers use *name caching* to optimize search costs. Each server maintains a cache of recently used names as well as a record of where the mapping information for that name was obtained. When a client asks the server to resolve a name, the server first checks to see if it has authority for the name according to the standard procedure. If not, the server checks its cache to see if the name has been resolved recently. Servers report cached information to clients, but mark it as a *nonauthoritative* binding, and give the domain name of the server, S, from which they obtained the binding. The local server also sends along additional information that tells the client the binding between S and an IP address. Therefore, clients receive answers quickly, but the information may be out-of-date. If efficiency is important, the client will choose to accept the nonauthoritative answer and proceed. If accuracy is important, the client will choose to contact the authority and verify that the binding between name and address is still valid.

Caching works well in the domain name system because name to address bindings change infrequently. However, they do change. If servers cached information the first time it was requested and never changed it, entries in the cache could become incorrect. To keep the cache correct, servers time each entry and dispose of entries that exceed a reasonable time. When the server is asked for the information after it has removed the entry from the cache, it must go back to the authoritative source and obtain the binding again. More important, servers do not apply a single fixed timeout to all entries, but allow the authority for an entry to configure its timeout. Whenever an authority responds to a request, it includes a *Time To Live* (TTL) value in the response that specifies how long it guarantees the binding to remain. Thus, authorities can reduce network overhead by specifying long timeouts for entries that they expect to remain unchanged, while improving correctness by specifying short timeouts for entries that they expect to change frequently.

Caching is important in hosts as well as local domain name servers. Many timesharing systems run a complex form of resolver code that attempts to provide even more efficiency than the server system. The host downloads the complete database of names and addresses from a local domain name server at startup, maintains its own cache of recently used names, and uses the server only when names are not found. Naturally, a host that maintains a copy of the local server database must check with the server periodically to obtain new mappings, and it must remove entries from its cache after they become invalid. However, most sites have little trouble maintaining consistency because domain names change so infrequently.

Keeping a copy of the local server's database in each host has several advantages. Obviously, it makes name resolution on local hosts extremely fast because it means the host can resolve names without any network activity. It also means that the local site has protection in case the local name server fails. Finally, it reduces the computational load on the name server, and makes it possible for a given server to supply names to more machines.

20.14 Domain Server Message Format

Looking at the details of messages exchanged between clients and domain name servers will help clarify how the system operates from the view of a typical application program. We assume that a user invokes an application program and supplies the name of a machine with which the application must communicate. Before it can use protocols like TCP or UDP to communicate with the specified machine, the application program must find the machine's IP address. It passes the domain name to a local resolver and requests an IP address. The local resolver checks its cache and returns the answer if one is present. If the local resolver does not have an answer, it formats a message and sends it to the server (i.e., it becomes a client). Although our example only involves one name, the message format allows a client to ask multiple questions in a single message. Each question consists of a domain name for which the client seeks an IP address, a specification of the query class (i.e., *internet*), and the type of object desired (e.g., *address*). The server responds by returning a similar message that contains answers to the questions for which the server has bindings. If the server cannot answer all questions, the response will contain information about other name servers that the client can contact to obtain the answers.

Responses also contain information about the servers that are authorities for the replies and the IP addresses of those servers. Figure 20.5 shows the message format.

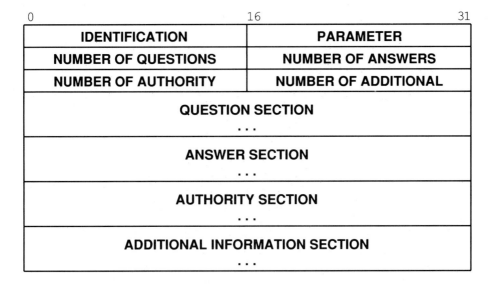

Figure 20.5 Domain name server message format. The question, answer, authority, and additional information sections are variable length.

As Figure 20.5 shows, each message begins with a fixed header that contains a unique *IDENTIFICATION* field that the client uses to match responses to queries. In the header, the field labeled *PARAMETER* specifies the operation requested and a response code, as shown in Figure 20.6 below.

The fields labeled *NUMBER OF* each give a count of entries in the corresponding sections that occur later in the message. For example, the field labeled *NUMBER OF QUESTIONS* gives the count of entries that appear in the *QUESTION SECTION* of the message.

The *QUESTION SECTION* contains queries for which answers are desired. The client fills in only the question section; the server returns the questions and answers in its response. Each question consists of a *QUERY DOMAIN NAME* followed by *QUERY TYPE* and *QUERY CLASS* fields, as Figure 20.7 shows.

Bit of PARAMETER field	Meaning
0	Operation: 0 Query 1 Response
1-4	Query Type: 0 Standard 1 Inverse 2 Completion 1 (now obsolete) 3 Completion 2 (now obsolete)
5	Set if answer authoritative
6	Set if message truncated
7	Set if recursion desired
8	Set if recursion available
9-11	Reserved
12-15	Response Type: 0 No error 1 Format error in query 2 Server failure 3 Name does not exist

Figure 20.6 The meaning of bits of the *PARAMETER* field in a domain name server message. Bits are numbered left to right starting at 0.

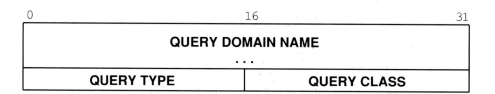

Figure 20.7 The format of entries in the question section of a domain name server message. The domain name is variable length. Clients fill in the questions; servers return them along with answers.

Although the *QUERY DOMAIN NAME* field has variable length, we will see in the next section that the internal representation of domain names makes it possible for the receiver to know the exact length. The *QUERY TYPE* encodes the type of the question (e.g., whether the question refers to a machine name or a mail address). The *QUERY CLASS* field allows domain names to be used for arbitrary objects because official Internet names are only one possible class. It should be noted that, although the diagram in Figure 20.5 follows our convention of showing formats in 32-bit multiples, the query domain name field may contain an arbitrary number of octets. No padding is used. Therefore, messages to or from domain name servers may contain an odd number of octets.

In a domain name server message, each of the *ANSWER SECTION*, *AUTHORITY SECTION*, and *ADDITIONAL INFORMATION SECTION* consists of a set of *resource records* that describe domain names and mappings. Each resource record describes one name. Figure 20.8 shows the format.

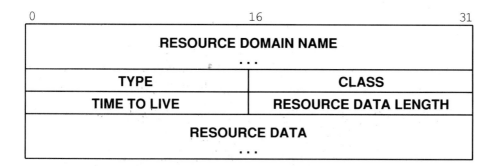

Figure 20.8 The format of resource records used in later sections of messages returned by domain name servers.

The *RESOURCE DOMAIN NAME* field contains the domain name to which this resource record refers. It may be an arbitrary length. The *TYPE* field specifies the type of the data included in the resource record; the *CLASS* field specifies it class. The *TIME TO LIVE* field contains an integer that specifies the number of seconds information in this resource record can be cached. It is used by clients who have requested a name binding and may want to cache the results. The last two fields contain the results of the binding, with the *RESOURCE DATA LENGTH* field specifying the count of octets in the *RESOURCE DATA* field.

20.15 Compressed Name Format

When represented in a message, domain names are stored as a sequence of labels. Each label begins with an octet that specifies its length. Thus, the receiver reconstructs a domain name by repeatedly reading a 1-octet length, *n*, and then reading a label *n* octets long. A length octet containing zero marks the end of the name.

Domain name servers often return multiple answers to a query and, in many cases, suffixes of the domain overlap. To conserve space in the reply packet, the name servers compress names by storing only one copy of each domain name. When extracting a domain name from a message, the client software must check each segment of the name to see whether it consists of a literal string (in the format of a 1-octet count followed by the characters that make up the name) or a pointer to a literal string. When it encounters a pointer, the client must follow the pointer to a new place in the message to find the remainder of the name.

Pointers always occur at the beginning of segments and are encoded in the count byte. If the top 2 bits of the 8-bit segment count field are 1s, the client must take the next 14 bits as an integer pointer. If the top two bits are zero, the next 6 bits specify the number of characters in the label that follow the count octet.

20.16 Abbreviation Of Domain Names

The telephone number hierarchy illustrates another useful feature of local resolution, viz., *name abbreviation*. Abbreviation provides a method of shortening names when the resolving process can supply part of the name automatically. Normally, a subscriber omits the area code when dialing a local telephone number. The resulting digits form an abbreviated name assumed to lie within the same area code as the subscriber's phone. Abbreviation also works well for machine names. Given a name like *xyz*, the resolving process can assume it lies in the same local authority as the machine on which it is being resolved. Thus, the resolver can supply missing parts of the name automatically. For example, within the Computer Science Department at Purdue, the abbreviated name

xinu

is equivalent to the full domain name

xinu.cs.purdue.edu

Most client software implements abbreviations with a *domain suffix list*. The local network manager configures a list of possible suffixes to be appended to names during lookup. When a resolver encounters a name, it steps through the list, appending each suffix and trying to look up the resulting name. For example, the suffix list for the Computer Science Department at Purdue includes:

.cs.purdue.edu
.cc.purdue.edu
.purdue.edu
null

Thus, local resolvers first append *cs.purdue.edu* onto the name *xinu*. If that lookup fails, they append *cc.purdue.edu* onto the name and look that up. The last suffix in the example list is the null string, meaning that if all other lookups fail, the resolver will attempt to look up the name with no suffix. Managers can use the suffix list to make abbreviation convenient or to restrict application programs to local names.

We said that the client takes responsibility for the expansion of such abbreviations, but it should be emphasized that such abbreviations are not part of the domain name system itself. The domain system only allows lookup of a fully specified domain name. As a consequence, programs that depend on abbreviations may not work correctly outside the environment in which they were built. We can summarize:

> *The domain name system only maps full domain names into addresses; abbreviations are not part of the domain name system itself, but are introduced by client software to make local names convenient for users.*

20.17 Inverse Mappings

We said that the domain name system can provide mappings other than machine name to IP address. *Inverse queries* allow the client to ask a server to map "backwards" by taking an answer and generating the question that would produce that answer. Of course, not all answers have a unique question. Even when they do, a server may not be able to provide it. Although inverse queries have been part of the domain system since it was first specified, they are generally not used because there is often no way to find the server that can resolve the query without searching the entire set of servers.

20.18 Pointer Queries

One form of inverse mapping is so obviously needed that the domain system supports a special domain and a special form of question called a *pointer query* to answer it. In a pointer query, the question presented to a domain name server specifies an IP address encoded as a printable string in the form of a domain name (i.e., a textual representation of digits separated by periods). A pointer query requests the name server to return the correct domain name for the machine with the specified IP address. Pointer queries are especially useful for diskless machines because they allow the system to obtain a high-level name given only an IP address. (We have already seen in Chapter 6 how a diskless machine can obtain its IP address.)

Pointer queries are not difficult to generate. If we think of an IP address written in dotted-decimal form, it has the following format:

$$aaa.bbb.ccc.ddd$$

To form a pointer query, the client rearranges the dotted decimal representation of the address into a string of the form:

$$ddd.ccc.bbb.aaa.in\text{-}addr.arpa$$

The new form is a name in the special *in-addr.arpa* domain†. Because the local name server may not be the authority for either the *arpa* domain or the *in-addr.arpa* domain, it may need to contact other name servers to complete the resolution. To make the resolution of pointer queries efficient, the Internet root domain servers maintain a database of valid IP addresses along with information about domain name servers that can resolve each address.

20.19 Object Types And Resource Record Contents

We have mentioned that the domain name system can be used for translating a domain name to a mail exchanger address as well as for translating a host name to an IP address. The domain system is quite general in that it can be used for arbitrary hierarchical names. For example, one might decide to store the names of available computational services along with a mapping from each name to the telephone number to call to find out about the corresponding service. Or one might store names of protocol products along with a mapping to the names and addresses of vendors that offer such products.

Recall that the system accommodates a variety of mappings by including a *type* in each resource record. When sending a request, a client must specify the type in its query†; servers specify the data type in all resource records they return. The type determines the contents of the resource record according to the table in Figure 20.9.

Type	Meaning	Contents
A	Host Address	32-bit IP address
CNAME	Canonical Name	Canonical Domain Name for an alias
HINFO	CPU & OS	Name of CPU and Operating System
MINFO	Mailbox info	Information about a mailbox or mail list
MX	Mail Exchanger	16-bit preference and name of host that acts as mail exchanger for the domain
NS	Name Server	Name of authoritative server for domain
PTR	Pointer	Domain name (like a symbolic link)
SOA	Start of Authority	Multiple fields that specify which parts of the naming hierarchy a server implements
TXT	Arbitrary text	Uninterpreted string of ASCII text

Figure 20.9 Domain Name System resource record types.

Most data is of type *A*, meaning that it consists of the name of a host attached to the Internet along with the host's IP address. The second most useful domain type, *MX*, is assigned to names used for electronic mail exchangers. It allows a site to specify multiple machines that are each capable of accepting mail. When sending electronic mail, the user specifies an electronic mail address in the form *user@domain-part*. The mail

---

†The octets of the IP address must be reversed when forming a domain name because IP addresses have the most significant octets first while domain names have the least-significant octets first.

†Queries can specify a few additional types (e.g., there is a query type that requests all resource records).

system uses the domain name system to resolve *domain-part* with query type *MX*. The domain system returns a set of resource records that each contain a preference field and a host's domain name. The mail system steps through the set from highest preference to lowest (lower numbers mean higher preference). For each *MX* resource record, the mailer extracts the domain name and uses a type *A* query to resolve that name to an IP address. It tries to contact the host and deliver mail. If the host is unavailable, the mailer will continue trying other hosts on the list.

To make lookup efficient, a server always returns additional bindings that it knows in the *ADDITIONAL INFORMATION SECTION* of a response. In the case of *MX* records, a domain server can use the *ADDITIONAL INFORMATION SECTION* to return type *A* resource records for domain names reported in the *ANSWER SECTION*. Doing so substantially reduces the number of queries a mailer sends to its domain server.

20.20 Obtaining Authority For A Subdomain

Before an institution is granted authority for an official second-level domain, it must agree to operate a domain name server that meets Internet standards. Of course, a domain name server must obey the protocol standards that specify message formats and the rules for responding to requests. The server must also know the addresses of servers that handle each subdomain (if any exist) as well as the address of at least one root server.

In practice, the domain system is much more complex than we have outlined. In most cases, a single physical server may handle more than one part of the naming hierarchy. For example, a single name server at Purdue University handles both the second-level domain *purdue.edu* as well as the geographic domain *laf.in.us*. A subtree of names managed by a given name server forms a *zone of authority*. Another practical complication arises because servers must be able to handle many requests, even though some requests take a long time to resolve. Usually, servers support concurrent activity, allowing work to proceed on later requests while earlier ones are being processed. Handling requests concurrently is especially important when the server receives a recursive request that forces it to send the request on to another server for resolution.

Server implementation is also complicated because the Internet authority requires that the information in every domain name server be replicated. Information must appear in at least two servers that do not operate on the same computer. In practice, the requirements are quite stringent: the servers must have no single common point of failure. Avoiding common points of failure means that the two name servers cannot both attach to the same network; they cannot even obtain electrical power from the same source. Thus, to meet the requirements, a site must find at least one other site that agrees to operate a backup name server. Of course, at any point in the tree of servers, a server must know how to locate both the primary and backup name servers for subdomains, and it must direct queries to a backup name server if the primary server is unavailable.

20.21 Summary

Hierarchical naming systems allow delegation of authority for names, making it possible to accommodate an arbitrarily large set of names without overwhelming a central site with administrative duties. Although name resolution is separate from delegation of authority, it is possible to create hierarchical naming systems in which resolution is an efficient process that starts at the local server even though delegation of authority always flows from the top of the hierarchy downward.

We examined the Internet domain name system, an example of a distributed, hierarchical naming scheme. Domain name servers map high-level domain names to IP addresses or to mail exchanger addresses. Clients begin by trying to resolve names locally. When the local server cannot resolve the name, the client must choose to work through the tree of name servers iteratively or request the local name server to do it recursively. Finally, we saw that the domain name system supports a variety of bindings including bindings from IP addresses to high-level names.

FOR FURTHER STUDY

Mockapetris [RFC 1034] discusses Internet domain naming in general, giving the overall philosophy, while Mockapetris [RFC 1035] provides a protocol standard for domain naming. Mockapetris [RFC 1101] discusses using the domain name system to encode network names and proposes extensions useful for other mappings. Older versions appeared in Mockapetris [RFC 882, 883, and 973]. Postel and Reynolds [RFC 920] states the requirements that an Internet domain name server must meet. Stahl [RFC 1032] gives administrators guidelines for establishing a domain, and Lottor [RFC 1033] provides guidelines for operating a domain name server. Finally, Partridge [RFC 974] relates domain naming to electronic mail addressing.

EXERCISES

20.1   Machine names should not be bound into the operating system at compile time. Explain why.

20.2   Would you prefer to use a machine that obtained its name from a remote file or from a name server? Why?

20.3   Why should each name server know the IP address of its parent instead of the domain name of its parent?

20.4   Devise a naming scheme that tolerates changes to the naming hierarchy. As an example, consider that two large companies each have an independent hierarchy and they merge. Can you arrange to have all previous names still work correctly?

20.5   Read the standard and find out how the domain name system uses *SOA* records.

20.6   The Internet domain naming system can also accommodate mailbox names. Find out how.

20.7   The standard suggests that when a program needs to find the domain name associated with an IP address, it should send an inverse query to the local server first and use domain *in-addr.arpa* only if that fails. Why?

20.8   How would you accommodate abbreviations in the domain naming scheme? Sketch name servers for two departments at each of two universities as well as a top-level name server. Explain how each server would treat each type of abbreviation.

20.9   Obtain the official description of the domain name system and build a client program. Look up the name *merlin.cs.purdue.edu.*

20.10   Extend the exercise above to include a pointer query. Try looking up the domain name for address *128.10.2.3* .

20.11   If we extended the domain name syntax to include a dot after the top-level domain, names and abbreviations would be unambiguous. What are the advantages and disadvantages of the extension?

21

The Socket Interface

21.1 Introduction

So far, we have concentrated on discussing the principles and concepts that underlie the TCP/IP protocols without specifying the interface between the application programs and the protocol software. This chapter reviews one example of an interface between application programs and TCP/IP protocols. There are two reasons for postponing the discussion of interfaces. First, in principle we must distinguish between the interface and TCP/IP protocols because the standards do not specify exactly how application programs interact with protocol software. Thus, the interface architecture is not standardized; its design lies outside the scope of the protocol suite. Second, in practice, it is inappropriate to tie the protocols to a particular interface because no single interface architecture works well on all systems. In particular, because protocol software resides in a computer's operating system, interface details depend on the operating system.

Despite the lack of a standard, reviewing an example will help us understand how programmers use TCP/IP. Although the example we have chosen is from the 4BSD UNIX operating system, it has become widely accepted and is used in many other systems. The reader should keep in mind that our goal is merely to give one concrete example, not to prescribe how interfaces should be designed. The reader should also remember that the operations listed here do not comprise a standard in any sense.

21.2 The UNIX I/O Paradigm And Network I/O

Developed in the late 1960s and early 1970s, UNIX was originally designed as a timesharing system for single processor computers. It is a process-oriented system in which application programs execute as user level processes. An application program interacts with the operating system by making *system calls*. From the programmer's point of view, system calls look and behave exactly like other procedure calls. They take arguments and return one or more results. Arguments can be values (e.g., an integer count) or pointers to objects in the application program (e.g., a buffer to be filled with characters).

The UNIX input and output (I/O) primitives, derived from those in Multics and earlier systems, follow a paradigm sometimes referred to as *open-read-write-close*. Before a user process can perform I/O operations, it calls *open* to specify the file or device to be used and obtains permission. The call to *open* returns a small integer *file descriptor*† that the process uses when performing I/O operations on the opened file or device. Once an object has been opened, the user process makes one or more calls to *read* or *write* to transfer data. *Read* transfers data into the user process; *write* transfers data from the user process to the file or device. Both *read* and *write* take three arguments that specify the file descriptor to use, the address of a buffer, and the number of bytes to transfer. After all transfer operations are complete, the user process calls *close* to inform the operating system that it has finished using the object (the operating system automatically closes all open objects if a process terminates without calling *close*).

21.3 Adding Network I/O to UNIX

Originally, UNIX designers cast all I/O operations in the open-read-write-close paradigm described above. The scheme included I/O for character-oriented devices like CRT terminals and block-oriented devices like disks and data files. Early implementations of TCP/IP under UNIX also used the open-read-write-close paradigm with a special file name, */dev/tcp*.

The group adding network protocols to 4BSD UNIX decided that because network protocols are more complex than conventional I/O devices, interaction between user processes and network protocols must be more complex than interactions between user processes and conventional I/O facilities. In particular, the protocol interface must allow programmers to create both server code that awaits connections passively as well as client code that forms connections actively. Furthermore, application programs sending datagrams may wish to specify the destination address along with each datagram instead of binding destinations at the time they call *open*. To handle all these cases, the designers chose to abandon the traditional UNIX open-read-write-close paradigm and added several new operating system calls as well as new library routines. Adding network protocols to UNIX increased the complexity of the I/O interface substantially.

---

†The term "file descriptor" arises because in UNIX all devices are mapped into the file system name space. In most cases, files, devices, and other I/O operations are indistinguishable.

Further complexity arises in the UNIX protocol interface because designers attempted to build a general mechanism to accommodate many protocols. For example, the generality makes it possible to have protocol software for both the TCP/IP protocols as well as the Xerox internet protocols (XNS), and to allow application programs to use either one or both. As a consequence, the application program cannot merely supply an address and expect the operating system to interpret it correctly. The application must explicitly specify that an address is an IP address.

21.4 The Socket Abstraction

The basis for network I/O in 4BSD UNIX centers on an abstraction known as the *socket*†. We think of a socket as a generalization of the UNIX file access mechanism that provides an endpoint for communication. As with file access, application programs request the operating system to create a socket when one is needed. The system returns a small integer that the application program uses to reference the newly created socket. The chief difference between file descriptors and socket descriptors is that the operating system binds a file descriptor to a specific file or device when the application calls *open*, but it can create sockets without binding them to specific destination addresses. The application can choose to supply a destination address each time it uses the socket (e.g., when sending datagrams), or it can choose to bind the destination address to the socket and avoid specifying the destination repeatedly (e.g., when making a TCP connection).

Whenever it makes sense, sockets perform exactly like UNIX files or devices, so they can be used with traditional operations like *read* and *write*. For example, once an application program creates a socket and creates a TCP connection from the socket to a foreign destination, the program can use *write* to send a stream of data across the connection (the application program at the other end can use *read* to receive it). To make it possible to use primitives like *read* and *write* with both files and sockets, the operating system allocates socket descriptors and file descriptors from the same set of integers and makes sure that if a given integer has been allocated as a file descriptor, it will not also be allocated as a socket descriptor.

21.5 Creating A Socket

The *socket* system call creates sockets on demand. It takes three integer arguments and returns an integer result:

$$result = socket(af, type, protocol)$$

Argument *af* specifies the protocol family to be used with the socket. That is, it specifies how to interpret addresses when they are supplied. Current families include the TCP/IP internet (AF_INET), Xerox Corporation PUP internet (AF_PUP), Apple Com-

---

†For now, we will describe sockets as part of the operating system because that is the way 4BSD UNIX provides them; later sections describe how other operating systems use library routines to provide a socket interface.

puter Incorporated Appletalk network (AF_APPLETALK), and UNIX file system (AF_UNIX) as well as many others.

Argument *type* specifies the type of communication desired. Possible types include reliable stream delivery service (SOCK_STREAM) and connectionless datagram delivery service (SOCK_DGRAM), as well as a raw type (SOCK_RAW) that allows privileged programs to access low-level protocols or network interfaces. Two additional types have been planned but not implemented.

Although the general approach of separating protocol families and types may seem sufficient to handle all cases easily, it does not. First, it may be that a given family of protocols does not support one or more of the possible service types. For example, the UNIX family has an interprocess communication mechanism called a *pipe* that uses a reliable stream delivery service, but has no mechanism for sequenced packet delivery. Thus, not all combinations of protocol family and service type make sense. Second, some protocol families have multiple protocols that support one type of service. For example, it may be that a single protocol family has two connectionless datagram delivery services. To accommodate multiple protocols within a family, the *socket* call has a third argument that can be used to select a specific protocol. To use the third argument, the programmer must understand the protocol family well enough to know the type of service each protocol supplies.

Because the designers tried to capture many of the conventional UNIX operations in their socket design, they needed a way to simulate the UNIX pipe mechanism. It is not necessary to understand the details of pipes; only one salient feature is important: pipes differ from standard network operations because the calling process creates both endpoints for the communication simultaneously. To accommodate pipes, the designers added a *socketpair* system call that takes the form:

socketpair(af, type, protocol, sarray)

Socketpair has one more argument than the *socket* procedure, *sarray*. The additional argument gives the address of a 2-element integer array. *Socketpair* creates two sockets simultaneously and places the two socket descriptors in the two elements of *sarray*. Readers should understand that *socketpair* is not meaningful when applied to the TCP/IP protocol family (it has been included here merely to make our description of the interface complete).

21.6 Socket Inheritance And Termination

UNIX uses the *fork* and *exec* system calls to start new application programs. It is a two-step procedure. In the first step, *fork* creates a separate copy of the currently executing application program. In the second step, the new copy replaces itself with the desired application program. When a program calls *fork*, the newly created copy inherits access to all open sockets just as it inherits access to all open files. When a program calls *exec*, the new application retains access to all open sockets. We will see that master servers use socket inheritance when they create slave servers to handle a specific connection. Internally, the operating system keeps a reference count associated with each socket, so it knows how many application programs (processes) have access to it.

Both the old and new processes have the same access rights to existing sockets, and both can access the sockets. Thus, it is the responsibility of the programmer to ensure that the two processes use the shared socket meaningfully.

When a process finishes using a socket it calls *close*. *Close* has the form:

close(socket)

where argument *socket* specifies the descriptor of a socket to close. When a process terminates for any reason, the system closes all sockets that remain open. Internally, a call to *close* decrements the reference count for a socket and destroys the socket if the count reaches zero.

21.7 Specifying A Local Address

Initially, a socket is created without any association to local or destination addresses. For the TCP/IP protocols, this means no local protocol port number has been assigned and no destination port or IP address has been specified. In many cases, application programs do not care about the local address they use and are willing to allow the protocol software to choose one for them. However, server processes that operate at a well-known port must be able to specify that port to the system. Once a socket has been created, a server uses the *bind* system call to establish a local address for it. *Bind* has the following form:

bind(socket, localaddr, addrlen)

Argument *socket* is the integer descriptor of the socket to be bound. Argument *localaddr* is a structure that specifies the local address to which the socket should be bound, and argument *addrlen* is an integer that specifies the length of the address measured in bytes. Instead of giving the address merely as a sequence of bytes, the designers chose to use a structure for addresses as Figure 21.1 illustrates.

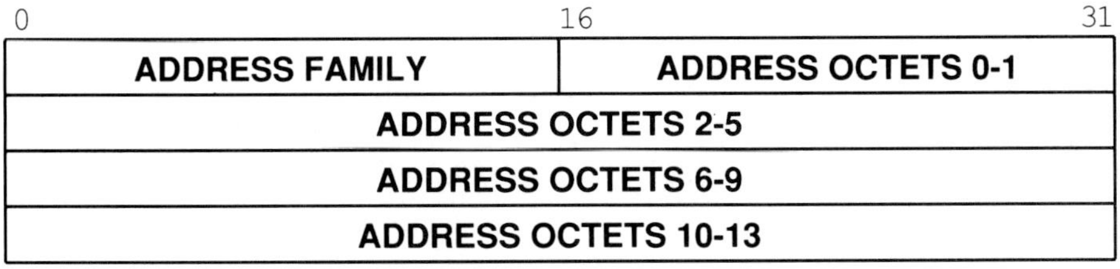

0	16	31
ADDRESS FAMILY	**ADDRESS OCTETS 0-1**	
ADDRESS OCTETS 2-5		
ADDRESS OCTETS 6-9		
ADDRESS OCTETS 10-13		

Figure 21.1 The *sockaddr* structure used when passing a TCP/IP address to the socket interface.

The structure, generically named *sockaddr*, begins with a 16-bit *ADDRESS FAMILY* field that identifies the protocol suite to which the address belongs. It is followed by an address of up to *14* octets. When declared in C, the socket address structure is a union of structures for all possible address families.

The value in the *ADDRESS FAMILY* field determines the format of the remaining address octets. For example, the value *2†* in the *ADDRESS FAMILY* field means the remaining address octets contain a TCP/IP address. Each protocol family defines how it will use octets in the address field. For TCP/IP addresses, the socket address is known as *sockaddr_in*. It includes both an IP address and a protocol port number (i.e., an internet socket address structure can contain both an IP address and a protocol port at that address). Figure 21.2 shows the exact format of a TCP/IP socket address.

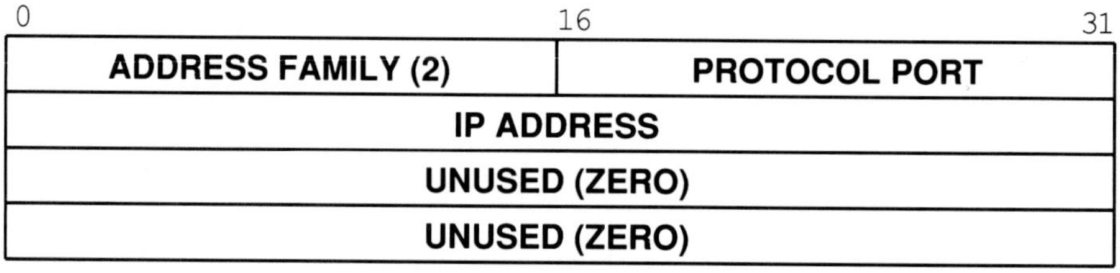

0	16	31
ADDRESS FAMILY (2)	PROTOCOL PORT	
IP ADDRESS		
UNUSED (ZERO)		
UNUSED (ZERO)		

Figure 21.2 The format of a socket address structure (sockaddr_in) when used with a TCP/IP internet address. The structure includes both an IP address and a protocol port at that address.

Although it is possible to specify arbitrary values in the address structure when calling *bind*, not all possible bindings are valid. For example, the caller might request a local protocol port that is already in use by another program, or it might request an invalid IP address. In such cases, the *bind* call fails and returns an error code.

21.8 Connecting Sockets To Destination Addresses

Initially, a socket is created in the *unconnected state*, which means that the socket is not associated with any foreign destination. The system call *connect* binds a permanent destination to a socket, placing it in the *connected state*. An application program must call *connect* to establish a connection before it can transfer data through a reliable stream socket. Sockets used with connectionless datagram services need not be connected before they are used, but doing so makes it possible to transfer data without specifying the destination each time.

The *connect* system call has the form:

connect(socket, destaddr, addrlen)

---

†UNIX uses the symbolic name *AF_INET* to denote TCP/IP addresses.

Argument *socket* is the integer descriptor of the socket to connect. Argument *destaddr* is a socket address structure that specifies the destination address to which the socket should be bound. Argument *addrlen* specifies the length of the destination address measured in bytes.

The semantics of *connect* depend on the underlying protocols. Selecting the reliable stream delivery service in the AF_INET family means choosing TCP. In such cases, *connect* builds a TCP connection with the destination and returns an error if it cannot. In the case of connectionless service, *connect* does nothing more than store the destination address locally.

21.9 Sending Data Through A Socket

Once an application program has established a socket, it can use the socket to transmit data. There are five possible operating system calls from which to choose: *send, sendto, sendmsg, write,* and *writev. Send, write,* and *writev* only work with connected sockets because they do not allow the caller to specify a destination address. The differences between the three are minor. *Write* takes three arguments:

write(socket, buffer, length)

Argument *socket* contains an integer socket descriptor (*write* can also be used with other types of descriptors). Argument *buffer* contains the address of the data to be sent, and argument *length* specifies the number of bytes to send. The call to *write* blocks until the data can be transferred (e.g., it blocks if internal system buffers for the socket are full). Like most system calls in UNIX, *write* returns an error code to the application calling it, allowing the programmer to know if the operation succeeded.

The system call *writev* works like *write* except that it uses a "gather write" form, making it possible for the application program to write a message without copying the message into contiguous bytes of memory. *Writev* has the form:

writev(socket, iovector, vectorlen)

Argument *iovector* gives the address of an array of type *iovec* that contains a sequence of pointers to the blocks of bytes that form the message. As Figure 21.3 shows, a length accompanies each pointer. Argument *vectorlen* specifies the number of entries in *iovector*.

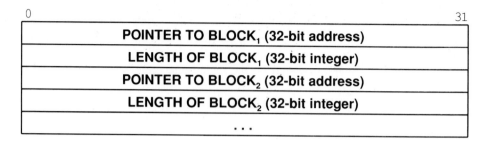

Figure 21.3 The format of an iovector of type iovec used with *writev* and *readv*.

The *send* system call has the form:

> send(socket, message, length, flags)

where argument *socket* specifies the socket to use, argument *message* gives the address of the data to be sent, argument *length* specifies the number of bytes to be sent, and argument *flags* controls the transmission. One value for *flags* allows the sender to specify that the message should be sent out-of-band on sockets that support such a notion. For example, recall from Chapter 12 that out-of-band messages correspond to TCP's notion of urgent data. Another value for *flags* allows the caller to request that the message be sent without using local routing tables. The intention is to allow the caller to take control of routing, making it possible to write network debugging software. Of course, not all sockets support all requests from arbitrary programs. Some requests require the program to have special privileges; others are simply not supported on all sockets.

System calls *sendto* and *sendmsg* allow the caller to send a message through an unconnected socket because they both require the caller to specify a destination. *Sendto*, which takes the destination address as an argument, has the form:

> sendto(socket, message, length, flags, destaddr, addrlen)

The first four arguments are exactly the same as those used with the *send* system call. The final two arguments specify a destination address and give the length of that address. Argument *destaddr* specifies the destination address using the *sockaddr_in* structure as defined in Figure 21.2.

A programmer may choose to use system call *sendmsg* in cases where the long list of arguments required for *sendto* makes the program inefficient or difficult to read. *Sendmsg* has the form:

> sendmsg(socket, messagestruct, flags)

where argument *messagestruct* is a structure of the form illustrated in Figure 21.4. The structure contains information about the message to be sent, its length, the destination address, and the address length. This call is especially useful because there is a corresponding input operation (described below) that produces a message structure in exactly the same format.

0   31

POINTER TO SOCKETADDR
SIZE OF SOCKETADDR
POINTER TO IOVEC LIST
LENGTH OF IOVEC LIST
POINTER TO ACCESS RIGHTS LIST
LENGTH OF ACCESS RIGHTS LIST

Figure 21.4 The format of message structure *messagestruct* used by *sendmsg*.

21.10 Receiving Data Through A Socket

Analogous to the five different output operations, 4BSD UNIX offers five system calls that a process can use to receive data through a socket: *read*, *readv*, *recv*, *recvfrom*, and *recvmsg*. The conventional UNIX input operation, *read*, can only be used when the socket is connected. It has the form:

read(descriptor, buffer, length)

where *descriptor* gives the integer descriptor of a socket or file descriptor from which to read data, *buffer* specifies the address in memory at which to store the data, and *length* specifies the maximum number of bytes to read.

An alternative form, *readv*, allows the caller to use a "scatter read" style of interface that places the incoming data in noncontiguous locations. *Readv* has the form:

readv(descriptor, iovector, vectorlen)

Argument *iovector* gives the address of a structure of type *iovec* (see Figure 21.3) that contains a sequence of pointers to blocks of memory into which the incoming data should be stored. Argument *vectorlen* specifies the number of entries in *iovector*.

In addition to the conventional input operations, there are three additional system calls for network message input. Processes call *recv* to receive data from a connected socket. It has the form:

recv(socket, buffer, length, flags)

Argument *socket* specifies a socket descriptor from which data should be received. Argument *buffer* specifies the address in memory into which the message should be placed, and argument *length* specifies the length of the buffer area. Finally, argument *flags* allows the caller to control the reception. Among the possible values for the *flags* argument is one that allows the caller to look ahead by extracting a copy of the next incoming message without removing the message from the socket.

The system call *recvfrom* allows the caller to specify input from an unconnected socket. It includes additional arguments that allow the caller to specify where to record the sender's address. The form is:

recvfrom(socket, buffer, length, flags, fromaddr, addrlen)

The two additional arguments, *fromaddr* and *addrlen*, are pointers to a socket address structure and an integer. The operating system uses *fromaddr* to record the address of the message sender and uses *fromlen* to record the length of the sender's address. Notice that the output operation *sendto*, discussed above, takes an address in exactly the same form as *recvfrom* generates. Thus, sending replies is easy.

The final system call used for input, *recvmsg*, is analogous to the *sendmsg* output operation. *Recvmsg* operates like *recvfrom*, but requires fewer arguments. Its form is:

recvmsg(socket, messagestruct, flags)

where argument *messagestruct* gives the address of a structure that holds the address for an incoming message as well as locations for the sender's address. The structure produced by *recvmsg* is exactly the same as the structure used by *sendmsg*, making them operate well as a pair.

21.11 Obtaining Local And Remote Socket Addresses

We said that newly created processes inherit the set of open sockets from the process that created them. Sometimes, a newly created process needs to determine the destination address to which a socket connects. A process may also wish to determine the local address of a socket. Two system calls provide such information: *getpeername* and *getsockname* (despite their names, both deal with what we think of as ''addresses'').

A process calls *getpeername* to determine the address of the peer (i.e., the remote end) to which a socket connects. It has the form:

getpeername(socket, destaddr, addrlen)

Argument *socket* specifies the socket for which the address is desired. Argument *destaddr* is a pointer to a structure of type *sockaddr* (see Figure 21.1) that will receive the socket address. Finally, argument *addrlen* is a pointer to an integer that will receive the length of the address. *Getpeername* only works with connected sockets.

System call *getsockname* returns the local address associated with a socket. It has the form:

getsockname(socket, localaddr, addrlen)

As expected, argument *socket* specifies the socket for which the local address is desired. Argument *localaddr* is a pointer to a structure of type *sockaddr* that will contain the address, and argument *addrlen* is a pointer to an integer that will contain the length of the address.

21.12 Obtaining And Setting Socket Options

In addition to binding a socket to a local address or connecting it to a destination address, the need arises for a mechanism that permits application programs to control the socket. For example, when using protocols that use timeout and retransmission, the application program may want to obtain or set the timeout parameters. It may also want to control the allocation of buffer space, determine if the socket allows transmission of broadcast, or control processing of out-of-band data. Rather than add new system calls for each new control operation, the designers decided to build a single mechanism. The mechanism has two operations: *getsockopt* and *setsockopt*.

System call *getsockopt* allows the application to request information about the socket. A caller specifies the socket, the option of interest, and a location at which to store the requested information. The operating system examines its internal data structures for the socket and passes the requested information to the caller. The call has the form:

getsockopt(socket, level, optionid, optionval, length)

Argument *socket* specifies the socket for which information is needed. Argument *level* identifies whether the operation applies to the socket itself or to the underlying protocols being used. Argument *optionid* specifies a single option to which the request applies. The pair of arguments *optionval* and *length* specify two pointers. The first gives the address of a buffer into which the system places the requested value, and the second gives the address of an integer into which the system places the length of the option value.

System call *setsockopt* allows an application program to set a socket option using the set of values obtained with *getsockopt*. The caller specifies a socket for which the option should be set, the option to be changed, and a value for the option. The call to *setsockopt* has the form:

setsockopt(socket, level, optionid, optionval, length)

where the arguments are like those for *getsockopt*, except that the *length* argument contains the length of the option being passed to the system. The caller must supply a legal value for the option as well as a correct length for that value. Of course, not all options apply to all sockets. The correctness and semantics of individual requests depend on the current state of the socket and the underlying protocols being used.

21.13 Specifying A Queue Length For A Server

One of the options that applies to sockets is used so frequently, a separate system call has been dedicated to it. To understand how it arises, consider a server. The server creates a socket, binds it to a well-known protocol port, and waits for requests. If the server uses a reliable stream delivery, or if computing a response takes nontrivial amounts of time, it may happen that a new request arrives before the server finishes responding to an old request. To avoid having protocols reject or discard incoming requests, a server must tell the underlying protocol software that it wishes to have such requests enqueued until it has time to process them.

The system call *listen* allows servers to prepare a socket for incoming connections. In terms of the underlying protocols, *listen* puts the socket in a passive mode ready to accept connections. When the server invokes *listen*, it also informs the operating system that the protocol software should enqueue multiple simultaneous requests that arrive at the socket. The form is:

$$listen(socket, qlength)$$

Argument *socket* gives the descriptor of a socket that should be prepared for use by a server, and argument *qlength* specifies the length of the request queue for that socket. After the call, the system will enqueue up to *qlength* requests for connections. If the queue is full when a request arrives, the operating system will refuse the connection by discarding the request. *Listen* applies only to sockets that have selected reliable stream delivery service.

21.14 How A Server Accepts Connections

As we have seen, a server process uses the system calls *socket*, *bind*, and *listen* to create a socket, bind it to a well-known protocol port, and specify a queue length for connection requests. Note that the call to *bind* associates the socket with a well-known protocol port, but that the socket is not connected to a specific foreign destination. In fact, the foreign destination must specify a *wildcard*, allowing the socket to receive connection requests from an arbitrary client.

Once a socket has been established, the server needs to wait for a connection. To do so, it uses system call *accept*. A call to *accept* blocks until a connection request arrives. It has the form:

$$newsock = accept(socket, addr, addrlen)$$

Argument *socket* specifies the descriptor of the socket on which to wait. Argument *addr* is a pointer to a structure of type *sockaddr*, and *addrlen* is a pointer to an integer. When a request arrives, the system fills in argument *addr* with the address of the client that has placed the request and sets *addrlen* to the length of the address. Finally, the system creates a new socket that has its destination connected to the requesting client and returns the new socket descriptor to the caller. The original socket still has a wild-card foreign destination and it still remains open. Thus, the master server can continue to accept additional requests at the original socket.

When a connection request arrives, the call to *accept* returns. The server can either handle requests iteratively or concurrently. In the iterative approach, the server handles the request itself, closes the new socket, and then calls *accept* to obtain the next connection request. In the concurrent approach, after the call to accept returns, the master server creates a slave to handle the request (in UNIX terminology, it forks a child process to handle the request). The slave process inherits a copy of the new socket, so it can proceed to service the request. When it finishes, the slave closes the socket and terminates. The original (master) server process closes its copy of the new socket after starting the slave. It then calls *accept* to obtain the next connection request.

The concurrent design for servers may seem confusing because multiple processes will be using the same local protocol port number. The key to understanding the mechanism lies in the way underlying protocols treat protocol ports. Recall that in TCP a pair of endpoints define a connection. Thus, it does not matter how many processes use a given local protocol port number as long as they connect to different destinations. In the case of a concurrent server, there is one process per client and one additional process that accepts connections. The socket the master server process uses has a wildcard for the foreign destination, allowing it to connect with an arbitrary foreign site. Each remaining process has a specific foreign destination. When a TCP segment arrives, it will be sent to the socket connected to the segment's source. If no such socket exists, the segment will be sent to the socket that has a wildcard for its foreign destination. Furthermore, because the socket with a wildcard foreign destination does not have an open connection, it will only honor TCP segments that request a new connection.

21.15 Servers That Handle Multiple Services

The 4BSD UNIX interface provides another interesting possibility for server design because it allows a single process to wait for connections on multiple sockets. The system call that makes such organization possible is called *select*, and it applies to I/O in general, not just to communication over sockets. *Select* has the form:

nready = select(ndesc, indesc, outdesc, excdesc, timeout)

In general, a call to *select* blocks waiting on one of a set of file descriptors to become ready. Argument *ndesc* specifies how many descriptors should be examined (the descriptors checked are always *0* through *ndesc*-1). Argument *indesc* is a pointer to a bit mask that specifies the file descriptors to check for input, argument *outdesc* is a pointer to a bit mask that specifies the file descriptors to check for output, and argument *excdesc* is a pointer to a bit mask that specifies the file descriptors to check for exception conditions. Finally, if argument *timeout* is nonzero, it is the address of an integer that specifies how long to wait for a connection before returning to the caller. A zero value for timeout forces the call to block until a descriptor becomes ready. Because the *timeout* argument contains the address of the timeout integer and not the integer itself, a process can request zero delay by passing the address of an integer that contains zero (i.e., a process can poll to see if I/O is ready).

A call to *select* returns the number of descriptors from the specified set that are ready for I/O. It also changes the bit masks specified by *indesc*, *outdesc*, and *excdesc* to inform the application which of the selected file descriptors are ready. Thus, before calling *select*, the caller must turn on those bits that correspond to descriptors to be checked. Following the call, all bits that remain set to *1* correspond to a ready file descriptor.

To communicate over more than one socket at a time, a process first creates all the sockets it needs and then uses *select* to determine which of them becomes ready for I/O first. Once it finds a socket has become ready, it uses the input or output procedures defined above to communicate.

21.16 Obtaining And Setting The Host Names

The 4BSD UNIX operating system maintains an internal host name. For machines on the Internet, the internal name is usually chosen to be the domain name for the machine's main network interface. The *gethostname* system call allows user processes to access the host name, and the *sethostname* system call allows privileged processes to set the host name. *Gethostname* has the form:

gethostname(name, length)

Argument *name* gives the address of an array of bytes where the name is to be stored, and argument *length* is an integer that specifies the length of the *name* array. To set the host name, a privileged process makes a call of the form:

sethostname(name, length)

Argument *name* gives the address of an array where the name is stored, and argument *length* is an integer that gives the length of the name array.

21.17 Obtaining And Setting The Internal Host Domain

The operating system maintains a string that specifies the naming domain under which a machine falls. When a site obtains authority for part of the domain name space, it invents a string that identifies its piece of the space and uses that string as the name of the domain. For example, machines in the domain

cs.purdue.edu

have names taken from the Arthurian legend. Thus, one finds machines like *merlin*, *arthur*, *guenevere*, and *lancelot*. The domain itself has been named *camelot*, so the operating system on each host in the group must be informed that it resides in the *camelot* domain. To do so, a privileged processes uses system call *setdomainname*, which has the form:

setdomainname(name, length)

Argument *name* gives the address of an array of bytes that contains the name of a domain, and argument *length* is an integer that gives the length of the name.

User processes call *getdomainname* to retrieve the name of the domain from the system. It has the form:

getdomainname(name, length)

where argument *name* specifies the address of an array where the name should be stored, and argument *length* is an integer that specifies the length of the array.

21.18 4BSD UNIX Network Library Calls

In addition to the system calls described above, 4BSD UNIX offers a set of library routines that perform useful functions related to networking. Figure 21.5 illustrates the difference between system calls and library routines. System calls pass control to the computer's operating system, while library routines are like other procedures that the programmer binds into a program.

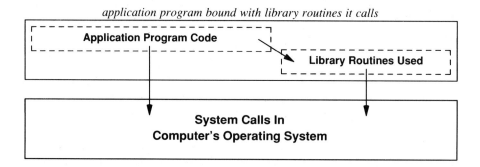

Figure 21.5 The difference between library routines, which are bound into an
application program, and system calls, which are part of the
operating system. A program can call either; library routines
can call other library routines or system calls.

Many of the 4BSD UNIX library routines provide database services that allow a
process to determine the names of machines and network services, protocol port
numbers, and other related information. For example, one set of library routines provides access to the database of network services. We think of entries in the services database as 3-tuples, where each 3-tuple contains the (human readable) name of a network
service, the protocol that supports the service, and a protocol port number for the service. Library routines exist that allow a process to obtain information from an entry
given any piece.

The next sections examine groups of library routines, explaining their purposes and
providing information about how they can be used. As we will see, the sets of library
routines that provide access to a sequential database follow a pattern. Each set allows
the application to: establish a connection to the database, obtain entries one at a time,
and close the connection. The three routines used for these three operations are named
setXent, *getXent*, and *endXent*, where *X* is the name of the database. For example, the
library routes for the host database are named *sethostent*, *gethostent*, and *endhostent*.
The sections that describe these routines summarize the calls without repeating the details of their use.

21.19 Network Byte Order Conversion Routines

Recall that machines differ in the way they store integer quantities and that the
TCP/IP protocols define a machine independent standard for byte order. 4BSD UNIX
provides four library functions that convert between the local machine byte order and
the network standard byte order. To make programs portable, they must be written to
call the conversion routines every time they copy an integer value from the local
machine to a network packet, or when they copy a value from a network packet to the
local machine.

All four conversion routines are functions that take a value as an argument and re-turn a new value with the bytes rearranged. For example, to convert a short (2-byte) in-teger from network byte order to the local host byte order, a programmer calls *ntohs* (network to host short). The format is:

$$localshort = ntohs(netshort)$$

Argument *netshort* is a 2-byte (16-bit) integer in network standard byte order and the result, *localshort*, is in local host byte order.

Unix calls 4 byte (32 bit) integers *longs*. Function *ntohl* (network to host long) converts 4-byte longs from network standard byte order to local host byte order. Pro-grams invoke it as a function, supplying a long integer in network byte order as an ar-gument:

$$locallong = ntohl(netlong)$$

Two analogous functions allow the programmer to convert from local host byte order to network byte order. Function *htons* converts a 2-byte (short) integer in the host's local byte order to a 2-byte integer in network standard byte order. Programs in-voke it as a function:

$$netshort = htons(localshort)$$

The final conversion routine, *htonl*, converts long integers to network standard byte order. Like the others, it is a function:

$$netlong = htonl(locallong)$$

It should be obvious that the conversion routines preserve the following mathemat-ical relationships:

$$netshort = htons(\ ntohs(netshort)\ )$$

and

$$localshort = ntohs(\ htons(localshort)\ )$$

Similar relationships hold for the long integer conversion routines.

21.20 IP Address Manipulation Routines

Because many programs translate between 32-bit IP addresses and the correspond-ing dotted decimal notation, the 4BSD UNIX library includes utility routines that per-form the translation. Procedures *inet_addr* and *inet_network* both translate from dotted decimal format to a 32-bit IP address. *Inet_addr* forms a full 32-bit IP address;

inet_network forms the network address with zeroes for the host part. They have the form:

$$address = inet\_addr(string)$$

and

$$address = inet\_network(string)$$

where argument *string* gives the address of an ASCII string that contains the number expressed in dotted decimal format. The dotted decimal form can have 1 to 4 segments of digits separated by periods (dots). If all 4 appear, each corresponds to a single byte of the resulting 32-bit integer. If less than 4 appear, the last segment is expanded to fill remaining bytes.

Procedure *inet_ntoa* performs the inverse of *inet_addr* by mapping a 32-bit integer to an ASCII string in dotted decimal format. It has the form:

$$str = inet\_ntoa(internetaddr)$$

where argument *internetaddr* is a 32-bit IP address, and *str* is the address of the result-ing ASCII version.

Often programs that manipulate IP addresses must combine a network address with the local address of a host on that network. Procedure *inet_makeaddr* performs such a combination. It has the form:

$$internetaddr = inet\_makeaddr(net, local)$$

Argument *net* is a 32-bit network IP address, and argument *local* is the integer representing a local host address on that network.

Procedures *inet_netof* and *inet_lnaof* provide the inverse of *inet_makeaddr* by separating the network and local portions of an IP address. They have the form:

$$net = inet\_netof(internetaddr)$$

and

$$local = inet\_lnaof(internetaddr)$$

where argument *internetaddr* is a 32-bit IP address.

21.21 Accessing The Domain Name System

A set of five library procedures comprise the 4BSD UNIX interface to the TCP/IP domain name system. Application programs that call these routines become clients of one domain name system, sending one or more servers requests and receiving responses.

The general idea is that a program makes a query, sends it to a server, and awaits an answer. Because many options exist, the routines have only a few basic parameters and use a global structure, *res*, to hold others. For example, one field in *res* enables debugging messages while another controls whether the code uses UDP or TCP for queries. Most fields in *res* begin with reasonable defaults, so the routines can be used without changing it.

A program calls *res_init* before using other procedures. The call takes no arguments:

$$res\_init()$$

Res_init reads a file that contains information like the name of the machine that runs the domain name server and stores the results in global structure *res*.

Procedure *res_mkquery* forms a domain name query and places it in a buffer in memory. The form of the call is:

$$res\_mkquery(op, dname, class, type, data, datalen, newrr, buffer, buflen)$$

The first seven arguments correspond directly to the fields of a domain name query. Argument *op* specifies the requested operation, *dname* gives the address of a character array that contains a domain name, *class* is an integer that gives the class of the query, *type* is an integer that gives the type of the query, *data* gives the address of an array of data to be included in the query, and *datalen* is an integer that gives the length of the data. In addition to the library procedures, UNIX provides application programs with definitions of symbolic constants for important values. Thus, programmers can use the domain name system without understanding the details of the protocol. The last two arguments, *buffer* and *buflen*, specify the address of an area into which the query should be placed and the integer length of the buffer area, respectively. Finally, in the current implementation, argument *newrr* is unused.

Once a program has formed a query, it calls *res_send* to send it to a name server and obtain a response. The form is:

$$res\_send(message, msglen, answer, anslen)$$

Argument *message* is a pointer to a buffer that holds the message to be sent (presumably, the application called procedure *res_mkquery* to form the message). Argument *msglen* is an integer that specifies the length. Argument *answer* gives the address in memory into which a response should be written, and argument *anslen* is an integer that specifies the length of the answer area.

In addition to routines that make and send queries, the 4BSD UNIX library contains two routines that translate domain names between conventional ASCII and the compressed format used in queries. Procedure *dn_expand* expands a compressed domain name into a full ASCII version. It has the form:

$$dn\_expand(msg, eom, compressed, full, fullen)$$

Argument *msg* gives the address of a domain name message that contains the name to be expanded, with *eom* specifying the end-of-message limit beyond which the expansion cannot go. Argument *compressed* is a pointer to the first byte of the compressed name. Argument *full* is a pointer to an array into which the expanded name should be written, and argument *fullen* is an integer that specifies the length of the array.

Generating a compressed name is more complex than expanding a compressed name because compression involves eliminating common suffixes. When compressing names, the client must keep a record of suffixes that have appeared previously. Procedure *dn_comp* compresses a full domain name by comparing suffixes to a list of previously used suffixes and eliminating the longest possible suffix. A call has the form:

> dn_comp(full, compressed, cmprlen, prevptrs, lastptr)

Argument *full* gives the address of a full domain name. Argument *compressed* points to an array of bytes that will hold the compressed name, with argument *cmprlen* specifying the length of the array. The argument *prevptrs* is the address of an array of pointers to previously compressed suffixes, with *lastptr* pointing to the end of the array. Normally, *dn_comp* compresses the name and updates *prevptrs* if a new suffix has been used.

Procedure *dn_comp* can also be used to translate a domain name from ASCII to the internal form without compressing (i.e., without removing suffixes). To do so, one invokes it with the *prevptrs* argument set to *NULL* (i.e., zero).

21.22 Obtaining Information About Hosts

Library procedures exist that allow a process to retrieve information about a host given either its domain name or its IP address. When used on a machine that has access to a domain name server, the library procedures make the process a client of the domain name system by sending a request to a server and waiting for a response. When used on systems that do not have access to the domain name system (e.g., a host not on the Internet), the routines obtain the desired information from a database kept on secondary storage.

Function *gethostbyname* takes a domain name and returns a pointer to a structure of information for that host. A call takes the form:

> ptr = gethostbyname(namestr)

Argument *namestr* is a pointer to a character string that contains a domain name for the host. The value returned, *ptr*, points to a structure that contains the following information: the official host name, a list of aliases that have been registered for the host, the host address type (i.e., whether the address is an IP address), the address length, and a list of one or more addresses for the host. More details can be found in the UNIX Programmer's Manual.

Function *gethostbyaddr* produces the same information as *gethostbyname*. The difference between the two is that *gethostbyaddr* accepts a host address as an argument:

$$ptr = gethostbyaddr(addr, len, type)$$

Argument *addr* is a pointer to a sequence of bytes that contain a host address. Argument *len* is an integer that gives the length of the address, and argument *type* is an integer that specifies the type of the address (e.g., that it is an IP address).

As mentioned earlier, procedures *sethostent*, *gethostent*, and *endhostent* provide sequential access to the host database.

21.23 Obtaining Information About Networks

Hosts running 4BSD UNIX either use the domain name system or keep a simple database of networks in their internet. The network library routines include five routines that allow a process to access the network database. Procedure *getnetbyname* obtains and formats the contents of an entry from the database given the domain name of a network. A call has the form:

$$ptr = getnetbyname(name)$$

where argument *name* is a pointer to a string that contains the name of the network for which information is desired. The value returned is a pointer to a structure that contains fields for the official name of the network, a list of registered aliases, an integer address type, and a 32-bit network address (i.e., an IP address with the host portion set to zero).

A process calls library routine *getnetbyaddr* when it needs to search for information about a network given its address. The call has the form:

$$ptr = getnetbyaddr(netaddr, addrtype)$$

Argument *netaddr* is a 32-bit network address, and argument *addrtype* is an integer that specifies the type of *netaddr*.

Procedures *setnetent*, *getnetent*, and *endnetent* provide sequential access to the network database.

21.24 Obtaining Information About Protocols

Five library routines provide access to the database of protocols available on a machine. Each protocol has an official name, registered aliases, and an official protocol number. Procedure *getprotobyname* allows a caller to obtain information about a protocol given its name:

$$ptr = getprotobyname(name)$$

Argument *name* is a pointer to an ASCII string that contains the name of the protocol for which information is desired. The function returns a pointer to a structure that has fields for the official protocol name, a list of aliases, and a unique integer value assigned to the protocol.

Procedure *getprotobynumber* allows a process to search for protocol information using the protocol number as a key:

$$ptr = getprotobynumber(number)$$

Finally, procedures *getprotoent*, *setprotoent*, and *endprotoent* provide sequential access to the protocol database.

21.25 Obtaining Information About Network Services

Recall from Chapter 12 that some UDP and TCP protocol port numbers are reserved for well-known services. For example, TCP port *43* is reserved for the *whois* service. *Whois* allows a client on one machine to contact a server on another and obtain information about a user that has an account on the server's machine. The entry for *whois* in the services database specifies the service name, *whois*, the protocol, *TCP*, and the protocol port number *43*. Five library routines exist that obtain information about services and the protocol ports they use.

Procedure *getservbyname* maps a named service onto a port number:

$$ptr = getservbyname(name, proto)$$

Argument *name* specifies the address of a string that contains the name of the desired service, and integer argument *proto* specifies the protocol with which the service is to be used. Typically, protocols are limited to TCP and UDP. The value returned is a pointer to a structure that contains fields for the name of the service, a list of aliases, an identification of the protocol with which the service is used, and an integer protocol port number assigned for that service.

Procedure *getservbyport* allows the caller to obtain an entry from the services database given the port number assigned to it. A call has the form:

$$ptr = getservbyport(port, proto)$$

Argument *port* is the integer protocol port number assigned to the service, and argument *proto* specifies the protocol for which the service is desired.

As with other databases, a process can access the services database sequentially using *setservent*, *getservent*, and *endservent*.

21.26 An Example Client

The following C programming example illustrates the 4BSD UNIX operating system interface to TCP/IP. It is a very simple implementation of a *whois* client and server. As defined in RFC 954, the *whois* service allows a client on one machine to obtain information about a user on a remote system. In this implementation, the client is an application program that a user invokes along with two arguments: the name of a remote machine, and the name of a user on that machine about whom information is desired. The client calls *gethostbyname* to map the remote machine name into an IP address and calls *getservbyname* to find the well-known port for the *whois* service. Once it has mapped the host and service names, the client creates a socket, specifying that the socket will use reliable stream delivery (i.e., TCP). The client then binds the socket to the *whois* protocol port on the specified destination machine.

```
/* whoisclient.c - main */

#include <stdio.h>
#include <sys/types.h>
#include <sys/socket.h>
#include <netinet/in.h>
#include <netdb.h>


/*-------------------------------------------------------------------
 * Program:      whoisclient
 *
 * Purpose:      UNIX application program that becomes a client for the
 *               Internet "whois" service.
 *
 * Use:          whois hostname username
 *
 * Author:       Barry Shein, Boston University
 *
 * Date:         January, 1987
 *
 *-------------------------------------------------------------------
 */
main(argc, argv)
int argc;                       /* standard UNIX argument declarations  */
char *argv[];
{
    int s;                      /* socket descriptor                    */
    int len;                    /* length of received data              */
    struct sockaddr_in sa;      /* Internet socket addr. structure      */
    struct hostent *hp ;        /* result of host name lookup           */
```

```
struct servent *sp ;           /* result of service lookup          */
char buf[BUFSIZ+1] ;           /* buffer to read whois information   */
char *myname;                  /* pointer to name of this program    */
char *host;                    /* pointer to remote host name        */
char *user;                    /* pointer to remote user name        */

myname = argv[0];
/*
 * Check that there are two command line arguments
 */
if(argc != 3) {
        fprintf(stderr, "Usage: %s host username\n", myname);
        exit(1);
}
host = argv[1];
user = argv[2];
/*
 * Look up the specified hostname
 */
if((hp = gethostbyname(host)) == NULL) {
        fprintf(stderr,"%s: %s: no such host?\n", myname, host);
        exit(1);
}
/*
 * Put host's address and address type into socket structure
 */
bcopy((char *)hp->h_addr, (char *)&sa.sin_addr, hp->h_length);
sa.sin_family = hp->h_addrtype;
/*
 * Look up the socket number for the WHOIS service
 */
if((sp = getservbyname("whois","tcp")) == NULL) {
        fprintf(stderr,"%s: No whois service on this host\n", myname);
        exit(1);
}
/*
 * Put the whois socket number into the socket structure.
 */
sa.sin_port = sp->s_port;
/*
 * Allocate an open socket
 */
if((s = socket(hp->h_addrtype, SOCK_STREAM, 0)) < 0) {
        perror("socket");
```

```
            exit(1);
    }
    /*
     * Connect to the remote server
     */
    if(connect(s, &sa, sizeof sa) < 0) {
            perror("connect") ;
            exit(1) ;
    }
    /*
     * Send the request
     */
    if(write(s, user, strlen(user)) != strlen(user)) {
            fprintf(stderr, "%s: write error\n", myname);
            exit(1);
    }
    /*
     * Read the reply and put to user's output
     */
    while( (len = read(s, buf, BUFSIZ)) > 0)
            write(1, buf, len);
    close(s);
    exit(0);
}
```

21.27 An Example Server

The example server is only slightly more complex than the client. It listens on the well-known ''whois'' port and returns information to any clients that request it. The information is taken from the UNIX password file on the server's machine.

```
/* whoisserver.c - main */

#include <stdio.h>
#include <sys/types.h>
#include <sys/socket.h>
#include <netinet/in.h>
#include <netdb.h>
#include <pwd.h>


/*-----------------------------------------------------------------
 * Program:     whoisserver
 *
```

```
 * Purpose:     UNIX application program that acts as a server for
 *              the "whois" service on the local machine.  It listens
 *              on well-known WHOIS port (43) and answers queries from
 *              clients.  This program requires super-user privilege to
 *              run.
 *
 * Use:         whois hostname username
 *
 * Author:      Barry Shein, Boston University
 *
 * Date:        January, 1987
 *
 *-------------------------------------------------------------------
 */

#define BACKLOG         5       /* # of requests we're willing to queue */
#define MAXHOSTNAME     32      /* maximum host name length we tolerate */

main(argc, argv)
int argc;                       /* standard UNIX argument declarations  */
char *argv[];
{
  int s, t;                     /* socket descriptors                   */
  int i;                        /* general purpose integer              */
  struct sockaddr_in sa, isa;   /* Internet socket address structure    */
  struct hostent *hp;           /* result of host name lookup           */
  char *myname;                 /* pointer to name of this program      */
  struct servent *sp;           /* result of service lookup             */
  char localhost[MAXHOSTNAME+1];/* local host name as character string  */

  myname = argv[0];
  /*
   * Look up the WHOIS service entry
   */
  if((sp = getservbyname("whois","tcp")) == NULL) {
      fprintf(stderr, "%s: No whois service on this host\n", myname);
      exit(1);
  }
  /*
   * Get our own host information
   */
  gethostname(localhost, MAXHOSTNAME);
  if((hp = gethostbyname(localhost)) == NULL) {
      fprintf(stderr, "%s: cannot get local host info?\n", myname);
```

```
        exit(1);
}
/*
 * Put the WHOIS socket number and our address info
 * into the socket structure
 */
sa.sin_port = sp->s_port;
bcopy((char *)hp->h_addr, (char *)&sa.sin_addr, hp->h_length);
sa.sin_family = hp->h_addrtype;
/*
 * Allocate an open socket for incoming connections
 */
if((s = socket(hp->h_addrtype, SOCK_STREAM, 0)) < 0) {
        perror("socket");
        exit(1);
}
/*
 * Bind the socket to the service port
 * so we hear incoming connections
 */
if(bind(s, &sa, sizeof sa) < 0) {
        perror("bind");
        exit(1);
}
/*
 * Set maximum connections we will fall behind
 */
listen(s, BACKLOG);
/*
 * Go into an infinite loop waiting for new connections
 */
while(1) {
        i = sizeof isa ;
        /*
         * We hang in accept() while waiting for new customers
         */
        if((t = accept(s, &isa, &i)) < 0) {
          perror("accept");
          exit(1);
        }
        whois(t);              /* perform the actual WHOIS service */
        close(t);
}
}
```

```
/*
 * Get the WHOIS request from remote host and format a reply.
 */
whois(sock)
int sock;
{
  struct passwd *p;
  char buf[BUFSIZ+1];
  int i;

  /*
   * Get one line request
   */
  if( (i = read(sock, buf, BUFSIZ)) <= 0)
      return;
  buf[i] = '\0';          /* Null terminate */
  /*
   * Look up the requested user and format reply
   */
  if((p = getpwnam(buf)) == NULL)
      strcpy(buf,"User not found\n");
  else
      sprintf(buf, "%s: %s\n", p->pw_name, p->pw_gecos);
  /*
   * Return reply
   */
  write(sock, buf, strlen(buf));
  return;
}
```

21.28 Summary

Because TCP/IP protocol software resides inside an operating system, the exact interface between an application program and TCP/IP protocols depends on the details of the operating system; it is not specified by the TCP/IP protocol standard. We examined the socket interface used in 4BSD UNIX, and saw that it adopted the UNIX open-read-write-close paradigm. To use TCP, a program must create a socket, bind addresses to it, accept incoming connections, and then communicate using the *read* or *write* primitives. Finally, when finished using a socket, the program must close it. In addition to the socket abstraction and system calls that operate on sockets, 4BSD UNIX includes library routines that help programmers create and manipulate IP addresses, convert integers between the local machine format and network standard byte order, and search for information such as network addresses.

The socket interface has become popular and is widely supported by many vendors. Vendors who do not offer socket facilities in their operating systems often provide a socket library that makes it possible for programmers to write applications using socket calls even though the underlying operating system uses a different set of system calls.

FOR FURTHER STUDY

More information on sockets can be found in the *UNIX Programmer's Manual*, where Section 2 contains a description of each UNIX system call and Section 3 contains a description of each library procedure. UNIX also supplies on-line copies of the manual pages through the *man* command. Leffler, Karels, McKusick, and Quarterman [1989] explore the UNIX system in more detail.

EXERCISES

21.1   Try running the sample *whois* client and server on your local system.

21.2   Build a simple server that accepts multiple concurrent connections (to test it, have the process that handles a connection print a short message, delay a random time, print another message, and exit).

21.3   When is the *listen* call important?

21.4   What procedures does your local system provide to access the domain name system?

21.5   Devise a server that uses a *single UNIX process* but handles multiple concurrent TCP connections. Hint: think of *select*.

21.6   Read about the AT&T System V Transport Library Interface (TLI) and compare it to the socket interface. What are the major conceptual differences?

21.7   Each operating system limits the number of sockets a given program can use at any time. How many sockets can a program create on your local system?

21.8   The socket/file descriptor mechanism and associated *read* and *write* operations can be considered a form of object-oriented design. Explain why.

21.9   Consider an alternative interface design that provides an interface for every layer of protocol software (e.g., the system allows an application program to send and receive raw packets without using IP, or to send and receive IP datagrams without using UDP or TCP). What are the advantages of having such an interface? The disadvantages?

22

Applications: Remote Login (TELNET, Rlogin)

22.1 Introduction

This chapter and the next four continue our exploration of internetworking by examining high-level internet services and the protocols that support them. These services form an integral part of TCP/IP. They determine how users perceive an internet and demonstrate the power of the technology.

We will learn that high-level services provide increased communication functionality, and allow users and programs to interact with automated services on remote machines and with remote users. We will see that high-level protocols are implemented with application programs, and we will learn how they depend on the network level services described in previous chapters. This chapter begins by examining remote login.

22.2 Remote Interactive Computing

We have already seen how the client–server model can provide specific computational services like a time-of-day service to multiple machines. Reliable stream protocols like TCP make possible interactive use of remote machines as well. For example, we can imagine building a server that provides a remote text editing service. To implement this service we would need a server that accepted requests to edit a file and a client to make such requests. To invoke the remote editor service, a user would execute the client program. The client would establish a TCP connection from the local machine to the server, and would then begin sending keystrokes to the server and reading screen output that the server sent back.

How can our imagined remote interactive editing service be generalized? The problem with using one server for each computational service is that machines quickly become clogged with server processes. We can eliminate most specialized servers and provide more generality by allowing the user to establish a login session on the remote machine and then execute commands. With a *remote login* facility, users have access to all the commands available on the remote system, and system designers need not provide specialized servers.

Of course, providing remote login may not be simple. Many timesharing systems were designed before networks became popular, so they expect login sessions only from directly connected terminals. On such systems, adding a remote login server requires modifying the machine's operating system. Building interactive client software may also be difficult. Consider, for example, systems that assign special meaning to some keystrokes. If the local system interprets Control–C to mean ''abort the currently executing command process,'' it may be impossible to pass Control–C to the remote machine. If the client does pass Control-C to the remote site, it may be impossible to abort the local client process.

Despite the technical difficulties, system programmers have managed to build remote login server software for most operating systems and to construct application programs that act as clients. Often, the client software overrides the local interpretation of all keys except one, allowing a user to interact with the remote machine exactly as one would from a locally connected terminal. The single key exception provides a way for a user to escape to the local environment and control the client (e.g., to abort the client). In addition, some remote login protocols recognize a set of *trusted hosts*, permitting remote login from such hosts without verifying passwords.

22.3 TELNET Protocol

The TCP/IP protocol suite includes a simple remote terminal protocol called *TELNET*. TELNET allows a user at one site to establish a TCP connection to a login server at another, and then it passes keystrokes from the user's terminal directly to the remote machine as if they had been typed at a terminal on the remote machine. TELNET also carries output from the remote machine back to the user's terminal. The service is called *transparent* because it gives the appearance that the user's terminal attaches directly to the remote machine.

Although TELNET is not sophisticated compared to some remote terminal protocols, it is widely available. Usually, TELNET client software allows the user to specify a remote machine either by giving its domain name or IP address. Because it accepts IP addresses, TELNET can be used with hosts even if a name-to-address binding cannot be established (e.g., when domain naming software is being debugged).

TELNET offers three basic services. First, it defines a *network virtual terminal* that provides a standard interface to remote systems. Client programs do not have to understand the details of all possible remote systems; they are built to use the standard interface. Second, it includes a mechanism that allows the client and server to negotiate options, and it provides a set of standard options (e.g., one of the options controls whether data passed across the connection uses the standard 7-bit ASCII character set or an 8-bit character set). Finally, TELNET treats both ends of the connection symmetrically. So, instead of forcing the client side to connect to a user's terminal, TELNET allows an arbitrary program to become a client. Furthermore, either end can negotiate options.

Figure 22.1 illustrates how application programs implement a TELNET client and server.

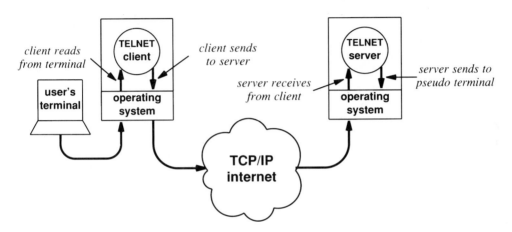

Figure 22.1 The path of data in a TELNET remote terminal session as it travels from the user's terminal to the remote operating system. Adding a TELNET server to a timesharing system usually requires modifying the operating system.

As the figure shows, when a user invokes TELNET, an application program on the user's machine becomes the client. The client establishes a TCP connection to the server over which they will communicate. Once the connection has been established, the client accepts keystrokes from the user's terminal and sends them to the server, while it concurrently accepts characters that the server sends back and displays them on the user's terminal. The server must accept a TCP connection from the client and then relay data between the TCP connection and the local operating system.

In practice, the server is more complex than the figure shows because it must handle multiple, concurrent connections. Usually, a master server process waits for new connections and creates a new slave to handle each connection. Thus, the 'TELNET server', shown in Figure 22.1, represents the slave that handles one particular connection. The figure does not show the master server that listens for new requests nor does it show the slaves handling other connections.

We use the term *pseudo terminal*† to describe the operating system entry point that allows a running program like the TELNET server to transfer characters to the operating system as if they came from a terminal. It is impossible to build a TELNET server unless the operating system supplies such a facility. If the system supports a pseudo terminal abstraction, the TELNET server can be implemented with application programs. Each slave server connects a TCP stream from one client to one particular pseudo terminal.

Arranging for the TELNET server to be an application level program has advantages and disadvantages. The most obvious advantage is that it makes modification and control of the server easier than if the code were embedded in the operating system. The obvious disadvantage is inefficiency. Each keystroke travels from the user's terminal through the operating system to the client program, from the client program back through the operating system and across the internet to the server machine. After reaching the destination machine, the data must travel up through the server's operating system to the server application program, and from the server application program back into the server's operating system at a pseudo terminal entry point. Finally, the remote operating system delivers the character to whatever application program the user is running. Meanwhile, output (including remote character echo if that option has been selected) travels back from the server to the client over the same path.

Readers who understand operating systems will appreciate that for the implementation shown in Figure 22.1, every keystroke requires the machines to switch process context several times. In most systems, an additional context switch is required because the operating system on the server's machine must pass characters from the pseudo terminal back to another application program (e.g., a command interpreter). Although context switching is expensive, the scheme is practical because users do not type at high speed.

22.4 Accommodating Heterogeneity

To make TELNET interoperate between as many systems as possible, it must accommodate the details of heterogeneous computers and operating systems. For example, some systems require lines of text to be terminated by the ASCII *carriage control* character (*CR*). Others require the ASCII *linefeed* (*LF*) character. Still others require the two-character sequence of CR-LF. In addition, most systems provide a way for a user logged in to an ordinary terminal to interrupt a running program. However, the keystroke used to generate the interrupt varies from system to system.

To accommodate heterogeneity, TELNET defines how data and command sequences are sent across the internet. The definition is known as the *network virtual terminal* (*NVT*). As Figure 22.2 illustrates, the client software translates keystrokes and command sequences from the user's terminal into NVT format and sends them to the server. Server software translates incoming data and commands from NVT format into the format the remote system requires. For data returning, the remote server translates from the remote machine's format to NVT, and the local client translates from NVT format to the local machine's format.

---

†UNIX calls the system entry point a *pseudo tty* because terminal devices are called *ttys*.

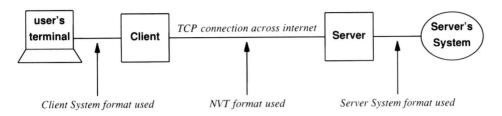

Figure 22.2 The Network Virtual Terminal (NVT) format used by TELNET.

The definition of NVT format is fairly straightforward. All communication involves 8-bit bytes. At startup, NVT uses the standard 7-bit USASCII representation for data and reserves bytes with the high order bit set for command sequences. The US-ASCII character set includes 95 characters that have "printable" graphics (e.g., letters, digits, punctuation marks, etc.), as well as 33 "control" codes. All printable characters are assigned the same meaning as in the standard USASCII character set. The NVT standard defines interpretations for control characters as shown in Figure 22.3†.

ASCII Control Code	Decimal Value	Assigned Meaning
NUL	0	No operation (has no effect on output)
BEL	7	Sound audible/visible signal (no motion)
BS	8	Move left one character position
HT	9	Move right to the next horizontal tab stop
LF	10	Move down (vertically) to the next line
VT	11	Move down to the next vertical tab stop
FF	12	Move to the top of the next page
CR	13	Move to the left margin on the current line
other control	–	No operation (has no effect on output)

Figure 22.3 The TELNET NVT interpretation of USASCII control characters.
TELNET does not specify the locations of tab stops.

In addition to the control character interpretation in Figure 22.3, NVT defines the standard line termination to be a two-character sequence *CR-LF*. When a user presses the key that corresponds to end-of-line on the local terminal (e.g., *ENTER* or *RETURN*), the TELNET client must map it into *CR-LF* for transmission. The TELNET server translates *CR-LF* into the appropriate end-of-line character sequence for the remote machine.

---

†The NVT interpretation of control characters follows their usual ASCII interpretation.

22.5 Passing Commands That Control The Remote Side

We said that most systems provide a mechanism that allows users to terminate a running program. Usually, the local operating system binds such mechanisms to a particular key or keystroke sequence. For example, unless the user specifies otherwise, 4BSD UNIX reserves the character generated by *CONTROL-C* as the interrupt key. Depressing *CONTROL-C* causes UNIX to terminate the executing program; the program does not receive *CONTROL-C* as input. The system may reserve other characters or character sequences for other control functions.

The TELNET NVT accommodates control functions by defining how they are passed from the client to the server. Conceptually, we think of NVT as accepting input from terminals that can generate more than 128 possible characters. We assume the user's terminal has virtual (imaginary) keys that correspond to the functions typically used to control processing. For example, NVT defines a conceptual "interrupt" key that requests program termination. Figure 22.4 lists the control functions the NVT allows.

Signal	Meaning
IP	Interrupt Process (terminate running program)
AO	Abort Output (discard any buffered output)
AYT	Are You There (test if server is responding)
EC	Erase Character (delete the previous character)
EL	Erase Line (delete the entire current line)
SYNCH	Synchronize (clear data path until TCP urgent data point, but do interpret commands)
BRK	Break (break key or attention signal)

Figure 22.4 The control functions TELNET NVT recognizes. Conceptually, the client receives these from a user in addition to normal data and passes them to the server's system where they must be interpreted.

In practice, most terminals do not provide extra keys for commands. Instead, individual operating systems or command interpreters have a variety of ways to generate them. We already mentioned the most common technique: binding an individual ASCII character to a control function so when the user presses the key, the operating system takes the appropriate action instead of accepting the character as input. The NVT designers chose to keep commands separate from the normal ASCII character set for two reasons. First, defining the control functions separately means TELNET has greater flexibility. It can transfer all possible ASCII character sequences between client and server as well as all possible control functions. Second, by separating signals from normal data, NVT allows the client to specify signals unambiguously – there is never confusion about whether an input character should be treated as data or as a control function.

To pass control functions across the TCP connection, TELNET encodes them using an *escape sequence*. An escape sequence uses a reserved octet to indicate that a control code octet follows. In TELNET, the reserved octet that starts an escape sequence is known as the *interpret as command (IAC)* octet. Figure 22.5 lists the possible commands and decimal encoding used for each.

Command	Decimal Encoding	Meaning
IAC	255	Interpret next octet as command (when the IAC octet appears as data, the sender doubles it and sends the 2-octet sequence IAC-IAC)
DON'T	254	Denial of request to perform specified option
DO	253	Approval to allow specified option
WON'T	252	Refusal to perform specified option
WILL	251	Agreement to perform specified option
SB	250	Start of option subnegotiation
GA	249	The "go ahead" signal
EL	248	The "erase line" signal
EC	247	The "erase character" signal
AYT	246	The "are you there" signal
AO	245	The "abort output" signal
IP	244	The "interrupt process" signal
BRK	243	The "break" signal
DMARK	242	The data stream portion of a SYNCH (always accompanied by TCP Urgent notification)
NOP	241	No operation
SE	240	End of option subnegotiation
EOR	239	End of record

Figure 22.5 Telnet commands and encoding for each. These codes only have meaning if preceded by an *IAC* character. When *IAC* occurs in the data it is sent twice.

As the figure shows, the signals generated by conceptual keys on an NVT keyboard each have a corresponding command. For example, to request that the server interrupt the executing program, the client must send the 2-octet sequence *IAC IP* (255 followed by 244). Additional commands allow the client and server to negotiate which options they will use and to synchronize communication.

22.6 Forcing The Server To Read A Control Function

Sending control functions along with normal data is not always sufficient to guarantee the desired results. To see why, consider the situation under which a user might send the *interrupt process* control function to the server. Usually, such control is only needed when the program executing on the remote machine is misbehaving and the user wants the server to terminate the program. For example, the program might be executing an endless loop without reading input or generating output. Unfortunately, if the application at the server's site stops reading input, operating system buffers will eventually fill and the server will be unable to write more data to the pseudo terminal. When this happens, the server must stop reading data from the TCP connection, causing its buffers to fill. Eventually, TCP on the server machine will begin advertising a zero window size, preventing data from flowing across the connection.

If the user generates an interrupt control function when buffers are filled, the control function will never reach the server. That is, the client can form the sequence *IAC IP* and write it to the TCP connection, but because TCP has stopped sending to the server's machine, the server will not read the control sequence. The point is:

> *TELNET cannot rely on the conventional data stream alone to carry control sequences between client and server, because a misbehaving application that needs to be controlled might inadvertently block the data stream.*

To solve the problem, TELNET uses an *out of band* signal. TCP implements out of band signaling with the *URGENT* mechanism. Whenever TELNET places a control function in the data stream, it also sends a *SYNCH* command. It appends a reserved octet called the *data mark*, and causes TCP to signal the server by sending a segment with the URGENT DATA bit set. Segments carrying urgent data bypass flow control and reach the server immediately. In response to an urgent signal, the server reads and discards all data until it finds the data mark. The server returns to normal processing when it encounters the data mark.

22.7 TELNET Options

Our simple description of TELNET omits one of the most complex aspects: options. In TELNET, options are negotiable, making it possible for the client and server to reconfigure their connection. For example, we said that the data stream passes 7-bit data and uses octets with the eighth bit set to pass control information like the *Interrupt Process* command. However, TELNET also provides an option that allows the client and server to pass 8-bit data (when passing 8-bit data, the reserved octet *IAC* must be doubled if it appears in the data). The client and server must negotiate, and both must agree to pass 8-bit data before such transfers are possible.

The range of TELNET options is wide: some extend the capabilities in major ways while others deal with minor details. For example, the original protocol was designed for a half-duplex environment where it was necessary to tell the other end to "go ahead" before it would send more data. One of the options controls whether TELNET operates in half- or full-duplex mode. Another option allows the server on a remote machine to determine the user's terminal type. The terminal type is important for software that generates cursor positioning sequences (e.g., a full screen editor executing on a remote machine).

Figure 22.6 lists several of the most commonly implemented TELNET options.

Name	Code	RFC	Meaning
Transmit Binary	0	856	Change transmission to 8-bit binary
Echo	1	857	Allow one side to echo data it receives
Suppress-GA	3	858	Suppress (no longer send) Go-ahead signal after data
Status	5	859	Request for status of a TELNET option from remote site
Timing-Mark	6	860	Request timing mark be inserted in return stream to synchronize two ends of a connection
Terminal-Type	24	884	Exchange information about the make and model of a terminal being used (allows programs to tailor output like cursor positioning sequences for the user's terminal)
End-of-Record	25	885	Terminate data sent with EOR code
Linemode	34	1116	Use local editing and send complete lines instead of individual characters

Figure 22.6 Commonly used TELNET options.

22.8 TELNET Option Negotiation

The way TELNET negotiates options is interesting. Because it sometimes makes sense for the server to initiate a particular option, the protocol is designed to allow either end to make a request. Thus, the protocol is said to be *symmetric* with respect to option processing. The receiving end either responds to a request with a positive acceptance or a rejection. In TELNET terminology, the request is *WILL X*, meaning *will you agree to let me use option X*; and the response is either *DO X* or *DON'T X*, meaning *I do agree to let you use option X* or *I don't agree to let you use option X*. The symmetry arises because *DO X* requests that the receiving party begin using option *X*, and *WILL X* or *WON'T X* means *I will start using option X* or *I won't start using it†*.

---

†To eliminate potential loops that arise when two sides each think the other's acknowledgement is a request, the protocol specifies that no acknowledgement be given to a request for an option that is already in use.

Another interesting negotiation concept arises because both ends are required to run an unenhanced NVT implementation (i.e., one without any options turned on). If one side tries to negotiate an option that the other does not understand, the side receiving the request can simply decline. Thus, it is possible to interoperate newer, more sophisticated versions of TELNET clients and servers (i.e., software that understands more options) with older, less sophisticated versions. If both the client and server understand the new options, they may be able to improve interaction. If not, they will revert to a less efficient, but workable style.

We can summarize:

> *TELNET uses a symmetric option negotiation mechanism to allow clients and servers to reconfigure the parameters controlling their interaction. Because all TELNET software understands a basic NVT protocol, clients and servers can interoperate even if one understands options another does not.*

22.9 Rlogin (4BSD UNIX)

The 4BSD UNIX system includes a remote login service, *rlogin*, that supports trusted hosts. It allows system administrators to choose a set of machines over which login names and file access protections are shared and to establish equivalences among user logins. Users can control access to their accounts by authorizing remote login based on remote host and remote user name. Thus, it is possible for a user to have login name *X* on one machine and *Y* on another, and still be able to remotely login from one of the machines to the other without typing a password each time.

Having automatic authorization makes remote login facilities useful for general purpose programs as well as human interaction. One variant of the 4BSD *rlogin* command, *rsh*, invokes a command interpreter on the remote UNIX machine and passes the command line arguments to the command interpreter, skipping the login step completely. The format of a command invocation using *rsh* is:

rsh *machine command*

Thus, typing

rsh merlin ps

on any of the machines in the Computer Science Department at Purdue University executes the *ps* command on machine *merlin* (with UNIX's standard input and standard output connected across the network to the user's terminal). The user sees the output as if he or she were logged into machine *merlin*. Because the user can arrange to have *rsh* invoke remote commands without prompting for a password, it can be used in programs as well as from the keyboard.

Because protocols like *rlogin* understand both the local and remote computing environments, they communicate better than general purpose remote login protocols like TELNET. For example, *rlogin* understands the UNIX notions of *standard input, standard output*, and *standard error*, and uses TCP to connect them to the remote machine. Thus, it is possible to type

```
rsh  merlin  ps  >  filename
```

and have output from the remote command redirected† into file *filename*. *Rlogin* also understands terminal control functions like flow control characters (typically Control–S and Control–Q). It arranges to stop output immediately without waiting for the delay required to send them across the network to the remote host. Finally, rlogin exports part of the user's environment to the remote machine, including information like the user's terminal type (i.e., the *TERM* variable). As a result, remote login sessions appear to behave almost exactly like local login sessions.

22.10 Summary

Much of the rich functionality associated with TCP/IP results from a variety of high-level services supplied by application programs. The high-level remote login protocols these programs use build on the basic services: unreliable datagram delivery and reliable stream transport. They usually follow the client-server model in which servers operate at known protocol ports so clients know how to contact them.

We reviewed two remote login systems: TELNET, the TCP/IP internet standard, and rlogin, a popular protocol used with 4BSD UNIX systems. TELNET provides a basic service. It allows the client to pass commands such as *interrupt process* as well as data to the server. It also permits client and server to negotiate many options. In contrast to TELNET, *rlogin* allows system managers and users more flexibility in establishing the equivalence of accounts on multiple machines, but it is restricted to UNIX systems.

FOR FURTHER STUDY

Many high-level protocols have been proposed, but only a few are in common use. Edge [1979] compares end-to-end protocols with the hop-by-hop approach. Saltzer, Reed, and Clark [1984] argues for having the highest level protocols perform end-to-end acknowledgement and error detection.

Postel [RFC 854] contains the TELNET remote login protocol specification. It was preceded by over three dozen RFCs that discuss TELNET options, weaknesses, experiments, and proposed changes, including Postel [RFC 764] that contains an earlier standard. Postel and Reynolds [RFC 855] gives a specification for options and considers subnegotiation. A lengthy list of options can be found in RFCs 856, 857, 858, 859,

---

†The ''greater than'' symbol is the usual UNIX syntax for directing the output of a command into a file.

860, 861, 884, 885, 1091, 1096, 1097, and 1116. The 4BSD UNIX program *tn3270* uses a TELNET-like mechanism to provide access to IBM computers running the VM/CMS operating system; Rekhter [RFC 1041] covers the TELNET option that permits communication with IBM 3270 displays.

EXERCISES

22.1 Experiment with both TELNET and rlogin. What are the noticeable differences?

22.2 Despite the large volume of notes written about TELNET, it can be argued that the protocol is still not well-defined. Experiment with TELNET: use it to reach a machine, *A*, and invoke TELNET on *A* to reach a second machine, *B*. Does the combination of two TELNET connections handle *line feed* and *carriage control* characters properly?

22.3 What is a remote procedure call?

22.4 Folklore says that operating systems come and go while protocols last forever. Test this axiom by surveying your local computing site to see whether operating systems or communication protocols have changed more frequently.

22.5 Build TELNET client software.

22.6 Use a TELNET client to connect your terminal to the TCP protocol port for *echo* or *chargen* on your local system to see what happens.

22.7 Read the TELNET standard and find out how the SYNCH operation works.

22.8 TELNET uses TCP's *urgent data* mechanism to force the remote operating system to respond to control functions quickly. Read the standard to find out which commands the remote server honors while scanning the input stream.

22.9 How can the symmetric DO/DON'T – WILL/WON'T option negotiation produce an endless loop of responses if the other party *always* acknowledges a request?

22.10 The text file for RFC 854 contains exactly 854 lines. Do you think there is any cosmic significance in this?

23

Applications: File Transfer And Access (FTP, TFTP, NFS)

23.1 Introduction

This chapter continues our exploration of application protocols. It examines the file access and transfer protocols that are part of the TCP/IP protocol suite. It describes their design and shows an example of a typical user interface. We will learn that the most widely used file transfer protocol builds on TCP, covered in Chapter 12, and TEL-NET, described in the previous chapter.

23.2 File Access And Transfer

Many network systems provide computers with the ability to access files on remote machines. Designers have explored a variety of approaches to remote access. Each approach optimizes for a particular set of goals. For example, some designs use remote file access to lower overall cost. In such architectures, a single, centralized *file server* provides secondary storage for a set of inexpensive *diskless computers*. Usually, the diskless machines are scientific workstations that communicate with the file server over a high-speed local area network. They run a conventional timesharing operating system but store files on the remote server instead of local disks. Diskless architectures have lower cost than equivalent architectures with disks because only the server needs expensive disk controller and disk drive hardware.

Some designs use remote storage to archive data. In such designs, users have conventional computers with local storage facilities and operate them as usual. Periodically the conventional computers send copies of files (or copies of entire disks) across a network to an archival facility, where they are stored in case of accidental loss.

Finally, some designs emphasize the ability to share data across multiple programs, multiple users, or multiple sites. For example, an organization might choose to have a single inventory database shared by all groups in the organization.

23.3 On-line Shared Access

File sharing comes in two distinct forms: *on-line access* and *whole-file copying*. Shared on-line access means allowing multiple programs to access a single file concurrently. Changes to the file take effect immediately and are available to all programs that access the file. Whole-file copying means that whenever a program wants to access a file it obtains a local copy. Copying is often used for read-only data, but if the file must be modified, the program makes changes to the local copy and transfers the modified file back to the original site.

Many users think that on-line data sharing can only be provided by a database system in which the database operates as a server and allows users (clients) to contact it from remote sites, but that is not what we have in mind. A file system that provides shared, on-line access from remote machines does not require the user to invoke special client programs. Instead, the operating system provides access to the shared file exactly like it provides access to local files. The user can execute any application program using the file as input or output. We say that the remote file is *integrated* with local files and that the entire file system provides *transparent access* to shared files.

The advantages of on-line access should be obvious: remote file access occurs with no visible changes in the environment. Users can access local and remote files with the same programs, allowing them to perform arbitrary computations on the shared data. The disadvantages are less obvious. Users may be surprised by the results. For example, consider an application program that uses both local and remote files. If the network or the remote machine is down, the application program may not work even though the user's machine is operating. Even if the remote machine is operating, it may be overloaded or the network may be congested, making the application program run extremely slowly, or communication protocols may report timeout conditions that the user does not expect. A user simply thinks that the program is unpredictable or unreliable.

Independent of user reaction, it is difficult to design and implement integrated, transparent file access. In a heterogeneous environment, it may be awkward or impossible to map file names from one system into the file namespace of another. Similarly, a remote file access mechanism must handle notions of ownership, authorization, and access protection. A heterogeneous environment makes each of these difficult. Finally, because file representations and allowed operations vary from machine to machine, it may be difficult or impossible to implement all operations on all files.

23.4 Sharing By File Transfer

The alternative to shared on-line access is transfer. Transfer schemes require a two-step process in which the user first obtains a local copy of a file and then operates on it. Most transfer mechanisms operate outside the user's local file system (i.e., they are not integrated). The user must invoke a special-purpose client program to transfer files. When invoking the client, the user specifies a remote computer on which the desired file resides and, usually, an authorization needed to obtain access (e.g., an account or password). The client contacts a server on the remote machine and requests a copy of the file. Once the transfer is complete, the user terminates the client and uses application programs on the local system to read or update the file. One advantage of whole-file copying lies in the efficiency of operations – once a program has obtained a copy of a remote file, it can manipulate the copy efficiently. Thus, many computations run faster with whole-file copying than with remote file access.

As with on-line sharing, whole-file transfer between heterogeneous machines can be difficult. The client and server must agree on authorization, notions of file ownership and access protections, and data formats. The latter is especially important because it may make inverse translations impossible. To see why, consider copying between two machines, *A* and *B*, that use different representations for floating point numbers as well as different representations for text files. As most programmers realize, it may be impossible to convert from one machine's floating point format to another's without losing precision. The same can happen with text files. Suppose system *A* stores text files as variable-length lines and system *B* pads text lines to a fixed length. Transferring a file from *A* to *B* and back can add padding to every line, making the final copy different from the original. However, automatically removing padding from the ends of lines during the transfer back to *A* will also make the copy different from the original for any files that had padding on some lines.

The exact details of representation differences and techniques to handle them depend on the computer systems involved. Furthermore, we have seen that not all representational differences can be accommodated – information can be lost when data must be translated from one representation to another. While it is not essential to learn about all possible representational differences, remembering that TCP/IP is designed for a heterogeneous environment will help explain some of the features of the TCP/IP file transfer protocols.

23.5 FTP: The Major TCP/IP File Transfer Protocol

File transfer is among the most frequently used TCP/IP applications, and it accounts for much network traffic. Standard file transfer protocols existed for the ARPANET before TCP/IP became operational. These early versions of file transfer software evolved into a current standard known as the *File Transfer Protocol* (*FTP*).

23.6 FTP Features

Given a reliable end-to-end transport protocol like TCP, file transfer might seem trivial. However, as the previous sections pointed out, the details of authorization and naming across heterogeneous machines make the protocol complex. In addition, FTP offers many facilities beyond the transfer function itself.

•Interactive Access. Although FTP is designed to be used by programs, most implementations provide an interactive interface that allows humans to easily interact with remote servers. For example, a user can ask for a listing of all files in a directory on a remote machine. Also, the client usually responds to input like ''help'' by showing the user information about possible commands that can be invoked.

•Format (representation) Specification. FTP allows the client to specify the type and format of stored data. For example, the user can specify whether a file contains text or binary integers and whether text files use the ASCII or EBCDIC character sets.

•Authentication Control. FTP requires clients to authorize themselves by sending a login name and password to the server before requesting file transfers. The server refuses access to clients that cannot supply a valid login and password.

23.7 FTP Process Model

Like other servers, most FTP implementations allow concurrent access by multiple clients. Clients use TCP to connect to the server. As described in Chapter 18, a single master server process awaits connections and creates a slave process to handle each connection. Unlike most servers, however, the slave process does not perform all the necessary computation. Instead, the slave accepts and handles the *control connection* from the client, but uses an additional process or processes to handle a separate *data transfer connection*. The control connection carries commands that tell the server which file to transfer. The data transfer connection, which also uses TCP as the transport protocol, carries all data transfers.

Usually, both the client and server create a separate process to handle the data transfer. While the exact details of the process architecture depend on the operating systems available, Figure 23.1 illustrates the concept:

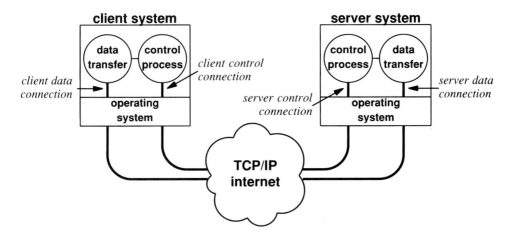

Figure 23.1 An FTP client and server with a TCP control connection between them and a separate TCP connection between their associated data transfer processes.

As the figure shows, the client control process connects to the server control process using one TCP connection, while the associated data transfer processes use their own TCP connection. In general, the control processes and the control connection remain alive as long as the user keeps the FTP "session" going. However, FTP establishes a new data transfer connection for each file transfer. In fact, many implementations create a new pair of data transfer processes, as well as a new TCP connection, whenever the server needs to send information to the client. The idea can be summarized:

> *Data transfer connections and the data transfer processes that use them can be created dynamically when needed, but the control connection persists throughout a session. Once the control connection disappears, the session is terminated and the software at both ends terminates all data transfer processes.*

Of course, client implementations that execute on personal computers may have a less complex structure because they cannot depend on an underlying operating system. Instead, such implementations often sacrifice generality by using a single application program to perform both the data transfer and control functions. However, such clients must still use multiple TCP connections, one for control and the other(s) for data transfer.

23.8 TCP Port Number Assignment

When a client forms an initial connection to a server, the client uses a random, locally assigned, protocol port number, but contacts the server at a well-known port (*21*). As we said in Chapter 18, many clients can contact a server with this scheme, because TCP uses both endpoints to identify a connection. The question arises, "When the control processes create a new TCP connection for a given data transfer, what protocol port numbers do they use?" Obviously, they cannot use the same pair of port numbers used in the control connection. Instead, the client obtains an unused port on its machine and uses it to contact the data transfer process on the server's machine. The data transfer process on the server machine can use the well-known port reserved for FTP data transfer (*20*). To insure that a data transfer process on the server connects to the correct data transfer process on the client machine, the server side must not accept connections from an arbitrary process. Instead, when it issues the TCP passive open request, it specifies the port that will be used on the client machine as well as the local port.

Finding a remote port might seem difficult, but now we can see why the protocol uses two connections: the client control process can obtain a random local port to be used in the file transfer, communicate the port number to the server over the control connection, wait for the server to establish a data transfer process accepting a connection from that port, and then start a transfer process on the client machine to make the connection. In general:

> *In addition to passing user commands to the server, FTP uses the control connection to allow client and server control processes to coordinate their use of dynamically assigned TCP protocol ports and the creation of data transfer processes that use those ports.*

What format should FTP use for data passing across the control connection? Although we could invent a new specification, FTP does not. It uses the TELNET network virtual terminal protocol described in Chapter 22. Unlike the full TELNET protocol, FTP does not allow option negotiation; it uses only the basic NVT definition. Thus, management of an FTP control connection is much simpler than management of a standard TELNET connection. Despite its limitations, using the TELNET definition instead of inventing a new one helps simplify FTP considerably.

23.9 The User's View Of FTP

Users view FTP as an interactive system. Once invoked, the client performs the following operations repeatedly: read a line of input, parse the line to extract a command and its arguments, and execute the command with the specified arguments. For example, to initiate the version of FTP available under 4BSD UNIX, the user invokes the *ftp* command:

% **ftp**

The local FTP client program begins and issues a prompt to the user. Following the prompt, the user can issue commands like *help*.

```
ftp> help
Commands may be abbreviated.   Commands are:

!                cr            macdef        proxy           send
$                delete        mdelete       sendport        status
account          debug         mdir          put             struct
append           dir           mget          pwd             sunique
ascii            disconnect    mkdir         quit            tenex
bell             form          mls           quote           trace
binary           get           mode          recv            type
bye              glob          mput          remotehelp      user
case             hash          nmap          rename          verbose
cd               help          ntrans        reset           ?
cdup             lcd           open          rmdir
close            ls            prompt        runique
```

To obtain more information about a given command the user types *help command* as in the following examples (output is shown in the same format as the program produces it):

```
ftp> help ls
ls              list contents of remote directory
ftp> help cdup
cdup            change remote working directory to parent directory
ftp> help glob
glob            toggle metacharacter expansion of local file names
ftp> help bell
bell            beep when command completed
```

To execute a command, the user types the command name:

```
ftp> bell
Bell mode on.
```

23.10 An Example Anonymous FTP Session

While the access authorization facilities in FTP make it secure, they can also be troublesome. Strict enforcement of FTP authorization prohibits people from accessing a file until they obtain a login and password for the computer on which the file resides. To provide unrestricted access to public files, many TCP/IP sites follow the convention of allowing *anonymous FTP*. Anonymous FTP access means the user does not need an account or password. Instead, the user specifies login name *anonymous* and password *guest*. The server allows anonymous logins, but restricts access to only publicly available files†.

Usually, users execute only a few FTP commands to establish a connection and obtain a file; few users have ever tried most commands. For example, suppose someone has placed an on-line copy of a text in file *tcpbook.tar* in the subdirectory *pub/comer* on machine *arthur.cs.purdue.edu*. A user logged in at another site as *usera* could obtain a copy of the file by executing the following:

```
% ftp arthur.cs.purdue.edu
Connected to arthur.cs.purdue.edu.
220 arthur.cs.purdue.edu FTP server (DYNIX V3.0.12) ready.
Name (arthur:usera): anonymous
331 Guest login ok, send ident as password.
Password: guest
230 Guest login ok, access restrictions apply.
ftp> get pub/comer/tcpbook.tar bookfile
200 PORT command okay.
150 Opening data connection for /bin/ls (128.10.2.1,2363) (7897088 bytes).
226 Transfer complete.
8272793 bytes received in 98.04 seconds (82 Kbytes/s)
ftp> close
221 Goodbye.
ftp> quit
```

In this example, the user specifies machine *arthur.cs.purdue.edu* as an argument to the FTP command, so the client automatically opens a connection and prompts for authorization. The user invokes anonymous FTP by specifying login *anonymous* and password *guest‡* (although our example shows the password that the user types, the ftp program does not display it on the user's screen).

After typing a login and password, the user requests a copy of a file using the *get* command. *Get* requires two arguments that specify the remote file name and a name for the local copy. In the example, the remote file name is *pub/comer/tcpbook.tar* and the local copy will be placed in *bookfile*. Once the transfer completes, the user types *close* to break the connection with the server and types *quit* to leave the client.

---

†In 4BSD UNIX systems, the server restricts anonymous FTP by changing the file system root to a small, restricted directory (*/usr/ftp*).

‡Usually, the server requests that the user supply identification in the form user@host, but this particular server has been configured to accept the password *guest*.

Intermingled with the commands the user types are informational messages from FTP. FTP messages always begin with a 3-digit number followed by text. Most come from the server; other output comes from the local client. For example, the message that begins *220* comes from the server and contains the domain name of the machine on which the server executes. The statistics that report the number of bytes received and the rate of transfer come from the client. In general:

> *Control and error messages between the FTP client and server begin with a 3-digit number followed by text. The software interprets the number; the text is meant for humans.*

The example session also illustrates a feature of FTP described earlier: its creation of new TCP connections for data transfer. Notice the *PORT* command in the output. The client *PORT* command reports that a new TCP port number has been obtained for use as a data connection. The client sends the port information to the server over the control connection; data transfer processes at both ends use the new port number when forming a connection. After the transfer completes, the data transfer processes at each end close the connection.

23.11 TFTP

Although FTP is the most general file transfer protocol in the TCP/IP suite, it is also the most complex and difficult to program. Many applications do not need the full functionality FTP offers, nor can they afford the complexity. For example, FTP requires clients and servers to manage multiple concurrent TCP connections, something that may be difficult or impossible on personal computers that do not have sophisticated operating systems.

The TCP/IP suite contains a second file transfer protocol that provides inexpensive, unsophisticated service. Known as the *Trivial File Transfer Protocol*, or *(TFTP)*, it is intended for applications that do not need complex interactions between the client and server. It restricts operations to simple file transfers and does not provide authentication. Because it is more restrictive, TFTP software is much smaller than FTP.

Small size is important in many applications. For example, manufacturers of diskless workstations can encode TFTP in read-only memory (ROM) and use it to obtain an initial memory image when the machine is powered on. The program in ROM is called the system *bootstrap*. The advantage of using TFTP is that it allows bootstrapping code to use the same underlying TCP/IP protocols that the operating system uses once it begins execution. Thus, it is possible for a computer to bootstrap from a server on another physical network.

Unlike FTP, TFTP does not need a reliable stream transport service. It runs on top of UDP or any other unreliable packet delivery system, using timeout and retransmission to ensure that data arrives. The sending side transmits a file in fixed size (*512* byte) blocks and awaits an acknowledgement for each block before sending the next. The receiver acknowledges each block upon receipt.

The rules for TFTP are simple. The first packet sent requests a file transfer and establishes the interaction between client and server – it specifies a file name and whether the file will be read (transferred to the client) or written (transferred to the server). Blocks of the file are numbered consecutively starting at *1*. Each data packet contains a header that specifies the number of the block it carries, and each acknowledgement contains the number of the block being acknowledged. A block of less than *512* bytes signals the end of file. It is possible to send an error message, either in the place of data or an acknowledgement; errors terminate the transfer.

Figure 23.2 shows the format of the five TFTP packet types. The initial packet must use operation codes *1* or *2*, specifying either a *read request* or a *write request*. The initial packet contains the name of the file as well as the access mode the client requests (*read* access or *write* access).

2-octet opcode	n octets	1 octet	n octets	1 octet
READ REQ. (1)	FILENAME	0	MODE	0

2-octet opcode	n octets	1 octet	n octets	1 octet
WRITE REQ. (2)	FILENAME	0	MODE	0

2-octet opcode	2 octets	up to 512 octets
DATA (3)	BLOCK #	DATA OCTETS...

2-octet opcode	2 octets
ACK (3)	BLOCK #

2-octet opcode	2 octets	n octets	1 octet
ERROR (5)	ERROR CODE	ERROR MESSAGE	0

Figure 23.2 The five TFTP message types. Fields are not shown to scale because some are variable length; an initial 2-octet operation code identifies the message format.

Once a *read* or *write* request has been made, the server uses the IP address and UDP protocol port number of the client to identify subsequent operations. Thus, neither *data* messages (the messages that carry blocks from the file) nor *ack* messages (the messages that acknowledge data blocks) need to specify the file name. The final message type illustrated in Figure 23.2 is used to report errors. Lost messages can be retransmitted after a timeout, but most other errors simply cause termination of the interaction.

TFTP retransmission is unusual because it is symmetric. Each side implements a timeout and retransmission. If the side sending data times out, it retransmits the last data block. If the side responsible for acknowledgements times out, it retransmits the last acknowledgement. Having both sides participate in retransmission helps ensure that transfer will not fail after a single packet loss.

While symmetric retransmission guarantees robustness, it can lead to excessive retransmissions. The problem, known as the *Sorcerer's Apprentice Bug*, arises when an acknowledgement for data packet k is delayed but not lost. The sender retransmits the data packet, which the receiver acknowledges. Both acknowledgements eventually arrive, and each triggers a transmission of data packet $k+1$. The receiver will acknowledge both copies of data packet k+1, and the two acknowledgements will each cause the sender to transmit data packet $k+2$. Once started, the cycle continues indefinitely with each data packet being transmitted exactly twice.

Although TFTP contains little except the minimum needed for transfer, it does support multiple file types. One interesting aspect of TFTP allows it to be integrated with electronic mail†. A client can specify to the server that it will send a file that should be treated as mail (with the *FILENAME* field taken to be the name of a mailbox to which the server should deliver the message).

23.12 NFS

Developed by Sun Microsystems Incorporated, the *Network File System* (*NFS*) provides on-line shared file access that is transparent and integrated; many TCP/IP sites use NFS to interconnect their computers' file systems. From the user's perspective, NFS is almost invisible. The user can execute an arbitrary application program and use arbitrary files for input or output. The file names themselves do not show whether the files are local or remote.

23.13 NFS Implementation

Figure 23.3 illustrates how NFS is imbedded in an operating system. When an application program executes, it calls the operating system to *open* a file, or to *store* and *retrieve* data in files. The file access mechanism accepts the request and automatically passes it to either the local file system software or to the NFS client, depending on whether the file is on the local disk or on a remote machine. When it receives a request, the client software uses the NFS protocol to contact the appropriate server on a remote machine and perform the requested operation. When the remote server replies, the client software returns the results to the application program.

---

†In practice, sites should not use TFTP to transport mail. Refer to Chapter 24 for details on electronic mail.

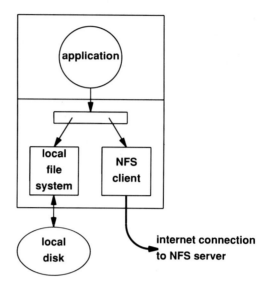

Figure 23.3 NFS code in an operating system. When application programs
request file operations, the operating system must pass the requests to the local file system or the NFS client software.

23.14 Remote Procedure Call (RPC)

Instead of defining the NSF protocol from scratch, the designers chose to build
three independent pieces: the NFS protocol itself, a general-purpose *Remote Procedure
Call (RPC)* mechanism, and a general-purpose *eXternal Data Representation (XDR)*.
Their intent was to separate the three to make it possible to use RPC and XDR in other
software (including application programs as well as other protocols).

From the programmer's point of view, NFS itself provides no new procedures that
a program can call. Instead, once a manager has configured NFS, programs access remote files using exactly the same operations as they use for local files. However, both
RPC and XDR provide mechanisms that programmers can use to build distributed programs. For example, a programmer can divide a program into a client side and a server
side that use RPC as the chief communication mechanism. On the client side, the programmer designates some procedures as *remote*, forcing the compiler to incorporate
RPC code into those procedures. On the server side, the programmer implements the
desired procedures and uses other RPC facilities to declare them to be part of a server.
When the executing client program calls one of the remote procedures, RPC automatically collects values for arguments, forms a message, sends the message to the remote
server, awaits a response, and stores returned values in the designated arguments. In
essence, communication with the remote server occurs automatically as a side-effect of

a procedure call. The RPC mechanism hides all the details of protocols, making it possible for programmers who know little about the underlying communication protocols to write distributed programs.

A related tool, XDR, provides a way for programmers to pass data among heterogeneous machines without writing procedures to convert among the hardware data representations. For example, not all computers represent 32-bit binary integers in the same format. Some store the most significant byte at the highest memory address, while others store the least significant byte at the highest address. Thus, if programmers use a network merely to move the bytes of an integer from one machine to another without rearranging them, the value of the integer may change. XDR solves the problem by defining a machine-independent representation. At one end of a communication channel, a program invokes XDR procedures to convert from the local hardware representation to the machine-independent representation. Once the data has been transferred to another machine, the receiving program invokes XDR routines to convert from the machine-independent representation to the machine's local representation.

The chief advantage of XDR is that it automates much of the data conversion task. Programmers do not need to type XDR procedure calls manually. Instead, they provide the XDR compiler with the declaration statements from the program for which data must be transformed, and the compiler automatically generates a program with the needed XDR library calls.

23.15 Summary

Shared access to data takes two forms: whole-file copying, and shared on-line access. The File Transfer Protocol, FTP, is the major transfer protocol in the TCP/IP suite. It uses whole-file copying and provides the ability for users to list directories on the remote machine as well as transfer files in either direction. The Trivial File Transfer Protocol, TFTP, provides a small, simple alternative to FTP for applications that need only file transfer. Because it is small enough to be contained in ROM, TFTP can be used for bootstrapping diskless workstations.

The Network File System (NFS) designed by Sun Microsystems Incorporated provides on-line shared file access. It uses UDP for message transport and builds on the Remote Procedure Call (RPC) and eXternal Data Representation (XDR) mechanisms. Because RPC and XDR are defined separately from NFS, programmers can use them to build distributed applications.

FOR FURTHER STUDY

Postel [RFC 959] contains the FTP protocol standard. Over three dozen RFCs comment on FTP, propose modifications, or define new versions of the protocol. Among them, Lottor [RFC 913] describes a Simple File Transfer Protocol. DeSchon and Braden [RFC 1068] shows how to use FTP third-party transfer for background file transfer.

The Trivial File Transfer Protocol described here comes from Sollins [RFC 783]; Finlayson [RFC 906] describes its use in bootstrapping computer systems.

Sun Microsystems has published three RFCs that define the Network File System and related protocols. RFC 1094 contains the standard for NFS, RFC 1057 defines RPC, and RFC 1014 specifies XDR.

EXERCISES

23.1   Why should file transport protocols compute a checksum on the file data they receive, even when using a reliable end-to-end stream transfer protocol like TCP?

23.2   Find out whether FTP computes a checksum for files it transfers.

23.3   What happens in FTP if the TCP connection being used for data transfer breaks but the control connection does not?

23.4   What is the chief advantage of using separate TCP connections for control and data transfer? (Hint: think of abnormal conditions.)

23.5   Outline a method that uses TFTP to bootstrap a diskless machine. Be careful. Exactly what IP addresses does it use at each step?

23.6   Implement a TFTP client.

23.7   Experiment with FTP or an equivalent protocol to see how fast you can transfer a file between two reasonably large systems across a local area network like an Ethernet. Try the experiment when the network is busy and when it is idle. Explain the result.

23.8   Try FTP from a machine to itself and then from the machine to another machine on the same local area network. Do the rates surprise you?

23.9   Compare the rates of transfer for FTP and NFS on a local area network. Can you explain the difference?

23.10 Examine the RPC definition. Does it handle datagram loss? duplication? delay? corruption?

23.11 Under what circumstances is the XDR scheme inefficient?

23.12 Consider translating floating point numbers from an internal form to an external form and back to an internal form. What are the tradeoffs in the choice of exponent and mantissa sizes in the external form?

24

Applications: Electronic Mail (822, SMTP)

24.1 Introduction

This chapter continues our exploration of internetworking by considering electronic mail service and the protocols that support it.

24.2 Electronic Mail

Most users first encounter computer networks when they send or receive electronic mail to or from a remote site. It is the most widely used application service. Indeed, many computer users never access networks except for electronic mail.

Mail is popular because it offers a fast, convenient method of transferring information. It can accommodate small notes or large voluminous memos, with a single mechanism. It should not surprise you to learn that more users send files with electronic mail than with file transfer programs.

Mail delivery is a new concept because it differs fundamentally from other uses of networks that we have discussed. In all our examples, network protocols send packets directly to destinations, using timeout and retransmission for individual segments if no acknowledgement returns. In the case of electronic mail, however, the system must provide for instances when the remote machine or the network connections have failed. A sender does not want to wait for the remote machine to become available before continuing work, nor does the user want to have the transfer abort merely because communication with the remote machine becomes temporarily unavailable.

To handle delayed delivery, mail systems use a technique known as *spooling*. When the user "sends" a mail message, the system places a copy in its private storage (spool†) area along with identification of the sender, recipient, destination machine, and time of deposit. The system then initiates the transfer to the remote machine as a background activity, allowing the sender to proceed with other computational activities. Figure 24.1 illustrates the idea.

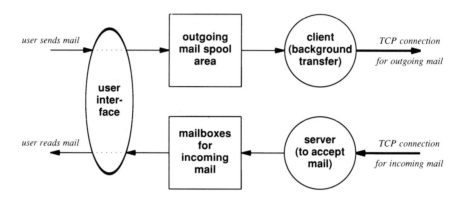

Figure 24.1 Conceptual components of an electronic mail system. The user invokes a user interface to deposit or retrieve mail; all transfers occur in the background.

The background mail transfer process becomes a client. It maps the destination machine name to an IP address and attempts to form a TCP connection to the mail server on the destination machine. If it succeeds, the transfer process passes a copy of the message to the remote server, which stores the copy in the remote system's spool area. Once the client and server agree that the copy has been accepted and stored, the client removes the local copy. If the transfer process cannot form a TCP connection, or if the connection fails, the transfer process records the time it tried delivery and terminates. The background transfer process sweeps through the spool area periodically, checking for undelivered mail. Whenever it finds a message, or whenever a user deposits new outgoing mail, it attempts delivery again. If the software finds that a mail message cannot be delivered after an extended time (e.g., 3 days), it returns the mail message to the sender.

---

†Mail spool areas are sometimes called *mail queue* areas even though the term is technically inaccurate.

24.3 Mailbox Names And Aliases

There are three important ideas hidden in our simplistic description of mail delivery. First, users specify recipients by giving a pair of identifiers that specify the *mail destination machine name* and a *mailbox address* on that machine. Second, the names used in such specifications are independent of other names assigned to machines. Usually, mailbox addresses are the same as the user's login id, and destination machine names are often the same as the machine's domain name, but that is not necessary. It is possible to assign a mailbox to a position of employment (e.g., making the mailbox identifier *department-chair* refer to whomever currently chairs the department). The domain name system supports a database and query type for mail destinations, making it possible to decouple mail destination names from the usual domain names used for machines. Third, our simplistic diagram fails to account for *mail processing* and *mail forwarding*, which include mail sent from one user to another on the same machine, and mail that arrives on a machine but which should be forwarded to another machine.

24.4 Alias Expansion And Mail Forwarding

Most systems provide *mail forwarding* software that includes a *mail alias expansion* mechanism. A mail forwarder allows the local site to map identifiers used in mail addresses to a set of one or more new mail addresses. Usually, after a user composes a message and names a recipient, the mail interface program consults the local aliases to replace the recipient with the mapped version before passing the message to the delivery system. Recipients for which no mapping has been specified remain unchanged. Similarly, the underlying mail system uses the mail aliases to map incoming recipient addresses.

Having aliases increases mail system functionality and convenience substantially. In mathematical terms, alias mappings can be many-one or one-many. For example, the alias system allows a single human to have multiple mail identifiers, including nicknames and positions, by mapping a set of identifiers to a single person. The system also allows a site to associate groups of recipients with a single identifier. Using aliases that map an identifier to a list of identifiers makes it possible to establish a mail *exploder* that accepts one incoming message and sends it to a large set of recipients. The set of recipients associated with an identifier is called an *electronic mailing list*. Not all the recipients on a list need to be local. Although it is uncommon, it is possible to have a mailing list at site, Q, with none of the recipients from the list located at Q. Expanding a mail alias into a large set of recipients is a popular technique used widely. Figure 24.2 illustrates the components of a mail system that support mail aliases and list expansion.

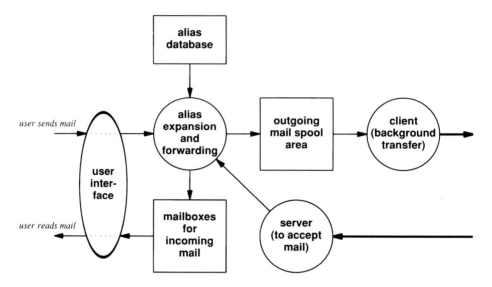

Figure 24.2 An extension of the mail system in Figure 24.1 that supports mail
aliases and forwarding. Both incoming and outgoing mail
passes through the alias expansion mechanism.

As Figure 24.2 shows, both incoming and outgoing mail passes through the mail
forwarder that expands aliases. Thus, if the alias database specifies that mail address x
maps to replacement y, alias expansion will rewrite destination address x, changing it to
y. The alias expansion program then looks to see whether y specifies a local or remote
address, so it knows whether to place the message in the incoming mail queue or outgoing mail queue.

Of course, mail alias expansion can be dangerous. Suppose two sites establish
conflicting aliases. For example, assume site A maps mail address x into mail address y
at site B, while site B maps mail address y into address x at site A. A mail message sent
to address x at site A could bounce forever between the two sites. Similarly, if the
manager at site A accidentally maps a user's login name at that site to an address at
another site, the user will be unable to receive mail. The mail may go to another user
or, if the alias specifies an illegal address, senders will receive error messages.

24.5 The Relationship Of Internetworking And Mail

Many commercial computer systems support electronic mail even though they do
not connect to the Internet. How do such systems differ from the mail system described
here? There are two crucial differences. First, a TCP/IP internet makes possible
universal delivery service. Second, electronic mail systems built on TCP/IP are in-

herently more reliable than those built from arbitrary networks. The first idea is easy to understand. TCP/IP makes possible universal mail delivery because it provides universal interconnection among machines. In essence, all machines attached to an internet behave as if attached to a single, vendor independent network. With the basic network services in place, devising a standard mail exchange protocol becomes easier.

The second claim, that using TCP/IP makes mail delivery more reliable than other mechanisms, needs explanation. The key idea here is that TCP provides end-to-end connectivity. That is, mail software on the sending machine acts as a client, contacting a server on the ultimate destination. Only after the client successfully transfers a mail message to the server does it remove the message from the local machine. Thus, direct, end-to-end delivery enforces the following principle:

> *Mail systems that use end-to-end delivery can guarantee that each mail message remains in the sender's machine until it has been successfully copied to the recipient's machine.*

With such systems, the sender can always determine the exact status of a message by checking the local mail spool area.

The alternative form of electronic mail delivery uses *mail gateways†*, sometimes called *mail bridges*, or *mail relays*, or *intermediate mail stops* to transfer messages. In such systems, the sender's machine does not contact the recipient's machine directly, but sends mail across one or more intermediate machines that forward it on.

The main disadvantage of using mail gateways is that they introduce unreliability. Once the sender's machine transfers a message to the first intermediate machine, it discards the local copy. Thus, while the message is in transit, neither the sender nor the recipient have a copy. Failures at intermediate machines may result in message loss without informing either the sender or recipient. Message loss can also result if the mail gateways route mail incorrectly. Another disadvantage of mail gateways is that they introduce delay. A mail gateway can hold messages for minutes, hours, or even days if it cannot forward them on to the next machine. Again, senders cannot determine where messages have been delayed, why they have not arrived, or how long the delay will last. The important point is that the sender and recipient must depend on machines over which they may have no control.

If mail gateways are less reliable than end-to-end delivery, why are they used? The chief advantage of mail gateways is interoperability. They provide connections among standard TCP/IP mail systems and other mail systems, as well as between TCP/IP internets and networks that do not support Internet protocols. Suppose, for example, that company *X* has a large internal network, and that employees use electronic mail, but that the network software they use does not support TCP/IP. Although it may be infeasible to make the company's network part of the connected Internet, it might be easy to place a mail gateway between the company's private network and the Internet, and to devise software that accepts mail messages from the local network and forwards them to the Internet.

---

†Readers should not confuse the concept of *mail gateway* with the concept of *IP gateway*, discussed earlier.

While the idea of mail gateways may seem somewhat clumsy, electronic mail has turned into such an important tool that users who do not have Internet access depend on them. CSNET provides an interesting example of mail gateway service. Started as an organization to help computer scientists obtain access to each other's research, CSNET members currently include universities, corporations, and sites in foreign countries. CSNET operates a mail gateway service that allows subscriber sites to send and receive mail across the Internet using only a dial-up modem. To do so, subscribers obtain mail system software from CSNET and install it on their machines. The mail gateway polls subscriber sites regularly using a dialup telephone connection, leaves mail that it has for the site, and picks up outgoing mail. The mail gateway, which connects directly to the Internet, sends the outgoing mail using standard techniques.

CSNET's mail delivery service illustrates that mail gateways can be a very effective way for users at disconnected sites to communicate. Well over 95% of the CSNET mail traffic is delivered in under 24 hours. A given site is able to improve its service by paying for more frequent dial-up connections. Thus, although the service is not as direct as end-to-end delivery, it can still be useful.

24.6 TCP/IP Standard For Electronic Mail Service

Recall that the goal of the TCP/IP protocol effort is to provide for interoperability across the widest range of computer systems and networks. To extend the interoperability of electronic mail, TCP/IP divides its mail standards into two sets. One standard specifies the format for mail messages†. The other specifies the details of electronic mail exchange between two computers. Keeping the two standards for electronic mail separate makes it possible to build mail gateways that connect TCP/IP internets to some other vendor's mail delivery system, while still using the same message format for both.

As anyone who has used electronic mail knows, each memo is divided into two parts: a header and a body, separated by a blank line. The TCP/IP standard for mail messages specifies the exact format of mail headers as well as the semantic interpretation of each header field; it leaves the format of the body up to the sender. In particular, the standard specifies that headers contain readable text, divided into lines that consist of a keyword followed by a colon followed by a value. Some keywords are required, others are optional, and the rest are uninterpreted. For example, the header must contain a line that specifies the destination. The line begins *To:* and contains the electronic mail address of the intended recipient on the remainder of the line. A line that begins *From:* contains the electronic mail address of the sender. Optionally, the sender may specify an address to which replies should be sent (i.e., to allow the sender to specify that replies should be sent to something other than the sender's usual address). If present, a line that begins *Reply-to:* specifies the address for replies. If no such line exists, the recipient will use information on the *From:* line as the return address.

The mail message format is chosen to make it easy to process and easy to transport across heterogeneous machines. Keeping the mail header format straightforward allows it to be used on a wide range of systems (including personal computers). Restricting

†Mail system experts often refer to the mail message format as "822" or "733" because RFC 822 contains the standard (RFC 733 was a former standard).

messages to readable text avoids the problems of selecting a standard binary representation and translating between the standard representation and the local machine's representation.

24.7 Electronic Mail Addresses

Anyone familiar with electronic mail knows that mail address formats seem chaotic. Thus, it can be difficult to determine a correct electronic mail address, or even to understand the sender's intentions. Within the connected Internet, addresses have a simple, easy to remember form:

local-part @ domain-name

where *domain-name* is the domain name of a mail destination† to which the mail should be delivered, and *local-part* is the address of a mailbox on that machine. For example, within the Internet, the author's electronic mail address is:

comer @ purdue . edu

However, mail gateways make addresses complex. Someone outside the Internet must either address the mail to the nearest mail gateway or have software that automatically does so. For example, someone outside the Internet using the CSNET mail relay machine might address the author as:

comer % purdue . edu @ relay . cs . net

The relay acts as a mail gateway between outside networks and the connected Internet. Once the mail reaches *relay . cs . net*, that machine extracts the *local-part* and uses it as a destination address. In this example, we are assuming that the relay machine maps the percent sign ''%'' into a commercial at sign ''@'' and resends the message.

The reason addresses become so complex when they include non-Internet sites is that the electronic mail address mapping function is local to each machine. Thus, some mail gateways require the local part to contain addresses of the form:

user % domain-name

while others require

user : domain-name

and still others use completely different forms. More important, electronic mail systems do not usually agree on conventions for precedence or quoting, making it impossible for a user to guarantee how addresses will be treated. For example, consider the electronic mail address

---

†Technically, the domain name specifies a *mail exchanger*, not a machine name.

comer % purdue . edu @ relay . cs . net

mentioned earlier. A site using the TCP/IP standard for mail would interpret the address to mean, ''send the mail to mail exchanger *relay . cs . net* and let that mail exchanger decide how to interpret *comer % purdue . edu*'' (the local part). In essence, those sites act as if the address were parenthesized:

(comer % purdue . edu) @ (relay . cs . net)

At sites that use *%* to separate user names from destination machines, the same address might mean, ''send the mail to user *comer* at the site given by the remainder of the address.'' That is, such sites act as if the address were parenthesized:

(comer) % (purdue . edu @ relay . cs . net)

We can summarize the problem:

> *Because each mail gateway determines the exact details of how it interprets and maps electronic mail addresses, there is no standard for addresses that cross mail gateway boundaries (i.e., that cross network boundaries).*

24.8 Pseudo Domain Addresses

In recent years, many networks have switched to domain-style names, even if they do not use domain name software. For example, many sites that have a connection to the UUCP network implement a pseudo-domain, *UUCP*, that allows users to specify mail addresses of the form:

uucp-style address **@** *uucp*

or a related form:

user **@** *uucp-site . uucp*

The local mail forwarding software recognizes the special addresses and translates them to the address syntax required by the UUCP network software. From the user's perspective, the advantage is clear: all electronic addresses have the same general format independent of the underlying communication network used to reach the recipient. Of course, such addresses only work where local mailers have been instructed to map them into appropriate forms and only when the appropriate transport mechanisms are available. Furthermore, even though pseudo-domain mail addresses have the same form as domain names, they can only be used with electronic mail – one cannot find IP addresses or mail exchanger addresses for them using the domain name system.

24.9 Simple Mail Transfer Protocol (SMTP)

In addition to message formats, the TCP/IP protocol suite specifies a standard for the exchange of mail between machines. That is, the standard specifies the exact format of messages a client on one machine uses to transfer mail to a server on another. The standard transfer protocol is known as *SMTP*, the *Simple Mail Transfer Protocol*. As you might guess, SMTP is simpler than an earlier *Mail Transfer Protocol, MTP*. The SMTP protocol focuses specifically on how the underlying mail delivery system passes messages across a link from one machine to another. It does not specify how the mail system accepts mail from a user or how the user interface presents the user with incoming mail. Also, SMTP does not specify how mail is stored or how frequently the mail system attempts to send messages.

SMTP is surprisingly simple. Communication between a client and server consists of readable text. Although SMTP rigidly defines the command format, humans can easily read a transcript of interactions between a client and server. Initially, the client establishes a reliable stream connection to the server and waits for the server to send a *220 READY FOR MAIL* message. (If the server is overloaded, it may delay sending the *220* message temporarily.) Upon receipt of the *220* message, the client sends a *HELO*† command. The end of a line marks the end of a command. The server responds by identifying itself. Once communication has been established, the sender can transmit one or more mail messages, terminate the connection, or request the server to exchange the roles of sender and receiver so messages can flow in the opposite direction. The receiver must acknowledge each message. It can also abort the entire connection or abort the current message transfer.

Mail transactions begin with a *MAIL* command that gives the sender identification as well as a *FROM:* field that contains the address to which errors should be reported. A recipient prepares its data structures to receive a new mail message, and replies to a *MAIL* command by sending the response *250*. Response *250* means that all is well. The full response consists of the text *250 OK*. As with other application protocols, programs read the abbreviated commands and 3-digit numbers at the beginning of lines; the remaining text is intended to help humans debug mail software.

After a successful *MAIL* command, the sender issues a series of *RCPT* commands that identify recipients of the mail message. The receiver must acknowledge each *RCPT* command by sending *250 OK* or by sending the error message *550 No such user here*.

After all *RCPT* commands, the sender issues a *DATA* command. The receiver responds with message *354 Start mail input* and specifies a sequence of characters used to terminate mail messages. The termination sequence consists of 5 characters: carriage return, line feed, period, carriage return, and line feed‡.

An example will make the SMTP exchange clear. Suppose user *Smith* at host *Alpha.EDU* sends a message to users *Jones*, *Green*, and *Brown* at host *Beta.GOV*. The SMTP client software on host *Alpha.EDU* contacts the SMTP server software on host *Beta.GOV* and begins the exchange shown in Figure 24.3.

---

†*HELO* is an abbreviation for ''hello.''
‡SMTP forbids the body of a mail message to have a period on a line by itself.

```
S: 220 Beta.GOV Simple Mail Transfer Service Ready
C: HELO Alpha.EDU
S: 250 Beta.GOV

C: MAIL FROM:<Smith@Alpha.EDU>
S: 250 OK

C: RCPT TO:<Jones@Beta.GOV>
S: 250 OK

C: RCPT TO:<Green@Beta.GOV>
S: 550 No such user here

C: RCPT TO:<Brown@Beta.GOV>
S: 250 OK

C: DATA
S: 354 Start mail input; end with <CR><LF>.<CR><LF>
C: ...sends body of mail message...
C: ...continues for as many lines as message contains
C: <CR><LF>.<CR><LF>
S: 250 OK

C: QUIT
S: 221 Beta.GOV Service closing transmission channel
```

Figure 24.3 Example of SMTP transfer from Alpha.EDU to Beta.GOV.
Lines that begin with ''C:'' are transmitted by the client (Al-
pha), while lines that begin ''S:'' are transmitted by the server.
In the example, machine Beta.GOV does not recognize the intended recipient Green.

In the example, the server rejects recipient *Green* because it does not recognize the
name as a valid mail destination (i.e., it is neither a user nor a mailing list). The SMTP
protocol does not specify the details of how the client handles such errors – the client
must decide. Although clients can abort the delivery completely if an error occurs,
most clients do not. Instead, they continue delivery to all valid recipients and then report problems to the original sender. Usually, the client reports errors using electronic
mail. The error message contains a summary of the error as well as the header of the
mail message that caused the problem.

Once a client has finished sending all the mail messages it has for a particular destination, the client may issue the *TURN*† command to turn the line around. If it does,
the receiver responds *250 OK* and assumes control of the line. With the roles reversed,
the side that was originally a server sends back any waiting mail messages. Whichever

---

†In practice, few mail servers use the *TURN* command.

side controls the interaction can choose to terminate the session. To do so, it issues a *QUIT* command. The other side responds with command *221*, which means it agrees to terminate. Both sides then close the TCP connection gracefully.

SMTP is much more complex than we have outlined here. For example, if a user has moved, the server may know about the user's new mailbox address. SMTP allows the server to choose to inform the client about the new address so the client can use it in the future. When informing the client about a new address, the server may choose to forward the mail that triggered the message, or it may request that the client take the responsibility for forwarding.

24.10 Summary

Electronic mail is among the most widely used application services. Like most TCP/IP services, it uses the client-server paradigm. Unlike most other services, however, the mail system buffers outgoing and incoming messages, allowing the transfer between client and server to occur in background while users continue with other activities.

The TCP/IP protocol suite provides separate standards for mail message format and mail transfer. The format, called *822*, is easy to understand because it uses a blank line to separate the message into a header and a body. The header consists of keyword-value pairs, with keywords like *From:* required and others optional.

The Simple Mail Transfer Protocol (SMTP) defines how the mail system on one machine transfers mail to the server on another. Messages sent between the client and server begin with a command (often a 3-digit number) that the programs use, followed by text that humans can read to understand the interaction.

FOR FURTHER STUDY

Quarterman and Hoskins [1986] discusses how mail gateways connect various networks. Quarterman [1990] contains more details. Partridge [1986] provides a more theoretical treatment of the problem.

The protocols described in this chapter are all specified in Internet RFCs. Postel [RFC 821] describes the Simple Mail Transfer Protocol and gives many examples. The exact format of mail messages is given by Crocker [RFC 822]. Partridge [RFC 974] discusses the relationship between mail routing and the domain name system. Sluizer [RFC 780] defines the older MTP protocol. Horton [RFC 976] proposes a standard for the UNIX UUCP mail system.

EXERCISES

24.1   Some mail systems force the user to specify a sequence of machines through which the message should travel to reach its destination. The mail protocol in each machine merely passes the message on to the next machine. List three disadvantages of such a scheme.

24.2   Find out if your computing systems allow you to invoke SMTP directly.

24.3   Build an SMTP client and use it to deliver a mail message.

24.4   See if you can send mail through the CSNET mail gateway and back to yourself.

24.5   Make a list of mail address forms that your site handles and write a set of rules for parsing them.

24.6   Find out how the Berkeley UNIX *sendmail* program can be used to implement a mail gateway.

24.7   Find out how often your local mail system attempts delivery and how long it will continue before giving up.

24.8   Many mail systems allow users to direct incoming mail to a program instead of storing it in a mailbox. Build a program that accepts incoming mail and sends a reply that tells the sender you are on vacation.

25

Applications: Internet Management (SNMP, CMOT)

25.1 Introduction

In addition to protocols that provide network level services and application programs that use those services, an internet needs software that allows managers to debug problems, control routing, and find computers that violate protocol standards. We refer to such activities as *internet management*. This chapter considers the ideas behind TCP/IP internet management software and presents two internet management protocols.

25.2 The Level Of Management Protocols

Many of the older wide area networks included management protocols as part of their link level protocols. If a packet switch began misbehaving, the network manager could instruct a neighboring packet switch to send it a special *control packet*. Control packets caused the receiver to suspend normal operation and respond to commands from the manager. The manager could interrogate the packet switch to identify problems, examine or change routes, test one of the communication interfaces, or reboot the switch. Once managers repaired the problem, they could instruct the switch to resume normal operations. Because management tools were part of the lowest level protocol, managers were often able to control switches even if higher level protocols failed.

Unlike a homogeneous wide area network, a TCP/IP internet does not have a single link level protocol. Instead, the internet consists of multiple physical networks interconnected by IP gateways. As a result, internet management differs from network management. First, a single manager can control heterogeneous gateways†. Second, the controlled entities may not share a common link level protocol. Third, the set of computers a manager controls may lie at arbitrary points in an internet. Thus, it may not be possible for the managers to communicate with machines they control unless the management software uses end-to-end transport connections. To summarize:

> *In a TCP/IP internet, IP gateways form the active switches that managers need to examine and control. Because gateways connect heterogeneous networks, protocols for internet management operate at the application level and use TCP/IP for message transport.*

Designing internet management software to operate at the application level has several advantages. Because the protocols can be designed without regard to the underlying network hardware, one set of protocols can be used for all networks. Because the protocols can be designed without regard to the gateway hardware, the same protocols can be used for all gateways. From a manager's point of view, having a single set of management protocols means uniformity – all gateways respond to exactly the same set of commands. Furthermore, because the management software uses IP for communication, a manager can control the gateways across an entire TCP/IP internet without having direct attachment to every physical network or gateway.

Of course, building management software at the application level also has disadvantages. Unless the operating system, IP software, and transport protocol software work correctly, the manager may not be able to contact the gateway. For example, if the gateway's routing table becomes damaged, it may be impossible to correct the table or reboot the machine from a remote site. If the operating system on a gateway crashes, it will be impossible to reach the application program that implements the internet management protocols even if the gateway can still field hardware interrupts and route packets.

25.3 Architectural Model

Despite the potential disadvantages, TCP/IP management software operates at the application level. Figure 25.1 illustrates the architectural model.

---

†Although managers can control both gateways and hosts, we will focus on control of gateways because they present the most complexity.

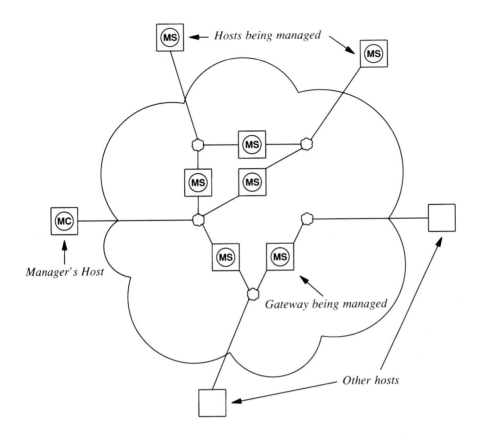

Figure 25.1 Internet management model. A manager invokes management
                client (MC) software that contacts management server (MS)
                software on gateways throughout the internet.

As the figure shows, each participating host or gateway runs a server program. A
manager invokes client software on the local host computer and specifies a server with
which it communicates. After the client contacts a server, it sends queries to obtain information or it sends commands to change conditions in the gateway. Of course, not all
gateways in a large internet fall under a single manager. Most managers only control a
few gateways at their local sites.

Internet management software uses an authentication mechanism to insure only authorized managers can access or control a particular gateway. Many management protocols support multiple levels of authorization, allowing a manager specific privileges on
each gateway. For example, a specific gateway could be configured to allow several
managers to obtain information while only allowing a select subset of them to change
information or control the gateway.

25.4 Protocol Architecture

TCP/IP network† management protocols divide the management problem into two parts and specify separate standards for each part. The first part concerns communication of information. Protocols specify how client software running on a manager's host communicates with a server. They define the format and meaning of messages clients and servers exchange as well as the form of names and addresses. The second part concerns the data being controlled. Standards specify which data items a gateway must keep as well as the names of the data items and the syntax used to express those names.

25.4.1 Standards For Network Management

Although the TCP/IP suite does not have a single official standard protocol for communication of management information, two draft standards‡ are currently co-recommended. The first, and by far the most widely used, is the *Simple Network Management Protocol* (*SNMP*); we will concentrate on it throughout this chapter. The second, known as *CMIP Over TCP* (*CMOT*), specifies using the ISO standard *Common Management Information Services/Common Management Information Protocol* (*CMIS/CMIP*) over a TCP connection.

25.4.2 Standards For Management Data

Both SNMP and CMOT specify that gateways being managed must keep status information that managers can access. Typically, the gateway keeps statistics on the status of its network interfaces, incoming and outgoing traffic, dropped datagrams, and error messages generated. Network management protocols allow managers to access these statistics.

25.5 Common Management Information Base

The two groups that proposed SNMP and CMOT initially cooperated to define a single standard for network management data. Known as the *Management Information Base* (*MIB*), the standard specifies the data items a host or gateway must keep and the operations allowed on each. For example, the MIB specifies that IP software must keep a count of all octets that arrive over each network interface, and it specifies that network management software can only read those values.

The initial MIB definition divides management information into eight categories as Figure 25.2 shows. The choice of categories is important because identifiers used to specify items include a code for the category.

---

†Technically, there is a distinction between internet management protocols and network management protocols. For a variety of reasons, however, TCP/IP internet management protocols are known as *network management* protocols; we will follow the accepted terminology.

‡A protocol is designated a *draft standard* as the last step before it becomes an official standard. Appendix C contains the details.

MIB category	Includes Information About
system	The host or gateway operating system
interfaces	Individual network interfaces
addr. trans.	Address translation (e.g., ARP mappings)
ip	Internet Protocol software
icmp	Internet Control Message Protocol software
tcp	Transmission Control Protocol software
udp	User Datagram Protocol software
egp	Exterior Gateway Protocol software

Figure 25.2 Categories of information in the MIB. The category is encoded in the identifier used to specify an object.

The advantage of keeping the MIB definition independent of the network management protocols should be clear – it allows vendors to incorporate software in their products that gathers statistics without requiring them to choose between the two proposed network management protocols. From a customer's point of view, a common MIB makes it possible to choose (or change) a network management protocol without changing the gateway software.

The main disadvantage of a common MIB lies in the consensus process: all groups specifying network management protocols must cooperate and agree on the information to be managed. Unfortunately, such cooperation is especially difficult among groups that are building competitive network management protocols. If one protocol handles more data items than another, a second group may object to placing the items in the MIB. Because the SNMP and CMOT groups were unable to agree on extensions to the original MIB, they each decided to define their own MIB extensions in 1989. The first extension, proposed by the SNMP group, is referred to as *MIB-II*. Further extensions to MIB-II, proposed by the CMOT group, are referred to as *MIB-II-OIM*.

25.6 Examples of MIB Variables

Although the exact definitions of the MIB and proposals for MIB-II are quite long, examining some of the data items they include will help clarify their contents. Figure 25.3 lists example MIB variables along with their categories.

MIB Variable	Category	Meaning
sysUpTime	system	Time since last reboot
ifNumber	interfaces	Number of network interfaces
ifMtu	interfaces	MTU for a particular interface
ipDefaultTTL	ip	Value IP uses in time-to-live field
ipInReceives	ip	Number of datagrams received
ipForwDatagrams	ip	Number of datagrams forwarded
ipOutNoRoutes	ip	Number of routing failures
ipReasmOKs	ip	Number of datagrams reassembled
ipFragOKs	ip	Number of datagrams fragmented
ipRoutingTable	ip	IP Routing table
icmpInEchos	icmp	Number of ICMP Echo Requests received
tcpRtoMin	tcp	Minimum retransmission time TCP allows
tcpMaxConn	tcp	Maximum TCP connections allowed
tcpInSegs	tcp	Number of segments TCP has received
udpInDatagrams	udp	Number of UDP datagrams received
egpInMsgs	egp	Number of EGP messages received

Figure 25.3 Examples of a few MIB variables along with their categories.

Values for most of the items listed in Figure 25.3 can be stored in a single integer. However, the MIB also defines more complex structures. For example, the MIB variable *ipRoutingTable* refers to a gateway's routing table. Additional MIB variables define the contents of a routing table entry and allow the network management protocols to reference the data for individual entries.

25.7 The Structure Of Management Information

In addition to the MIB standard, which specifies specific network management variables and their meanings, a separate standard specifies a set of rules used to define and identify MIB variables. The rules are known as the *Structure of Management Information (SMI)* specification. To keep network management protocols simple, the SMI places restrictions on the types of variables allowed in the MIB, specifies the rules for naming those variables, and creates rules for defining variable types. For example, the SMI standard includes definitions of terms like *IpAddress* (defining it to be a 4-octet string) and *Counter* (defining it to be an integer in the range of 0 to $2^{32} - 1$), and specifies that they are the terms used to define MIB variables. More important, the rules in the SMI describe how the MIB refers to tables of values (e.g., the IP routing table).

25.8 Formal Definitions Using ASN.1

The SMI standard specifies that all MIB variables must be defined and referenced using ISO's *Abstract Syntax Notation 1 (ASN.1†)*. ASN.1 is a formal language that has two main features: a notation used in documents that humans read, and a compact encoded representation of the same information used in communication protocols. In both cases, the precise, formal notation removes any possible ambiguities from both the representation and meaning. For example, instead of saying that a variable contains an integer value, a protocol designer who uses ASN.1 must state the exact form and range of numeric values. Such precision is especially important when implementations include heterogeneous computers that do not all use the same representations for data items.

Besides keeping standards documents unambiguous, ASN.1 also helps ease the implementation of network management protocols and guarantees interoperability. It defines precisely how to encode both names and data items in a message. Thus, once the documentation of a MIB has been expressed using ASN.1, the human readable form can be translated directly and mechanically into the encoded form used in messages. In summary:

> *The TCP/IP network management protocols use a formal notation called ASN.1 to define names and types for variables in the management information base. The precise notation makes the form and contents of variables unambiguous.*

25.9 Structure And Representation Of MIB Object Names

We said that ASN.1 specifies how to represent both data items and names. However, understanding the names used for MIB variables requires us to know about the underlying namespace. Names used for MIB variables are taken from the *object identifier* namespace administered by ISO and CCITT (another international organization that specifies communication standards). The key idea behind the object identifier namespace is that it provides a namespace in which all possible objects can be named. The namespace is not restricted to variables used in network management – it includes names for arbitrary objects (e.g., each international protocol standard document has a name).

The object identifier namespace is *absolute (global)*, meaning that names are structured to make them globally unique. Like most namespaces that are large and absolute, the object identifier namespace is hierarchical. Authority for parts of the namespace is subdivided at each level, allowing individual groups to obtain authority to assign some of the names without consulting a central authority for each assignment‡.

The root of the object identifier hierarchy is unnamed, but has three direct descendants managed by: ISO, CCITT, and jointly by ISO and CCITT. The descendants are assigned both short text strings and integers to identify them (the text strings are used

---

†ASN.1 is usually pronounced by reading the dot: 'A-S-N dot 1'.

‡Readers should recall from the Domain Name System discussion in Chapter 20 how authority for a hierarchical namespace is subdivided.

when humans need to understand object names; computer software uses the integers to form compact, encoded representations of the names). ISO has allocated one subtree for use by other national or international standards organizations (including U.S. standards organizations), and the U.S. National Institute for Standards and Technology† has allocated a subtree for the U.S. Department of Defense. Finally, the IAB has petitioned the Department of Defense to allocate it a subtree in the namespace.

Figure 25.4 illustrates pertinent parts of the object identifier hierarchy and shows the position of the node used by TCP/IP network management protocols.

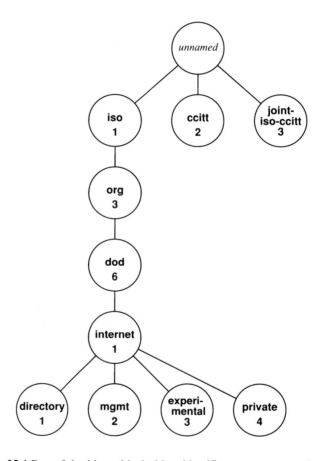

Figure 25.4 Part of the hierarchical object identifier namespace used to name MIB variables. An object's name consists of the numeric labels along a path from the root to the object.

---

†NIST was formerly the National Bureau of Standards.

The name of an object in the hierarchy is the sequence of numeric labels on the nodes along a path from the root to the object. The sequence is written with periods separating the individual components. For example, the name *1.3.6.1.1* denotes the node labeled *directory*. The MIB has been assigned a node under the *internet* management subtree with label *mib* and numeric value *1*. Because all MIB variables fall under that node, they all have names beginning with the prefix *1.3.6.1.2.1*.

Earlier we said that the MIB groups all variables into eight categories. The exact meaning of the categories can now be explained: they are the eight subtrees of the *mib* node of the object identifier namespace. Figure 25.5 illustrates the idea by showing part of the naming subtree under the *mib* node.

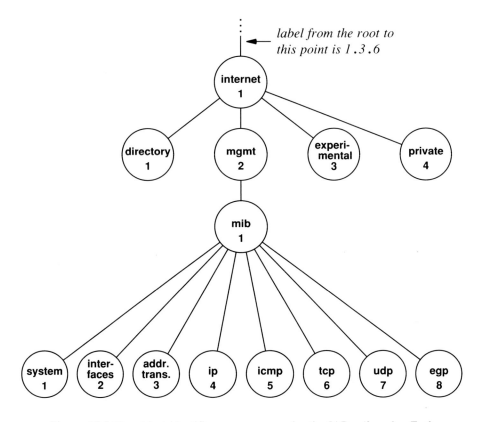

Figure 25.5 The object identifier namespace under the IAB *mib* node. Each subtree corresponds to one of the eight categories of MIB variables.

Two examples will make the naming syntax clear. Figure 25.5 shows that the category labeled *ip* has been assigned the numeric value *4*. Thus, the names of all MIB variables corresponding to IP have an identifier that begins with the prefix *1.3.6.1.2.1.4*. If one wanted to write out the textual labels instead of the numeric representation, the name would be:

$$iso.org.dod.internet.mgmt.mib.ip$$

A MIB variable named *ipInReceives* has been assigned numeric identifier *3* under the *ip* node in the namespace, so its name is

$$iso.org.dod.internet.mgmt.mib.ip.ipInReceives$$

and the corresponding numeric representation is:

$$1.3.6.1.2.1.4.3$$

When network management protocols use names of MIB variables in messages, each name has a suffix appended. For simple variables, the suffix *0* refers to the instance of the variable with that name. So, when it appears in a message sent to a gateway, the numeric representation of *ipInReceives* is

$$1.3.6.1.2.1.4.3.0$$

which refers to the instance of *ipInReceives* on that gateway. Note that there is no way to guess the numeric value or suffix assigned to a variable. One must consult the published standards to find which numeric values have been assigned to each object type. Thus, programs that provide mappings between the textual form and underlying numeric values do so entirely by consulting tables of equivalences – there is no closed-form computation that performs the transformation.

As a second, more complex example, consider the MIB variable *ipAddrTable*, which contains a list of the IP addresses for each network interface. The variable exists in the namespace as a subtree under *ip*, and has been assigned the numeric value *20*. Therefore, a reference to it has the prefix

$$iso.org.dod.internet.mgmt.mib.ip.ipAddrTable$$

with a numeric equivalent

$$1.3.6.1.2.1.4.20$$

In programming language terms, we think of the IP address table as a one-dimensional array, where each element of the array consists of a structure (record) that contains five items: an IP address, the integer index of an interface corresponding to the entry, an IP subnet mask, an IP broadcast address, and an integer that specifies the maximum datagram size that the gateway will reassemble. Of course, not all gateways have such an array in memory. The gateway may keep this information in many variables or may need to follow pointers to find it. However, the MIB provides a naming for the array as if it existed, and allows network management software on individual gateways to map table references into appropriate internal variables.

Using ASN.1 style notation, we can define *ipAddrTable*:

$$\text{ipAddrTable} \ ::= \ \text{SEQUENCE OF IpAddrEntry}$$

where *SEQUENCE* and *OF* are keywords that define an ipAddrTable to be a one-dimensional array of *IpAddrEntry*s. Each entry in the array is defined to consist of five fields (the definition assumes that *IpAddress* has already been defined).

$$
\begin{aligned}
&\text{IpAddrEntry} \ ::= \ \text{SEQUENCE \{} \\
&\quad \text{ipAdEntAddr} \\
&\qquad \text{IpAddress,} \\
&\quad \text{ipAdEntIfIndex} \\
&\qquad \text{INTEGER,} \\
&\quad \text{ipAdEntNetMask} \\
&\qquad \text{IpAddress,} \\
&\quad \text{ipAdEntBcastAddr} \\
&\qquad \text{IpAddress,} \\
&\quad \text{ipAdEntReasmMaxSize} \\
&\qquad \text{INTEGER (0..65535)} \\
&\text{\}}
\end{aligned}
$$

Further definitions must be given to assign numeric values to *ipAddrEntry* and to each item in the *IpAddrEntry* sequence. For example, the definition

$$\text{ipAddrEntry \{ ipAddrTable 1 \}}$$

specifies that *ipAddrEntry* falls under *ipAddrTable* and has numeric value *1*. Similarly, the definition

$$\text{ipAdEntNetMask \{ ipAddrEntry 3 \}}$$

assigns *ipAdEntNetMask* numeric value *3* under *ipAddrEntry*.

We said that *ipAddrTable* was like a one-dimensional array. However, there is a significant difference in the way programmers use arrays and the way network management software uses tables in the MIB. Programmers think of an array as a set of elements that have an index used to select a specific element. For example, the programmer might write *xyz[3]* to select the third element from array *xyz*. ASN.1 syntax does not use integer indices. Instead, MIB tables append a suffix onto the name to select a specific element in the table. For our example of an IP address table, the standard specifies that the suffix used to select an item consists of an IP address. Syntactically, the IP address (in dotted decimal notation) is concatenated onto the end of the object name to form the reference. Thus, to specify the network mask field in the IP address table entry corresponding to address 128.10.2.3, one uses the name:

iso.org.dod.internet.mgmt.mib.ip.ipAddrTable.ipAddrEntry.ipAdEntNetMask.128.10.2.3

which, in numeric form, becomes

$$1.3.6.1.2.1.4.20.1.3.128.10.2.3$$

Although concatenating an index to the end of a name may seem awkward, it provides a powerful tool that allows clients to search tables without knowing the number of items or the type of data used as an index. The next section shows how network management protocols use this feature to step through a table one element at a time.

25.10 Simple Network Management Protocol

Network management protocols specify communication between the network management client program a manager invokes and a network management server program executing on a host or gateway. In addition to defining the form and meaning of messages exchanged and the representation of names and values in those messages, network management protocols also define administrative relationships among gateways being managed. That is, they provide for authentication of managers.

One might expect network management protocols to contain a large number of commands. Some early protocols, for example, supported commands that allowed the manager to: *reboot* the system, *add* or *delete* routes, *disable* or *enable* a particular network interface, or *remove cached address bindings*. The main disadvantage of building management protocols around commands arises from the resulting complexity. The protocol requires a separate command for each operation on a data item. For example, the command to delete a routing table entry differs from the command to disable an interface. As a result, the protocol must change to accommodate new data items.

SNMP takes an interesting alternative approach to network management. Instead of defining a large set of commands, SNMP casts all operations in a *fetch-store paradigm*†. Conceptually, SNMP contains only two commands that allow a manager to fetch a value from a data item or store a value into a data item. All other operations are defined as side-effects of these two operations. For example, although SNMP does not have an explicit *reboot* operation, an equivalent operation can be defined by declaring a data item that gives the time to next reboot and allowing the manager to assign it a value (including zero).

The chief advantages of using a fetch-store paradigm are stability, simplicity, and flexibility. SNMP is especially stable because its definition remains fixed, even though new data items are added to the MIB and new operations are defined as side-effects of storing into those items. SNMP is simple to implement, understand, and debug because

---

†The fetch-store paradigm comes from a management protocols known as HEMS. See Partridge and Trewitt [RFCs 1021, 1022, 1023, and 1024] for details.

it avoids the complexity of having special cases for each command. Finally, SNMP is especially flexible because it can accommodate arbitrary commands in an elegant framework.

From the manager's point of view, of course, SNMP remains hidden. The user interface to network management software can phrase operations as imperative commands (e.g., *reboot*). Thus, there is little visible difference between the way a manager uses SNMP and other protocols.

As Figure 25.6 shows, SNMP offers more than the two operations we have described.

Command	Meaning
get-request	Fetch a value from a specific variable
get-next-request	Fetch a value without knowing its exact name
get-response	Reply to a fetch operation
set-request	Store a value in a specific variable
trap	Reply triggered by an event

Figure 25.6 The set of possible SNMP operations. *Get-next-request* allows the manager to iterate through a table of items.

Operations *get-request*, *get-response*, and *set-request* provide the basic fetch and store operations (as well as replies to those operations). SNMP specifies that operations must be *atomic*, meaning that if a single SNMP message specifies operations on multiple variables, the server either performs all operations or none of them. In particular, no assignments will be made if any of them are in error. The *trap* operation allows managers to program servers to send information when an event occurs. For example, an SNMP server can be programmed to send a manager a *trap* message whenever one of the attached networks becomes unusable (i.e., an interface goes down).

25.10.1 Searching Tables Using Names

We said that ASN.1 does not provide mechanisms for declaring arrays or indexing them in the usual sense. However, it is possible to denote individual elements of a table by appending a suffix to the object identifier for the table. Unfortunately, a client program may wish to examine entries in a table for which it does not know all valid suffixes. The *get-next-request* operation allows a client to iterate through a table without knowing how many items the table contains. The rules are quite simple. When sending a *get-next-request*, the client supplies a prefix of a valid object identifier, *P*. The server examines the set of object identifiers for all variables it controls, and responds by sending a *get-response* command for the one that has object identifier lexicographically greater than *P*. Because the MIB uses suffixes to index tables, a client can send the prefix of an object identifier corresponding to a table and receive the first element in the table. The client can send the name of the first element in a table and receive the second, and so on.

Consider an example search. Recall that the *ipAddrTable* uses IP addresses to identify entries in the table. A client that does not know which IP addresses are in the table on a given gateway cannot form a complete object identifier. However, it can still use the *get-next-request* operation to search the table by sending the prefix:

iso . org . dod . internet . mgmt . mib . ip . ipAddrTable . ipAddrEntry . ipAdEntNetMask

which, in numeric form, is

$$1.3.6.1.2.1.4.20.1.3$$

The server returns the network mask field of the first entry in *ipAddrTable*. The client uses the full object identifier returned by the server to request the next item in the table.

25.11 SNMP Message Format

Unlike most TCP/IP protocols, SNMP messages do not have fixed fields. Instead, they use the standard ASN.1 encoding. Thus, they can be difficult for humans to decode and understand. After examining the SNMP message definition in ASN.1 notation, we will review the ASN.1 encoding scheme briefly, and see an example of an encoded SNMP message.

An SNMP message consists of three main parts: a protocol *version*, an SNMP *community* identifier (used to group together the gateways managed by a given manager), and a *data* area. The data area is divided into *protocol data units* (*PDUs*). Each PDU consists of a request (sent by client) or a response (sent by server). Figure 25.7 shows how the message can be described in ASN.1 notation.

```
SNMP-Message  ::=
    SEQUENCE  {
        version  INTEGER  {
            version-1  (0)
        },
        community
            OCTET STRING,
        data
            ANY
    }
```

Figure 25.7 The SNMP message format in ASN.1 notation. The *data* area contains one or more protocol data units.

The five types of protocol data units are further described in ASN.1 notation in Figure 25.8.

SNMP-PDUs ::=
CHOICE {
        get-request
                GetRequest-PDU,
        get-next-request-PDU
                GetNextRequest-PDU,
        get-response
                GetResponse-PDU,
        set-request
                SetRequest-PDU,
        trap
                Trap-PDU,
}

Figure 25.8 The ASN.1 definitions of an SNMP PDU. The syntax for each request type must be specified further.

The definition specifies that each protocol data unit consists of one of the five request or response types. To complete the definition of an SNMP message, we must further specify the syntax of the five individual types. For example, Figure 25.9 shows the definition of a *get request*.

GetRequest-PDU ::= [0]
        IMPLICIT SEQUENCE {
                request-id
                        RequestID,
                error-status
                        ErrorStatus,
                error-index
                        ErrorIndex,
                variable-bindings
                        VarBindList
        }

Figure 25.9 The definition of a GetRequest-PDU.

Further definitions in the standard specify the remaining undefined terms. *Request-ID* is defined to be a 4-octet integer (used to match responses to queries). Both *Error-Status* and *ErrorIndex* are single octet integers which contain the value zero in a request. Finally, *VarBindList* contains a list of object identifiers for which the client seeks values. In ASN.1 terms, the definitions specify that *VarBindList* is a sequence of pairs of object name and value. ASN.1 represents the pairs as a sequence of two items. Thus, in the simplest possible request, *VarBindList* is a sequence of two items: a name and a *null*.

25.12 Example Encoded SNMP Message

The encoded form of ASN.1 uses variable-length fields to represent items. In general, each field begins with a header that specifies the type of object and its length in bytes. For example, Figure 25.10 shows the string of encoded octets in a *get-request* message for data item *sysDescr* (numeric object identifier *1.3.6.1.2.1.1.1*).

```
   30        29        02        01        00
SEQUENCE  len=41   INTEGER   len=1    vers=0


   04        06        70        75        62        6C        69        63
 string    len=6      p         u         b         l         i         c


   A0        1C        02        04        05        AE        56        02
getreq.    len=28   INTEGER   len=4    -------  request  id  -------


   02        01        00        02        01        00
INTEGER    len=1    status   INTEGER   len=1  error index


   30        0E        30        0C        06        08
SEQUENCE  len=14   SEQUENCE  len=12   objectid  len=8


   2B        06        01        02        01        01        01        00
   1.3   .    6    .    1    .    2    .    1    .    1    .    1    .    0


   05        00
 null     len=0
```

Figure 25.10 The encoded form of a *get-request* for data item *sysDescr* with octets shown in hexadecimal and their meaning below. Related octets have been grouped onto lines; they are contiguous in the message.

As Figure 25.10 shows, the message starts with a code for *SEQUENCE* which has a length of 41 octets. The first item in the sequence is a 1-octet integer that specifies the protocol *version*. The *community* field is stored in a character string, which in the example, is a 6-octet string that contains the word *public*.

The *GetRequest-PDU* occupies the remainder of the message. The initial code specifies a *get-Request* operation. Because the high-order bit is turned on, the interpretation is *context specific*. That is, the hexadecimal value *A0* only specifies a *getRequest-PDU* when used in an SNMP message; it is not a universally reserved value.

Following the request octet, the length octet specifies the request is *28* octets long. The request id is *4* octets, but each of the error status and index are one octet. Finally, the sequence of pairs contains one binding, a single object identifier bound to a *null* value. The identifier is encoded as expected except that the first two numeric labels are combined into a single octet.

25.13 Summary

Network management protocols allow a manager to monitor and control gateways and hosts. A network management client program executing on the manager's workstation contacts one or more servers running on the computers to be controlled. Because an internet consists of heterogeneous machines and networks, TCP/IP management software executes as application programs and uses internet transport protocols (e.g., UDP) for communication between clients and servers.

The TCP/IP protocol suite has two co-recommended draft standard network management protocols: CMOT and SNMP. CMOT uses the ISO CMIS/CMIP protocols over a TCP connection. SNMP defines a simple management protocol that provides two basic operations: fetch a value from a variable or store a value into a variable. In SNMP, all operations occur as side-effects of storing values into variables.

Initially, both SNMP and CMOT used a common definition of variables to be controlled. The set of variables was known as the common Management Information Base, or MIB. MIB variables are described using ASN.1, a formal language that provides a concise encoded form as well as a precise human-readable notation for names and objects. ASN.1 uses a hierarchical namespace to guarantee that all MIB names are globally unique while still allowing subgroups to assign parts of the namespace. Recently, the two groups have each proposed their own MIB extensions.

FOR FURTHER STUDY

Case, Fedor, Schoffstall, and Davin [RFC 1157] contains the standard for SNMP. OSI standards [1988a] and [1988b] specify CMIS and CMIP. Warrier and Besaw [RFC 1095] contains the CMOT standard that specifies how to use CMIS/CMIP over TCP/IP. Schoffstall, Davin, Fedor, and Case [RFC 1089] discusses using SNMP over Ethernet.

ISO [May 87a] and [May 87b] contain the standard for ASN.1 and specify the encoding. McCloghrie and Rose [RFC 1156] specifies the MIB, while McCloghrie and Rose [RFC 1155] contains the SMI rules for naming MIB variables. Rose [RFC 1158] proposes a MIB-II for use with SNMP, while the Internet draft by LaBarre [December 1989] contains a proposal from the CMOT group.

An older proposal for a network management protocol called HEMS can be found in Trewitt and Partridge [RFCs 1021, 1022, 1023, and 1024]. Davin, Case, Fedor, and Schoffstall [RFC 1028] specifies a predecessor to SNMP known as the Simple Gateway

Monitoring Protocol (SGMP). Cerf [RFC 1052] clarifies the IAB recommendations and plans for evolving Internet management protocols.

EXERCISES

25.1   Capture an SNMP packet with a network analyzer and decode the fields.

25.2   Read the standard to find out how ASN.1 encodes the first two numeric values from an object identifier in a single octet. Why does it do so?

25.3   Read the specification for CMIP. How many commands does it support?

25.4   Suppose the MIB designers needed to define a variable that corresponded to a 2-dimensional array. How can ASN.1 notation accommodate references to such a variable?

25.5   What are the advantages and disadvantages of defining globally unique ASN.1 names for MIB variables?

25.6   If you have SNMP client code available, try using it to read MIB variables in a local gateway. What is the advantage of allowing arbitrary managers to read variables in all gateways?

25.7   Read the MIB specification to find the definition of variable *ipRoutingTable* that corresponds to an IP routing table. Design a program that will use SNMP to contact *n* gateways and see if any entries in their routing tables cause a routing loop. Exactly what ASN.1 names do you generate?

26

Summary Of Protocol Dependencies

26.1 Introduction

TCP/IP has spawned many more protocols than we can discuss in a single text. Well-known distributed systems like the Andrew file system, which provides remote file access, the X-window system, which allows client programs to paint text and graphics on bit-mapped displays, and many distributed database systems all use TCP/IP protocols. In general, each of these systems defines its own application protocol and relies on TCP or UDP for end-to-end transport. In fact, any programmer who builds a distributed application using TCP/IP defines yet another application-level protocol.

While it is not important to know all protocols, it is important to understand which protocols exist and how they can be used. This chapter provides a brief summary of the relationships among the major protocols we have discussed and shows which ones are available for use by application programs.

26.2 Protocol Dependencies

The chart in Figure 26.1 shows dependencies among the major protocols we have discussed. Each enclosed polygon corresponds to one protocol and resides directly above the polygons representing protocols that it uses. For example, the mail protocol, SMTP, depends on TCP, which depends on IP.

Users

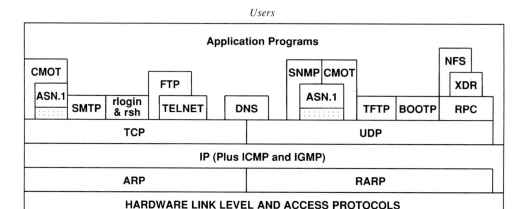

Figure 26.1 Dependencies among higher level TCP/IP protocols. A protocol
uses those protocols that lie directly below it. Application programs can use all protocols above IP.

Several parts of the diagram need further explanation. The bottom layer represents
all protocols that the hardware provides. This level includes all hardware protocols, and
ranges from media access to logical link allocation. As we have throughout this text,
we will assume that any packet transfer system can be included in this layer as long as
IP can use it to transfer datagrams. Thus, if a system is configured to send datagrams
through a tunnel, the entry to the tunnel is treated like a hardware interface, despite its
software implementation.

The second layer from the bottom lists ARP and RARP. Of course, not all
machines or network technologies use them. ARP is most often used on Ethernets;
RARP is seldom used except for diskless machines. Other address binding protocols
may occur here, but none are currently in widespread use.

The third layer from the bottom contains IP. It includes the required error and
control message protocol, ICMP, and the optional multicast group management protocol
IGMP. Note that IP is the only protocol that spans an entire layer. All higher-level
protocols must use IP to send outgoing datagrams, and all lower-level protocols deliver
incoming information to it. IP is shown with a direct dependency on the hardware layer
because it needs to use the hardware link or access protocols to transmit datagrams after
it uses ARP to bind addresses.

TCP and UDP comprise the transport layer. Of course, new transport protocols
have been suggested, but none has been widely accepted yet.

The application layer shows complex dependencies among the various application protocols. Recall, for example, that FTP uses the network virtual terminal definitions from TELNET to define communication on its control connection, and TCP to form data connections. Thus, the diagram shows FTP depending on both TELNET and TCP. The domain name system (DNS) uses both UDP and TCP for communication, so the diagram shows both dependencies. Sun's NFS depends on the external data representation (XDR) and remote procedure call (RPC) protocols

The network management protocols have more complex dependencies than most protocols. Both SNMP and CMOT depend on *Abstract Syntax Notation* (ASN.1). Furthermore, because CMOT can use either TCP or UDP for transport, it appears in two places in the diagram.

Because ASN.1 simply describes a syntax and a namespace, it does not depend on either TCP or UDP. Thus, the diagram shows no direct dependence between ASN.1 and UDP or TCP, even though it shows CMOT and SNMP depending on both ASN.1 and a transport protocol. In fact, many details have been omitted in our depiction of CMOT; it also depends heavily on OSI protocols that are not shown.

26.3 Application Program Access

Most systems limit application program access to lower-level protocols. Usually, an application program can only use TCP or UDP, or it can execute other protocols that use them (e.g., SMTP). An application may need special privilege to open specific ports, but that is different from restricting access completely. Access to lower-level protocols is much more restricted. Many systems simply do not have mechanisms that allow an application program to access IP directly; almost none allow application programs to access lower-level protocols like ARP. Despite the usual limitations, our diagram suggests that application should have access to IP (one of the exercises explores this further).

Some systems provide special purpose mechanisms that permit an application program to interact with lower protocol layers. For example, a mechanism known as the *packet filter* allows privileged programs to affect frame demultiplexing. Using the packet filter primitives, an application program establishes the criteria used to capture packets (e.g., the application program specifies that it wishes to capture all packets with a given value in the *type* field of the frame). Once the operating system accepts the filter command, it begins placing all packets that match the specified type on a queue. The application program uses another part of the packet filter mechanism to extract packets from the queue. For such systems, the diagram should be changed to show application access at all levels.

26.4 Summary

Much of the rich functionality associated with the TCP/IP protocol suite results from a variety of high-level services supplied by application programs. The high-level protocols these programs use build on the basic services: unreliable datagram delivery and reliable stream transport. They usually follow the client-server model in which servers operate at known protocols ports so clients know how to contact them.

The highest levels of protocols provide user services like file and mail transfer and remote login. The chief advantages of having an internet on which to build such services are that it provides universal connectivity and simplifies the application protocols. In particular, when used by two machines that attach to an internet, end-to-end transport protocols can guarantee that a client program on the source machine communicates directly with a server on the destination machine. Because services like electronic mail use the end-to-end transport connection, they do not need to rely on intermediate machines to forward (whole) messages.

We have seen a variety of application level protocols and the complex dependencies among them. Earlier, we said that although many application protocols have been defined, electronic mail, file transfer, and remote login services account for most use.

FOR FURTHER STUDY

One of the issues underlying protocol layering revolves around the optimal location of protocol functionality. Edge [1979] compares end-to-end protocols with the hop-by-hop approach. Saltzer, Reed, and Clark [1984] argues for having the highest level protocols perform end-to-end acknowledgement and error detection.

In a series of papers, Mills proposes application protocols for clock synchronization and reports on experiments [RFCs 956, 957, and 958].

EXERCISES

26.1   It is possible to translate some application protocols into others? For example, it might be possible to build a program that accepts an FTP request, translates it to a TFTP request, passes the result to a TFTP server to obtain a file, and translates the reply back to FTP form for transmission to the original source. What are the advantages and disadvantages of such protocol translation?

26.2   Consider the translation described in the previous question. Which pairs of protocols in Figure 26.1 are amenable to such translations?

26.3   Figure 26.1 suggests that some application programs invoked by users may need access to IP. Find examples of such programs. (Hint: think of ICMP.)

26.4   Where does EGP fit into the diagram in Figure 26.1?

26.5   Read about protocol dependencies used by CMOT and expand the diagram to include them.

26.6   Find out whether your local operating system allows a single process to accept both TCP connections and UDP requests.

26.7   Choose a complex application like the *X window system* and find out which protocols it uses.

26.8   Where does RIP fit into the diagram in Figure 26.1?

26.9   The diagram in Figure 26.1 shows that FTP depends on TELNET. Does your local FTP client invoke the TELNET program or does the FTP client contain a separate implementation of the TELNET protocol?

27

TCP/IP Internet Research And Engineering Problems

27.1 Introduction

Evolution of TCP/IP technology is intertwined with evolution of the connected Internet for several reasons. First, the Internet is the largest installed TCP/IP internet, so many problems related to scale arise in the Internet before they surface in other TCP/IP internets. Second, funding for TCP/IP research and engineering comes from agencies that need to use the operational Internet, so they tend to fund projects which impact the Internet. Third, most researchers engaged in TCP/IP work have connections to the Internet and use it daily. Thus, they have immediate motivation to solve problems that will improve service and extend functionality.

With tens of thousands of users at over a thousand sites depending on the connected Internet as part of their daily work environment, it might seem that the Internet is a completely stable production facility. We have passed the early stage of development in which every user was also an expert and entered a stage in which few users understand the technology. Despite appearances, however, neither the Internet nor the TCP/IP protocol suite is static. New groups interconnect their networks and find new ways to use the technology. Researchers discover ways to solve networking problems, and engineers find ways to improve the underlying mechanisms. In short, the technology continues to evolve.

The purpose of this chapter is to consider the ongoing evolutionary process and quickly survey a few of the current research and engineering efforts. Whether the projects reviewed here become integral parts of the technology in the next years or decades is unimportant; the goal is to give the reader some intuition for the scope of research and engineering projects associated with the Internet and TCP/IP protocols at a given point in time. While some of these issues will surely fade, others will rise.

27.2 The Forces Stimulating Evolution

In a broad sense, four types of change stimulate the evolution of TCP/IP technology and the Internet architecture, as Figure 27.1 illustrates. No single thrust dominates the technology.

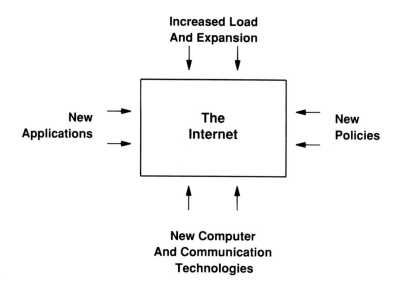

Figure 27.1 The four types of change that stimulate evolution of Internet technology.

27.2.1 Increased load and expansion

As the user population grows, load increases. Of course, some increase in load arises when new sites are added to the Internet. Load can also increase when groups at existing sites suddenly start using the facilities. As individuals gain access to an internet, they stimulate new interactions among existing users. In any case, load is increasing faster than the population. As a result of load, engineers and researchers seek ways to obtain better service from existing facilities.

27.2.2 New technologies

Like most technically oriented groups, researchers working on TCP/IP protocols maintain a keen interest in new technologies. As new minicomputers become available, researchers use them as packet switches and gateways. Besides conventional packet switching networks that use leased communication lines, TCP/IP research has studied point-to-point satellite communication, multiple station synchronized satellite communication, and communication using packet radio networks. More recently, researchers have studied voice and video teleconferencing. Thus, researchers have used new technologies to expand internetworking and improve its capacity to meet increased load. More important, research has produced innovative technology (e.g., the Butterfly multiprocessor, used as a gateway).

27.2.3 New policies

Adding new groups of users differs from merely increasing the load because it results in new administrative authorities. Changes in authority produce changes in administrative policies and mandate new mechanisms to enforce those policies. As we have seen, both the architecture of the connected Internet gateway system and the protocols it uses are evolving away from a centralized core model. Evolution will continue as more national backbone networks attach, producing increasingly complex policies regulating interaction. When multiple corporations connect their private TCP/IP internets, they face similar problems as they try to define policies for interaction and then find mechanisms to enforce those policies. Thus, many of the research and engineering efforts surrounding TCP/IP focus on finding ways to accommodate new administrative groups.

27.2.4 New applications

One of the most exciting frontiers of research, new applications often demand facilities or services that the current protocols cannot provide. They stimulate researchers to reconsider both the assumptions underlying TCP/IP internet architecture and protocols as well as the details of the services the protocols provide.

Although we have listed the four types of stimuli separately, it should be obvious that they interact. A new communication technology may make it possible to support an entirely new set of applications which, in turn, may entice an entirely new group of users to become interested in using TCP/IP and connecting their internet to others. Or it may happen that the need to support increased load stimulates research that yields a new communication technology. Thus, it can be difficult to determine the exact motivation for a change.

To make the discussion more concrete, the next sections provide examples of current research and engineering problems. Each section poses an important unanswered question and describes some of the ongoing work surrounding it.

27.3 Routing In An Expanded Internet

Perhaps the most important short-term problem Internet engineers face is success. The Internet was designed and built as a research prototype. Early estimates suggested the Internet should support dozens of networks and hundreds of host computers. By 1990, the size had reached over one thousand active networks and over one hundred thousand hosts. But numbers alone do not accurately reveal the problem: the rate of growth changed dramatically from the slow, steady pace of early years to a sudden explosion in connectivity. Observations reported at IETF meetings from the period between late summer of 1987 and the spring of 1988 show the growth rate averaged 10% per month, with several months of 15% growth. For over six years, the number of active networks has doubled every 13.5 to 14 months.

The engineering and research questions underlying rapid expansion are complex, but one is quite apparent:

> *Will the current Internet routing mechanisms operate with an order of magnitude more hosts and networks, and if not, what must be done to accommodate growth?*

Recall that the core routing model requires at least some gateways to have tables that contain all IP network addresses. We already saw that it is impossible to partition a core without introducing the possibility of routing loops. However, it might be possible to use hierarchical routing or other schemes.

The subnet routing scheme described in Chapter 16 is a form of hierarchical routing that was invented to help solve the problem of routing in an expanded Internet. If every site used subnet addressing, the size of gateway routing tables would grow more slowly, making it possible to use current technology longer. Thus, work on subnetting will continue until it becomes a well-understood and integral part of all IP implementations.

A working group has proposed the Open Shortest Path First (OSPF) routing algorithm as a new Interior Gateway Protocol (IGP) that scales well to handle routing in large regional or corporate internets. While that working group continues to refine and test OSPF, another working group has investigated an *Open Distance-Vector* (ODV) routing algorithm. The idea was to explore the possibility of using a simpler algorithm for cases where OSPF proved to be too complex.

Still other research and engineering groups have begun the study of policy-based routing. The question they ask is:

> *How can routing mechanisms accommodate administrative polices on network access, use of bandwidth, and priority?*

The issue of how to account for traffic is related to the question of speed and routing. The key problem is efficiency: while it is possible to build software that implements arbitrary administrative policies, such software can require each gateway to perform a complicated computation every time it routes a packet. Thus, we seek a compromise – a mechanism that remains efficient while providing sufficient support for most administrators.

27.4 Finding Users

As the number of users on any internet increases, it becomes difficult to locate information about a given individual. For example, when the Internet began, the Network Information Center published a directory of all users along with their postal and electronic mail addresses. The latter is especially important because without an exact electronic mail address, no delivery is possible. However, at the current population size and growth rate, printed directories are hopelessly inadequate. The central question has become:

> *How can we automate mechanisms for storing and locating information about individual users?*

It is easy to see how to build client and server software that allows one to access an on-line database of user names, addresses, and telephone numbers. The NIC has such a database, as does CSNET. Unfortunately, centralized facilities have two major drawbacks: the information becomes out of date quickly because users do not take an active interest in updating their entries, and the central server is a bottleneck through which all traffic must pass (a central server also causes the entire system to fail if it is unavailable).

It is more challenging to design a system that can expand indefinitely, allows fairly broad database queries (e.g., to find all users with first name "Peter"), and keeps the information current. The problem is known as the *white pages problem*, the name being a reference to the white pages of a U.S. telephone book. Several research and engineering groups are conducting experiments with white pages services. One group is experimenting with an implementation of the OSI *X.500* directory service. Another is using the *Profile* white pages mechanism. Both experiments use an architecture built around distributed on-line servers. Taking a different approach, researchers at Purdue University are exploring a 2-level hierarchy in which the top level, called a *Directory Location Service* (*DLS*), provides information about the locations of white pages services. When a user requests information about an individual, the user must supply some hint(s) about the individual's organization. Client software at the user's site contacts the DLS and passes along the hints to obtain a list of potential organizations and the servers those organizations operate (along with information about which protocols each server uses). The user then selects one or more organizations, and the client software contacts servers for those organizations to ask about the individual.

27.5 Finding Services

We said that many groups are working on the problem of locating an individual. A related problem occurs when a user wants to locate services available on an internet. For example, in the beginning of the connected Internet, it was possible to send out mail to all sites or even to submit an RFC that requested information about which hosts offered which services. As the Internet expanded, manual schemes became hopelessly inadequate.

This problem, known as the *yellow pages problem*, can be summarized:

> *How can we automate mechanisms for storing and locating informa-*
> *tion about services offered by hosts in an internet?*

Researchers are examining automated ways to allow hosts to advertise services that are available and to locate services on other hosts. The ultimate goal is to have a system in which any user can find desired computational services quickly and invoke those services with little overhead. The problem differs from the domain name lookup problem because multiple hosts offer a given service, and because services change more frequently than host names.

27.6 Managing Networks

Expansion also affects management of the connected Internet and the networks that comprise it. Early management schemes consisted of cooperation among researchers who built and used the Internet. Gateways came from very few vendors who each devised whatever monitoring or control software they thought was needed. If a particular host or protocol implementation caused problems, researchers cooperated to identify the problem, and then simply discussed it with whoever was responsible for the offending host. Since those early days, the Internet has grown in complexity as well as size. Now, many vendors manufacture gateways, protocols, and application software. Many systems programmers install, modify, and maintain TCP/IP protocol software. Clearly, automated methods are needed to manage internets.

The management question becomes:

> *How can we create automated, vendor independent mechanisms that*
> *will allow network managers to monitor and control traffic across an*
> *entire internet?*

Chapter 25 discussed current network management tools and suggested that development continues on these tools. In addition, other groups are exploring related areas of network management: *alert management*, *LAN management*, and *network operation center tools*.

Alert management refers to automation of the analysis of warning and log messages. For example, it is possible to have gateways emit messages whenever events occur like congestion, arrival of an illegal datagram, or arrival of a conflicting ARP message (one machine answers ARP requests for two distinct IP addresses). Accumulating long lists of such messages does little to help in managing a network because a human can overlook significant facts or trends. Groups working on this problem hope to automate the analysis by providing software that will watch trends and identify significant problems for the manager.

27.7 Automatic Configuration

The installation and operation of TCP/IP software still requires considerable expertise. The question arises:

*Can we automate the installation and operation of TCP/IP software
so a user can attach a machine to a network and begin using it
without requiring manual configuration?*

The ultimate goal of work on this problem is automatic configuration. That is, researchers expect to produce TCP/IP protocols and support software so sophisticated that it allows users to connect their computer to an internet without relying on experts to manage software, configuration parameters, or routing tables.

Several research and engineering groups have begun work that will automate a particular aspect of the process. For example, one working group is exploring *dynamic host configuration*. Dynamic host configuration means designing new protocols that allow a host to obtain or register all necessary name and address information automatically. We have seen that a host can already use ICMP to obtain a subnet mask, and it can even use limited broadcast addressing to find the network address. Finally, the host can use RARP to obtain its IP address. However, a host cannot currently obtain its domain name or mail forwarding information automatically.

Related working groups are exploring two more aspects of automatic configuration. The *gateway discovery* group is working on protocols that will allow a host to discover which gateway(s) it can use. Most of the currently available routing software requires a manager to manually configure the address of a default gateway. The gateway discovery protocol will allow a host to discover the addresses of local gateways and to continually test those gateways to find out which ones are available at any time.

Another working group is exploring *MTU† discovery*. The idea is to invent ways for a host to discover the minimum MTU along a path to a given destination. The optimal TCP segment size depends on the MTU because datagrams larger than the MTU will be fragmented, and datagrams smaller then the MTU have unnecessary overhead. Thus, if the MTU is known, TCP can optimize throughput by making segments as large as will fit in a datagram less than or equal to the MTU. Similarly, application programs using UDP can optimize throughput by using the MTU along a path to choose datagram size.

---

†Recall that the Maximum Transmission UNIT (MTU) refers to the largest amount of data that can be transported in a single network packet.

Finding the MTU between source and destination can be difficult because not all datagrams follow the same route. Furthermore, as networks fail or routes change, the MTU can change. Thus, MTU discovery produces an approximation, and a dynamic protocol may be needed to update the MTU continually.

27.8 New Applications

The birth of any new technology stimulates creative people to find new ways to use it. TCP/IP is no exception. As soon as users become comfortable with the technology, they begin to apply it to their everyday tasks. They imagine new uses of existing technology and dream of how slightly more advanced technology will make their work even easier. There are more new applications driving TCP/IP than can be covered here. Instead of a survey, we will concentrate on a handful of research projects. These projects have been selected because they illustrate both innovation and utility.

Readers who lack firsthand experience with existing Internet facilities may find new applications difficult to appreciate. To make sure everyone begins from a common point of view, we will spend a short time reviewing an existing service, electronic mail, and the way people with Internet access use it. While the discussion presents one point of view, that of a scientist, most of the activities described are common to most professional jobs.

Electronic mail forms an integral part of most Internet users' professional environment. People who have access to the Internet quickly begin to depend on electronic mail as their primary form of business communication. For experienced users, it is difficult to imagine a world without it. Scientists, for example, use electronic mail to exchange technical papers and scientific data, to debate technical ideas, to announce new results to colleagues, to schedule national meetings, to submit research proposals, and to replace most telephone conversations. Besides using electronic mail for interactions among distant parties, the scientist uses it to contact local groups like the accounting office or purchasing agent. The advantages are obvious: electronic communication provides a written record, and it is much faster than postal delivery. By integrating local and remote communication, the scientist is able to have a uniform environment for conducting business. Unlike a telephone, electronic mail does not require the two correspondents to rendezvous at exactly the same time. Finally, electronic mail allows a user to define sets of colleagues, so memos can be distributed to a group as easily as to an individual.

As an example, consider a group of scientists working together on a project. They can use electronic mail to distribute periodic progress reports or conduct technical discussions. When they do decide to meet face to face, the person who volunteers to make local arrangements can use electronic mail to collect information about arrival and departure times, inform the group about travel and hotel accommodations, and distribute a meeting agenda. Participants can send in suggestions for additions or changes to the agenda. After the meeting, the secretary can use electronic mail to send minutes of the meeting to the chairperson for approval and, after approval, to the entire group. Finally the scientists can use electronic mail to send progress summaries to funding agencies.

For people with Internet access, such communication is not fantasy. It is part of their everyday work environment. The point is that Internet users depend on electronic mail the way most professionals depend on a telephone. It has been integrated into their working environment and has made major changes in the way they conduct daily business.

Now that we understand the current state of communication by electronic mail and how it is used in the Internet, we can appreciate the excitement generated by some of the new research projects. The question driving all of these investigations is:

> *How can we make substantial improvements in electronic communication while retaining all the features that have made electronic mail so popular and successful?*

The answers require imagination and engineering skill because we are seeking mechanisms that go far beyond current capabilities and yet remain economical enough for most users to obtain. We will discuss five areas of research that pose different solutions.

Integrated text and graphics. There is an obvious and immediate need for standards that will allow participants to send more than simple text messages. Several research and engineering projects are examining ways to integrate graphics into electronic mail. The goal is to make it easy for users to send line drawings or images along with text. Although research prototypes have been built that demonstrate feasibility, the goal is to make such facilities accessible using commercially available hardware. Researchers are looking for ways to represent images without making them hardware dependent. The objective is to define an abstraction for images that makes it possible to have a compact representation (to make transmission across an internet efficient), while still accommodating a wide variety of underlying hardware displays (to make mapping onto any given hardware efficient and easy).

Voice mail. A second interesting area of research focuses on the question of how to integrate spoken voice with electronic mail. Novice users often express disappointment in electronic mail because they cannot convey emotion (e.g., tone of voice) along with messages. Some users send textual clues to alleviate the problem (e.g., the sideways smiley face `` :-) '' to indicate humor), but such clues do not solve the problem completely. The result is that electronic memos or replies are often misinterpreted. While the lack of inflection can make electronic mail frustrating, users appreciate the ability to read electronic mail at their leisure instead of being interrupted by telephone calls. A specific question is:

> *How can one record voice and send it along with electronic mail?*

Although digitized voice storage has been well understood for many years, new technologies make possible low-cost digitizing and playback equipment. Thus, adding digital voice to electronic mail has become more interesting. The success of current research projects will make it possible to have digitizing and playback equipment widely available.

Integrated telephone services. Once mechanisms and standards are in place for voice storage, it becomes natural to interconnect computers and telephones. We can imagine an automated system that works like an answering machine except that it digitizes the incoming message, so it can be sent through electronic mail. A user traveling in a distant city could arrange to have the telephone server answer the phone, digitize phone messages, forward them to the recipient, and then accept responses from the recipient along with instructions that cause the server to return the calls and play the recorded responses.

Video mail. Once available electronic mail systems include graphics and digitized voice, it is natural to ask whether video can be included as well. The basic hardware technology exists. Powerful workstations have appeared that allow one to display real time video in a window on their bit mapped displays. Storing and transporting video requires substantially more resources than voice because video uses much higher bandwidth. Some research projects are looking for ways to compress the amount of bandwidth needed for real time video, while others are examining how users react to slow-speed video.

Because applications like video cannot be added to the existing Internet without changing the performance, some researchers are experimenting to see how well current protocols perform with new applications. One interesting project conducted at The Massachusetts Institute of Technology has turned the experiment around and considered what new protocols are needed to support the efficient transfer of large bulk data across an internet. The protocol is called *NETBLT*†. A preliminary version has already become recognized as an experimental protocol in the TCP/IP protocol suite.

NETBLT tries to achieve better throughput by controlling the rate at which packets enter an internet. The idea comes from the observation that when bursts of traffic clog communication paths, each burst results in many lost packets that require retransmission. NETBLT tries to avoid unnecessary retransmissions by sending groups of packets with precisely controlled interpacket and intergroup delays.

Teleconferencing. The logical extension of integrating voice and video with electronic mail is a real time voice and video delivery service. If such a delivery service were available, it could be used for *teleconferencing*, in which geographically diverse users conduct business by having video and voice display of each other.

Internet researchers use the WIDEBAND network regularly to conduct video conferences in which groups at two or more sites conduct a joint business meeting. Although such experiments demonstrate exciting possibilities, they also show fundamental limits of the TCP/IP protocols. Indeed, for teleconferencing to work well, special purpose protocols must be used as well as special purpose communication links. Thus, one of the main questions becomes:

> *How can we adapt TCP/IP protocols to accommodate new applications that need high bandwidth communication paths?*

One group is exploring this topic under the name *connection-oriented IP*. They have begun examining ways to add the benefits of connection oriented protocols to IP's con-

---

†NETBLT is pronounced "net blit."

nectionless delivery service. Related research at Massachusetts Institute of Technology and Purdue have defined higher-level abstractions that transport protocols can use to reserve resources in underlying networks.

27.9 High-Speed Communication Technologies

The advent of a new communication technology always stimulates curiosity. When that technology promises to increase communication bandwidth several orders of magnitude, while simultaneously decreasing the error rate, then it becomes revolutionary. One communication technology with those properties is collectively called *fiber optics*. Glass fiber can be used to interconnect two computers, to build local area networks, to build metropolitan area networks, or to provide high capacity trunk connections in wide area networks.

Fiber technology comes at a crucial time for TCP/IP and the connected Internet: just as the demand for higher capacity interconnection has begun to exceed the capacity of existing backbone networks. With fiber, it is possible to substantially increase the bandwidth of interconnections. The motivation is to improve performance of existing applications as well as to allow new applications that are now impossible. Thus, researchers and engineers ask two questions:

> *What minor changes are needed to allow existing TCP/IP protocols to use higher speed backbone interconnections effectively? What major changes or additions must be made to TCP/IP protocols to accommodate new applications that need higher throughput than is now possible?*

The NETBLT protocol research discussed above provides an example of how researchers are attacking the second question. Related research has focused on special protocols that obtain high throughput when using satellite links. The Internet includes both point-to-point satellite connections (SATNET) as well as a synchronized, multistation satellite system (WIDEBAND) that uses a slotted reservation protocol. The latter has sufficient bandwidth to deliver video and voice traffic (i.e. it can support teleconferencing).

The most dramatic consequence of increased communication bandwidth is its effect on packet switching technology. To understand why, consider one of the packet switches in a network that uses *DS1 speed*† leased line interconnections. Imagine incoming traffic from a single leased line that operates at 100% capacity. The amount of computation required in the packet switch is proportional to the number of packets switched. Thus, the packet switch must do more computation per unit time if packet sizes are small (because more packets arrive per unit time).

How fast must a packet switch operate to handle a DS1 line? Consider switching IP datagrams that carry TCP segments. Recall that such datagrams have an IP header followed by a TCP segment header, followed by data. As a result, the smallest da-

---

†DS1 speed lines operate at 1.544 Mbps and are often called *T1* lines after a standard low-level protocol commonly used with them.

tagram (e.g., those that carry one octet of TELNET data) is approximately 40 octets long. Dividing the line speed by 40 octets of 8 bits per octet shows that the packet switch must handle approximately 4800 packets per second. Of course, a packet switch must also handle traffic in at least two directions simultaneously and should be able to accommodate multiple connections. Thus, a general purpose packet switch needs a total switching capacity well above 10000 packets per second.

Most current packet switches have only a single CPU. The fastest single CPU systems are capable of switching an aggregate of between 2000 and 5000 packets per second, clearly not enough for DS1 speed lines. DS1 speed is only the beginning, however, because fiber optics can handle speeds of tens of gigabits per second. Accommodating such speeds requires entirely new packet switching technologies. The question becomes:

> *How can new processing technologies make it possible to switch packets at speeds comparable with the transmission speeds provided by fiber optic interconnects?*

Several Internet research projects are investigating packet switching, with the most interesting concentrating on designs that eventually avoid electronics and use only optical switches. It is interesting to note that the advent of such switches may eventually force changes in IP because in its present form, gateways must read and change the IP header when switching the datagram.

27.10 Reliable Transactions

We said that while TCP provides reliable delivery, there is no reliable datagram service because UDP provides only unreliable delivery. Some applications that only use datagram service also need a guarantee of reliable delivery. The question arises:

> *Can we devise a single, general purpose protocol that supports reliable datagram transfer in an internet environment while retaining the efficiency of current datagram protocols?*

A current research project is exploring such a protocol. It has resulted in a preliminary draft specification and prototype implementation. Early measurements show that the protocol, known as *VMTP*, performs well, adapts to internet delays, and supports a wide variety of applications. If the results continue to be positive, VMTP may become a TCP/IP standard on which transaction processing systems can be built.

27.11 Security

We said that TCP/IP makes universal interoperability possible. In many environments, however, managers need to limit interoperability to keep data private. We refer to all such restrictions under the general heading of *security*. Making a TCP/IP internet secure can be more difficult than making a single computer secure, because it provides much more powerful communication facilities. The question becomes:

> *How can an organization using TCP/IP insure that its computers and data are secure from unwanted or unauthorized access?*

One group has explored the question of how to make mail transport secure by providing an experimental facility for *privacy enhanced mail*. The idea is to have a mechanism that allows the sender to encrypt a message and send it across an open internet (an internet in which arbitrary users on intermediate machines can spy on packets), without allowing anyone but the intended recipient to decrypt it.

Related work on packet filtering in gateways has produced a variety of mechanisms that allow managers to provide explicit access control lists. An access list specifies a set of machines or networks between which the gateway will route datagrams. The gateway must verify the source and destination addresses of each datagram with the access control mechanism before it routes the datagram. If the address is not allowed, the gateway discards the datagram. In most implementations, the gateway can be configured to report attempted violations to the manager. Thus, it is possible to use address filters to control communication among machines. Groups continue to explore how to provide additional security control in TCP/IP internets.

27.12 Summary

Neither the connected Internet nor the TCP/IP protocols it uses are static. Through its Research and Engineering Task Forces, the Internet Activities Board fosters active, ongoing research and engineering efforts that keep the technology stretching and evolving. The stimulus for change occurs as increased use forces improvements to maintain service, as new applications demand more from the underlying technology, as new technologies make it possible to provide new services, and as new groups extend the architectural and functional basis. This chapter examined a few of the many problems that arise because the Internet is growing and adapting to new applications, technologies, and groups of users. It discussed a few of the many engineering and research projects aimed at solving those problems.

FOR FURTHER STUDY

Arnon [RFC 1019] discusses representations for mathematical equations. Mills and Braun [1987] describes some of the problems created by NSFNET. Reynolds *et al* [October 1985] discusses multimedia experiments. Crowley *et al* [June 1987] focuses on a multimedia mail system that integrates graphics, voice, and text. Clark *et al* [1987] describes the NETBLT protocol, and Lambert [RFC 1030] reports the results of experiments using it.

The IETF holds regular meetings and publishes the proceedings [Gross 1989]. The IRSG workshop on high-speed networks reported by Partridge [RFC 1152] considers how new, higher-speed technologies will affect network research and existing protocols. Also see Lynch and Jacobsen [1987-] for timely discussions.

EXERCISES

27.1 Categorize the research and engineering problems discussed in this chapter under the four types of change shown in figure 27.1.

27.2 Among protocols in the TCP/IP suite, TELNET is extremely old. Find out what changes/improvements the IETF TELNET working group is exploring.

27.3 Read the proceedings of the latest IETF meeting to find a list of all active working groups. Summarize the major emphasis.

27.4 Find out how your site handles network security.

27.5 If a packet filter uses only IP addresses to prevent access, it cannot easily be used to allow outgoing TCP connections while preventing incoming connections. Explain.

27.6 If your site runs privacy-enhanced mail, experiment to see if you can find a disadvantage.

Appendix 1

A Guide To RFCs

Introduction

Most of the written information about TCP/IP and the connected Internet, including its architecture, protocols, and history, can be found in a series of reports known as *Request For Comments* or *RFC*s. An informal, loosely coordinated set of notes, RFCs are unusually rich in information and color. Before we consider the more serious aspects of RFCs, it is fitting that we take a few minutes to pay attention to the colorful side. A good place to begin is with Cerf's poem *'Twas the Night Before Start-up* (RFC 968), a humorous parody that describes some of the problems encountered when starting a new network. Knowing not to take itself too seriously has pervaded the Internet effort. Anyone who can remember both their first Internet meeting, filled with networking jargon, and Lewis Carroll's *Jabberwocky*, filled with strangely twisted English, will know exactly why D. L. Covill put them together in *ARPAWOCKY* (RFC 527). Anyone that has read Knuth's *The Art Of Computer Programming* may chuckle over RFC 473 asking where on the ARPANET one could execute MIX programs. We can imagine Pickens filled with pride when responding with RFC 485, *MIX and MIXAL at UCSB*. The University of California at Santa Barbara wasn't alone in offering MIX to the world. In RFC 494, Walden provides a list of all hosts on the network that supported MIX programming.

Other RFCs seem equally frivolous. Interspersed amid the descriptions of ideas that would turn out to dramatically change networking, we find notes like RFC 416, written in early November, 1972: *The ARC System will be Unavailable for Use During Thanksgiving Week*. It says exactly what you think it says. Or consider Crispin's tongue-in-cheek humor found in RFC 748, which describes the *TELNET Randomly-Lose Option* (a proposed option for TELNET that makes it randomly drop characters). If notes like that do not seem insignificant, think about the sixty-six RFCs listed as *nev-*

er issued. They were all assigned a number and had an author, but none ever saw the light of day. All that remains are the holes in the numbering scheme, preserved as little reminders of ideas that vaporized or work that remains incomplete.

Even after the silly, lighthearted, and useless RFCs have been removed, the remaining documents do not conform to most standards for scientific writing. Unlike scholarly scientific journals that concentrate on identifying papers of important archival interest, screening them carefully, and filing them for posterity, RFCs provide a record of ongoing conversations among the principals involved in designing, building, measuring, and using the ARPANET and, later, the connected Internet. The reader understands at once that RFCs include the thoughts of researchers on the leading edge of technological innovation, not the studied opinions of scholars who have completely mastered a subject. The authors are not always sure of the consequences of their proposals, or even of the contents, but they clearly realize the issues are too complex to understand without community discussion.

Despite the inconsistencies in RFCs that sometimes make them difficult for beginners to understand, the RFC mechanism has evolved and now works extremely well. Because they are available electronically, information is propagated to the community quickly. Because they span a broad range of interests, practitioners as well as designers contribute. Because they record informal conversations, they capture discussions and not merely final conclusions. Even the disagreements and contradictory proposals are useful in showing what the designers considered before settling on a given protocol (and readers interested in the history of a particular idea or protocol can use RFCs to follow it from its inception to its current state).

Importance Of Host And Gateway Requirements Documents

Unlike most RFCs, which concentrate on a single idea or protocol, three special RFCs cover a broad range of protocols. These special documents are entitled *Requirements for Internet Gateways* and *Requirements for Internet Hosts* (parts 1 and 2).

The requirements documents were published in the late 1980s, after many years of experience with the TCP/IP protocols, and are considered a major revision to the protocol standards. In essence, requirement documents each review many protocols. They point out known weaknesses or ambiguities in the RFCs that define the protocols, state conventions that have been adopted by vendors, document problems that occur in practice, and list solutions to those problems that have been accumulated through experience. RFCs for individual protocols have *not* been updated to include changes and updates from the requirements documents. Thus, readers must be careful to always consult the requirements documents when studying a particular protocol.

How To Obtain An RFC Over The Internet

RFCs are available electronically from the Internet Network Information Center. The Internet domain name for the host that provides the archive is:

NIC.DDN.MIL

To obtain a copy of the text file for an RFC directly from the archive, you must use the File Transfer Protocol (FTP) on a computer attached to the Internet. After invoking FTP on your local computer system, you need to supply retrieval commands. Issue the *user* command to identify yourself to the FTP server and supply a user name *guest* and password *anonymous* when asked. Once the server recognizes you, use the *get* command to retrieve a file named†

<rfc>rfc$N$.txt

where N is the number of the RFC desired. For example, to obtain a copy of RFC 822, retrieve file

<rfc>rfc822.txt

The file you retrieve will contain ASCII text with a form feed character separating pages and newline (line feed) characters separating lines. Except for the newline and form feed characters, the entire file contains printable text that can be rendered with a conventional line printer. No line drawings or other special graphics are included.

The following command script illustrates how one might use FTP to retrieve RFCs under 4BSD UNIX:

---

†A few RFCs are only available in postscript; their names end in *.ps*

```
#! /bin/sh
#
# rfc - 4BSD UNIX (Bourne) shell script to obtain copies of RFCs,
#       keeping a local cache for subsequent requests.
#
# use: rfc number [number...]
#
PATH=/bin:/usr/bin:/usr/ucb
PUB=/usr/pub/RFC
NIC=nic.ddn.mil
for i
do      if test ! -r $PUB/$i -o $i = "-index"
        then echo Retrieving RFC $i from $NIC >&2
#
# invoke FTP under 4BSD UNIX and feed it retrieval commands as input.
#
                ftp -n $NIC  >/dev/null 2>&1 <<!
user anonymous guest
get <rfc>rfc$i.txt $PUB/$i
quit
!
#
# Have obtained file; give copy to user if retrieval was successful.
#
        if test -r $PUB/$i
        then cat $PUB/$i
        else echo Could not retrieve RFC $i 1>&2
        fi
done
```

The script shown above does more than use FTP to retrieve an RFC. It leaves a copy of the RFC in directory */usr/pub/RFC*. The advantage of keeping a local copy of an RFC is that subsequent requests are much faster than the first because they do not use FTP nor do they pass information across the Internet. If the script finds one of the requested RFCs in the cache, it merely presents the user with a copy. Note that the script does not look in the cache when retrieving the special file *-index* because the index contains a list of all RFCs and changes as new RFCs appear.

How To Obtain An RFC Through Electronic Mail

Both the Internet NIC and the NFSNET Network Service Center (NNSC), located at Bolt, Beranek, and Newman Inc. in Cambridge Massachusetts, operate information servers that can respond to electronic mail messages. That is, you send electronic mail to a special address, a computer program reads the mail and consults its database of information, and the computer program sends the answer back in electronic mail. The address of the information servers are:

info-server@ sh.cs.net

and

service@ nic.ddn.mil

These databases contain text documents for RFCs along with other information. To obtain an RFC, you must mail one of these information servers an electronic message.

Obtaining RFCs By Mail From The NSFNET Network Service Center

To obtain an RFC from the NNSC, you must mail a message where the first line specifies the keyword *REQUEST:* followed by the value *rfc*. The second line specifies the keyword *TOPIC:* followed by the integer number of the RFC to retrieve. For example, to retrieve RFC 822, you send the mail message:

REQUEST: rfc
TOPIC: 822

If you need more information on NNSC's info-server, you can send *REQUEST: help*. To obtain help with RFCs only, send a message in which the request is *rfc* and the topic is *help*.

Obtaining RFCs By Mail From The NIC

To obtain an RFC from the NIC by electronic mail, you must mail a message to the server with a subject field that specifies the RFC you want. For example, to obtain RFC 822, you send a mail message with subject field:

RFC 822

If you want more information on the NIC mail information service, send a message with subject field *help* and you will receive a 1-page description of how to use the service.

How To Obtain A Paper Copy Of An RFC

People without access to any electronic networks can still obtain copies of RFCs from the NIC. Their telephone number is 1-800-235-3155. Before calling, use this appendix to make a list of the RFCs needed.

Browsing Through RFCs

There are several indexes that can help one browse through RFCs. First, as we mentioned above, the file *<rfc>rfc-index.txt* contains an accurate list of all RFCs listed in reverse chronological order. It is kept at the archive along with text files for the RFCs. Anyone can obtain the index file using FTP or by mail; users who plan to browse through RFCs usually obtain the index first to verify that they know about the latest RFCs. Second, many RFCs contain summaries or indexes of other RFCs. For example, RFC 899 contains an index of all RFCs numbered 800 through 899, in reverse chronological order. Third, readers often need to know which RFC contains the latest version of some official Internet protocol or which protocols are official and which are unofficial. To accommodate such needs, the Internet Activities Board periodically publishs a new RFC entitled *IAB Official Protocol Standards*, which provides a list of all protocols that have been adopted as TCP/IP standards, as of the time of its publication, along with the number of the most recent RFC describing each protocol. Appendix *C* contains a list of the IAB protocol standards at the time of publication of this text as well as an explanation of the standardization process.

The group at The University of Southern California's Information Sciences Institute responsible for documenting TCP/IP standards publishes important information periodically in RFCs entitled *Internet Numbers*†. The Internet numbers RFCs contain values used in various fields of the official protocols (e.g., the Internet numbers RFC specifies that the *protocol* field in an IP datagram header must contain the value *6* when the datagram contains a TCP segment).

Despite the available indexes, browsing through RFCs can be difficult, especially when the reader is searching for information pertinent to a given topic. Reading a chronological list of all RFCs becomes tedious, but there is no mechanism that allows one to find related groups of RFCs. To exacerbate the problem, information on a given topic may be spread across many years. Browsing through a chronological index of RFCs is particularly difficult because titles do not provide sufficient identification of the information in an RFC. (How could one guess that *Leaving Well Enough Alone* pertains to FTP?) Finally, having multiple RFCs with a single title (e.g., Internet Numbers) can be confusing because the reader cannot easily tell whether a document is out of date without checking the archive.

---

†The *Internet Numbers* RFCs were formerly entitled *Assigned Numbers*.

RFCs Arranged By Topic

The final section of this appendix provides some help in finding information in RFCs because it contains a list of the first 1150 RFCs arranged by topic. Readers can find an earlier topical index in RFC 1000, which also includes an annotated chronological listing of the first 1000 RFCs. Although long, RFC 1000 is highly recommended as a source of authoritative and valuable critique. Its introduction is especially fascinating. Recalling the origin of RFCs along with the origin of the ARPANET, it captures the spirit of adventure and energy that still characterizes the Internet.

RFCs Organized By Major Category And Subtopic
(Also see RFC 1000 for and earlier version)

1. Administrative

1a. Assigned Internet Numbers (official values used by protocols)

1117, 1062, 1020, 1010, 997, 990, 960, 943, 923, 900, 870, 820, 790, 776, 770, 762, 758, 755, 750, 739, 717, 604, 503, 433, 349, 322, 317, 204, 179, 175, 167.

1b. Official IAB Standards and Other Lists of Protocols

1130, 1100, 1083, 1011, 991, 961, 944, 924, 901, 880, 840, 694, 661, 617, 582, 580, 552.

774 - Internet Protocol Handbook Table of Contents

1c. Meeting Notes and Minutes

1152 - Workshop report: Internet research steering group workshop on very-high-speed networks

1077 - Critical issues in high bandwidth networking

1019 - Report of the Workshop on Environments for Computational Mathematics

1017 - Network requirements for scientific research: Internet task force on scientific computing

898 - Gateway Special Interest Group Meeting Notes

808, 805, 469 - Computer Mail Meeting Notes

910, 807 - Multimedia Mail Meeting Notes

585 - ARPANET Users Interest Working Group Meeting

549, 396, 282, 253 - Graphics Meeting Notes

371 - International Computer Communications Conference

327 - Data and File Transfer Workshop Notes

316 - Data Management Working Group Meeting Report

164, 131, 116, 108, 101, 082, 077, 066, 063, 037, 021 - Network Working Group Meeting

1d. Meeting Announcements and Group Overviews

1120 - Internet Activities Board

828 - Data Communications: IFIP's International "Network" of Experts

631 - Call for Papers: International Meeting on Minicomputers and Data Communication

584 - Charter for ARPANET Users Interest Working Group

1e. Distribution Lists

1f. Policies Documents

1124 - Policy issues in interconnecting networks

1087 - Ethics and the Internet

1052 - IAB recommendations for the development of Internet network management standards

1039 - DoD statement on Open Systems Interconnection protocols

980 - Protocol Document Order Information

952, 810, 608 - Host Table Specification

945 - A DoD Statement on the NRC Report

902 - ARPA-Internet Protocol Policy

849 - Suggestions for Improved Host Table Distribution

678 - Document Formats

602 - The Stockings Were Hung by the Chimney With Care

115 - Some Network Information Center Policies on Handling Documents

053 - An Official Protocol Mechanism

1g. Request for Comments Administrative

1150 - F.Y.I. on F.Y.I.: Introduction to the F.Y.I. notes

1111 - Request for comments on Request for Comments: Instructions to RFC authors

1000 - Request For Comments reference guide

999, 899, 800, 699 - Requests for Comments Summary

825 - Request for Comments on Requests for Comments

629 - Scenario for Using the Network Journal

628 - Status of RFC Numbers and a Note on Pre-assigned Journal Numbers

598, 200, 170, 160, 100, 084 - RFC Index

1h. Bibliographies

1012 - Bibliography of Request For Comments 1 through 999

829 - Packet Satellite Technology Reference Sources

290 - Computer Network and Data Sharing: A Bibliography

243 - Network and Data Sharing Bibliography

1i. Other

637 - Change of Network Address for SU-DSL

634 - Change in Network Address for Haskins Lab

616 - Latest Network Maps

609 - Statement of Upcoming Move of NIC/NLS Service

590 - MULTICS Address Change

588 - London Node is Now Up

551 - NYU, ANL, and LBL Joining the Net

2. Requirements Documents And Major Protocol Revisions

2a. Host requirements

2b. Gateway requirements

1009 - Requirements for Internet gateways

2c. Other

3. Network Interface Level (Also see Section 8)

3a. Address Binding (ARP, RARP)

1027 - Using ARP to implement transparent subnet gateways

3b. Internet Protocol over another network (encapsulation)

1149 - Standard for the transmission of IP datagrams on avian carriers
1103 - Proposed standard for the transmission of IP datagrams over FDDI
       Networks
1088 - Standard for the transmission of IP datagrams over NetBIOS networks
1055 - Nonstandard for transmission of IP datagrams over serial lines: SLIP
1051 - Standard for the transmission of IP datagrams and ARP packets over
       ARCNET networks
1044 - Internet Protocol on Network System's HYPERchannel: Protocol
       specification
1042 - Standard for the transmission of IP datagrams over IEEE 802 networks
948 - Two Methods for the Transmission of IP Datagrams Over IEEE 802.3
       Networks
907 - Host Access Protocol
903 - A Reverse Address Resolution Protocol
895 - A Standard for the Transmission of IP Datagrams over Experimental
       Ethernet Networks
894 - A Standard for the Transmission of IP Datagrams over Ethernet
       Networks
893 - Trailer Encapsulations
891 - Internet Protocol on DC Networks
877 - A Standard for the Transmission of IP Datagrams Over Public Data
       Networks
826 - Address Resolution Protocol
796 - Address Mappings
795 - Service Mappings

3c. Other

4. Internet Level

4a. Internet Protocol (IP)

4b. Internet Control Message Protocol (ICMP)

4c. Internet Group Management Protocol (IGMP)

4d. Routing and Gateway Algorithms (GGP, RIP, OSPF)

4e. Other

5. Host Level

5a. User Datagram Protocol (UDP)

5b. Transmission Control Protocol (TCP)

5c. Point-To-Point Protocols

5d. Reliable Datagram Protocols (RDP, VMTP)

5e. Transaction Protocols and Distributed Operating Systems

5f. Protocols For Personal Computers (NETBIOS)

5g. Other

6. Application Level

6a. Telnet Protocol (TELNET)

6b. Telnet Options

6c. File Transfer and Access Protocols (FTP, TFTP, SFTP, NFS)

6d. Domain Name System

6e. Mail and Message Systems (SMTP)

6f. Facsimile and Bitmaps

6g. Graphics and Window Systems

6h. Data Management

6i. Remote Job Entry (NETRJE, NETRJS)

338 - EBCDIC/ASCII Mapping for Network RJE
307 - Using Network Remote Job Entry
283 - NETRJT - Remote Job Service Protocol for TIPS
105 - Network Specification for Remote Job Entry and Remote Job Output
        Retrieval at UCSB

6j. Remote Procedure Call (RPC)

1057 - RPC: Remote Procedure Call Protocol specification version 2
1050 - RPC: Remote Procedure Call Protocol specification

6k. Time And Date (NTP)

1129 - Internet time synchronization: The Network Time Protocol
1128 - Measured performance of the Network Time Protocol in the Internet
        system
1119 - Network Time Protocol (version 2) specification and implementation
1059 - Network Time Protocol (version 1) specification and implementation
958, 957, 956 - Network Time Protocol
868 - Time Server Protocol
867 - Daytime Protocol
778 - DCNET Time Server Protocol
738 - Time Server
685 - Response Time in Cross-network Debugging
034 - Some Brief Preliminary Notes on the ARC Clock
032 - Some Thoughts on SRI's Proposed Real Time Clock
028 - Time Standards

6l. Presentation and Representation (XDR)

1014 - XDR: External Data Representation standard
1003 - Issues in defining an equations representation standard

6m. Network Management (SNMP, CMOT, MIB)

1109 - Report of the second Ad Hoc Network Management Review Group
1095 - Common Management Information Services and Protocol over TCP/IP
        (CMOT)
1089 - SNMP over Ethernet
1076 - HEMS monitoring and control language
1067 - Simple Network Management Protocol
1156, 1066 - Management Information Base for network management of
        TCP/IP-based internets
1155, 1065 - Structure and identification of management information for
        TCP/IP-based internets
1028 - Simple Gateway Monitoring Protocol

7. Program Documentation

7a. General

8. Network Specific (also see section 3)

8a. ARPANET

8b. Host Front End Protocols

8c. ARPANET NCP (Obsolete predecessor of TCP/IP)

8d. ARPANET Initial Connection Protocol

202 - Possible Deadlock in ICP

197 - Initial Connection Protocol - Revised

161 - A Solution to the Race Condition in the ICP

151, 148, 143, 127, 123 - A Proferred Official ICP

150 - The Use of IPC Facilities

145 - Initial Connection Protocol Control Commands

093 - Initial Connection Protocol

080 - Protocol and Data Formats

066 - 3rd Level Ideas and Other Noise

8e. USENET

1036 - Standard for interchange of USENET messages

8f. Other

1132 - Standard for the transmission of 802.2 packets over IPX networks

935 - Reliable Link Layer Protocols

916 - Reliable Asynchronous Transfer Protocol

914 - Thinwire Protocol

824 - The Cronus Virtual Local Network

9. Measurement

9a. General

573 - Data and File Transfer - Some Measurement Results

557 - Revelations in Network Host Measurements

546 - Tenex Load Averages for July 1973

462 - Responding to User Needs

415 - TENEX Bandwidth

392 - Measurement of Host Costs for Transmitting Network Data

352 - TIP Site Information Form

308 - ARPANET Host Availability Data

286 - Network Library Information System

274 - Establishing a Local Guide for Network Usage

214, 193 - Network Checkout

198 - Site Certification - Lincoln Labs

182 - Compilation of List of Relevant Site Reports

180 - File System Questionnaire

156 - Status of the Illinois Site (Response to RFC 116)

153 - SRI ARC-NIC Status

152 - SRI Artificial Intelligence Status Report

9b. Surveys

9c. Statistics

12. Site Documentation

12a. General

30, 27, 24, 16, 10, 3 - Documentation Conventions

13. Protocol Standards By Other Groups Of Interest To The Internet

13a. ANSI

570 - Experimental Input Mapping Between NVT ASCII and UCSB Online System

183 - The EBCDIC Codes and Their Mapping to ASCII

020 - ASCII Format for Network Interchange

13b. CCITT

987 - Mapping Between X.400 and RFC 822

874 - A Critique of X.25

13c. NRC

942 - Transport Protocols for Department of Defense Data Networks

939 - Executive Summary of the NRC Report on Transport Protocols for Department of Defense Data Networks

13d. ISO

1139 - Echo function for ISO 8473

1008 - Implementation guide for the ISO Transport Protocol

1007 - Military supplement to the ISO Transport Protocol

995 - End System to Intermediate System Routing Exchange Protocol for Use in Conjunction with ISO 8473

994 - Final Text of DIS 8473, Protocol for Providing the Connectionless Mode Network Service

982 - Guidelines for the Specification of the Structure of the Domain Specific Part (DSP) of the ISO Standard NSAP Address

941 - Addendum to the Network Service Definition Covering Network Layer Addressing

926 - Protocol for Providing the Connectionless-Mode Network Services

905 - ISO Transport Protocol Specification (ISO DP 8073)

892 - ISO Transport Protocol

873 - The Illusion of Vendor Support

14. Interoperability With Other Applications And Protocols

14a. Protocol Translation And Bridges

1086 - ISO-TP0 bridge between TCP and X.25

1029 - More fault tolerant approach to address resolution for a Multi-LAN system of Ethernets

14b. Tunneling And Layering

1090 - SMTP on X.25

1089 - SNMP over Ethernet

1085 - ISO presentation services on top of TCP/IP based internets

1070 - Use of the Internet as a subnetwork for experimentation with the OSI network layer

1006 - ISO transport services on top of the TCP: Version: 3

1002 - Protocol standard for a NetBIOS service on a TCP/UDP transport: Detailed specifications

1001 - Protocol standard for a NetBIOS service on a TCP/UDP transport: Concepts and methods

14c. Mapping of Names, Addresses and Identifiers

1148, 1138 Mapping between X.400(1988) / ISO 10021 and RFC 822

1069 - Guidelines for the use of Internet-IP addresses in the ISO Connectionless-Mode Network Protocol

1026 - Addendum to RFC 987: (Mapping between X.400 and RFC-822)

987 - Mapping Between X.400 and RFC 822

14d. Other

15. Miscellaneous

15a. General

1121 - Act one - the poems

1118 - Hitchhikers guide to the Internet

1015 - Implementation plan for interagency research Internet

16. Unissued

16a. Never Issued

853, 723, 715, 711, 710, 709, 693, 682, 676, 673, 670, 668, 665, 664, 650, 649, 648, 646, 641, 639, 605, 583, 575, 572, 564, 558, 554, 541, 540, 536, 517, 507, 502, 484, 481, 465, 444, 428, 427, 424, 397, 383, 380, 375, 358, 341, 337, 284, 279, 277, 275, 272, 262, 261, 260, 259, 258, 257, 248, 244, 220, 201, 159, 092, 026, 014

16b. Not yet Issued

1147, 1142, 1140, 1108, 1099, 1061, 1060

Appendix 2

Glossary Of Internetworking Terms and Abbreviations

TCP/IP Terminology

Like most large enterprises, TCP/IP has a language all its own. A curious blend of networking jargon, protocol names, project names, and names of government agencies, the language is both difficult to learn and difficult to remember. To outsiders, discussions among the cognoscenti sound like meaningless babble laced with acronyms at every possible opportunity. Even after a moderate amount of exposure, readers may find that specific terms are difficult to understand. The problem is compounded because some terminology is loosely defined and because the sheer volume is overwhelming.

This glossary helps solve the problem by providing short definitions for terms used throughout the Internet. It is not intended as a tutorial for beginners. Instead, we focus on providing a concise reference to make it easy for those who are generally knowledgeable about networking to look up the meaning of specific terms or acronyms quickly. Readers will find it substantially more useful as a reference after they have studied the text than before.

A Glossary of Terms and Abbreviations
In Alphabetical Order

733

See 822.

822

The TCP/IP standard format for electronic mail messages. Mail experts often refer to "822 messages." The name comes from RFC 822 that contains the specification. 822 format was previously known as 733 format.

1822

The (old) protocol that specifies how a host computer attached to the ARPANET sends and receives packets. In particular, the protocol describes the connection and interaction between a host computer and an ARPANET packet switch. The name *1822* was taken from the number of the technical report by BBN that describes the protocol.

ACK

Abbreviation for *Acknowledgement*.

acknowledgement

A response sent by a receiver to indicate successful reception of information. Acknowledgements may be implemented at any level including the physical level (using voltage on one or more wires to coordinate transfer), at the link level (to indicate successful transmission across a single hardware link), or at higher levels (e.g., to allow an application program at the final destination to respond to an application program at the source).

active open

The operation that a client performs to establish a TCP connection with a server at a known address.

address mask

A bit mask used to select bits from an IP address for subnet addressing. The mask is 32 bits long and selects the network portion of the IP address and one or more bits of the local portion.

address resolution

Conversion of an IP address into a corresponding physical address. Depending on the underlying network, resolution may require broadcasting on a local network. See ARP.

ANSI

(*American National Standards Institute*) A group that defines U.S. standards for the information processing industry. ANSI participates in defining network protocol standards.

ARP

(*Address Resolution Protocol*) The TCP/IP protocol used to dynamically bind a high level IP Address to a low-level physical hardware address. ARP is only across a single physical network and is limited to networks that support hardware broadcast.

ARP hack

See *proxy ARP*.

ARPA

(*Advanced Research Projects Agency*) Former name of DARPA, the government agency that funded the ARPANET and, later, the connected Internet. The group within ARPA with responsibility for the ARPANET was IPTO (*Information Processing Techniques Office*), later ISTO (*Information Systems Technology Office*), located at 1400 Wilson Blvd, Arlington, VA.

ARPANET

A pioneering long haul network funded by ARPA (later DARPA) and built by BBN. It served from 1969 through 1990 as the basis for early networking research as well as a central backbone during development of the Internet. The ARPANET consisted of individual packet switching nodes interconnected by leased lines. Also see PSN, Internet.

ARQ

(*Automatic Repeat Request*) Any protocol that uses positive and negative acknowledgements with retransmission techniques to ensure reliability. The sender automatically repeats the request if it does not receive an answer.

Assigned Numbers

The RFC document that specifies (usually numeric) values used by TCP/IP protocols.

authority zone

A part of the domain name hierarchy for which a single name server is the authority.

autonomous confederation

A set of autonomous systems grouped together because they trust network reachability/routing information obtained from one another more than they trust network reachability/routing information obtained from other autonomous systems.

autonomous system

A collection of gateways and networks that fall under one administrative entity and cooperate closely to propagate network reachability (and routing) information among themselves using an interior gateway protocol of their choice. Gateways within an autonomous system have a high degree of trust. Before two autonomous systems can communicate, one gateway in each system sends reachability information to a gateway in the other.

baseband

Characteristic of any network technology like Ethernet that uses a single carrier frequency and requires all stations attached to the network to participate in every transmission. See broadband.

baud

Literally, the number of times per second the signal can change on a transmission line. Commonly, the transmission line uses only two signal states (e.g., two voltages), making the baud rate equal to the number of bits per second that can be transferred. The underlying transmission technique may use some of the bandwidth, so it may not be the case that users experience data transfers at the line's specified bit rate. For example, because asynchronous lines require 10 bit-times to send an 8-bit character, a 9600 bps asynchronous transmission line can only send 960 characters per second.

BBN

(*Bolt, Beranek, and Newman, Incorporated*) The Cambridge, MA company responsible for development, operation, and monitoring of the ARPANET and, later, Internet core gateway system, CSNET Coordination and Information Center (CIC), and NSFNET Network Service Center (NNSC). BBN works on DARPA research contracts and has contributed much to TCP/IP and the connected Internet.

Berkeley broadcast

A reference to a nonstandard IP broadcast address that uses all zeros in the host portion instead of all ones. The name arises because the technique was introduced and propagated in Berkeley's BSD UNIX.

best-effort delivery

Characteristic of network technologies that do not provide reliability at link levels. Best-effort delivery systems work well with TCP/IP internets because IP assumes that the underlying network provides unreliable connectionless delivery. The combination of IP and UDP protocols provides best-effort delivery service to application programs.

big endian

A format for storage or transmission of binary data in which the most-significant byte (bit) comes first. The TCP/IP standard network byte order is big endian. Also see *little endian*.

BISYNC

(*BInary SYNchronous Communication*) An early, low-level protocol developed by IBM and used to transmit data across a synchronous communication link. Unlike most modern link level protocols, BISYNC is byte-oriented, meaning that it uses special characters to mark the beginning and end of frames. BISYNC is often called BSC, especially in commercial products.

BITNET

(*Because It's Time NETwork*) A low cost, low speed network started at City University of New York, that eventually connected to over 200 universities before it was merged with CSNET to produce CREN. BITNET attached to EARN in Europe. The technology consists of (mostly IBM) mainframe computers interconnected by 9600 bps leased lines. The fundamental paradigm is remote job entry: one machine sends a set of card images which the receiver treats as a remote job to be executed. When the job runs, it produces a new set of card images and sends them on to the next site, where they are treated as a remote job. BITNET provides services like electronic mail by building a remote job that invokes the mailer router program. At each node, the mailer examines the message, chooses a route, and encapsulates the message in a new job that it sends over the chosen route.

bps

(*bits per second*) A measure of the rate of data transmission.

bridge

A computer that connects two or more networks and forwards packets among them. Usually, bridges operate at the physical network level. For example, an Ethernet bridge connects two physical Ethernet cables and forwards from one cable to the other exactly those packets that are not local. Bridges differ from repeaters because bridges store and forward complete packets while repeaters forward electrical signals. They differ from IP gateways or IP routers because they use physical addresses instead of IP addresses.

broadband

Characteristic of any network technology that multiplexes multiple, independent network carriers onto a single cable (usually using frequency division multiplexing). For example, a single 50 mbps broadband cable can be divided into five 10 mbps carriers, with each treated as an independent Ethernet. The advantage of broadband is less cable; the disadvantage is higher cost for equipment at connections. See baseband.

broadcast

A packet delivery system that delivers a copy of a given packet to all hosts that attach to it is said to broadcast the packet. Broadcast may be implemented with hardware (e.g., as in Ethernet) or with software (e.g., as in Cypress).

BSC

(*Binary Synchronous Communication*) See BISYNC.

catastrophic network event

See Ethernet meltdown.

Chernobylgram

(*Chernobyl datagram*) A packet so malformed that it causes the receiving system to "meltdown" (i.e. crash).

CCIRN

(*Coordinating Committee for Intercontinental Research Networking*) An international group that helps coordinate international cooperation on internetworking research and development. See FRICC.

CCITT

(*Consultative Committee on International Telephony and Telegraphy*) An international organization that sets standards for interconnection of telephone equipment. It defined the standards for X.25 network protocols. (Note: in Europe, PTTs offer both voice telephone services and X.25 network services).

checksum

A small, integer value computed from a sequence of octets by treating them as integers and computing the sum. A checksum is used to detect errors that result when the sequence of octets is transmitted from one machine to another. Typically, protocol software computes a checksum and appends it to a packet when transmitting. Upon reception, the protocol software verifies the contents of the packet by recomputing the checksum and comparing to the value sent. Many TCP/IP protocols use a 16-bit checksum computed with one's complement arithmetic with all integer fields in the packet stored in network byte order.

client-server

The model of interaction in a distributed system in which a program at one site sends a request to a program at another site and awaits a response. The requesting program is called a client; the program satisfying the request is called the server. It is usually easier to build client software than server software.

CMOT

(*CMip/cmis Over Tcp*) The use of ISO CMIP/CMIS network management protocols to manage gateways in a TCP/IP internet. CMOT is a co-recommended standard with SNMP. Also see MIB and SNMP.

connection

The path between two protocol modules that provides reliable stream delivery service. In a TCP/IP internet, a connection extends from a TCP module on one machine to a TCP module on the other.

connectionless service

Characteristic of the packet delivery service offered by most hardware and by the Internet Protocol (IP). The connectionless service treats each packet or datagram as a separate entity that contains the source and destination address. Usually, connectionless services can drop packets or deliver them out of sequence.

core gateway

One of a set of gateways operated by the Internet Network Operations Center (INOC) at BBN. Gateways in the core system exchange routing updates periodically to ensure that their routing tables remain consistent. The core forms a central part of Internet routing in that all groups must advertise paths to their networks to core gateways using the Exterior Gateway Protocol.

CRC

(*Cyclic Redundancy Code*) A small, integer value computed from a sequence of octets used to detect errors that result when the sequence of octets is transmitted from one machine to another. Typically, packet switching network hardware computes a CRC and appends it to a packet when transmitting. Upon reception, the hardware verifies the contents of the packet by recomputing the CRC and comparing to the value sent. Although more expensive to compute, a CRC detects more errors than a checksum that uses additive methods.

CREN

(*Consortium for Research and Education Network*) The name of the organization that resulted when BITNET and CSNET merged.

CSMA

(*Carrier Sense Multiple Access*) A characteristic of network hardware that operates by allowing multiple stations to contend for access to a transmission medium by listening to see if it is idle.

CSMA/CD

(*Carrier Sense Multiple Access with Collision Detection*) A characteristic of network hardware that uses CSMA access combined with a mechanism that allows the hardware to detect when two stations simultaneously attempt transmission. Ethernet is an example of a well-known network based on CSMA/CD technology.

CSNET

(*Computer Science NETwork*) A network that offered mail delivery service using di- alup telephone, as well as Internet connectivity using X25NET and Cypress. CSNET offered other services like a registry of members and a domain name server for member institutions that could not run their own. Initially funded by the Nation- al Science Foundation, CSNET became self sufficient before it merged with BIT- NET to form CREN.

DARPA

(*Defense Advanced Research Projects Agency*) Formerly called ARPA. The govern- ment agency that funded research and experimentation with the ARPANET, and later, the connected Internet. The group within DARPA responsible for the AR- PANET is ISTO (*Information Systems Techniques Office*), formerly IPTO (*Informa- tion Processing Techniques Office*), located at 1400 Wilson Blvd, Arlington, VA.

DARPA Internet

See Internet.

datagram

see IP datagram.

DCA

(*Defense Communication Agency*) The government agency responsible for installa- tion of Defense Data Network (e.g., ARPANET and MILNET) lines and PSNs. DCA writes contracts for operation of the DDN and pays for network services.

DCE

(*Data Communications Equipment*) Term X.25 protocol standards apply to switch- ing equipment that forms a packet switched network to distinguish it from the com- puters or terminals that connect to the network. Also see DTE.

DDCMP

(*Digital Data Communication Message Protocol*) The link level protocol Digital Equipment Corporation uses in their network products. DDCMP operates over serial lines, delimits frames by a special character, and includes checksums at the link level. It was relevant to TCP/IP because the original NSFNET used DDCMP over its backbone lines.

DDN

(*Defense Data Network*) Used loosely to refer to the MILNET, ARPANET, and the TCP/IP protocols they use. More literally, it is the MILNET and associated parts of the connected Internet that connect military installations.

demultiplex

To separate from a common input into several outputs. Demultiplexing occurs at many levels. Hardware demultiplexes signals from a transmission line based on time or carrier frequency to allow multiple, simultaneous transmissions across a single physical cable. IP software demultiplexes incoming datagrams, sending each to the appropriate high-level protocol module or application program.

directed broadcast address

An IP address that specifies "all hosts" on a specific network. A single copy of a directed broadcast is routed to the specified network where it is broadcast to all machines on that network.

DNS

(*Domain Name System*) The on-line distributed database system used to map human-readable machine names into IP addresses. DNS servers throughout the connected Internet implement a hierarchical namespace that allows sites freedom in assigning machine names and addresses. DNS also supports separate mappings between mail destinations and IP addresses.

domain

A part of the DNS naming hierarchy. Syntactically, a domain name consists of a sequence of names (labels) separated by periods (dots).

dotted decimal notation

The syntactic representation for a 32-bit integer that consists of four 8-bit numbers written in base 10 with periods (dots) separating them. Many TCP/IP application programs accept dotted decimal notation in place of destination machine names.

DSAB

(*Distributed Systems Architecture Board*) A group of approximately 12 researchers analogous to the IAB that explored distributed systems. The DSAB disbanded when the IAB reorganized in 1989.

DTE

(*Data Terminal Equipment*) Term X.25 protocol standards apply to computers and/or terminals to distinguish them from the packet switching network to which they connect. Also see DCE.

EARN

(*European Academic Research Network*) A network using BITNET technology to connect universities and research labs in Europe. EARN interconnects with BIT-NET in the U.S. and allows electronic mail transfer as well as remote job entry.

Ethernet meltdown

An event that causes saturation or near saturation on an Ethernet. It usually results from illegal or misrouted packets and typically lasts only a short time. As an example, consider an IP datagram directed to a nonexistent host and delivered via hardware broadcast to all machines on the network. Gateways receiving the broadcast will send out ARP packets in an attempt to find the host and deliver the datagram.

EGP

(*Exterior Gateway Protocol*) The protocol used by a gateway in one autonomous system to advertise the IP addresses of networks in that autonomous system to a gateway in another autonomous system. Every autonomous system must use EGP to advertise network reachability to the core gateway system.

EIA

(*Electronics Industry Association*) A standards organization for the electronics industry. Known for RS232C and RS422 standards that specify the electrical characteristics of interconnections between terminals and computers or between two computers.

encapsulation

The technique used by layered protocols in which a lower level protocol accepts a message from a higher level protocol and places it in the data portion of the low level frame. Encapsulation often means that packets traveling across a physical network have a sequence of headers in which the first header comes from the physical network frame, the next from the Internet Protocol (IP), the next from the transport protocol, and so on.

epoch date

A point in history chosen as the date from which time is measured. TCP/IP uses January 1, 1900, Universal Time (formerly called Greenwich Mean Time) as its epoch date. When TCP/IP programs exchange date or time of day they express time as the number of seconds past the epoch date.

Ethernet

A popular local area network technology invented at the Xerox Corporation Palo Alto Research Center. An Ethernet itself is a passive coaxial cable; the interconnections contain all active components. Ethernet is a best-effort delivery system that uses CSMA/CD technology. Xerox Corporation, Digital Equipment Corporation, and Intel Corporation developed and published the standard for 10 Mbps Ethernet. Originally, the coaxial cable specified for Ethernet was a 1/2 inch diameter heavily shielded cable. However, many office environments now use a lighter coaxial cable sometimes called *thinnet* or *cheapernet*. It is also possible to run Ethernet over shielded twisted pair cable.

EACK

(*Extended ACKnowledgement*) See SACK.

fair queueing

A well-known technique for controlling congestion in gateways. Called ''fair'' because it restricts every host to an equal share of gateway bandwidth. Fair queueing is not completely satisfactory because it does not distinguish between small and large hosts or between hosts with few active connections and those with many.

FARNET

(*Federation of American Research Networks*) The organization formed by managers of NSFNET mid-level networks to help them benefit from sharing experiences.

FCCSET

(*Federal Coordinating Council for Science, Engineering, and Technology*) A government group noted for its report that calls for high-speed computing and high-speed networking research.

FDDI

(*Fiber Distribution Data Interface*) An emerging standard for a network technology based on fiber optics that has been established by the American National Standards Institute (ANSI). FDDI specifies a 100 mbps data rate using 1300 nanometer light wavelength and limits networks to approximately 200 km in length, with repeaters every 2 km or less. The access control mechanism uses token ring technology.

FDM

(*Frequency Division Multiplexing*) The method of passing multiple, independent signals across a single medium by assigning each a unique carrier frequency. Hardware to combine signals is called a multiplexor; hardware to separate them is called a demultiplexor.

file server

A process running on a computer that provides access to files on that computer to programs running on remote machines. The term is often applied loosely to computers that run file server programs.

flat namespace

Characteristic of any naming in which object names are selected from a single set of strings (e.g., street names in a typical city). Flat naming contrasts with hierarchical naming in which names are divided into subsections that correspond to the hierarchy of authority that administers them (e.g., telephone numbers that are divided into area code, exchange, and subscriber).

flow control

Control of the rate at which hosts or gateways inject packets into a network or internet, usually to avoid congestion. Flow control mechanisms can be implemented at various levels. Simplistic schemes like ICMP source quench simply ask the sender to cease transmission until congestion ends. More complex schemes vary the transmission rate continuously.

FNC

(*Federal Networking Council*) The group of representatives from those federal agencies involved in the development and use of federal networking, especially those networks using TCP/IP, and the connected Internet. The FNC coordinates research and engineering. Current members include representatives from DOD, DOE, DARPA, NSF, NASA, and HHS.

fragment

One of the pieces that results when an IP gateway divides an IP datagram into smaller pieces for transmission across a network that cannot handle the original datagram size. Fragments use the same format as datagrams; fields in the IP header declare whether a datagram is a fragment, and if so, the offset of the fragment in the original datagram. IP software at the receiving end must reassemble fragments into complete datagrams.

frame

Literally, a packet as it is transmitted across a serial line. The term derives from character oriented protocols that added special start-of-frame and end-of-frame characters when transmitting packets. We use the term throughout this book to refer to the objects that physical networks transmit, even if the network does not use traditional framing. (X.25 networks use the term to specifically refer to the format of data transferred between a host and a packet switch.)

FRICC

(*Federal Research Internet Coordinating Committee*) The former name of the Federal Networking Council. See FNC.

FTP

(*File Transfer Protocol*) The TCP/IP standard, high-level protocol for transferring files from one machine to another. Usually implemented as application level programs, FTP uses the TELNET and TCP protocols. The server side requires a client to supply a login identifier and password before it will honor requests.

Fuzzball

Term applied to both a piece of gateway software and the Digital Equipment Corporation LSI-11 computer on which it runs. The original NSFNET backbone used fuzzballs as packet switches.

FYI

(*For Your Information*) A subset of the REFs that are not technical standards or descriptions of protocols. FYIs convey general information about topics related to TCP/IP or the connected Internet.

gated

(*GATEway Daemon*) A program that runs under 4BSD UNIX on a gateway to allow the gateway to collect information from within one autonomous system using RIP, HELLO, or other interior gateway protocols, and to advertise routes to another autonomous system using the exterior gateway protocol, EGP.

gateway

A special purpose, dedicated computer that attaches to two or more networks and routes packets from one to the other. In particular, an IP gateway routes IP datagrams among the networks to which it connects. Gateways route packets to other gateways until they can be delivered to the final destination directly across one physical network. The term is loosely applied to any machine that transfers information from one network to another, as in *mail gateway*. Although the original literature used the term *gateway*, vendors often call them *IP routers*.

gateway requirements

A document that specifies requirements for an IP gateway. The gateway requirements document clarifies how a gateway routes traffic, and is intended to improve interoperability among gateways produced by multiple vendors. It has been published as an RFC.

GGP

(*Gateway to Gateway Protocol*) The protocol core gateways use to exchange routing information, GGP implements a distributed shortest path routing computation. Under normal circumstances, all GGP participants will reach a steady state in which the routing information at all gateways agrees. GGP is now obsolete.

GOSIP

(*Government Open Systems Interconnection Profile*) A U.S. government procurement document that specifies agencies may use OSI protocols in new networks after August 1991. Although GOSIP was originally thought to eliminate the use of TCP/IP on government internets, clarifications have specified that government agencies can continue to use TCP/IP.

hardware address

The low-level addresses used by physical networks. Each type of network hardware has its own addressing scheme. For example, Ethernet uses 48-bit hardware addresses assigned by the vendor, while proNET-10 uses small integer hardware addresses assigned when a connection to the network is installed.

HDLC

(*High level Data Link Control*) A link level protocol standard by ISO. CCITT later adapted HDLC for its link access protocol (LAP) used with X.25 networks. HDLC was relevant to TCP/IP because ARPANET used it to transfer frames between the host and PSN.

HELLO

The protocol used by a group of cooperative, trusting packet switches to allow them to discover minimal delay routes. It was relevant to TCP/IP because fuzzballs on the NSFNET backbone used it.

HEMS

(*High-level Entity Management System*) A generalization of early host monitoring protocols used for internet management. HEMS is not used. See CMOT, HMP, MIB, and SNMP.

hierarchical routing

Routing that is based on a hierarchical addressing scheme. Most TCP/IP routing is based on a 2-level hierarchy in which an IP address is divided into a network portion and a host portion. Gateways use only the network portion until the datagram reaches a gateway that can deliver it directly. Subnetting introduces additional levels of hierarchical routing.

HMP

(*Host Monitoring Protocol*) A protocol used by the Internet Network Operations Center to monitor computers. It was pertinent because the operations center used HMP to monitor Internet gateways. Also see CMOT, MIB, and SNMP.

hop count

A measure of distance between two points in an internet. A hop count of *n* means that *n* gateways separate the source and destination.

host

Any (end-user) computer system that connects to a network. Hosts range in size from personal computers to supercomputers. Also see gateway.

host requirements

A long document that contains a revision and update of many TCP/IP protocols. The host requirements document is published in a pair of RFCs.

IAB

(*Internet Activities Board*) A group of approximately 12 people who set policy and standards for TCP/IP and the connected Internet. The IAB was reorganized in 1989, with technical people moved to research and engineering subgroups. See IRTF and IETF.

ICCB

(*Internet Control and Configuration Board*) A predecessor to the IAB.

ICMP

(*Internet Control Message Protocol*) An integral part of the Internet Protocol (IP) that handles error and control messages. Specifically, gateways and hosts use ICMP to send reports of problems about datagrams back to the original source that sent the datagram. ICMP also includes an echo request/reply used to test whether a destination is reachable and responding.

IEN

(Internet Engineering Notes) A series of notes developed in parallel to RFCs and available across the Internet from the NIC. IENs contain many of the early thoughts on TCP/IP and the Internet.

IETF

(Internet Engineering Task Force) A group of people concerned with short-term and medium-term problems with TCP/IP and the connected Internet. The IETF chairperson is a member of the IAB. The IETF is divided into six areas which are further divided into working groups. Each area has an independent manager. Also see IAB and IESG.

IESG

(Internet Engineering Steering Group) A committee consisting of the IETF chairperson and the six area managers. The IESG coordinates activities among the IETF working groups. Also see IAB and IRSG.

IGP

(Interior Gateway Protocol) The generic term applied to any protocol used to propagate network reachability and routing information within an autonomous system. Although there is no single standard IGP, RIP is among the most popular.

IMP

(Interface Message Processor) Former name of packet switches used in the ARPANET. An IMP became known as Packet Switching Nodes. See PSN.

INOC

(Internet Network Operations Center) A subgroup of the NOC at BBN that monitors and controls the Internet core gateway system. The INOC measures traffic flow, tests reachability, monitors routing tables, and controls downloading of the new gateway software.

International Organization for Standardization

See ISO.

internet

Physically, a collection of packet switching networks interconnected by gateways along with protocols that allow them to function logically as a single, large, virtual network. When written in upper case, Internet refers specifically to the connected Internet and the TCP/IP protocols it uses.

Internet

The collection of networks and gateways, including the MILNET and NSFNET, that use the TCP/IP protocol suite and function as a single, cooperative virtual network. The Internet provides universal connectivity and three levels of network services: unreliable, connectionless packet delivery; reliable, full duplex stream delivery; and application level services like electronic mail that build on the first two. The Internet reaches many universities, government research labs, and military installations and over a dozen countries.

Internet address

See IP address.

Internet Engineering Notes

See IEN.

Internet Protocol

See IP.

interoperability

The ability of software and hardware on multiple machines from multiple vendors to communicate meaningfully. This term best describes the goal of internetworking, namely, to define an abstract, hardware independent networking environment that makes it possible to build distributed computations that interact at the network transport level without knowing the details of underlying technologies.

IP

(*Internet Protocol*) The TCP/IP standard protocol that defines the IP datagram as the unit of information passed across an internet and provides the basis for connectionless, best-effort packet delivery service. IP includes the ICMP control and error message protocol as an integral part. The entire protocol suite is often referred to as TCP/IP because TCP and IP are the two most fundamental protocols.

IP address

The 32-bit address assigned to hosts that want to participate in a TCP/IP internet. IP addresses are the abstraction of physical hardware addresses just as an internet is an abstraction of physical networks. Actually assigned to the interconnection of a host to a physical network, an IP address consists of a network portion and a host portion. The partition makes routing efficient.

IP datagram

The basic unit of information passed across a TCP/IP internet. An IP datagram is to an internet as a hardware packet is to a physical network. It contains a source and destination address along with data.

IRTF

(*Internet Research Task Force*) A group of people working on research problems related to TCP/IP and the connected Internet. The IRTF is divided into a set of research groups. The IRTF chairperson is a member of the IAB.

IRSG

(*Internet Research Steering Group*) A committee consisting of the IRTF research group chairpersons plus the IRTF chairperson, who set direction and coordinate research related to TCP/IP and the connected Internet.

ISDN

(*Integrated Services Digital Network*) The name of a proposed digital network that telephone carriers intend to provide. It will combine voice and digital network services through a single medium, making it possible to offer customers digital data services as well as voice connections. The CCITT controls ISDN's definition and protocol standards.

ISO

(*International Organization for Standardization*) An international body that drafts, discusses, proposes, and specifies standards for network protocols. ISO is best know for its 7-layer reference model that describes the conceptual organization of protocols and its slowly emerging suite of protocols for Open System Interconnection. The OSI protocols most like the TCP/IP protocol suite are known as *TP-4/IP*.

ISODE

(*ISO Development Environment*) Software that provides an ISO transport level protocol interface on top of TCP/IP. ISODE is designed to allow researchers to experiment with ISO's higher-level OSI protocols before an internet exists that supports the lower levels of the OSI suite.

Karn's algorithm

An algorithm that allows transport protocols to distinguish between good and bad round-trip time samples and thus improve round-trip estimations.

kbps

(*Kilo Bits Per Second*) A measure of the rate of data transmission. Also see mbps and baud.

LAN

(*Local Area Network*) Any physical network technology that operates at high speed (usually tens of megabits per second through several gigabits per second) over short distances (up to a few thousand meters). Examples include Ethernet and proNET-10. See MAN and WAN.

LAP/LAPB

A modified form of HDLC that CCITT chose as the link level protocol for X.25 networks. LAPB provides for the reliable transfer of a packet from a host to an X.25 packet switch, which then forwards the packet on to its destination. The protocol has evolved through several versions, with relative stability since LAPB replaced LAPA. Also see X.25 and HDLC.

level 1

A reference to the hardware interface level of communication. The name is derived from the ISO 7-layer reference model. Level 1 specifications refer to physical connections, including pin configuration and voltages on wires.

level 2

A reference to link level communication (e.g., frame formats) or link level connections derived from the ISO 7-layer reference model. For long haul networks, level 2 refers to the communication between a host computer and a network packet switch (e.g., HDLC/LAPB). For local area networks, level 2 refers to physical frame format and addressing. Thus, a level 2 address is a physical frame address (e.g., an Ethernet address).

level 3

A reference to transport level communication derived from the ISO 7-layer reference model. For TCP/IP internets, level 3 refers to IP and the IP datagram format. Thus, a level 3 address is an IP address.

little endian

A format for storage or transmission of binary data in which the least-significant byte (bit) comes first. See *big endian*.

mail bridge

Used loosely to refer to any mail gateway. Technically, a mail bridge screens mail passing between two networks to ensure that it meets administrative constraints. In particular, mail bridges between the ARPANET and MILNET did not permit arbitrary mail flow.

mail exploder

Part of an electronic mail system that accepts a piece of mail and a list of addresses as input and sends a copy of the message to each address on the list. Most electronic mail systems incorporate a mail exploder to allow users to define mailing lists locally.

mail gateway

A machine that connects to two or more electronic mail systems (especially dissimilar mail systems on two different networks) and transfers mail messages among them. Mail gateways usually capture an entire mail message, reformat it according to the rules of the destination mail system, and then forward the message. See mail bridge.

MAN

(*Metropolitan Area Network*) Any of several new physical network technologies that operate at high speeds (usually hundreds of megabits per second through several gigabits per second) over distances sufficient for a metropolitan area. See LAN and WAN.

management information base

See MIB

martians

Humorous term applied to packets that turn up unexpectedly on the wrong network, usually because of incorrect routing tables.

maximum segment size

A term used with TCP, it refers to the largest amount of data from the stream that can be transmitted at one time (e.g., to allow a sender with limited buffer space to restrict the size of incoming packets). Sender and receiver negotiate maximum segment size.

maximum transfer unit

See MTU.

mbps

(*Millions of Bits Per Second*) A measure of the rate of data transmission.

MIB

(*Management Information Base*) The set of variables (database) that a gateway running CMOT or SNMP maintains. Managers can fetch or store into these variables. MIB-II refers to an extended management database that contains variables not shared by both CMOT and SNMP. See also CMOT and SNMP.

mid-level net

One of several networks funded by the National Science Foundation. Mid-level networks operate autonomously but connect to the NSFNET backbone. Mid-level nets are sometimes called regional networks.

MILNET

(*MILitary NETwork*) Originally part of the ARPANET, MILNET was partitioned in 1984 to make it possible for military installations to have reliable network service while the ARPANET continued to be used for research. MILNET uses exactly the same hardware and protocol technology as ARPANET. Under normal circumstances, MILNET is part of the connected Internet.

MOTIS

The ISO version of the X.400 mail standard.

MTU

(*Maximum Transfer Unit*) The largest amount of data that can be transferred across a given physical network. For local area networks like the Ethernet, the MTU is determined by the network hardware. For long haul networks that use serial lines to interconnect packet switches, the MTU is determined by software.

multi-homed host

A host using TCP/IP that has connections to two or more physical networks. Multi-homed hosts can function as gateways if their routing tables are assigned correct values for routes.

multicast

A technique that allows copies of a single packet to be passed to a selected subset of all possible destinations. Some hardware (e.g., Ethernet) supports multicast by allowing a network interface to belong to one or more multicast groups. Broadcast is a special form of multicast in which the subset of machines to receive a copy of a packet consists of the entire set. IP supports an internet multicast facility.

Nagle's algorithm

Used to refer to two separate congestion control algorithms used with TCP. One algorithm reduces the sending window in the face of congestion; the other limits the transmission of datagrams containing small segments.

NAK

(*Negative Acknowledgement*) A response from the recipient of data to the sender of that data to indicate that the transmission was unsuccessful (e.g., that the data was corrupted by transmission errors). Usually, a NAK triggers retransmission of the lost data. NAKs can be sent at the link level between two machines that communicate directly, or they can be sent at the transport level between the original source and ultimate destination. Also see ACK.

name resolution

The process of mapping a name into a corresponding address. The domain name system provides a mechanism for naming computers in which programs use remote name servers to resolve machine names into IP addresses for those machines.

NASA Science Internet

See NSI.

NASA Science Network

See NSN.

NetBIOS

(*Network Basic Input Output System*) NetBIOS is the standard interface to networks on IBM PC and compatible personal computers. In a TCP/IP internet, NetBIOS refers to a set of guidelines that describes how to map NetBIOS operations into equivalent TCP/IP operations. For example, one of the NetBIOS naming operations maps into domain name system interactions.

NETBLT

(*NETwork BLock Transfer*) A transport level, flow controlled, bulk data transfer protocol used with TCP/IP internets. NETBLT controls the rate at which data is sent to allow a steady, high speed flow.

network byte order

The TCP/IP standard for transmission of integers that specifies the most significant byte appears first (big endian). Sending machines are required to translate from the local integer representation to network byte order, and receiving machines are required to translate from network byte order to the local machine representation.

network management

See CMOT, MIB, and SNMP.

NFS

(*Network File System*) A protocol developed by SUN Microsystems that uses IP to allow a set of cooperating computers to access each other's file systems as if they were local. The key advantage of NFS over conventional file transfer protocols is that NFS hides the differences between local and remote files by placing them in the same name space. NFS was designed for UNIX systems, but has been implemented on many other systems, including personal computers like the IBM PC and Apple MacIntosh.

NIC

(*Network Information Center*) A group at SRI International, Menlo Park, CA, responsible for providing users with information about TCP/IP and the connected Internet. The machine named *NIC.DDN.MIL* serves as the on-line repository for RFCs and other documents related to TCP/IP.

NIST

(*National Institute of Standards and Technology*) Formerly, the National Bureau of Standards. NIST is one standards organization within the US that establishes standards for network protocols.

NOC

(*Network Operations Center*) The organization at BBN that monitors and controls several networks that form part of the connected Internet, including the MILNET, and at least one X.25 based network.

NREN

(*National Education and Research Network*) The planned successor to the connected Internet that will provide high-speed access to scientific and educational institutions.

NSF

(*National Science Foundation*) A government agency that has funded the development of a cross country backbone network as well as regional networks designed to connect scientists to the connected Internet. NSF has also funded individual researchers working in the network area as well as large projects spanning multiple institutions like CSNET.

NSFNET

(*National Science Foundation NETwork*) Loosely used to describe collectively the cross country backbone, mid-level networks, and supercomputer consortia networks that have all been started with NSF seed funds. In a narrow sense, NSFNET refers only to the national backbone network NSF funds.

NSI

(*NASA Science Internet*) A computer networking project started by NASA's Office of Space Science and Applications. It contains two major networks, SPAN and NSN. Only NSN uses TCP/IP. See also NSN, SPAN.

NSN

(*NASA Science Network*) The component of NSI that uses TCP/IP. NSN is part of the connected Internet.

OSF

(*Open Software Foundation*) A consortium of hardware manufacturers who attempt to set common standards for open systems, including operating systems and networks.

OSI

(*Open Systems Interconnection*) A reference to protocols, specifically ISO standards, for the interconnection of cooperative computer systems. When the term is used generically, TCP/IP is a type of OSI protocol; when referring to ISO standards, TCP/IP is not an OSI protocol.

packet

The unit of data sent across a packet switching network. The term is used loosely. While some TCP/IP literature uses it to refer specifically to data sent across a physical network, other literature views an entire TCP/IP internet as a packet switching network and describes IP datagrams as packets.

PAD

(*Packet Assembler Disassembler*) A term used with X.25 networks that refers to a terminal multiplexor device that forms a connection between terminals and hosts across an X.25 network. A PAD accepts characters from a conventional terminal and sends them across an X.25 network; it accepts packets from an X.25 network, extracts characters, and displays them on a terminal.

PDN

(*Public Data Network*) A network service offered by a common carrier. Typically, PDNs use X.25 protocols. See TELENET

PING

(*Packet InterNet Groper*) The name of a program used with TCP/IP internets to test reachability of destinations by sending them an ICMP echo request and waiting for a reply. The term is now used like a verb as in, "please ping host A to see if it is alive."

port

See protocol port.

positive acknowledgement

See ACK.

promiscuous ARP

See proxy ARP.

proNET-10

A commercially available local area network that operates at 10 Mbps using token ring technology.

protocol

A formal description of message formats and the rules two or more machines must follow to exchange those messages. Protocols can describe low-level details of machine to machine interfaces (e.g., the order in which the bits from a byte are sent across a wire), or high-level exchanges between application programs (e.g., the way in which two programs transfer a file across an internet). Most protocols include both intuitive descriptions of the expected interactions as well as more formal specifications using finite state machine models.

protocol port

The abstraction that transport protocols use to distinguish among multiple destinations within a given host computer. TCP/IP protocols identify ports using small positive integers. Usually, the operating system allows an application program to specify which port it wants to use. Some ports are reserved for standard services (e.g., electronic mail).

proxy ARP

The technique in which one machine, usually a gateway, answers ARP requests intended for another by supplying its own physical address. By pretending to be another machine, the gateway accepts responsibility for routing packets to it. The purpose of proxy ARP is to allow a site to use a single IP network address with multiple physical networks.

PSN

(*Packet Switching Node*) The name of an ARPANET packet switch; PSNs were formerly called IMPs. PSNs were implemented with BBN C30 or BBN C300 minicomputers and executed packet switching software under control of the Network Operation Center at BBN. Each PSN connected to from 1 to 16 host computers.

PUP

(*Parc Universal Packet*) In the internet system developed by Xerox Corporation, a PUP is the fundamental unit of transfer, like the IP datagram is in a TCP/IP internet. The name was derived from the name of the laboratory at which the Xerox internet was developed, the Palo Alto Research Center (PARC).

RARP

(*Reverse Address Resolution Protocol*) The TCP/IP protocol a diskless machine uses at startup to find its IP address. The machine broadcasts a request that contains its physical hardware address and a server responds by sending the machine its IP address. RARP takes its name and message format from another IP address resolution protocol, ARP.

RDP

(*Reliable Datagram Protocol*) A protocol that provides reliable datagram service on top of the standard unreliable datagram service that IP provides. RDP is not among the most widely implemented TCP/IP protocols.

regional net

The original term applied to NSFNET mid-level networks.

repeater

A hardware device that copies electrical signals from one Ethernet to another. Typically, sites that have repeaters use them to connect a physical Ethernet cable on each floor of a building to a backbone cable. The chief disadvantage of a repeater compared to a bridge is that it transfers electrical noise as well as packets. At most, two repeaters can appear between any two machines connected to an Ethernet.

research group

The term applied to committees organized under the Internet Research Task Force (IRTF). Each research group studies a single problem or issue. See working group.

RFC

(*Request For Comments*) The name of a series of notes that contain surveys, measurements, ideas, techniques, and observations, as well as proposed and accepted TCP/IP protocol standards. RFCs are edited but not refereed. They are available on-line from the Network Information Center.

RIP

(*Routing Information Protocol*) The protocol used by Berkeley 4BSD UNIX systems to exchange routing information among a (small) set of computers. Usually, the participating machines all attach to a single local area network. Implemented by the UNIX program *routed*, RIP derives from an earlier protocol of the same name developed at Xerox.

RJE

(*Remote Job Entry*) The service offered by many networks that allows one to submit a (batch) job from a remote site. Although TCP/IP has a protocol for RJE service, it is not very popular because most machines now support timesharing instead of batch job processing.

rlogin

(Remote LOGIN) The service offered by Berkeley 4BSD UNIX systems that allows users of one machine to connect to other UNIX systems across an internet and interact as if their terminals connected to the machines directly. Although rlogin offers essentially the same service as TELNET, it is superior because the software passes information about the user's environment (e.g., terminal type) to the remote machine.

round trip time

See RTT.

route

In general, a route is the path that network traffic takes from its source to its destination. In a TCP/IP internet, each IP datagram is routed separately; the route a datagram follows may include many gateways and many physical networks.

routed

(*Route Daemon*) A program that runs under 4BSD UNIX to propagate routes among machines on a local area network. It uses the RIP protocol. Pronounced ''route-d.''

router

Generically, any machine responsible for making decisions about which of several paths network traffic will follow. When used with TCP/IP, the term refers specifically to an IP gateway that routes datagrams using IP destination addresses. Thus, at the lowest level, a physical network bridge is a router because it chooses whether to pass packets from one physical wire to another. Within a long haul network, each individual packet switch is a router because it chooses routes for individual packets. In a TCP/IP internet, each IP gateway is a router because it uses IP destination addresses to choose routes.

RS232

A standard by EIA that specifies the electrical characteristics of slow speed interconnections between terminals and computers or between two computers. The specification limits speed to 20 Kbps and distance to 500 feet, but many manufacturers support speeds of 38.4 Kbps and/or longer distances. Although the standard commonly used is RS232C, most people refer to it as RS232.

RTT

(*Round Trip Time*) A measure of delay between two hosts. The round trip time consists of the total time taken for a single packet or datagram to leave one machine, reach the other, and return. In most packet switching network delays vary as a result of congestion. Thus, measures of round trip times usually give averages which may have high standard deviation.

SACK

(*Selective ACKnowledgement*) An acknowledgement mechanism used with sliding window protocols that allows the receiver to acknowledge packets received out of order, but within the current sliding window. The TCP sliding window protocol could be improved if it used selective acknowledgement. Also called extended acknowledgement.

SDLC

(*Synchronous Data Link Control*) A predecessor of HDLC defined by IBM Corporation and used in their SNA network products.

segment

The unit of transfer sent from TCP on one machine to TCP on another. Each segment contains part of a stream of bytes being sent between the machines as well as additional fields that identify the current position in the stream and contain a checksum to ensure validity of received data.

selective acknowledgement

See SACK.

SGMP

(*Simple Gateway Monitoring Protocol*) A predecessor of SNMP.

silly-window syndrome

A condition that can arise in TCP in which the receiver keeps advertising a small window and the sender keeps sending small segments to fill it. The resulting transmission of small segments makes inefficient use of network bandwidth.

sliding window

Characteristic of those protocols that, when sending a stream of bytes, allow the sender to transmit up to n packets before an acknowledgement arrives. After the sender receives an acknowledgement for the first outstanding packet, it "slides" the packet window along the stream and sends another. Values for n are usually on the order of 10.

SMTP

(*Simple Mail Transfer Protocol*) The TCP/IP standard protocol for transferring electronic mail messages from one machine to another. SMTP specifies how two mail systems interact and the format of control messages they exchange to transfer mail.

SNA

(*System Network Architecture*) The name applied to an architecture and a class of network products offered by IBM Corporation. SNA does not interoperate with TCP/IP.

SNMP

(*Simple Network Monitoring Protocol*) A standard protocol used to monitor IP gateways and the networks to which they attach. SNMP defines a set of variables that the gateway must keep and specifies that all operations on the gateway are a side-effect of fetching or storing to the data variables. Also see CMOT and MIB.

socket

The abstraction provided by Berkeley 4BSD UNIX that allows an application program to access the TCP/IP protocols. An application opens a socket, specifies the service desired (e.g., reliable stream delivery), binds the socket to a specific destination, and then sends or receives data.

source quench

A congestion control technique in which a machine experiencing congestion sends a message back to the source of the packets causing the congestion requesting that the source stop transmitting. In a TCP/IP internet, gateways use ICMP source quench to stop or reduce the transmission of IP datagrams.

source route

A route that is determined by the source. TCP/IP implements source routing by using an option field in an IP datagram. The source fills in a sequence of machines that the datagram must visit along its trip to the destination. Each gateway along the path honors source routing by following the list of machines to visit instead of following the usual route to the destination.

SPAN

(*Space Physics Analysis Network*) Part of the NASA Science Internet that uses DECNET protocols.

subnet address

An extension of the IP addressing scheme that allows a site to use a single IP network address for multiple physical networks. Outside of the site using subnet addressing, routing continues as usual by dividing the destination address into a network portion and local portion. Gateways and hosts inside a site using subnet addressing interpret the local portion of the address by dividing it into a physical network portion and host portion.

SYN

(*SYNchronizing segment*) The first segment sent by the TCP protocol, it is used to synchronize the two ends of a connection in preparation for opening a connection.

TAC

(*Terminal Access Controller*) A program and a piece of hardware that connects terminals to the Internet, usually using dialup modem connections. In essence, a TAC is a host computer that accepts terminal connections from dialup lines and allows the user to invoke Internet remote login software (e.g., TELNET). TACs were formerly called TIPs.

TCP

(*Transmission Control Protocol*) The TCP/IP standard transport level protocol that provides the reliable, full duplex, stream service on which many application protocols depend. TCP allows a process on one machine to send a stream of data to a process on another. It is connection-oriented in the sense that before transmitting data, participants must establish a connection. Software implementing TCP usually resides in the operating system and uses the IP protocol to transmit information across the underlying internet. It is possible to terminate (shut down) one direction of flow across a TCP connection, leaving a one-way (simplex) connection. The entire protocol suite is often referred to as TCP/IP because TCP and IP are the two most fundamental protocols.

TCP/IP Internet Protocol Suite

The official name of the TCP/IP protocols.

TDM

(*Time Division Multiplexing*) A technique used to multiplex multiple signals onto a single hardware transmission channel by allowing each signal to use the channel for a short time before going on to the next one. Also see FDM.

TDMA

(*Time Division Multiple Access*) A method of network access in which time is divided into slots and each node on the network is assigned one of the slots. Because all nodes using TDMA must synchronize exactly (even though the network introduces propagation delays between them), TDMA technologies are difficult to design and the equipment is expensive.

TELENET

A public packet switched network using the CCITT X.25 protocols owned and operated by GTE. CSNET's X25NET used TELENET.

TELNET

The TCP/IP standard protocol for remote terminal connection service. TELNET allows a user at one site to interact with a remote timesharing system at another site as if the user's terminal connected directly to the remote machine. That is, the user invokes a TELNET application program that connects to a remote machine, prompts for a login id and password, and then passes keystrokes from the user's terminal to the remote machine and displays output from the remote machine on the user's terminal.

TFTP

(*Trivial File Transfer Protocol*) The TCP/IP standard protocol for file transfer with minimal capability and minimal overhead. TFTP depends only on the unreliable, connectionless datagram delivery service (UDP), so it can be used on machines like diskless workstations that keep such software in ROM and use it to bootstrap themselves.

time to live

See TTL.

token ring

When used in the generic sense, a type of network technology that controls media access by passing a distinguished packet, called a token, from machine to machine. A computer can only transmit a packet when holding the token. When used in a specific sense, it refers to the token ring network hardware produced by IBM.

TP-4/IP

A term often given to the ISO protocol suite that closely resembles TCP/IP. Both TCP and ISO TP-4 protocols provide reliable stream delivery service using basically the same techniques of positive acknowledgement and retransmission.

trailer protocol

A nonconventional method of encapsulating IP datagrams for transmission across a local area network (e.g., Ethernet). Trailer protocols place the "header" at the end of the packet, so the operating system can arrange to have the network hardware deposit incoming datagrams with the data area starting on a page boundary. The technique saves on the overhead of copying datagrams once they arrive.

transceiver

A device that connects a host interface to a local area network (e.g., Ethernet). Ethernet transceivers contain analog electronics that apply signals to the cable and sense collisions.

TTL

(*Time To Live*) A technique used in best-effort delivery systems to avoid endlessly looping packets. For example, each IP datagram is assigned an integer time to live when it is created. IP gateways decrement the time to live field when they process a datagram and discard the datagram if the time to live counter reaches zero.

type of service routing

A routing scheme in which the choice of path depends on the characteristics of the underlying network technology as well as the shortest path to the destination. In principle, the Internet Protocol (IP) accommodates type of service routing because datagrams contain a type of service request field. In practice, few gateways honor type of service requests.

UART

(*Universal Asynchronous Receiver and Transmitter*) An electronic device consisting of a single chip that can send or receive characters on asynchronous serial communication lines that use RS232. UARTs are flexible because they have control lines that allow the designer to select parameters like transmission speed, parity, number of stop bits, and modem control. UARTs appear in terminals, modems, and on the I/O boards in computers that connect the computer to terminal(s).

UCBCAST

See Berkeley broadcast.

UDP

(*User Datagram Protocol*) The TCP/IP standard protocol that allows an application program on one machine to send a datagram to an application program on another machine. UDP uses the Internet Protocol (IP) to deliver datagrams. Conceptually, the important difference between UDP datagrams and IP datagrams is that UDP includes a protocol port number, allowing the sender to distinguish among multiple destinations (application programs) on the remote machine. In practice, UDP also includes a checksum over the data being sent.

universal time

The international standard time reference that was formerly called Greenwich Mean Time. It is also called universal coordinated time.

UUCP

(*Unix to Unix Copy Program*) An application program developed in the mid 1970s for version 7 UNIX that allows one UNIX timesharing system to copy files to or from another UNIX timesharing system over a single (usually dialup) link. Because UUCP is the basis for electronic mail transfer in UNIX, the term is often used loosely to refer to UNIX mail transfer.

VAN gateway

(*Value Added Network gateway*) The gateway that interconnects the commercial X.25 network service offered by GTE Telenet and the connected Internet. The VAN gateway supports CSNET's X25NET, allowing subscribers to pass IP datagrams across X.25, through the VAN, and onto the Internet.

virtual circuit

See connection.

VMTP

(*Versatile Message Transaction Protocol*) A protocol developed to provide, among other facilities, efficient, reliable datagram communication service at the user level. Unlike most programs that use UDP, programs using VMTP do not have to implement time out, retransmission, or estimation of network delays because the VMTP protocol provides reliable end-to-end datagram delivery.

WAN

(*Wide Area Network*) Any physical network technology that spans large geographic distances. Also called long-haul networks, WANs usually operate at slower speeds and have significantly higher delays than networks that operate over shorter distances. See LAN and MAN.

well-known port

Any of a set of protocol port numbers preassigned for specific uses by transport level protocols (i.e., TCP and UDP). Servers follow the well-known port assignments so clients can locate them. Examples of well-known port numbers include ports assigned to echo servers, time servers, remote login (TELNET) servers, and file transfer (FTP) servers.

window

See sliding window.

working group

The term applied to groups under the Internet Engineering Task Force (IETF).

X

See X-Window System.

X.25

The CCITT standard protocol for transport level network service. Originally designed to connect terminals to computers, X.25 provides a reliable, stream transmission service that can support remote login. The X25NET service offered by CSNET demonstrates that it is possible to run TCP/IP protocols, IP in particular, over an X.25 network. X.25 is most popular in Europe.

X25NET

(*X.25 NETwork*) A service offered by CSNET that passes IP traffic between a subscriber site and the Internet using X.25.

X.400

The CCITT protocol for electronic mail that is expected to become widely accepted. The current version is X.400(88) because it was defined in 1988. Work is underway to make TCP/IP mail systems interoperate with X.400.

XDR

(*eXternal Data Representation*) The standard for a machine independent data structure representation developed by SUN Microsystems, Incorporated. To use XDR, a sender translates from the local machine representation to the standard external representation and a receiver translates from the external representation to the local machine representation.

XNS

(*Xerox Network Standard*) The term used collectively to refer to the suite of internet protocols developed by researchers at Xerox Corporation. Although similar in spirit to the TCP/IP protocols, XNS uses different packet formats and terminology.

X-Window System

A software system developed at MIT for presenting and managing output on bit-mapped displays. Each window consists of a rectangular region of the display that contains textual or graphical output. X allows application programs on a variety of computers to display output in separate windows on a single display. X uses a program called a window manager to allow the user to create, move, overlap, and destroy windows.

zone of authority

Term used in the domain name system to refer to the group of names for which a given name server is an authority. Each zone must be supplied by two name servers that have no common point of failure.

Appendix 3

Standardization And Official TCP/IP Protocol Standards

Introduction

Early in the development of TCP/IP and the Internet, no formal standardization process existed. Documentation for TCP/IP protocols was published in RFCs, and the RFC review process served to scrutinize documentation and standardize protocols. A version of the RFCs for TCP/IP was collected into a three volume set entitled *DDN Protocol Handbook*, dated December 1985†. Several earlier versions of the material appeared between 1978 and 1985, in a small bound set with a yellow cover entitled *Internet Protocol Transition Workbook* dated March 1982. All of the early documents are now obsolete; even minor parts of the DDN Protocol Handbook have changed. Although the major protocols remain relatively stable, research and engineering efforts constantly find new ways to interpret or implement them. The host requirements documents (RFCs 1122 and 1123) update many protocols and clarify some of the remaining ambiguities.

Recently, the IAB has begun to take a more active role in defining the standards. Every three months it publishes an RFC, entitled *IAB Official Protocol Standards*, that specifies the standardization process and lists specific protocol standards. The IAB standards RFC is the official source of information on standardization, and the most recent version should be consulted for the latest lists of protocol standards.

This appendix provides a summary of the standardization process along with a snapshot of the official protocols from 1990. It is not intended to replace the protocol standards RFC, but merely to help the reader grasp the scope of the TCP/IP protocol suite. Indeed, the IAB's Official Protocol Standard RFC gives much more information

---

†This is the set with white covers, approximately 5 inches thick.

about the standardization process and the intention of the IAB for individual protocols. It is required reading for anyone who wants to know the details of protocol status.

Protocol State

The IAB assigns each protocol in the TCP/IP suite a *state* and a *status* A protocol's assigned state specifies whether it is currently: an accepted standard, being considered for standardization, or is not on the "standards track." The table in figure A3.1 summarizes the possible states.

State	Meaning
Initial	The protocol has been submitted for consideration.
Proposed Standard	The protocol has been proposed as a standard and it is currently undergoing an initial screening.
Draft Standard	The protocol has passed an initial review and can be considered in semi-final form. At least two independent implementations will be constructed and the RFC document describing it will be reviewed. Implementors can expect changes before final standardization.
Standard	The protocol has been reviewed and accepted as a full standard. It is officially part of the TCP/IP protocol suite.
Experimental	The protocol is not being considered for standardization but has been used in experiments.
Historic	The protocol is considered obsolete and is not currently used.

Figure A3.1 The possible states of a TPC/IP protocol and the meaning of each.

Normally, protocols submitted for consideration must pass through technical review by appropriate working groups of the IETF before the IAB will vote to promote them through the standards process†. Figure A3.2 shows the possible transitions among states and the IAB action required for each. When a protocol is submitted for review, the designer must request that it be considered for standardization.

---

†Although it is not recommended, it is possible for protocols developed by vendors to become standards without IETF review.

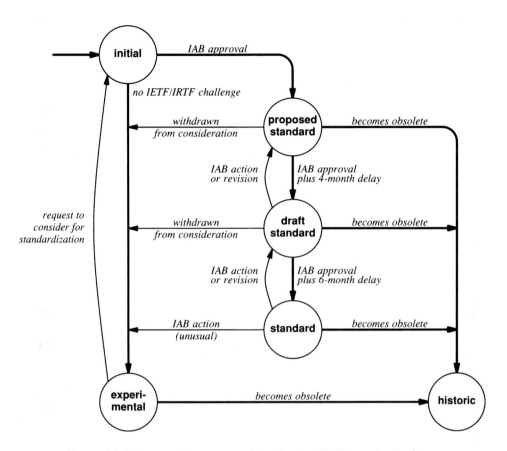

Figure A3.2 The possible state transitions in the TCP/IP standardization process and the actions required for each. Darkened paths represent the normal transitions.

The Status Of A Protocol

The IAB assigns a *status* to each protocol to specify under what conditions the protocol should be used. The table in Figure A3.3 lists the possible status assignments along with the meaning of each.

Status	Meaning
Required	All hosts and gateways using TCP/IP must implement this protocol.
Recommended	All hosts and gateways are encouraged to implement this protocol.
Elective	Hosts and gateways may choose to implement or not implement this protocol.
Limited use	This protocol is not intended for general use. For example, an experimental protocol may be limited to groups involved in the experiment.
Not Recommended	The use of this protocol is not recommended. For example, obsolete protocols are not recommended.

Figure A3.3 The possible status assigned to a protocol and the meaning of each.

Interaction Of Protocol State And Status

Although the IAB can assign state and status independently, not all combinations make sense. Most protocols begin the standardization process classified as *(proposed standard, elective)*. The IAB may move the protocol to *(draft standard, elective)* after appropriate review, or it may decided to change the status to *recommended* before the protocol becomes a draft standard.

As an alternative, protocols that are not intended to become standards usually start as *(experimental, not recommended)*. Their status may change to *limited use* or even *elective*, even if they remain experimental.

The table in Figure A3.4 summarizes the valid combinations of protocol state and status.

State	Protocol Status				
	Req.	**Rec.**	**Elect.**	**Limited**	**Not Rec.**
Standard	•	●	●		
Draft Std.	•	•	●		
Proposed Std.		•	●	•	
Experimental			•	●	•
Historic				•	●

Figure A3.4 The valid combinations of protocol state and protocol status. A nonempty entry shows that the combination is feasible; the size of the bullet in each table entry shows how likely it is to find a protocol with that combination.

Protocol Standardization And RFC Publication

Because all protocol standards are published as RFCs, the RFC publication process reflects the protocol standardization process. When the RFC editor receives an RFC that describes a protocol, it must be reviewed by the appropriate group to insure that the classification of protocol state and status are correct before it can be published. Refer to the IAB Official Protocol Standards RFC for details on how an RFC is processed.

Internet Standard Protocols

This section lists those protocols that have been designated *standard* by the IAB in 1990. It includes documents that are a required part of the TCP/IP standards even if they do not pertain to a specific protocol.

Protocol	Description	Status	RFC
–	Assigned Numbers	Req.	1060
–	Gateway Requirements	Req.	1009
–	Host Requirements - Communications	Req.	1122
–	Host Requirements - Applications	Req.	1123
IP	Internet Protocol	Req.	791
–	IP Subnet Extension	Req.	950
–	IP Broadcast Datagrams	Req.	919
–	IP Broadcast Datagrams with Subnets	Req.	922
ICMP	Internet Control Message Protocol	Req.	792
IGMP	Internet Group Multicast Protocol	Rec.	1112
UDP	User Datagram Protocol	Rec.	768
TCP	Transmission Control Protocol	Rec.	793
SMI	Structure of Management Information	Rec.	1155
MIB	Management Information Base	Rec.	1156
SNMP	Simple Network Management Protocol	Rec.	1157
DOMAIN	Domain Name System	Rec.	1034,1035
TELNET	TELNET Protocol	Rec.	854
FTP	File Transfer Protocol	Rec.	959
SMTP	Simple Mail Transfer Protocol	Rec.	821
MAIL	Format of Electronic Mail Messages	Rec.	822
CONTENT	Content Type Header Field	Rec.	1049
EGP	Exterior Gateway Protocol	Rec.	904
ECHO	Echo Protocol	Rec.	862
NTP	Network Time Protocol	Rec.	1119
NETBIOS	NetBIOS Service Protocols	Elect.	1001,1002
DISCARD	Discard Protocol	Elect.	863
CHARGEN	Character Generator Protocol	Elect.	864
QUOTE	Quote of the Day Protocol	Elect.	865
USERS	Active Users Protocol	Elect.	866
DAYTIME	Daytime Protocol	Elect.	867
TIME	Time Server Protocol	Elect.	868

Network-Specific Standard Protocols

This section lists TCP/IP standards that apply to specific network technologies. In particular, each of these protocols specifies *encapsulation*. Usually, the standard specifies how to encapsulate IP datagrams for transmission over a specific network. However, the list also includes protocols that specify how to encapsulate non-IP packets.

Protocol	Description	Status	RFC
ARP	Address Resolution Protocol	Elect.	826
RARP	Reverse Address Resolution Protocol	Elect.	903
IP-ARPA	Internet Protocol on ARPANET	Elect.	B1822
IP-WB	Internet Protocol on Wideband Net	Elect.	907
IP-X25	Internet Protocol on X.25 Nets	Elect.	877
IP-E	Internet Protocol on Ethernets	Elect.	894
IP-EE	Internet Protocol on Exp. Ethernets	Elect.	895
IP-IEEE	Internet Protocol on IEEE 802	Elect.	1042
IP-DC	Internet Protocol on DC Networks	Elect.	891
IP-HC	Internet Protocol on Hyperchannel	Elect.	1044
IP-ARC	Internet Protocol on ARCNET	Elect.	1051
IP-SLIP	Transmission of IP over Serial Lines	Elect.	1055
IP-NETBIOS	Transmission of IP over NETBIOS	Elect.	1088
IP-FDDI	Transmission of IP over FDDI	Elect.	1103
IP-IPX	Transmission of 802.2 over IPX Nets	Elect.	1132

Draft Standard Protocols

This section lists all protocols classified as draft standards as of 1990.

Protocol	Description	Status	RFC
–	Mail Privacy: Procedures	Elect.	1113
–	Mail Privacy: Key Management	Elect.	1114
–	Mail Privacy: Algorithms	Elect.	1115
CMOT	Common Management Information Services and Protocol over TCP/IP	Rec.	1095
BOOTP	Bootstrap Protocol	Rec.	951,1048, 1084
RIP	Routing Information Protocol	Elect.	1058
TP-TCP	ISO Transport Service on top of TCP	Elect.	1006
NICNAME	WhoIs Protocol	Elect.	954
TFTP	Trivial File Transfer Protocol	Elect.	783

Proposed Standard Protocols

This section lists all protocols classified as *proposed standard*.

Protocol	Description	Status	RFC
MIB-II	MIB-II	Elect.	–
IP-CMPRS	Compressing TCP/IP Headers	Elect.	1144
–	Echo for ISO-8473	Elect.	1139
PPP	Point to Point Protocol	Elect.	1134
OSPF	Open Shortest Path First Routing	Elect.	1131
SUN-NFS	Network File System Protocol	Elect.	1094
POP3	Post Office Protocol, Version 3	Elect.	1081, 1082
SUN-RPC	Remote Procedure Call Protocol	Elect.	1057
PCMAIL	PCmail Transport Protocol	Elect.	1056
NFILE	A File Access Protocol	Elect.	1037
–	Mapping between X.400(84) and RFC-822	Elect.	987, 1026
NNTP	Network News Transfer Protocol	Elect.	977
HOSTNAME	HOSTNAME Protocol	Elect.	953
SFTP	Simple File Transfer Protocol	Elect.	913
RLP	Resource Location Protocol	Elect.	887
FINGER	Finger Protocol	Elect.	742
SUPDUP	SUPDUP Protocol	Elect.	734

Experimental Protocols

This section lists all protocols classified as *experimental*.

Protocol	Description	Status	RFC
EHF-MAIL	Encoding Header Field for Mail	Elect.	1154
DMF-MAIL	Digest Message Format for Mail	Elect.	1153
RDP	Reliable Data Protocol	Limit.	908, 1151
–	Mapping between X.400(88) and RFC-822	Elect.	1148
TCP-ACO	TCP Alternate Checksum Option	Not Rec.	1146
–	Mapping full 822 to Restricted 822	Elect.	1137
BGP	Border Gateway Protocol	Limit.	1105
IP-DVMRP	IP Distance Vector Multicast Routing	Not Rec.	1075
TCP-LDP	TCP Extensions for Long Delay Paths	Limit.	1072
IMAP2	Interactive Mail Access Protocol	Limit.	1064
IP-MTU	IP MTU Discovery Options	Not Rec.	1063
VMTP	Versatile Message Transact. Protocol	Elect.	1045
COOKIE-JAR	Authentication Scheme	Not Rec.	1004
NETBLT	Bulk Data Transfer Protocol	Not Rec.	998
IRTP	Internet Reliable Transact. Protocol	Not Rec.	938
AUTH	Authentication Service	Not Rec.	931
LDP	Loader Debugger Protocol	Not Rec.	909
ST	Stream Protocol	Limit.	IEN119
NVP-II	Network Voice Protocol	Limit.	memo
PVP	Packet Video Protocol	Limit.	memo

Historic Protocols

This section lists all protocols that the IAB has classified as *historic* in 1990. All of these protocols are considered obsolete.

Protocol	Description	Status	RFC
SGMP	Simple Gateway Monitor. Protocol	Not Rec.	1028
HEMS	High Level Entity Management	Not Rec.	1021
STATSRV	Statistics Server	Not Rec.	996
POP2	Post Office Protocol, Version 2	Not Rec.	937
RATP	Reliable Async. Transfer Protocol	Not Rec.	916
THINWIRE	Thinwire Protocol	Not Rec.	914
HMP	Host Monitoring Protocol	Not Rec.	869
GGP	Gateway Gateway Protocol	Not Rec.	823
RTELNET	Remote Telnet Service	Not Rec.	818
CLOCK	DCNET Time Server Protocol	Not Rec.	778
MPM	Internet Message Protocol	Not Rec.	759
NETRJS	Remote Job Service	Not Rec.	740
NETED	Network Standard Text Editor	Not Rec.	569
RJE	Remote Job Entry	Not Rec.	407
XNET	Cross Net Debugger	Not Rec.	IEN158
NAMESERVER	Host Name Server Protocol	Not Rec.	IEN116
MUX	Multiplexing Protocol	Not Rec.	IEN90
GRAPHICS	Graphics Protocol	Not Rec.	N24308

Appendix 4

Examples Of Internet Information Archives

Introduction

The connected Internet offers a wide variety of information archives and services. In addition to the NIC (*nic.ddn.mil*), which is the official repository for RFCs, Internet drafts, and other information about TCP/IP, sites like the NSFNET Service Center (*nnsc.nsf.net*) supply copies of important documents as well as general information like the *Internet Resource Guide*.

This appendix lists the names of a few of the many computers in the Internet on which information archives reside, along with a brief description of information available on each. The intention is to provide an example list. Readers are encouraged to obtain updated copies of this information periodically.

Internet Anonymous FTP Sites

All the information listed here is posted to *comp.misc*, *comp.sources.wanted*, and *alt.sources.wanted* on Usenet, and is available by anonymous FTP from the following sites.

Machine Name	IP address
acns.nwu.edu	129.105.49.1
pine.circa.ufl.edu	128.227.128.55
ssyx.ucsc.edu	128.114.133.1

Using Anonymous FTP

To use anonymous FTP, supply login name *anonymous* and password *guest*:

> user name: anonymous
> password: guest

Alternatively, you can supply your login name in place of the password.

Site administrators for the sites listed below have made their systems available without funding or outside support. Please respect their wishes and restrict FTP access to non-prime hours (approximately 7 PM through 6 AM, local time for the site).

Site Name	IP Address	Description
ads.com	128.229.30.16	internet mailing lists
aeneas.mit.edu	18.71.0.38	kerberos
ahwahnee.stanford.edu	36.56.0.208	pcip interface specs
allspice.lcs.mit.edu	18.26.0.115	RFC 1056 (PCMAIL) code, MIT snmp
ames.arc.nasa.gov.	128.102.18.3	mmdf, popd
anise.acc.com	129.192.64.22	Berkeley utilities ported to A/UX,
apple.com	130.43.2.2	tech-notes, worm papers
argus.stanford.edu	36.56.0.151	netinfo
arisia.xerox.com	13.1.100.206	TCP/IP, IDA sendmail kit
bitsy.mit.edu	18.72.0.3	MIT worm paper
bmc1.bmc.uu.se	130.238.96.1	drivers over Decnet, X25 and SLIP for CMU TCP/IP version 6.3
bodega.stanford.edu	36.14.0.200	highspeed networking papers
boombox.micro.umn.edu	128.101.95.95	POP2 email server (hypercard link to boombox.micro.umn.edu unix host)
chalmers.se	129.16.1.1	RFCs, sunet information (runs whois server)
citi.umich.edu	35.1.128.16	CITI macIP
clouso.crim.ca	192.26.210.1	CA domain reg.
clutx.clarkson.edu	128.153.4.3	net kit
clvms.clarkson.edu	128.153.4.4	CMU TCP V6.3 for VMS V5 VMODEM
columbia.edu	128.59.16.1	NEST network simulation testbed

cs.toronto.edu	128.100.1.65	NETINFO, DOMAIN, IETF INET-DRAFTS, logging ftpd, sunOS SLIP, UofT BIND, X applications
cs.utah.edu	128.110.4.21	Worm Tour
cunixc.cc.columbia.edu	128.59.40.130	MM mailer, CAP/KIP
dept.csci.unt.edu	129.120.1.2	TX Packet Radio Society
devvax.tn.cornell.edu	192.35.82.200	tn3270, gated
dopey.cs.unc.edu	128.109.136.82	sunOS 3.5 traceroute
emx.utexas.edu	128.83.1.33	net directory
eru.mt.luth.se	130.240.0.9	gated
expo.lcs.mit.edu	18.30.0.212	X
ftp.uu.net	192.48.96.2	Internet drafts, Internet Resource Guide, BSD sources
funet.fi	128.214.1.1	isode, pc nfs server, telnet & ftp-resolver binaries, RFCs BSD sources
gargoyle.uchicago.edu	128.135.20.100	named-kit
gregorio.stanford.edu	36.8.0.11	vmtp-ip, ip-multicast
gumby.dsd.trw.com	129.193.72.50	some RFCs, network progs
gwen.cs.purdue.edu	128.10.2.8	cypress
hogg.cc.uoregon.edu	128.223.32.9	NorthWestNet site info
husc6.harvard.edu	128.103.1.56	pcip, ucb tahoe
icarus.cns.syr.edu	128.230.1.49	misc Syr U. and other doc.
ipac.caltech.edu	131.215.139.35	gated, sendmail, named
jade.berkeley.edu	128.32.136.9	NNTP, ping
jyu.fi	128.214.7.5	etherprint
kolvi.hut.fi	130.233.160.32	ka9q, packet radio
kth.se	130.237.72.201	misc, sendmail 5.61 w/ida
lancaster.andrew.cmu.edu	128.2.13.21	CMU PCIP, RFC1073 telnetd, RFC1048
larry.mcrcim.mcgill.edu	132.206.4.3	RFCs, X, local nameserver
lilac.berkeley.edu	128.32.136.12	POP3 for BSD/Ultrix/sunOS
loke.idt.unit.no	129.241.1.103	net directories
ncnoc.concert.net	128.109.193.1	misc local network info
nic.ddn.mil	10.0.0.51	netinfo, RFCs, IEN, IETF
nic.mr.net	192.12.250.5	Minnesota Regional Net traffic data
nis.nsf.net	35.1.1.48	MERIT & NSFNET info
nisc.nyser.net	192.33.4.10	Nysernet, IETF
nnsc.nsf.net	128.89.1.178	Network Info, Internet Resource Guide
noc.byu.edu	128.187.7.2	byu-telnet
oddjob.uchicago.edu	128.135.4.2	NNTP, Sendmail, Ethernet

omnigate.clarkson.edu	128.153.4.2	PS maps of Domain system
orville.nas.nasa.gov	129.99.20.2	hyperchannel net device driver
osi.ncsl.nist.gov	129.6.48.100	misc OSI info
p6xje.ldc.lu.se	130.235.133.7	NCSA telnet 2.2ds, PC net.
pine.circa.ufl.edu	128.227.128.55	RFCs, worm papers
psuvax1.cs.psu.edu	128.118.6.2	network/hosts stuff
rohini.telecomm.umn.edu	128.101.55.1	UMN hostables
safe.stanford.edu	36.44.0.193	3COM/Interlan 4.X BSD UNIX
sh.cs.net	192.31.103.3	NetLists, NetMaps, etc. (lots)
sics.se	192.16.123.90	gated, isode, packet radio, ping code
sol.ctr.columbia.edu	128.59.64.40	ethernet code & docs
spot.colorado.edu	128.138.238.1	netinfo: pgs & RFCs
sun.soe.clarkson.edu	128.153.12.3	Packet Driver, PCIP
sunic.sunet.se	192.36.125.2	RFCs, nntp, sendmail, ntp
sutcase.case.syr.edu	128.230.32.2	TCP-related items
trout.nosc.mil	26.1.0.3	X11R3, popd
trwind.trw.com	129.4.16.70	NNStat, cisco, isode, ka9q, named, sendmail, traceroute
twg.com	26.5.0.73	network-related items
ucdavis.ucdavis.edu	128.120.2.1	dSLIP, POP2, NetHop, UCDwhois, UCDMail, IETF-PPP records
umaxc.weeg.uiowa.edu	128.255.64.80	NCSA telnet, sendmail
valhalla.ee.rochester.edu	128.151.160.11	RFCs, Net load balancer
vgr.brl.mil	128.20.1.1	ping+record route, ttcp, mon, pmon
vx2.gba.nyu.edu	128.122.130.85	PC telnet
watmsg.waterloo.edu	129.97.129.9	pd BSD
zaphod.ncsa.uiuc.edu	128.174.20.50	NCSA Telnet source

Bibliography

ABRAMSON, N. [1970], The ALOHA System – Another Alternative for Computer Communications, *Proceedings of the Fall Joint Computer Conference.*

ABRAMSON, N. and F. KUO (EDS.) [1973], *Computer Communication Networks,* Prentice Hall, Englewood Cliffs, New Jersey.

ANDREWS, D. W., and G. D. SHULTZ [1982], A Token-Ring Architecture for Local Area Networks: An Update, *Proceedings of Fall 82 COMPCON,* IEEE.

BALL, J. E., E. J. BURKE, I. GERTNER, K. A. LANTZ, and R. F. RASHID [1979], Perspectives on Message-Based Distributed Computing, *IEEE Computing Networking Symposium,* 46-51.

BBN [1981], A History of the ARPANET: The First Decade, *Technical Report* Bolt, Beranek, and Newman, Inc.

BBN [December 1981], Specification for the Interconnection of a Host and an IMP (revised), *Technical Report 1822,* Bolt, Beranek, and Newman, Inc.

BERTSEKAS D. and R. GALLAGER [1987], *Data Networks,* Prentice-Hall, Englewood Cliffs, New Jersey.

BIRRELL, A., and B. NELSON [February 1984], Implementing Remote Procedure Calls, *ACM Transactions on Computer Systems,* 2(1), 39-59.

BOGGS, D., J. SHOCH, E. TAFT, and R. METCALFE [April 1980], Pup: An Internetwork Architecture, *IEEE Transactions on Communications.*

BORMAN, D., [April 1989], Implementing TCP/IP on a Cray Computer, *Computer Communication Review,* 19(2), 11-15.

BROWN, M., N. KOLLING, and E. TAFT [November 1985], The Alpine File System, *Transactions on Computer Systems,* 3(4), 261-293.

BROWNBRIDGE, D., L. MARSHALL, and B. RANDELL [December 1982], The Newcastle Connections or UNIXes of the World Unite!, *Software – Practice and Experience,* 12(12), 1147-1162.

CERF, V., and E. CAIN [October 1983], The DOD Internet Architecture Model, *Computer Networks.*

CERF, V., and R. KAHN [May 1974], A Protocol for Packet Network Interconnection, *IEEE Transactions of Communications*, Com-22(5).

CERF, V. [October 1989], A History of the ARPANET, *ConneXions, The Interoperability Report*, 480 San Antonio Rd, Suite 100, Mountain View, California.

CHERITON, D. R. [1983], Local Networking and Internetworking in the V-System, *Proceedings of the Eighth Data Communications Symposium*.

CHERITON, D. R. [April 1984], The V Kernel: A Software Base for Distributed Systems, *IEEE Software*, 1(2), 19-42.

CHERITON, D. [August 1986], VMTP: A Transport Protocol for the Next Generation of Communication Systems, *Proceedings of ACM SIGCOMM '86*, 406-415.

CHERITON, D., and T. MANN [May 1984], Uniform Access to Distributed Name Interpretation in the V-System, *Proceedings IEEE Fourth International Conference on Distributed Computing Systems*, 290-297.

CHESSON, G. [June 1987], Protocol Engine Design, *Proceedings of the 1987 Summer USENIX Conference*, Phoenix, AZ.

CLARK, D. [December 1985], The structure of Systems Using Upcalls, *Proceedings of the Tenth ACM Symposium on Operating Systems Principles*, 171-180.

CLARK, D., M. LAMBERT, and L. ZHANG [August 1987], NETBLT: A High Throughput Transport Protocol, *Proceedings of ACM SIGCOMM '87*.

COHEN, D., [1981], On Holy Wars and a Plea for Peace, *IEEE Computer*, 48-54.

COMER, D. E. and J. T. KORB [1983], CSNET Protocol Software: The IP-to-X25 Interface, *Computer Communications Review*, 13(2).

COMER, D. E. [1984], *Operating System Design – The XINU Approach*, Prentice-Hall, Englewood Cliffs, New Jersey.

COMER, D. E. [1987], *Operating System Design Vol II. – Internetworking With XINU*, Prentice-Hall, Englewood Cliffs, New Jersey.

COMER, D. E., T. NARTEN, and R. YAVATKAR [April 1987], The Cypress Network: A Low-Cost Internet Connection Technology, *Technical Report TR-653*, Purdue University, West Lafayette, IN.

COMER, D. E., T. NARTEN, and R. YAVATKAR [1987], The Cypress Coaxial Packet Switch, *Computer Networks and ISDN Systems*, vol. 14:2-5, 383-388.

COTTON, I. [1979], Technologies for Local Area Computer Networks, *Proceedings of the Local Area Communications Network Symposium*.

CROWLEY, T., H, FORSDICK, M. LANDAU, and V. TRAVERS [June 1987], The Diamond Multimedia Editor, *Proceedings of the 1987 Summer USENIX Conference, Phoenix, AZ*.

DALAL Y. K., and R. S. PRINTIS [1981], *48-Bit Absolute Internet and Ethernet Host Numbers, Proceedings of the Seventh Data Communications Symposium*.

DEERING S. E., and D. R. CHERITON [May 1990], *Multicast Routing in Datagram Internetworks and Extended LANs, ACM Transactions on Computer Systems, 8(2)*.

DENNING P. J., [September-October 1989], *The Science of Computing: Worldnet*, in American Scientist, 432-434.

DENNING P. J., [November-December 1989], *The Science of Computing: The ARPANET After Twenty Years*, in American Scientist, 530-534.

DIGITAL EQUIPMENT CORPORATION., INTEL CORPORATION, and XEROX CORPORATION [September 1980], *The Ethernet: A Local Area Network Data Link Layer and Physical Layer Specification.*

DION, J. [Oct. 1980], The Cambridge File Server, *Operating Systems Review,* 14(4), 26-35.

DRIVER, H., H. HOPEWELL, and J. IAQUINTO [September 1979], How the Gateway Regulates Information Control, *Data Communications.*

EDGE, S. W. [1979], Comparison of the Hop-by-Hop and Endpoint Approaches to Network Interconnection, in *Flow Control in Computer Networks,* J-L. GRANGE and M. GIEN (EDS.), North-Holland, Amsterdam, 359-373.

EDGE, S. [1983], An Adaptive Timeout Algorithm for Retransmission Across a Packet Switching Network, *Proceedings of ACM SIGCOMM '83.*

ENSLOW, P. [January 1978], What is a 'Distributed' Data Processing System? *Computer,* 13-21.

FALK, G. [1983], The Structure and Function of Network Protocols, in *Computer Communications, Volume I: Principles,* CHOU, W. (ED.), Prentice-Hall, Englewood Cliffs, New Jersey.

FARMER, W. D., and E. E. NEWHALL [1969], An Experimental Distributed Switching System to Handle Bursty Computer Traffic, *Proceedings of the ACM Symposium on Probabilistic Optimization of Data Communication Systems,* 1-33.

FCCSET [November 1987], A Research and Development Strategy for High Performance Computing, *Report from the Executive Office of the President and Office of Science and Technology Policy.*

FEDOR, M. [June 1988], GATED: A Multi-Routing Protocol Daemon for UNIX, *Proceedings of the 1988 Summer USENIX conference*, San Francisco, California.

FEINLER, J., O. J. JACOBSEN, and M. STAHL [December 1985], *DDN Protocol Handbook Volume Two, DARPA Internet Protocols,* DDN Network Information Center, SRI International, 333 Ravenswood Avenue, Room EJ291, Menlo Park, California.

FRANK, H., and W. CHOU [1971], Routing in Computer Networks, *Networks,* 1(1), 99-112.

FRANK, H., and J. FRISCH [1971], *Communication, Transmission, and Transportation Networks,* Addison-Wesley, Reading, Massachusetts.

FRANTA, W. R., and I. CHLAMTAC [1981], *Local Networks,* Lexington Books, Lexington, Massachusetts.

FRICC [May 1989], *Program Plan for the National Research and Education Network*, Federal Research Internet Coordinating Committee, US Department of Energy, Office of Scientific Computing report ER-7.

FRIDRICH, M., and W. OLDER [December 1981], The Felix File Server, *Proceedings of the Eighth Symposium on Operating Systems Principles,* 37-46.

FULTZ, G. L., and L. KLEINROCK, [June 14-16, 1971], Adaptive Routing Techniques for Store-and-Forward Computer Communication Networks, presented at *IEEE International Conference on Communications,* Montreal, Canada.

GERLA, M., and L. KLEINROCK [April 1980], Flow Control: A Comparative Survey, *IEEE Transactions on Communications.*

GOSIP [April 1989], U.S. Government Open Systems Interconnection Profile (GOSIP) version 2.0, GOSIP Advanced Requirements Group, National Institute of Standards and Technology (NIST).

GRANGE, J-L., and M. GIEN (EDS.) [1979], *Flow Control in Computer Networks,* North-Holland, Amsterdam.

GREEN, P. E. (ED.) [1982], *Computer Network Architectures and Protocols,* Plenum Press, New York.

HINDEN, R., J. HAVERTY, and A. SHELTZER [September 1983], The DARPA Internet: Interconnecting Heterogeneous Computer Networks with Gateways, *Computer.*

INTERNATIONAL ORGANIZATION FOR STANDARDIZATION [June 1986a], Information processing systems — Open Systems Interconnection — *Transport Service Definition,* International Standard number 8072, ISO, Switzerland.

INTERNATIONAL ORGANIZATION FOR STANDARDIZATION [July 1986b], Information processing systems — Open Systems Interconnection — *Connection Oriented Transport Protocol Specification,* International Standard number 8073, ISO, Switzerland.

INTERNATIONAL ORGANIZATION FOR STANDARDIZATION [May 1987a], Information processing systems — Open Systems Interconnection — *Specification of Basic Specification of Abstract Syntax Notation One (ASN.1),* International Standard number 8824, ISO, Switzerland.

INTERNATIONAL ORGANIZATION FOR STANDARDIZATION [May 1987b], Information processing systems — Open Systems Interconnection — *Specification of Basic Encoding Rules for Abstract Syntax Notation One (ASN.1),* International Standard number 8825, ISO, Switzerland.

INTERNATIONAL ORGANIZATION FOR STANDARDIZATION [May 1988a], Information processing systems — Open Systems Interconnection — *Management Information Service Definition, Part 2: Common Management Information Service,* Draft International Standard number 9595-2, ISO, Switzerland.

INTERNATIONAL ORGANIZATION FOR STANDARDIZATION [May 1988a], Information processing systems — Open Systems Interconnection — *Management Information Protocol Definition, Part 2: Common Management Information Protocol,* Draft International Standard number 9596-2.

JAIN, R. [January 1985], On Caching Out-of-Order Packets in Window Flow Controlled Networks, *Technical Report,* DEC-TR-342, Digital Equipment Corporation.

JAIN, R. [March 1986], Divergence of Timeout Algorithms for Packet Retransmissions, *Proceedings Fifth Annual International Phoenix Conference on Computers and Communications,* Scottsdale, AZ.

JAIN, R. [October 1986], A Timeout-Based Congestion Control Scheme for Window Flow-Controlled Networks, *IEEE Journal on Selected Areas in Communications,* Vol. SAC-4, no. 7.

JAIN, R., K. RAMAKRISHNAN, and D-M. CHIU [August 1987], Congestion Avoidance in Computer Networks With a Connectionless Network Layer. *Technical Report,* DEC-TR-506, Digital Equipment Corporation.

JENNINGS, D. M., L. H. LANDWEBER, and I. H. FUCHS [February 28, 1986], Computer Networking for Scientists and Engineers, *Science* vol 231, 941-950.

JUBIN, J. and J. TORNOW [January 1987], The DARPA Packet Radio Network Protocols, *IEEE Proceedings.*

KAHN, R. [November 1972], Resource-Sharing Computer Communications Networks, *Proceedings of the IEEE,* 60(11), 1397-1407.

KARN, P., H. PRICE, and R. DIERSING [May 1985], Packet Radio in the Amateur Service, *IEEE Journal on Selected Areas in Communications,*

KARN, P., and C. PARTRIDGE [August 1987], Improving Round-Trip Time Estimates in Reliable Transport Protocols, *Proceedings of ACM SIGCOMM '87.*

KENT, C., and J. MOGUL [August 1987], Fragmentation Considered Harmful, *Proceedings of ACM SIGCOMM '87.*

KLINE, C. [August 1987], Supercomputers on the Internet: A Case Study, *Proceedings of ACM SIGCOMM '87.*

KOCHAN, S. G., and P. H. WOODS [1989], *UNIX Networking,* Hayden Books, Indianapolis, IN.

LABARRE, L. (ED.) [December 1989], OSI Internet Management: Management Information Base, *Internet Draft <IETF.DRAFTS>DRAFT-IETF-SNMP-MIB2-01.TXT,* DDN Network Information Center, SRI International, Ravenswood, CA.

LAMPSON, B. W., M. PAUL, and H. J. SIEGERT (EDS.) [1981], *Distributed Systems Architecture and Implementation (An Advanced Course),* Springer-Verlag, Berlin.

LANZILLO, A. L., and C. PARTRIDGE [January 1989], Implementation of Dial-up IP for UNIX Systems, *Proceedings 1989 Winter USENIX Technical Conference,* San Diego, CA.

LAQUEY, T. L., [July 1989], *User's Directory of Computer Networks,* Digital Press, Bedford, MA.

LAZAR, A. [November 1983], Optimal Flow Control of a Class of Queuing Networks in Equilibrium. *IEEE Transactions on Automatic Control,* Vol. AC-28:11.

LEFFLER, S., M. McKUSICK, M. KARELS, and J. QUARTERMAN [1989], *The Design and Implementation of the 4.3BSD UNIX Operating System, Addison Wesley, 1989.*

LYNCH, D. C., and O. J. JACOBSEN (PUBLISHER and EDITOR) [1987-], ConneXions, the Interoperability Report, Interop Incorporated,, 480 San Antonio Rd, Suite 100, Mountain View, California.

LYNCH, D. C., (PRESIDENT) [1987-], The Annual Interop Conference *Interop Incorporated,* 480 San Antonio Rd, Suite 100, Mountain View, California.

MCNAMARA, J. [1982], *Technical Aspects of Data Communications,* Digital Press, Digital Equipment Corporation, Bedford, Massachusetts.

MCQUILLAN, J. M., I. RICHER, and E. ROSEN [May 1980], The New Routing Algorithm for the ARPANET, *IEEE Transactions on Communications,* (COM-28), 711-719.

MERIT [November 1987], Management and Operation of the NSFNET Backbone Network: A Proposal Funded by the National Science Foundation and the State of Michigan, *MERIT Incorporated,* Ann Arbor, Michigan.

METCALFE, R. M., and D. R. BOGGS [July 1976], Ethernet: Distributed Packet Switching for Local Computer Networks, *Communications of the ACM,* 19(7), 395-404.

MILLER, C. K., and D. M. THOMPSON [March 1982], Making a Case for Token Passing in Local Networks, *Data Communications.*

MILLS, D., and H-W. BRAUN [August 1987], The NSFNET Backbone Network, *Proceedings of ACM SIGCOMM '87.*

MITCHELL, J., and J. DION [April 1982], A Comparison of Two Network-Based File Servers, *Communications of the ACM*, 25(4), 233-245.

MORRIS, R. [1979], Fixing Timeout Intervals for Lost Packet Detection in Computer Communication Networks, *Proceedings AFIPS National Computer Conference*, AFIPS Press, Montvale, New Jersey.

NAGLE, J. [April 1987], On Packet Switches With Infinite Storage, *IEEE Transactions on Communications*, Vol. COM-35:4.

NARTEN, T. [Sept. 1989], Internet Routing, *Proceedings ACM SIGCOMM '89.*

NEEDHAM, R. M. [1979], System Aspects of the Cambridge Ring, *Proceedings of the ACM Seventh Symposium on Operating System Principles*, 82-85.

NELSON, J. [September 1983], 802: A Progress Report, *Datamation.*

OPPEN, D., and Y. DALAL [October 1981], The Clearinghouse: A Decentralized Agent for Locating Named Objects, Office Products Division, XEROX Corporation.

PARTRIDGE, C. [June 1986], Mail Routing Using Domain Names: An Informal Tour, *Proceedings of the 1986 Summer USENIX Conference*, Atlanta, GA.

PARTRIDGE, C. [June 1987], Implementing the Reliable Data Protocol (RDP), *Proceedings of the 1987 Summer USENIX Conference*, Phoenix, Arizona.

PETERSON, L. [1985], *Defining and Naming the Fundamental Objects in a Distributed Message System*, Ph.D. Dissertation, Purdue University, West Lafayette, Indiana.

PIERCE, J. R. [1972], Networks for Block Switching of Data, *Bell System Technical Journal*, 51.

POSTEL, J. B. [April 1980], Internetwork Protocol Approaches, *IEEE Transactions on Communications*, COM-28, 604-611.

POSTEL, J. B., C. A. SUNSHINE, and D. CHEN [1981], The ARPA Internet Protocol, *Computer Networks.*

QUARTERMAN, J. S. [1990], *The Matrix: Computer Networks and Conferencing Systems Worldwide*, Digital Press, Digital Equipment Corporation, Maynard, MA.

QUARTERMAN, J. S., and J. C. HOSKINS [October 1986], Notable Computer Networks, *Communications of the ACM*, 29(10).

REYNOLDS, J., J. POSTEL, A. R. KATZ, G. G. FINN, and A. L. DESCHON [October 1985], The DARPA Experimental Multimedia Mail System, *IEEE Computer.*

RITCHIE, D. M., and K. THOMPSON [July 1974], The UNIX Time-Sharing System, *Communications of the ACM*, 17(7), 365-375; revised and reprinted in *Bell System Technical Journal*, 57(6), [July-August 1978], 1905-1929.

ROSE, M. (ED.) [October 1989], Management Information Base for Network Management of TCP/IP-based Internets, *Internet Draft <IETF.DRAFTS>DRAFT-IETF-OIM-MIB2-00.TXT*, DDN Network Information Center, SRI International, Ravenswood, CA.

ROSENTHAL, R. (ED.) [November 1982], *The Selection of Local Area Computer Networks*, National Bureau of Standards Special Publication 500-96.

SALTZER, J. [1978], Naming and Binding of Objects, *Operating Systems, An Advanced Course,* Springer-Verlag, 99-208.

SALTZER, J. [April 1982], Naming and Binding of Network Destinations, *International Symposium on Local Computer Networks,* IFIP/T.C.6, 311-317.

SALTZER, J., D. REED, and D. CLARK [November 1984], End-to-End Arguments in System Design, *ACM Transactions on Computer Systems,* 2(4), 277-288.

SCHWARTZ, M., and T. STERN [April 1980], *IEEE Transactions on Communications,* COM-28(4), 539-552.

SHOCH, J. F. [1978], Internetwork Naming, Addressing, and Routing, *Proceedings of COMPCON.*

SHOCH, J. F., Y. DALAL, and D. REDELL [August 1982], Evolution of the Ethernet Local Computer Network, *Computer.*

SNA [1975], *IBM System Network Architecture – General Information,* IBM System Development Division, Publications Center, Department E01, P.O. Box 12195, Research Triangle Park, North Carolina, 27709.

SOLOMON, M., L. LANDWEBER, and D. NEUHEGEN [1982], The CSNET Name Server, *Computer Networks* (6), 161-172.

STALLINGS, W. [1984], *Local Networks: An Introduction,* Macmillan Publishing Company, New York.

STALLINGS, W. [1985], *Data and Computer Communications,* Macmillan Publishing Company, New York.

SWINEHART, D., G. MCDANIEL, and D. R. BOGGS [December 1979], WFS: A Simple Shared File System for a Distributed Environment, *Proceedings of the Seventh Symposium on Operating System Principles,* 9-17.

TANENBAUM, A. [1981], *Computer Networks: Toward Distributed Processing Systems,* Prentice-Hall, Englewood Cliffs, New Jersey.

TICHY, W., and Z. RUAN [June 1984], Towards a Distributed File System, *Proceedings of Summer 84 USENIX Conference,* Salt Lake City, Utah, 87-97.

TOMLINSON. R. S. [1975], Selecting Sequence Numbers, *Proceedings ACM SIGOPS/SIGCOMM Interprocess Communication Workshop,* 11-23, 1975.

WARD, A. A. [1980], TRIX: A Network-Oriented Operating System, *Proceedings of COMPCON,* 344-349.

WATSON, R. [1981], Timer-Based Mechanisms in Reliable Transport Protocol Connection Management, *Computer Networks,* North-Holland Publishing Company.

WEINBERGER, P. J. [1985], The UNIX Eighth Edition Network File System, *Proceedings 1985 ACM Computer Science Conference,* 299-301.

WELCH, B., and J. OSTERHAUT [May 1986], Prefix Tables: A Simple Mechanism for Locating Files in a Distributed System, *Proceedings IEEE Sixth International Conference on Distributed Computing Systems,* 1845-189.

WILKES, M. V., and D. J. WHEELER [May 1979], The Cambridge Digital Communication Ring, *Proceedings Local Area Computer Network Symposium.*

XEROX [1981], Internet Transport Protocols, *Report XSIS 028112,* Xerox Corporation, Office Products Division, Network Systems Administration Office, 3333 Coyote Hill Road, Palo Alto, California.

ZHANG, L. [August 1986], Why TCP Timers Don't Work Well, *Proceedings of ACM SIGCOMM '86.*

Index